The Beverage Testing Institute's
Buying Guide
to Inexpensive Wines

Other Publications from the Beverage Testing Institute
and Sterling Publishing Co., Inc.

Buying Guide to Imported Wines

Buying Guide to the Wines of North America

Buying Guide to Spirits

Buying Guide to Beer

The Beverage Testing Institute's

Buying Guide to Inexpensive Wines

Edited by Charles Laverick

Sterling Publishing Co., Inc.
New York

Library of Congress Cataloging-in-Publication Data Available

10   9   8   7   6   5   4   3   2   1

Published by Sterling Publishing Company, Inc.
387 Park Avenue South, New York, N.Y. 10016
© 1999 by the Beverage Testing Institute
Distributed in Canada by Sterling Publishing
$^{c}/_{o}$ Canadian Manda Group, One Atlantic Avenue, Suite 105
Toronto, Ontario, Canada M6K 3E7
Distributed in Great Britain and Europe by Cassell PLC
Wellington House, 125 Strand, London WC2R 0BB, England
Distributed in Australia by Capricorn Link (Australia) Pty Ltd.
P.O. Box 6651, Baulkham Hills, Business Centre, NSW 2153, Australia

Sterling ISBN 0-8069-2861-1

Acknowledgements

Wine ratings produced by Marc Dornan and Charles Laverick of BTI, with the help of regular guest panelists Bob Bansberg (Ambria), Kevin Cahoon (Langdon & Shiverick), Alan Dikty (Applied Beverage Technologies), Tom Hyland (North Shore Wine News), Phil Matievic (Frugal Wine Co.), and Tim Wermerling (Wermerling & Co.). Tasting notes written by Marc Dornan and Charles Laverick. Chapter introductions written by Sean Ludford, Micronesia's preeminent resident wine critic. Charles Laverick wrote other introductory material, with editing by Jim Clark, Alan Dikty, Marc Dorman, and Charles Laverick. Graphic design and layout was done by Kelley Witzemann of Jokerman Studio in Chicago with assistance from Sharon B. Dang. Special thanks to Jon Winsell of BTI for his tireless technical assistance and able coordination between all involved (He deserves a vacation and some time at home with his daughter, Julia). Also, thanks to Richard Cooper of BTI for his general support and the simple fact that he acquires our samples. No Coop, no book.

BTI is a team effort. Further thanks must go to Debra Bernstein and Rochelle Calhoun for their administrative support and Gary Nei, Pat Welsh, and Burt Eisenberg, members of the board who have put their money where our mouths are. By purchasing this book, you have moved us ever closer to repaying them. Consider buying another one, wine books make great stocking-stuffers.

Finally, last but certainly not least, we are all indebted to Craig Goldwyn, founder and longtime president of BTI, who has made the rather unusual transition from wine critic to webmaster. It was he who had the guts to start BTI (in his basement) in 1981, despite the advice of pundits long forgotten. Through the lean years he stuck it out, only recently to realize the fruits of his sacrifices. His stubborn nature and determination are reflected in all that BTI does today. He is one of a kind—give him a bump.

The Beverage Testing Institute's
Buying Guide
to Inexpensive Wines

Introduction

by Charles Laverick

Wine has gotten expensive. We may wish that it wasn't the case, but it's a fact that is hard to deny. Taking advantage of an unprecedented economic roll, producers in most of the world's glamorous wine growing regions have raised prices at a rate considerably above that of inflation. It is not uncommon to have the price of a particular wine doubling over the course of three or four vintages. We have often been asked the question by consumers, "Yes, but is it worth it?" The answer is that it is worth it if you are willing to pay the price for a very expensive wine—either because you truly enjoy it, or you want to impress someone. Our rhetorical response then usually ends with "Is a Rolls Royce worth 15 Hyundais?"

However, for those of you who just like wine, don't subscribe to a phalanx of lifestyle-masquerading-as-wine magazines, and have no one to impress but yourself, all does not have to be gloom and doom. There are a number of producers around the world who have kept a lid on prices, some chronically undervalued wine styles and regions, and even the odd national wine industry that has made a specialty of trying to make good wines for reasonable prices and offer consumers value for money. (Australia comes to mind.) This is where this book comes in handy. It is a simple guide to currently available, BTI recommended (scoring 80 and up) wines from around the world that cost $15 or less. Now, when faced with a wall of Chardonnays, you can whip out this trusty book and be sure that you get value for your hard-earned money.

This book is arranged in the same way that many consumers buy wine: first by general type (sparkling, red, white, etc.), then by grape variety or style (Cabernet, Merlot, Chardonnay, and so on). If you like Chardonnay, the Chardonnay chapter will give you a general introduction to value Chardonnays from around the world—the where, what, and how—and lots of Chardonnay reviews arranged by categories such as where they're from. This format also encourages experimentation, as we suggest good value Chardonnays to try, not only from California but from all corners of the globe. Why not a Chardonnay from South Africa or Italy for a change of pace? We have reviewed over 7,000 wines in the last year, and distilled that down to over 1,500 wines that won't kill you, or your pocketbook, arranged the way you buy wine to begin with. No muss, no fuss.

About BTI

The Beverage Testing Institute (BTI) was founded in 1981, with a mission to create fair and reliable reviews. This led to the institute publishing a well-respected magazine, *International Wine Review*, from 1984 through 1990. Subsequently, the results of BTI tastings were featured first in *Wine & Spirits* magazine, and then in *Wine Enthusiast* magazine as an independently produced buying guide. Other publications, including the *Chicago Tribune* and the *Washington Post*, have showcased BTI reviews over the years.

In 1994, BTI began to review beer and spirits in addition to wine. Today, we are the largest full-time beverage review body in the world. In 1999 BTI will review more than 10,000 wines, beers, and spirits. We produce a bimonthly publication, *Tastings, The Journal*, which carries up-to-the-minute reviews and insight from the world of wine, beer, and spirits. *Tastings, The Journal* is supported by our website, Tastings.com, which contains hundreds of articles, links to all things gustatory, including thousands of winery and brewery listings, and a database of over 30,000 of our recent reviews, linked to retailers around the country so that you don't have to pull your hair out looking for that hard to find wine. Additionally, Tastings.com features the Insiders Club, a subscription service that alerts consumers to highly rated products from upcoming issues of *Tastings, The Journal*. This puts you ahead of the crowd, before those products sell out. To subscribe, or to get more information about either *Tastings, The Journal* or the Insiders Club at Tastings.com, email us at journal@tastings.com; write to us at Beverage Testing Institute, 310 South Peoria Street, Suite 504A, Chicago, IL 60607; or phone us at 312-226-7857.

In addition to these endeavors, BTI produces a range of books. These include *Buying Guide to the Wines of North America, Buying Guide to Imported Wines, Buying Guide to Inexpensive Wines from Around the World, Buying Guide to Beer,* and *Buying Guide to Spirits*. They are all published by Sterling Publishers. Other publications that currently carry our reviews and musings include *Restaurant Hospitality* magazine, *All About Beer* magazine, Epicurious—the website of *Bon Appetit* and *Gourmet* magazines, AOL at keyword "Drinks," and Foofoo.com, to name a few.

BTI employs eight people on a full time basis. BTI, in no particular order, is: Craig Goldwyn-web guy/guru, Jon Winsell-operations/man of databases, Richard Cooper-marketing/man of cigars, Charles Laverick-wine/outdoorsman, Marc Dornan-wine/beer/resident alien, Catherine Fallis-Journal/woman of words, Debra Bernstein-whip cracker/chef, Rochelle Calhoun-teamster/Latin dance instructor and Señor Alan Dikty-man of letters/spirits. As a group, we spend lots of time listening to Johnny Cash.

How BTI Reviews Are Created

My name is Charles Laverick. I am responsible for wine reviews at the Beverage Testing Institute, but I don't do it alone, and that is the difference between a BTI review and a review from a wine critic who is working alone. My colleague, Marc Dornan, sits in on nearly all reviewing sessions, as does an invited guest panelist chosen specifically for expertise in a given region. This panel of three convenes on a daily basis at 9:30 a.m. to conduct our wine reviews, and uses a proprietary methodology, which insures that BTI reviews are both consistent and meaningful.

The Quality Question

There are two widely used scales in the product-testing universe. These are the qualitative assessment scale and the consumer acceptance scale. While a consumer scale asks the taster whether or not they like a particular product and if so to what degree, a qualitative scale is focused on a given product's quality vis-à-vis its peers (i.e., Qualitative: "In the world of Cabernet is this a world-class product?" Consumer: "Do you personally care for Cabernet or the flavors of this Cabernet in particular?").

Other critics don't fit neatly into either category, but tend to put a great deal of weight on their personal wine preferences, regardless of style. After some experimentation, we have come to the conclusion that a strict qualitative scale does the job better, as it more accurately reflects the consumer's understanding of the 100-point scale to which our reviews are ultimately translated. A 90 score signifies an excellent wine in the wider context of the wines of the world. Do consumers, or even professionals, like the flavors caused by malolactic fermentation in Chardonnay? Herbal Sauvignons? Oak-driven reds? We think these questions are best left to marketing professionals. Instead, a BTI panelist will look at any style of wine as valid. We are not in an endless quest for thick wines with lots of oak or any other uniform wine style. We believe diversity should be celebrated and endeavor not to set out on any stylistic crusades or frame qualitative decisions along purely stylistic guidelines. A BTI panelist will set aside any personal prejudices about particular wine styles (oaked Chablis, modern Barolo, New Zealand Sauvignon, etc.) and judge wines solely on their own merits. Using this challenging set of criteria necessitates a small, well-trained cadre of tasting professionals.

Three's Company

While a consumer approach requires a broad base of panelists to get an accurate sample size, a qualitative approach requires a small number of professionals who specialize in whatever varietal or region is being addressed, and have demonstrated expertise as such. A BTI panel will most always contain exactly three panelists. Why three? Relying on a single taster carries with it a certain risk. After all everyone has a bad day. However, panels have their faults as well. Chief among them is the "law of averages." Two panelists give a product low marks while two give a product high marks—the net result? The data "averages" to describe a middle-of-the-road product, what none of the four originally thought. Borrowing an approach from the Australian show system (clever, those Antipodeans), we use a panel of three. This eliminates the inherent problem of averaging; helping to guarantee that what we print is what we meant to say. That's not to say that we won't on occasion have an extra individual in the room. Unlike some reviewers, we make a point of being transparent, welcome qualified visitors, and are happy to have them "audit" a session. Additionally, new panelists, or those without depth of experience in the category du jour will always "audit" the tasting (meaning their scores won't count) until such time as they are deemed ready. In order to achieve and maintain the desired level of consistency, the panel of three contains our two in-house tasting directors and one specifically invited expert for the "guest slot." This allows us to review very large categories with most panelists seeing the majority of, if not all, wines in that category. Finally, all panelists undergo a rigorous warm-up exercise that is not only educational, but allows each individual to determine whether or not they are "up to snuff" for the day's tasting. If there is the slightest doubt, that panelist is expected to disqualify himself before the tasting, and be replaced by one of the other trained in-house tasters whom we have on hand.

A Banded Approach

The scoring system that our panelists use is quite narrow, and hence our scoring tends to be highly repeatable. A score is given only after a thorough, objective assessment of a wine's qualities. We have devised a system based on the bands in the 100-point scale, which are widely recognized and roughly correspond to a five-star style system. These bands are:

96–100	Superlative
90–95	Exceptional
85–89	Highly Recommended
80–84	Recommended
<80	Not Recommended

After this thorough assessment of a wine's characteristics, a panelist is asked to place it in one of four quality bands in each of two rounds. All wines are intially tasted under "first round" parameters using a qualitative assessment that does not assess points for certain elements that are then added, but instead looks at overall quality. The first-round scale is as such:

Round One

1 - A wine that one would not recommend in the wider context of today's global wine market (<80 points)

2 - A wine of sound commercial quality, though not overly exciting (80–84)

3 - A very good wine showing style and character, yet probably not of the highest merit (85–89)

4 - A wine that may be at the highest quality levels (potentially 90+)

Those wines that receive at least two scores of 4 are sent to the "merit round" whose scale is as follows:

Round Two

3 - A very good wine, yet upon comparison with examples of the highest

quality, not of the highest merit (88–89 points)

4 - A truly excellent wine, of style and distinction (90–92)

5 - An outstanding wine, though not quite one of the world's finest (93–95)

6 - A world-class wine, providing one of the world's great wine experiences (96–100)

This banded approach allows our tasters to think in broad terms of general quality without getting mixed up in the minutiae of adding up points for "ageability," "color," or "aftertaste." We, just like the consumer, are addressing the wine in question only in its totality. Further, individual tasters do not have to concern themselves with what constitutes the differences between an 88 or an 86 or a 90 and a 91. Finally, one of the chief advantages of this system is the large percentage of wines tasted more than once. To witness, wines scoring over the critical 90 point barrier are without exception tasted twice, a virtual guarantee that a wine rated as such will be deserving of the accolades. Also, after the first round, all wines that show a wide disparity in scoring between panelists (controversial) are re-tasted at a later date under first round parameters, as are many low scoring wines.

A Novel Permutation

Final scores are reached using a novel mapping process that does not average the three scores but instead uses the mode, a statistic much closer to what the panelists, as a group, are really saying. If, for instance, a wine in the first round receives three scores of "3," it is placed in the upper center of the (85–89) band and given a final score of 88 points. Should the third score be a 4 or a 2, the wine in question would be given an 89 or an 86, respectively. The third score is used to move the final score up or down within the same band. Again, permutations that are controversial will be re-tasted. While the need to further narrow down scores within bands is a topic of some debate in the industry, we have taken the position that it is still in the consumer's interest to do so for the top four recommended bands: 80–84, 85–89, 90–95, and 96–100. Wines falling in the lowest band (<80) are simply noted as not recommended (NR) and no further breakdown is attempted. We realize that there are many conflicting views about the 100-point scale, but feel that we have devised the fairest system going for reaching individual points on that scale.

Description Is Key

In our continued attempt to lead the consumer "beyond the scores," we have been putting ever-greater emphasis on our descriptive evaluations. In order to continue this process, and also to insure thorough and consistent assessments, we use a comprehensive evaluation form in our tasting room. These forms translate directly to the final "tasting notes" that we try to print with every recommended wine. (In instances where space doesn't permit this, all notes can be found on our website, www.tastings.com.) This form places an emphasis on objective structural information from color through intensity of finish. It covers several vital parameters and is amended with a final qualitative comment. This insures that all of our tasting notes are consistent in style, yet readable, while accurately conveying stylistic information to the consumer.

In order to make this descriptive information as consistent as possible (not to mention our qualitative assessments) we continue to rely heavily on our state-of-the-art tasting facility in Chicago. This room was specially designed to minimize external factors, and maximize our panelists concentration. Tasting at the same time of day, blind, under the same conditions, our panel continually works under ideal conditions. Hand in hand with our scorecard, we have specially designed tasting aids in order to standardize our tasting vocabularies. To this end we have even gone to the length of installing a state-of-the-art natural lighting system, paired with a standardized color palate for ever-greater consistency. If all this sounds fanatical, it's because we are fanatical. Our institute is unique in the world of wine. We provide the world's only full-time professional reviewing service. This is not a contest, and couldn't be further from your typical "set 'em up and knock 'em down" wine fair. We take what we do seriously and train rigorously, both out of respect for producers and with an eye to providing the most trustworthy reviews a consumer can find.

Special Reports

Occasionally, we must travel to a wine region in order to cover it in a timely fashion. The best example would be Bordeaux, where we taste the new vintage directly from the barrel on an annual basis, because the wine is sold in the futures market before it is bottled. These field tastings are referred to as "Special Reports," and an "SR" next to the tasting note designates reviews created in this fashion. This is to tell the reader that the review was not created under the ideal circumstances that we have established at our tasting lab in Chicago. Further, if the wine being reviewed was a barrel sample (a wine that has not finished aging or undergone the rigors of bottling), the score will be shown as a range—for instance 90–95. This is to make it clear to the reader that wines at this stage of evolution are tricky to evaluate, and that we are only aiming to put it into a general qualitative range based on its potential. Even when in the field, however, we strive to maintain as much of our methodology as possible, including a penchant for tasting blind. Lamentably, this is not always possible and that is why we do the vast majority of our tastings in Chicago where we can control all external factors.

Ten Things You Need to Know about Buying, Storing, and Serving Wine

1. Drink what you like.

Don't be intimidated. If you like a bit of sweetness to your wine, revel in it. If you just don't like red wine no matter what Morley Safer has to say, don't sweat it. Figure out what type of wine you like and get on with it. There are great examples of wine made in all styles. You pay for it and it should make you happy. If someone who presumes to know more than you do about wine gives you a hard time, get rid of them by referring to them as "cork dork" repeatedly or tell them that their Cabernet would be better on the rocks (see point ten).

2. Find a good retailer.

There are tons of wine shops around the country, both large and small, with people who are genuinely interested in wine waiting to answer your questions. If no one is willing to answer your questions, it is not a good wine shop. If they tell you what you should buy without asking you some fundamental questions—like what you like—it is not a good wine shop. In the end this person can steer you in the right direction and prevent the condition known as "overwhelming choice panic." Making a friend at a wine shop also may give you access to the allocated stuff that never hits the shelves. Your chances of getting a better wine for your money at a wine specialist (with assistance) as opposed to a grocery store (without assistance) are pretty good—plus you don't have to wait for an adult to come over and ring you up.

3. Pull from the bottom.

When in the wine shop, you will often notice that the wine is displayed vertically with a bottle on top and more of the same kind underneath it. Don't take the bottle on top; pull one from underneath. There are two reasons for this. One is that wine is sensitive to light, and fluorescent light in particular (hence the added protection of green or brown bottles). If your wine has been sitting there for a long time it may not be in quite the same condition as those that are a little more sheltered. Second, your new friend the retailer will have to come over and put one of the bottles from underneath in the display spot so that the next person knows what's there. This may endanger your chances of getting free samples and other handouts.

4. Beware the window and the vertical bottle.

Wine is not only sensitive to light; it is also sensitive to heat. If the wine shop in question is 90 degrees in the summer or the wine is sitting on a shelf in front of a window, it is not a good wine shop. The heat will degrade the wine rather quickly, while constant temperature swings provided by exposure to sun, followed by cooler temperatures at night will accelerate the wine's demise at an alarming rate. Heat damaged wines can sometimes be spotted by the fact that the wine will have expanded and popped the cork up out of the bottle a half inch or so. In bad cases, there may even be a bit of "seepage." Finally, wines that don't have a high turnover rate should be stored horizontally not upright. This is because when upright, the cork is no longer in contact with the wine. After some time the cork will dry out and contract, losing its seal. If the wine is then stored horizontally for a long period of time the wine may seep out the side. A sign of seepage (a sticky residue or stain) on the neck of the bottle under the capsule is not a good sign. If it is an old or rare wine, a cool, constant temperature over the years and horizontal storage should be prerequisites. If it seems like an unbelievable deal, there may be a reason. Show restraint.

5. Thou shalt not put wine near furnace.

When you bring wine home, don't forget everything you just learned. Wine does not like light, heat, temperature swings, or vibration. If you intend to keep it for a while don't put it next to the furnace. If it's a bottle for tonight, or next week, or next month, don't worry (real extremes excluded). If you intend to keep some wine around for a while though, find a decent spot for it. Storage doesn't have to be expensive. Put it on its side in a cool basement, or in a cooler part of the house that is usually dark, such as a closet. Though you may hear that ideal storage conditions are 55 degrees F and about 70% humidity (to keep the cork moist and maintain the seal—very dry climates can dry a cork from the outside over a very extended period of time), the reality is that wine stored at a constant temperature of even 70 or 72 degrees F should be just fine. Remember that wild swings in temperature are worse. That being said, if you are a big shooter who invests lots of money, a cooling unit that also controls humidity is probably in order, especially if you are likely to have wine sitting around for a long time. It becomes a sickness, trust me. Plus, when you go to auction wine because you realize that your grandchildren will still be well provisioned with what you have left, the auction house will check "provenance." Has the wine been well stored over its lifetime? Poor cellar conditions will translate to lower bids. Seepage or popped corks probably mean rejection.

6. The myth of food pairing.

Cork dorks (see point one) like nothing better than to prattle on about food pairing. These inane people have given the average consumer the idea that they can't drink a particular wine without this or that type of food. Serving wine can lead to agitation and a condition known as corkophobia, whereby a wine's owner is afraid to pop the cork because they have been incapacitated by the thought of making a food pairing blunder. Here's the scoop. Drink what you like with food you like. While it is true that certain combinations may heighten the qualities of both food and wine, it is an impractical nightly ritual, and most wine is not meant to be a special occasion beverage. Rarely will a combination prove truly disastrous, and if you don't notice anyway does it really matter? One final inside secret. I am a wine critic. At home I drink red wine 95% of the time. I usually have wine with dinner. I do not have a breast of Muscovy duck sliced razor thin, dressed with a compote of rare Moroccan cherries and served on a melange of juvenile central Asian grains to go with a specific wine because it worked for someone else who is paid to come up with this drivel. Sometimes I have fish. Sometimes I have cheeseburgers. I then have a glass of red and never give it a second thought.

7. Get a grip on the glass.

Glassware has become a hot topic recently. There are companies that have designed specific glasses for every conceivable type of wine, from Napa Valley

Chardonnay to Chianti between two and three point five years of age grown on young vines and harvested on a Thursday under a waxing moon. Simple really, once the evil crystal cartels have their claws in you, you will have to buy a glass for every bottle you bring home. Where will you put them after a while? Also, with the profits they will be making from your initial purchases, they will design ever more perfect and riveting glasses, compelling you to buy them, always in search of glass-wine nirvana. The result of this spiraling descent into the fluffy cloud that is wine crystal? You will be penniless and on the street, with only a bottle, a paper bag, and your MD 20/20 super-sommelier 6450 glass to console you. To avoid this fate get yourself a set of simple glasses. Ideally, they should be tulip shaped and stemmed, with a slight taper inward toward the rim. This is so that when you give the wine a little swirl and put your nose to the top of the glass, the aromas will be right there for you. Don't fill the glass beyond a half to a third full for the simple reason that when you give it a little swirl you will spill it on yourself, or your date. If you like to drink your wine out of pewter tankards and it makes you happy, that's okay too, otherwise clear glass is a good idea, not these funny colored things that don't let you see the color of your wine. Since we actually evaluate wine for a living, we have researched glassware quite thoroughly. After lots of experimentation, we settled on the Riedel red wine glass from their "Overture" series. It works well for all types of wine, even Champagne, as the winemaker of Dom Perignon was amused to learn when visitng our office.

8. To decant or not to decant?

Rich red wines or ports that have been aged for five years or so—sometimes a little less, sometimes a lot more—can throw a sediment. This happens when some of the "stuffing" (technical term) falls out of solution as a dark-colored sandy-type substance, and settles on the bottom of the bottle. The problem is that when the bottle is shaken the wine turns cloudy and takes on a sort of gritty astringency when you drink it. The same effect can be had when the unshaken sediment from the bottom of the bottle is poured into your glass. How to solve this problem? Decanting. Get a carafe, or a decanter, or a water pitcher—anything that can hold the contents of the bottle. Light a candle or place the container over some other source of light. Take the bottle, which has been resting on its side or placed upright a couple days before to allow "sedimental relocation" (hint), and open it while resisting the urge to shake it violently. Slowly pour from the bottle into the container with the neck of the bottle strategically positioned over the light source. It will look dark at first but don't panic. When about half the wine is poured out you will note the red color of the wine and be able to see clearly through to the light. Keep pouring, slowly tilting the bottle, and near the end you will notice a dark curl of sediment creeping up the bottle. Before it hits the neck, stop pouring. Congratulations, you have "decanted." Throw the little bit that's left out or cook with it. Decanting can also be done when drinking a youthful, full-bodied red that is muted and tannic. The interchange with oxygen helps to "open" the wine, simulating years of age in an hour or two. Be warned the cork dork who says that a wine bottle should be opened, then left on the table to "breathe." How much oxygen do you think 750 ml of wine gets from a dime-sized air space over an hour? Rather less than it will get from the act of pouring it into your glass I can assure you.

9. Don't serve it too cold.

Now that you are about to drink the wine that you have bought, stored, decanted, and generally fussed over—or not—do yourself a favor. Don't leave it on ice or in the arctic reaches of the refrigerator until it is so cold that you wouldn't want to put your tongue on the bottle. You are drinking a nice wine because good wine smells and tastes like something. If you don't like the taste of wine, however, over-chilling is a good tactic. It has the effect of dulling the wine's aromas and flavors. To chill, but not over-chill, an hour in the fridge is fine. In a restaurant, if the wine has been on ice for a while or a waiter brings you an arctic bottle and sets it back in the ice bucket, just pull it out and put it on the table. It will warm throughout the meal and open up in a few minutes time. While cold temperatures are something to watch with whites, Champagne is a bit of an exception. Champagne, due to its carbonation, has a tendency to be a bit rough at warmer temperatures, sort of like warm Coca-Cola. Bubbly needs a pretty good chill. If it is a really good Champagne (usually, but not always expensive is key here) don't over chill it for the same reasons as with whites, it will usually have a bit of age to it that has dulled the carbonation anyway. You paid the extra money because you think it tastes better than Cold Duck. Don't treat it like Cold Duck.

10. Or too hot.

You may have heard that red wines are best served at room temperature. This is true, but only partially. The adage meant European room temperature, and that usually referred to Britain. If you haven't been in a typical English home, take my word for it, it's chilly. There are Eskimos in Alaska who keep warmer igloos. The fact of the matter is a rich, high-alcohol (anything over 13%) red takes on a hot, rather aggressive profile where the alcohol dulls the aromas, at temperatures much above 70 or 72 degrees F. This is particularly true of the big, rich, ripe reds being produced in California, Australia, and other warm climate regions. When we taste reds at BTI, we serve them at about 67 or 68 degrees F. When talking about something like Zinfandel, the difference is like night and day. At home I keep wines at cellar temperature, but if I have something that seems a bit warm, I'll throw the bottle in the fridge for ten minutes or so. Try heavy reds both ways, you'll be instantly converted. I even find that an ice cube can rescue a heavy red from being served too warm, particularly at a cocktail party or in the heat of summer. Many restaurants have the nasty habit of chilling the whites beyond recognition and then storing the reds somewhere above the grill, particularly in the United States. Even in France; however, they have not quite got the hang of it. At one particularly well-known French restaurant that shall remain nameless, I was subjected to a Cote-Rotie that had been stored near the restaurant's exquisite wood-burning fire. The remedy, of course, was to ask for an ice bucket on which the decanter could rest for a few minutes and an ice cube for the wine in my glass. The inverse came later in the meal, with an old bottle of Sauternes that was being subjected to the polar treatment. The bottle was pulled and allowed to rest on the table. I gave no speeches and never treat such instances as a big deal, but that is how these wines show best. Even if it gave the sommelier something to snicker at for months on end, it made my dining companions and me happy. In the end, with wine, that's all that matters.

one

Sparkling Wines

Introduction   22
Reviews   24
  Cava   24
  French Sparklers   25
  U.S. Sparklers
   Brut   26
   Blanc de Blancs   26
   Blanc de Noirs   27
   Other U.S. Sparklers 27
  Other Great
Value Sparklers   28
  Italian Sparklers:
Moscato d'Asti and
Asti Spumante   28

Introduction: Great Value Sparkling Wines

It launches ships, celebrates matrimony, announces the arrival of a newborn, and says congratulations to a job promotion. It is sparkling wine, an indispensable catalyst for any special occasion. Winston Churchill said of Champagne, "In success you deserve it and in defeat you need it."

Among all of sparkling wine's opportunities to pass our lips, perhaps one stands above all others—the ringing in of a new year. The beginning of the new millennium is the greatest New Year's party of our lifetime, and the greatest party in memory calls for the perfect sparkling wine. This has resulted in unprecedented demand for sparkling wine and Champagne at all price levels. Sweet, dry, pink, or white, we need a sparkler that will satisfy our palates and delight our friends without tumbling us into financial ruin before the Y2K bug does.

Champagne, Anyone?

Champagne, in the American lexicon, is often misused to refer to any sparkling wine. Champagne is actually a strictly designated wine-producing region northeast of Paris in France. It is not technically accurate (or legally permissible in much of the world) to label sparkling wines made outside of the Champagne region as Champagne. Unfortunately, true Champagne is outside of value boundaries. Typically, a Champagne house's least expensive offerings sell for approximately $25 a bottle, and their top wines often sell for four or more times that amount. However, there is no need for despair, as many affordable, high-quality sparkling wines are produced throughout the world. Most notably, the United States and Spain are reliable sources for well-made dry sparkling wines at reasonable prices. For those with a preference for something sweeter, Italy may have just the right bubbly.

Most of the world's sparkling wines fall into one of two categories based on how they are made, *Méthode Champenoise*, or the Charmat process (also known as the "bulk method"). As the name indicates, Méthode Champenoise is the French term used to describe wines made by the traditional Champagne method. This unique process creates the wine's signature bubbles by way of a secondary fermentation that takes place in the bottle after the addition of yeast and sugar to a still wine. The result is a secondary fermentation, which produces alcohol, carbon dioxide (bubbles), and sediment that is ultimately removed in a procedure known as disgorging. Outside of Champagne, wines made by Méthode Champenoise are not always produced from the traditional Champagne grapes—Chardonnay, Pinot Noir, and Pinot Meunier. However, many U.S. producers of sparkling wine restrict themselves to the classic Champagne varietals.

The Charmat process involves a secondary fermentation in a large tank or vat. When the wine has achieved its desired carbonation and flavor, it is then filtered and bottled under pressure to retain its bubbles. This method is far less costly and cumbersome than Méthode Champenoise, but it represents a big step down in quality, with refinement being the first casualty.

Styles

Within the sparkling wine category, several variations exist. These styles are most often indicated on the label and are as follows:

Brut. This is a French term used to describe or identify the driest sparkling wines, with the exception of rare bottlings labeled "Brut Zero" or "Natural." Confusingly, Brut is drier than wines labeled "Extra Dry."

Extra Dry. Slightly sweeter than Brut, typically containing a very moderate amount of sugar, which manifests itself in a rounded, less tart palate feel.

Demi Sec. Sweet wines often used with dessert. These wines are not seen as often as Brut or Extra Dry.

Blanc de Blanc. Literally, white wine from white grapes. In the context of Champagne, and most U.S. Méthode Champenoise wines, it indicates a sparkling wine made entirely from Chardonnay. This may seem to be redundant and unnecessary because virtually all of the world's white wines are made from white grapes, but the delineation is important considering that two of the three traditional Champagne grapes are black. The resulting wines are typically more steely and fresh than those made from a blend of black and white grapes, and they often display a more pronounced yeasty quality.

Blanc de Noir. Literally, white wine from black grapes. Red wines acquire their color from pigments within the skin of the grape. Clear juice is obtained from red grapes when they are carefully crushed, allowing the juice to immediately separate from the skins. In the context of Champagne and most U.S. Méthode Champenoise wines, it indicates a sparkling wine made entirely from Pinot Noir and Pinot Meunier. Many Blanc de Noir wines are not entirely free of color, exhibiting a faint copper tint or pinkish hue.

Regions

Spain is the world's foremost supplier of value-priced Méthode Champenoise wines. These lovely sparkling wines are known as *Cava*, and largely come from the Penedés region of

Great Value Sparkling Wines at a Glance

Number of Wines Recommended:

51

Countries Represented:

7

northern Spain. In the past decade Cavas have become extremely popular in the United States. They are made in a variety of styles; consult the accompanying tasting notes to assist in choosing one to your liking. Regardless of style, Cava rarely exceeds $15 a bottle.

Asti

Asti Spumante is Italy's best known sparkling wine. Spumante is the Italian term for "foaming" or "sparkling," and Asti is an important wine-growing area in the Piedmont region of northern Italy. Recently, however, producers in Asti have dropped the word Spumante and now refer to these wines simply as Asti. Nearly all Asti is produced by the Charmat process, known locally as autoclave. The wines are made entirely from the Moscato di Canelli grape. Asti is unique among sparkling wines in that it is made directly from grape juice as opposed to a finished dry wine, in the manner of Champagne and its imitators. This results in a very fresh, grapey tasting wine. Asti is always bottled with a healthy portion of residual sugar, ranging from 7.5% to 9%. In addition to Asti Spumante, the Asti region is known for Moscato d'Asti, a lightly sparkling wine with a hint of sweetness, soft bubbles, and amazingly fresh, intense aromas. Vintage is of little concern with these Italian sparkling wines, but they should be bought and consumed when they are young.

Other Sparkling Wines

Many U.S. sparkling wines are made with Champagne as the model. In fact, a number of famous producers from Champagne and Spain are involved in U.S. sparkling wine production, either as partners or owner/operators. Virtually all styles of Champagne are replicated in the United States, many of them with great success. Woefully, this success has driven up prices, as most bottlings sell in the mid-$20 range, and some higher. Keeping true to the French model, many producers adhere to a multi-tier approach. For U.S. producers, this places their simplest offering in the value range, while their top wines sell for Champagne-like prices.

When buying value sparkling wines, vintage is generally not a factor because most are not vintage dated. With the given style information, you should be able to locate a wine that suits your taste. Beyond the obvious uses as a celebratory beverage, sparkling wines are very versatile at the table. They are unquestionably a fabulous apéritif, perhaps the best. Bubbly is often a great choice with seafood—either complementing fresh shellfish or serving to cut a rich dish such as lobster with drawn butter.

Reviews

Cava

88 • *Montsarra (Spain) NV Cava Brut, Penedés. $11.99.*
Bright deep yellow-gold. Moderately full-bodied. Balanced acidity. Spicy, mature aromas show an oxidized character that follows through on the richly flavored, nutty palate with an elegant bead and a lingering, complex finish.

86 • *Sumarroca (Spain) NV Cava Extra Brut, Penedés. $8.99.*
Pale green-straw. Medium-bodied. Full acidity. Big beaded carbonation. Lively mouthfeel with juicy, direct flavors. Finishes with lean minerally notes. Well-balanced, refreshing style.

Scale: Superlative (96-100), Exceptional (90-95), Highly Recommended (85-89), Recommended (80-84), Not Recommended (Under 80)

86 • Segura Viudas (Spain) NV Aria Cava Brut, Penedés. $8.99.
Bright green-gold. Medium-bodied. Full acidity. Fresh green apple aromas lead a fruit-forward palate with a juicy, direct appeal and a clean finish. A snappy aperitif style.

86 • Freixenet (Spain) NV Cordon Negro Brut Cava, Penedés. $7.99.
Pale greenish straw hue. Medium-bodied. Balanced acidity. Mildly floral aromas. Juicy, appealing, simple flavors have an apple and lemon cream character. The mouthfeel shows a degree of creamy richness.

86 • Freixenet (Spain) NV Carta Nevada Cava Brut, Penedés. $6.99.
Bright yellow-gold. Medium-bodied. Balanced acidity. Yellow apples and butter aromas follow through well on the palate with sweet juicy flavors. Finishes with an intriguing spicy note.

84 • Sumarroca (Spain) NV Cava Brut, Penedés. $8.99.
Pale platinum cast. Medium-bodied. Full acidity. Apples, minerals. Clean, direct and juicy with straightforward flavors and medium-beaded carbonation.

81 • Segura Viudas (Spain) NV Reserva Heredad Cava Brut, Penedés 1.1% rs. $15.
Bright gold-yellow. Medium-bodied. Balanced acidity. Yellow apple notes with yeasty overtones follow through on the palate. Full-flavored and lengthy, with finely beaded carbonation.

81 • Marques de Gelida (Spain) NV Cava Brut, Penedés. $7.50.
Pale gold. Moderately light-bodied. Moderately extracted. Citrus, minerals. Light and zesty with a clean citrusy flavor profile that finishes quickly. Effervescence seems frothy and large-beaded in the mouth. Shows lingering mineral notes on the finish.

81 • Freixenet (Spain) NV Brut de Noirs Cava, Penedés. $8.99.
Bright raspberry red. Medium-bodied. Balanced acidity. Perfumed raspberry and cherry aromas lead a juicy, fruity palate with appealing generosity of flavors.

French Sparklers

89 • Jean-Pierre Bechtold (France) NV Collection Robert Beltz, Cremant d'Alsace. $15.
Bright yellow-gold. Balanced acidity. Attractive doughy aromas lead a bright, peachy mouthful of fruit flavors, showing good weight and persistence. Very hedonistic; this should find wide appeal.

84 • Jean-Marc Bernhard (France) NV Brut Reserve, Cremant d'Alsace. $15.
Pale straw hue. Moderately light-bodied. Balanced acidity. A soft, quaffable style with a hint of dryness and restrained acids. Mousse and mouthfeel show effervescence on the low side, making for a very creamy style.

83 • Bouvet (France) NV Rose Excellence, Brut, France. $12.99.
Pale salmon hue. Medium-bodied. Full acidity. Austere aromas lead bright citric flavors, with very subtle dried red-fruit accents that persist through the finish. Quite elegant, with minerally notes on the finish.

81 • Grandin (France) NV Brut, France. $9.99.
Bright yellow-gold. Medium-bodied. Moderately extracted. Faintly smoky, herbal aromas. Very fizzy carbonation, with bright, sweet citrus flavors and a clean finish. Very friendly.

81 • Divinaude (France) NV Cuvee Imperiale, Blanquette de Limoux. $10.
Medium gold-straw hue. Medium-bodied. Rich, rounded mouthfeel, with creamy, apple flavors that linger briefly. Shows very ripe flavors, with softer acids.

81 • Bouvet (France) NV Signature Brut, France. $11.99.
Bright yellow-straw hue. Medium-bodied. Full acidity. Smoky, mildly sweaty aromas lead a brisk, tart, citric palate with good concentration and fine carbonation. Minerally, lean finish.

81 • Baron de Bellac (France) NV Carte Verte, Brut, France. $5.99.

Bright pale platinum cast. Moderately light-bodied. Moderately extracted. Flowers, juicy tropical fruit. A faint floral nose leads a bland, unexciting mouthful of faintly juicy flavors.

U.S. Brut

88 • Chateau Frank (NY) 1991 Brut, Finger Lakes. $15.

Medium straw hue. Medium-bodied. Tropical fruits, citrus, smoke. Soft, bready aromas. Elegant, juicy flavors have an impressively fruity center, with yeast complexity emerging on the finish.

87 • Piper Sonoma (CA) NV Brut, Sonoma. $14.

Bright straw cast. Medium-bodied. Full acidity. Toast, citrus peel. Forward aromas feature a subtle yeast accent. Crisp, bright, and austere through the finish, yet it shows fine biscuity nuances.

86 • Glenora (NY) NV Brut, New York. $12.99.

Pale gold. Moderately full-bodied. Ripe citrus, minerals. Full smoky, citrusy aromas lead a generously proportioned palate, with the accent on crisp fruit flavors. A substantial and rounded style.

86 • Cap Rock (TX) NV Sparkling Wine, American. $12.99.

Bright yellow-straw hue. Medium-bodied. Tropical fruit, grass, minerals. Floral, grassy aromas follow through on the palate, with a decidedly grassy finish. Nonclassical flavors are refreshing and generous through the midpalate.

83 • Korbel (CA) NV Natural Sparkling Wine, California. $12.99.

Pale yellow-gold. Medium-bodied. Citrus zest, canned pears. Powdery, zesty aromas follow through on the palate, with a gripping, dry finish giving some authority. Full, crisp carbonation.

83 • Gruet (NM) NV Brut, New Mexico. $14.

Medium yellow-straw hue. Medium-bodied. Full acidity. Minerals, citrus. Refined and quite aromatic. Very full, fine-beaded carbonation with rounded, yet intense flavors that have a spicy, toasty quality persisting through the finish. Very distinctive, unique flavors.

83 • Gloria Ferrer (CA) NV Brut, Sonoma County. $15.

Bright pale gold. Medium-bodied. Full acidity. Grapefruit, yeast. Steely, bright citrus aromas have a fresh, yeasty note that follows through on the flavor-packed palate and persistent finish. Shows lively, medium-beaded carbonation.

81 • Wente (CA) NV Brut Reserve, Arroyo Seco. $14.

Pale yellow-gold. Medium-bodied. Citrus, minerals. Vibrant, zesty aromas. Very lively, clean flavors, with a strong citrus cut through the finish. Shows lively, large-beaded carbonation. An aperitif style.

81 • Ste. Chapelle (ID) NV Brut, Idaho. $7.99.

Pale straw. Moderately light-bodied. Flowers, white citrus. High-toned floral aromas lead a leaner-styled palate, with full-beaded carbonation and mildly grassy flavors through the finish.

U.S. Blanc de Blancs

86 • Tribaut (CA) NV Blanc de Blancs Brut, California. $9.

Deep gold. Medium-bodied. Full acidity. Subtly extracted. Butter, minerals. Rather overtly mature, with big, toasty aromas that follow through with buttery richness on the palate. The finish is short. Although the maturity is exaggerated, this has attractive character.

85 • Glenora (NY) 1993 Blanc de Blancs, New York. $12.99.

Pale greenish straw cast. Medium-bodied. Minerals, chalk, citrus zest. Reserved and elegant, with understated citrusy flavors. Balanced and lean, with a judicious level of carbonation, a sense of roundness, and mild, sweet fruity notes on the finish.

83 • Korbel (CA) NV Chardonnay Brut, California. $12.99.

Medium yellow straw. Medium-bodied. Spice, tropical fruits. Yeasty, spicy aromas lead a generously flavored palate showing weight and some citrus length. The flavors are very attractive, though the bubbles are rather large.

U.S. Blanc de Noirs

90 • Piper Sonoma (CA) NV Blanc de Noir, Sonoma. $15.

Deep straw cast. Moderately full-bodied. Yeast, toast, bread dough. Forward, mature aromatics are complex and yeasty. Smooth and supple in the mouth, with a silky texture. This seems very generous and developed, with signs of extended bottle age.

86 • Gloria Ferrer (CA) NV Blanc de Noirs, Carneros. $15.

Pale copper with a subtle pinkish overtone. Full-bodied. Full acidity. Highly extracted. Minerals, red fruits. Aromatically reserved, with a forceful and austere mouthfeel featuring vibrant carbonation. Intense and racy through the finish.

84 • Gruet (NM) NV Blanc de Noirs, New Mexico. $14.

Pale straw with a slight copper tinge. Moderately full-bodied. Full acidity. Fruit, citrus, minerals. Carries a fruity overtone throughout. Lush and generous in the mouth, with an ample mouthfeel. Well-balanced and flavorful, this would partner well with food.

82 • Windsor (CA) 1996 Blanc de Noir, Sonoma County. $14.

Pale pink cast. Medium-bodied. Minerals, citrus zest. Aromatically reserved, with a full and racy mouthfeel. Well-balanced and rich, with fruity overtones through the finish.

80 • Tribaut (CA) NV Blanc de Noirs Brut, California. $9.

Deep gold. Full-bodied. Full acidity. Highly extracted. Butter, blanched almonds. Maderized aromas lead to a coarse and rustic mouthfeel, with aggressive carbonation.

Other U.S. Sparklers

86 • Firelands (OH) NV Riesling, Lake Erie. $10.95.

Bright yellow-straw cast. Medium-bodied. Full acidity. Citrus, tropical fruits, minerals. Quite aromatic, with bright, Riesling-like flavors. Firm and frothy in the mouth, with refreshing acidity and a hint of sweetness to round things out.

84 • Ste. Chapelle (ID) NV Sparkling, Johannisberg Riesling, Idaho 2.75% rs. $7.99.

Pale platinum cast. Moderately full-bodied. Full acidity. Highly extracted. Citrus peel, minerals. Pleasantly aromatic, with a firm and tart impression on the palate. Bright, angular, and citrusy through the finish.

84 • L. Mawby (MI) NV Blanc de Blanc Brut, Michigan. $15.

Bright yellow-gold. Moderately full-bodied. Full acidity. Highly extracted. Cream, toast, butter. Ripe and opulent aromas are unusual but complex. Firm and intense in the mouth, with aggressive carbonation and a flavorful finish.

84 • Korbel (CA) NV Rouge Sparkling Wine, California. $12.99.

Pale cherry red. Medium-bodied. Rose petals, cherries. Floral, dark fruit impression is conveyed on the nose and palate with the very slightest suggestion of dry tannin on the finish. Novel, but undeniably appealing.

83 • Chateau Frank (NY) NV Celebre Cremant, Finger Lakes. $10.

Bright green-straw cast. Moderately light-bodied. Full acidity. Citrus, tropical fruits. Forward, fruity aromas lead a crisp and vibrant mouthfeel. Finishes with a touch of sweetness that will appeal to those who do not favor drier styles.

82 • Cook's (CA) NV Spumante, American 8% rs. $4.29.

Green-straw cast. Medium-bodied. Full acidity. Lime, minerals, tropical fruits. Aromatic and forward, with bright, Moscato-like flavors. Crisp and zesty in the mouth, with a hint of sweetness through the finish.

Other Great Value Sparklers

89 • Seaview (Australia) 1997 Brut, South Eastern Australia. $8.

Pale yellow-straw cast. Medium-bodied. Balanced acidity. Moderately extracted. Bread, biscuit, citrus. Mature toasty aromas follow through on the palate, showing a rounded style and a touch of phenolic dryness on the finish. Very flavorful and appealing.

88 • Orlando (Australia) NV Carrington Rose Brut, Australia. $8.99.

Pale red-pink hue. Medium-bodied. Red fruits, citrus. Raspberry and strawberry aromas lead a crisp citric acid palate with red fruit accents that linger on the finish. Very tasty and straightforward.

87 • Seaview (Australia) NV Sparkling Shiraz-Cabernet, South Eastern Australia. $12.

Bright ruby purple. Medium-bodied. Moderately extracted. Pepper, black fruits, vanilla. Youthful Shiraz aromas have an oaky backnote. Flavorful and crisp, with dark bramble fruit flavors that finish with a note of dry tannins. Intense.

86 • Villiera (South Africa) NV Tradition Carte Rouge Brut, South Africa. $12.

Brilliant straw hue with finely beaded bubbles and a thin mousse. Attractive yeast and cream aromas. A crisp entry leads a rich, creamy, moderately full-bodied mouthfeel with vibrant acidity. Clean, lengthy finish. Drink now.

83 • Magnotta (Canada) NV Moscato Superiore. $6.

Pale straw hue. Typical varietal aromas show a floral, fruity quality. A frothy, well-carbonated entry leads a light-bodied palate with bright acids cutting through the residual sweetness. A crisp, quite dry style that remains fresh through the finish.

Italian Sparklers: Moscato d'Asti and Asti Spumante

89 • Mondoro (Italy) NV Spumante, Asti 8.2% rs. $14.

Bright platinum cast. Moderately light-bodied. Full acidity. Subtly extracted. Moderately tannic. Tropical fruits, citrus, chalk. Extremely aromatic with very pure Moscato flavors. Light, racy, and clean, with sweetness nicely counterbalanced by the acidity.

87 • Bera (Italy) 1996 Moscato d'Asti. $14.50.

Bright platinum cast. Light-bodied. Full acidity. Subtly extracted. Tropical fruits, toast. Quite highly carbonated for a Moscato, more closely resembling a fully sparkling wine. This takes the edge off the sweetness and makes it seem fairly dry. Very clean, precise and well focused.

85 • Ceretto (Italy) 1996 Santo Stefano, Moscato d'Asti. $15.

Bright straw cast. Moderately light-bodied. Full acidity. Subtly extracted. Green herbs, citrus. A tad restrained aromatically, with a decided herbal streak throughout. Well balanced and clean, with a very precise character.

83 • Opici (Italy) NV Spumante, Asti . $11.99.

Pale straw cast. Medium-bodied. Full acidity. Moderately extracted. Citrus, toast. Light, fruity, and racy, with strong citric flavors and mouthwatering acidity. Very clean and straightforward in the finish.

83 • Martini & Rossi (Italy) NV Spumante, Asti 9% rs. $12.

Bright platinum hue. Medium-bodied. Full acidity. Subtly extracted. Tropical fruits, toast. Extremely crisp in style with a bracing edge. Very clean through the finish with fairly well-defined Moscato flavors.

82 • Tosti (Italy) NV Spumante, Asti . $8.99.

Pale straw hue. Moderately light-bodied. Full acidity. Moderately extracted. Lanolin, citrus, toast. Not quite as fresh and fruit centered as some that have a fuller character. Relatively dry through the finish.

80 • Icardi (Italy) 1997 La Rosa Selvatica, Moscato d'Asti. $15.

Bright platinum cast. Light-bodied. Full acidity. Subtly extracted. Citrus, yeast, butter. A little unusual aromatically, with a yeasty focus. Quite sweet on entry.

Scale: Superlative (96-100), Exceptional (90-95), Highly Recommended (85-89), Recommended (80-84), Not Recommended (Under 80)

two

Chardonnay

Introduction	30
Reviews	32
White Burgundies	32
Other French Chardonnays	33
Aussie Chardonnays	34
Canadian Chardonnays	37
Italian Chardonnays	38
South African Chardonnays	39
South American Chardonnays	39
U.S. Chardonnays	41
Other Great Value Chardonnays	47

Introduction: Great Value Chardonnay

Chardonnay is the world's most recognized and requested white wine, so much so that it is effectively a cliché. This popularity is exaggerated in the United States, where Chardonnay has become synonymous with white wine. Why is Chardonnay so popular? First and foremost, Chardonnay is not only capable of producing some of the world's greatest white wines, it grows virtually anywhere. It is also a straightforward wine to produce. Chardonnay is made at all price points, but has also reached the pinnacle of quality in many nations and several continents, not only in its native France. Even the most strident Francophile will concede that California and Australia have produced some world-class examples of Chardonnay. More open-minded souls would further make note of Italy, South America, South Africa, and U.S. states other than California. Chardonnay simply has mass flavor appeal. Other varietals may present more distinctive personalities: Sauvignon Blanc with its aggressive herbal flavors and gripping acidity; Gewürztraminer, filling the nose and palate with hints of rosewater and spice; or Viognier in its wildly exotic, unctuous manifestations. Chardonnay strikes a middle chord that translates to universal magnetism and a marketer's dream.

In the global sea of Chardonnay, bargains abound. Chardonnay is present in every market segment, from the ridiculously expensive to the virtual steal. South America (Argentina and Chile) continues to be one of the world's most reliable suppliers of affordable Chardonnay. While many premium labels from Australia and the U.S. have risen to a high price plateau, marketers cannot ignore the huge under $15 wine market. At present, no nation is out of the value Chardonnay game, not even France. Differences in both style and price are as much, if not more, a product of winemaking decisions, rather than of location. This is not to say that fruit from cool climate nations such as Austria does not differ from that of California's hot Central Valley, but Chardonnay, perhaps more than any other variety, is the winemaker's equivalent of a blank white canvas.

Making Chardonnay

Left to its own devises, Chardonnay is simple, fresh, and clean, with fruit ranging in flavors from apple and pear in cooler regions, to tropical fruit flavors in hot climates. The winemaker's decision to use oak or not greatly impacts both flavor and price. Oak barrels are expensive. Chardonnay is often left on its lees—the sediment precipitated during fermentation. This imparts a toasty bread-like flavor. This process, which is sometimes indicated on the label as *Sur Lie*, takes time, and time equals money. A major contributor to flavor is the use of a secondary fermentation, known technically as malolactic fermentation. This secondary fermentation is bacteria-induced and creates no additional alcohol. Instead, it converts one kind of acid, malic, which is found in granny smith apples, to lactic. another softer acid, which is found in milk. In addition to acid conversion, malolactic fermentation creates a natural compound called diacetyl. Diacetyl is used by margarine producers to make their product taste like butter. It does the same for Chardonnay. These processes increases the cost, particularly if done with an artisan's touch.

Scale: Superlative (96-100), Exceptional (90-95), Highly Recommended (85-89), Recommended (80-84), Not Recommended (Under 80)

Regions

Value hunting for Chardonnay in France is still possible. Much of the variety's native home of Burgundy is off limits, as these wines are among the world's most expensive whites. However, two regions of Burgundy, Chablis and the Mâcon (which includes Mâcon-Villages and St. Veran), continue to offer moderately priced wines. Not surprisingly, these two regions do little to manipulate their wines. Little or no oak is used. In Chablis, a mighty debate is underway concerning the use of oak. Much of the value wine from this region is of the no oak ilk. In addition to Chablis and Mâcon, consumers may want to investigate Chardonnay from the Côte Chalonnaise, which includes the wines of Givry, Mercurey, Montagny, and Rully. Most often these wines are value priced, and in good vintages, such as '95, '96, and '97 they can represent incredible values in the world of Burgundy. Outside of Burgundy, an increasing number of Vin de Pays, French regional wines, are becoming available. These wines are extraordinarily consumer friendly because of their approachable flavors, varietal labeling (as in the New World), and attractive prices.

Staying in Europe, Italy has jumped on the Chardonnay bandwagon, producing some excellent examples of the variety. Many New World-inspired, oaky, buttery monsters have been released at equally monstrous prices. Values do exist, primarily in the North, from regions such as the Veneto, Lombardy, and Trentino. The wines are typically straightforward and delicious with enough crisp acidity to make them agreeable food companions.

Australian Chardonnay has a great deal in common with California Chardonnay. Both have cool and hot spots, climatically speaking, that offer all spectrums of fruit flavors from apples to pineapples. Oak is often used for both barrel fermentation and aging. American oak imparts a more aggressively toasty vanilla flavor that is prevalent in many Australian Chardonnays. In recent years, however, Australians have begun to rethink their Chardonnay styles, and the big, thick, buttery, oaky styles seem to be on the wane. Lighter wines

Great Value

Chardonnays

at a Glance

Number of Wines
Recommended:

188

Countries
Represented:

14

with fresher flavors are coming into vogue. As in America, many value Chardonnays from Australia are clean, forward, and unpretentious, showing true varietal fruit and acid. This is a recurring theme among value Chardonnays, which is carried on in other Southern Hemisphere examples, from both South America and South Africa.

Value Chardonnay from the United States crosses all geographic boundaries. California, due largely to its incredible number of wineries and labels, dominates the Chardonnay scene, value and otherwise. In addition to the popularity of flashy oak flavors, tropical fruit flavors from warmer regions are in vogue. This often results in Chardonnay from cooler states and regions fetching lower prices. Value hunters should seek out Chardonnay from Washington and New York. Oregon, although cool, is in fashion as it is considered by connoisseurs to be America's answer to Burgundy. In California the regions of Carneros, the Russian River Valley, and Santa Barbara are considered top regions for Chardonnay, which translates to higher-priced grapes and more costly wines. Cool regions such as Monterey and Mendocino, although greatly respected, tend to offer a greater percentage of values. Additionally, wines with broader designations such as California, North Coast, or Central Coast are most often competitively priced.

Using Chardonnay

Regarding pairing Chardonnay with food, value seekers are ahead of the game. Pricey and flashy Chardonnay from the New World tends to be fat and sweet, with plenty of oak, butter, and spice. On their own they are interesting, if heavy. With food they are clumsy, dominating, and largely incompatible. Value Chardonnays are often more restrained, with clean fruit balanced by crisp acidity. These wines work with a great deal of dishes from fish to fowl. Crisp, simple Chardonnay also works well as an aperitif, stimulating the palate rather than drowning it. When buying value Chardonnay from California, Australia, and South America, vintage is not usually a concern, so you can be confident with the current release. Ask your wine merchant to assist you with vintage preferences from Washington, New York, Oregon, and Europe.

Reviews

White Burgundies

91 • Michel Barat (France) 1996 "Cote de Lechet" Premier Cru, Chablis. $15.
Pale straw cast. Medium-bodied. Full acidity. Moderately extracted. Minerals, citrus peel. Pleasantly aromatic, with a clean and racy palate feel. Generous and flavorful finish with good length.

88 • Simonnet-Febvre (France) 1996 Chablis. $15.
Pale straw hue with a greenish cast. Medium-bodied. Full acidity. Moderately extracted. Minerals. Aromatically closed but light, clean, and quite racy on the palate with a vibrant finish. Textbook.

84 • Michel Barat (France) 1996 Chablis. $12.
Pale straw color. Medium-bodied. Full acidity. Highly extracted. Minerals. Pleasantly aromatic, with a clean, well- structured presence on the palate. Taut and crisp.

84 • *Bernard Defaix (France) 1996 Petit Chablis. $14.*
Pale yellow-straw hue. Moderately light-bodied. Full acidity. Moderately extracted.
Flint, citrus, minerals. Clean minerally nose reveals a lighter-framed palate. Quite
straightforward with a somewhat short finish.

83 • *Michel Picard (France) 1996 Mâcon Villages. $11.99.*
Pale straw. Medium-bodied. Balanced acidity. Moderately extracted. Apples, minerals.
Fresh, varietally correct aromas follow through on the palate. Decent mouthfeel, with
no oak influences.

83 • *Georges Duboeuf (France) 1997 Chardonnay, Saint-Veran. $9.*
Pale straw cast. Medium-bodied. Full acidity. Moderately extracted. Minerals, earth.
Forward aromas carry a residual hint of sulphur that blows off with aeration. Firm,
intense, and crisp in the mouth with vibrant balancing acidity.

83 • *Bernard Defaix (France) 1996 Chablis. $13.*
Bright straw hue with a greenish cast. Medium-bodied. Full acidity. Moderately extracted.
Citrus peel, dried herbs. Pleasantly aromatic with a straightforward palate feel and solid
grip.

83 • *Alain Geoffroy (France) 1996 Chablis. $14.50.*
Pale yellow-straw hue. Moderately light-bodied. Balanced acidity. Moderately extracted.
Clean, mildly tropical Chardonnay aromas follow through on the palate. Very nice,
but it has no minerally Chablis character to speak of. Ripe and highly quaffable.

82 • *Michel Barat (France) 1996 "Vaillons" Premier Cru, Chablis. $15.*
Bright straw hue. Medium-bodied. Full acidity. Moderately extracted. Minerals.
Aromatically reserved, with a zesty attack. Fades somewhat at the finish. Pleasant, but
could use a bit more grip.

82 • *Georges Duboeuf (France) 1997 Chardonnay, Mâcon-Villages. $8.*
Bright straw cast. Medium-bodied. Full acidity. Moderately extracted. Minerals, earth,
butter. Shows a slight earthy aspect to the nose. Lean and crisp in the mouth. Rounds
out toward the finish.

**81 • *Reine Pedauque (France) 1996 "Les Chevaliers de la Reine,"
Chardonnay, Bourgogne. $10.99.***
Pale yellow-straw hue. Medium-bodied. Balanced acidity. Moderately extracted. Lemons,
minerals. Good mouthfeel, with some nutty notes through the finish. Firm and minerally.

81 • *Louis Latour (France) 1996 Blanc, Givry. $13.*
Medium gold-straw hue. Medium-bodied. Balanced acidity. Moderately extracted. Mildly
oaked. Mildly toasty nose. Rounded mouthfeel has hints of phenolic astringency that
emerge on the finish. Quaffable, showing some edges..

Other French Chardonnays

**87 • *Louis Latour (France) 1996 Grand Ardèche, Chardonnay,
Vin de Pays des Coteaux de L'Ardèche. $13.***
Bright pale gold. Moderately full-bodied. Full acidity. Highly extracted. Moderately
oaked. Vanilla, smoke, yeast. Quite aromatic, with a toasty oak accent and yeasty flavors
throughout. Full and rich, yet crisp through the finish.

86 • *Michel Picard (France) 1996 Chardonnay, Vin de Pays d'Oc. $9.99.*
Bright gold. Moderately full-bodied. Balanced acidity. Moderately extracted. Cream,
toast, minerals. Ripe and rounded in style, with enough acidity to lend a sense of balance.
Nicely textured and flavorful.

85 • *Gallerie (France) 1996 Chardonnay, Vin de Pays de L'Hérault. $6.99.*
Bright gold. Moderately full-bodied. Full acidity. Moderately extracted. Mildly oaked.
Tropical fruits, spice, minerals. Forward fruit flavors are accented by judicious use of
oak. Full and flavorful, yet crisp and well balanced through the finish.

83 • Vichon (France) 1996 Mediterranean, Chardonnay, Vin de Pays d'Oc. $10.

Bright straw cast. Moderately light-bodied. Full acidity. Subtly extracted. Minerals, citrus fruits. Aromatically reserved, with a crisp and lively mouthfeel and no discernible oak influence. A refreshing quaffer.

83 • Marquise de Lassime (France) 1997 Chardonnay, Vin de Pays du Jardin de la France. $4.99.

Pale straw hue. Medium-bodied. Full acidity. Moderately extracted. Lemon, minerals. Tart, lean citrus flavors grip the palate. Finishes quickly, though the flavors are crisp and precise.

83 • La Baume (France) 1996 Chardonnay, Vin de Pays d'Oc. $6.99.

Bright greenish gold. Medium-bodied. Full acidity. Moderately extracted. Dried herbs, minerals. Forward aromatics carry a distinct herbal edge. Lean, crisp, and zesty through the finish.

83 • Jenard (France) 1997 Caves des Papes, Chardonnay, Vin de Pays d'Oc. $7.99.

Pale gold. Medium-bodied. Full acidity. Moderately extracted. Minerals, citrus. Lean, crisp, and clean, with a crisp, minerally character. A pleasant aperitif style.

83 • Georges Duboeuf (France) 1997 Chardonnay, Vin de Pays d'Oc. $6.99.

Pale straw cast. Medium-bodied. Full acidity. Moderately extracted. Mildly oaked. Toast, minerals, smoke. Shows just a hint of wood in the nose. Light and crisp in the mouth, with a zesty finish.

83 • Abarbanel (France) 1997 Chardonnay, Vin de Pays d'Oc. $10.

Pale straw cast. Medium-bodied. Full acidity. Moderately extracted. Dried herbs, minerals. Carries an herbal accent throughout. Light in weight, but features a rounded texture.

82 • Lucien Deschaux (France) 1996 Chardonnay, Vin de Pays d'Oc. $6.99.

Bright straw cast. Medium-bodied. Full acidity. Moderately extracted. Mildly oaked. Smoke, toast. Features a decided wood accent to the flavors, but remains light, crisp, and lively in the mouth.

81 • l'Orval (France) 1996 Chardonnay, Vin de Pays d'Oc. $6.99.

Pale greenish gold. Medium-bodied. Full acidity. Moderately extracted. Talc, tropical fruits. Ripe tropical aromas lead a lighter-styled, crisp mouthfeel. Vibrant finish.

81 • Domaine de Triennes (France) 1996 Chardonnay, Vin de Pays du Var. $12.99.

Deep yellow-gold. Full-bodied. Full acidity. Highly extracted. Minerals, lacquer, blanched almonds. Aromatically reserved, with a hint of maderization or a phenolic quality. Quite full and angular through the finish.

Aussie Chardonnays

91 • Lindemans (Australia) 1997 Chardonnay, Padthaway. $12.

Bright gold-yellow. Medium-bodied. Balanced acidity. Moderately extracted. Vanilla, minerals, citrus zest. Bright smoky aromas follow through to a crisp, zesty palate with subtle smoky notes pervading the finish. Well balanced and intensely flavorful, with very stylish winemaking evident.

90 • Seppelt (Australia) 1997 Corella Ridge, Chardonnay, Victoria. $14.

Bright yellow-straw cast. Moderately full-bodied. Full acidity. Moderately extracted. Moderately oaked. Brown spices, yeast, citrus. Forward aromatics show a measure of complexity. Ripe and zesty with a big yeasty quality throughout. Fine grip and intensity through the finish.

89 • Redbank (Australia) 1997 Long Paddock, Chardonnay, Victoria. $9.

Bright straw cast. Medium-bodied. Balanced acidity. Moderately extracted. Minerals, apples, vanilla. Understated but generous, with a precise set of clean fruit flavors. Elegant and well balanced through the finish.

Scale: Superlative (96-100), Exceptional (90-95), Highly Recommended (85-89), Recommended (80-84), Not Recommended (Under 80)

89 • *Cockatoo Ridge (Australia) 1998 Chardonnay, Australia. $9.*
Pale straw cast. Moderately full-bodied. Full acidity. Moderately extracted. Bananas, peaches, minerals. Shows an attractive tropical note to the nose. Full in the mouth with an overlay of acidity. The finish is clean and crisp.

88 • *Penfolds (Australia) 1997 The Valleys, Chardonnay, South Australia. $12.*
Bright yellow-straw cast. Moderately full-bodied. Balanced acidity. Moderately extracted. Mildly oaked. Lemon cream, butter, yeast. Forward aromas show a pleasant nutty, leesy quality. Generous in the mouth with lemony acidity lending balance. Rounded and buttery through the finish.

88 • *Deakin Estate (Australia) 1996 Alfred, Chardonnay, Victoria. $8.*
Deep gold. Moderately full-bodied. Balanced acidity. Moderately extracted. Toasted oak, butter. Heavily oak-accented aromas with a buttery note that follows through on the palate. Quite flavorful and textured.

87 • *Sheldrake (Australia) 1996 Chardonnay, Western Australia. $12.*
Dark gold. Medium-bodied. Balanced acidity. Moderately extracted. Butterscotch, pear. Developed aromas lead a bright, textured palate with pearlike flavors persisting through the finish. A rich and flavorful style that is drinking well now.

87 • *David Wynn (Australia) 1997 Chardonnay, South Eastern Australia. $13.*
Bright gold. Moderately full-bodied. Balanced acidity. Moderately extracted. Moderately oaked. Brown spices, cream, citrus. Quite fragrant, with a spicy oak overlay and a ripe, creamy palate feel. Shows some crispness toward the finish ,with fine acid intensity.

86 • *Wynns (Australia) 1997 Coonawarra Estate, Chardonnay, Coonawarra. $12.*
Pale yellow-straw hue. Medium-bodied. Full acidity. Moderately extracted. Citrus zest, apples, minerals. In the nose this is crisp and lively, though it shows some drier flavors on the intense, zesty finish. Well structured.

86 • *Tyrrell's (Australia) 1997 Old Winery, Chardonnay, South Eastern Australia. $9.99.*
Deep gold. Moderately full-bodied. Full acidity. Moderately extracted. Bread dough, citrus, cream. Subtle bready aromas lead a surprisingly zesty palate with an overlay of crisp acidity. Tart and juicy through the finish.

86 • *Jacob's Creek (Australia) 1998 Chardonnay, South Eastern Australia. $7.99.*
Bright yellow-straw cast. Medium-bodied. Balanced acidity. Moderately extracted. Minerals, yeast, citrus. Bright leesy aromas lead a clean, angular mouthfeel with a vibrant, crisp, moderately weighty finish.

85 • *Wolf Blass (Australia) 1998 Chardonnay, South Australia. $11.99.*
Pale straw cast. Medium-bodied. Full acidity. Moderately extracted. Blanched almonds, minerals. Developed aromatics hint at a degree of maturity. Lean and austere in the mouth, with a touch of bitterness through the finish.

84 • *Seppelt (Australia) 1997 Reserve Bin, Terrain Series, Chardonnay, South Eastern Australia. $8.*
Bright gold. Medium-bodied. Full acidity. Moderately extracted. Minerals, citrus zest, spice. Rather subdued aromatically with a hint of spice. Lean and angular in the mouth with a crisp, refreshing finish.

84 • *Seaview (Australia) 1997 Chardonnay, McLaren Vale. $8.*
Bright straw cast. Medium-bodied. Full acidity. Moderately extracted. Mildly oaked. Citrus, yeast, spice. Pleasantly aromatic with a core of citric flavors and gentle spicy nuances. Rounded yet crisp in the mouth with a lengthy, flavorful finish.

84 • *Marienberg (Australia) 1996 Reserve, Chardonnay,* ***South Eastern Australia. $12.***

Deep yellow-gold. Moderately full-bodied. Balanced acidity. Highly extracted. Heavily oaked. Brown spices, roasted nuts, blanched almonds. Forward aromas carry a developed, nutty quality. In the mouth it is large framed and marked by oak flavors through a drying, angular finish.

84 • *Goundrey (Australia) 1997 Unwooded, Chardonnay,* ***South East Australia. $14.***

Pale straw cast. Medium-bodied. Balanced acidity. Moderately extracted. Citrus, dried herbs, minerals. Crisp and lively with a ripe yet angular mouthfeel. Generous and flavorful through the finish.

84 • *Evans Wine Co. (Australia) 1996 Chardonnay, Hunter Valley. $12.99.*

Bright yellow-straw cast. Medium-bodied. Full acidity. Moderately extracted. Yeast, citrus, minerals. Aromas show yeast complexity and vibrant notes that follow through on the palate. Quite structured, with a firm backbone. This might improve over the short to medium term.

84 • *Chateau Reynella (Australia) 1996 Chardonnay, McLaren Vale. $12.99.*

Deep straw cast. Moderately full-bodied. Balanced acidity. Moderately extracted. Heavily oaked. Brown spices, citrus. Quite fragrant, with a big toasty oak overlay that runs through the palate. Full but zesty in the mouth, with crispness through the finish.

84 • *Callara (Australia) 1997 Reserve Bin, Chardonnay,* ***South Eastern Australia. $7.***

Deep gold. Moderately full-bodied. Balanced acidity. Moderately extracted. Bread, cream, tropical fruits. Rich and lush, with a weighty, ripe palate feel. Not overly flavorful, but extravagantly textured. Lobster, anyone?

84 • *Bulletin Place (Australia) 1998 Chardonnay,* ***South Eastern Australia. $9.99.***

Bright yellow-gold. Moderately full-bodied. Full acidity. Moderately extracted. Butter, citrus, pears. Quite fragrant, with a rich palate feel balanced by zesty acidity. The finish is angular and vibrant.

84 • *Alice White (Australia) 1997 Chardonnay, South Eastern Australia. $7.*

Bright golden cast. Moderately full-bodied. Balanced acidity. Moderately extracted. Bread dough, pears. Understated aromas lead a ripe, almost fat mouthfeel that flattens toward the finish. Texturally nice though the fruit flavors do not quite match the weight.

83 • *Wyndham (Australia) 1997 Bin 222, Chardonnay,* ***South Eastern Australia. $8.99.***

Bright yellow-gold. Moderately full-bodied. Full acidity. Moderately extracted. Minerals, citrus. Aromatically reserved with a full but angular mouthfeel. Lean and crisp through the finish.

83 • *Hermitage Road (Australia) 1996 Chardonnay,* ***South Eastern Australia. $10.***

Bright gold. Moderately full-bodied. Balanced acidity. Moderately extracted. Mildly oaked. Cream, spice, citrus. Ripe and fragrant with a rich, juicy mouthfeel. Shows a judiciously oaked spicy quality throughout.

82 • *Oxford Landing (Australia) 1998 Chardonnay, Australia. $8.*

Pale yellow-straw cast. Moderately light-bodied. Full acidity. Moderately extracted. Bananas, minerals. Forward aromas show a big buttery influence, though the flavors are lean on the palate, with some zesty character on the light finish.

82 • *Hardys (Australia) 1997 Signature, Chardonnay,* ***South Eastern Australia. $9.99.***

Deep straw cast. Medium-bodied. Balanced acidity. Subtly extracted. Dried herbs, blanched almonds. Lean aromas have an herbal, leesy quality. On the palate this is lighter in style and not deeply fruity, with a lean finish.

81 • Penfolds (Australia) 1997 Koonunga Hill, Chardonnay,
South Eastern Australia. $9.
Bright yellow-straw cast. Moderately full-bodied. Balanced acidity. Moderately extracted.
Sweet herbs, minerals. Aromatically reserved with steely mineral flavors and a generous
texture. Fades toward the clean finish.

81 • McGuigan (Australia) 1997 Cold Fermented, Bin 7000, Chardonnay,
South Eastern Australia. $12.
Bright gold. Medium-bodied. Full acidity. Moderately extracted. Minerals, citrus.
Aromatically subdued with a full but lean palate feel. Rather austere through the finish
with a hint of bitterness.

81 • Diamond Ridge (Australia) 1997 Chardonnay,
South Eastern Australia. $8.
Bright yellow-gold. Moderately full-bodied. Balanced acidity. Moderately extracted.
Tropical fruits, smoke. Fat, tropical aromas lead a buttery, rich palate lifted with a touch
of acidity on the finish. Fruit flavors are not quite matched by the weight of this wine.

81 • Abbey Vale (Australia) 1997 Chardonnay, Margaret River. $14.
Bright straw hue. Medium-bodied. Full acidity. Moderately extracted. Tart apple,
minerals. Aromas show a sour apple note that follows through on the palate. Quite
tart and angular through the quick finish.

80 • Tatachilla (Australia) 1997 Chardonnay, McLaren Vale. $13.99.
Deep straw cast. Medium-bodied. Low acidity. Subtly extracted. Earth, wool, apple.
Unusual aromas show woolly accents. Rather fat and round in the mouth with lighter
fruit flavors and a quick finish. Drink soon.

Canadian Chardonnays

88 • Peller Estates (Canada) 1997 Founder's Series, Chardonnay,
Niagara Peninsula. $10.
Dark golden-yellow hue. Subtle vanilla, cream, and spice aromas belie mild wood
treatment. A soft attack leads to a medium-bodied palate with gentle acidity. Rich
harmonious finish. Elegant and well-balanced. Drink now.

86 • Magnotta (Canada) 1997 Barrel Fermented, Chardonnay, Ontario. $12.
Rich golden yellow hue. Forward spice and vanilla aromas belie generous wood
treatment. A firm attack leads to a moderately full-bodied palate and a lingering
buttery finish. A rich but well-balanced style. An ideal match for lobster, crab, or any
rich white fish. Drink now.

86 • Calona (Canada) 1997 Artist Series, Chardonnay,
Okanagan Valley. $8.25.
Brilliant yellow-straw cast. Generous pleasant spice and vanilla aromas belie hefty
wood treatment. A supple attack leads to a medium-bodied palate with balanced
acidity through a persistent oaky finish. A clean, flavorful, oaky style. Drink now.

84 • Mission Hill (Canada) 1997 Grand Reserve, Chardonnay, Okanagan
Valley. $12.
Luminous golden yellow hue. Subtle, clean spice and citrus aromas. A crisp attack leads
to a medium-bodied palate with racy acidity through a snappy, vibrant finish. A clean and
racy Chard with the slightest hint of wood derived flavors. Drink now.

84 • Carriage House (Canada) 1997 Chardonnay, Okanagan Valley. $14.
Brilliant yellow-straw hue. Subdued cream and pear aromas. A firm attack leads to a
medium-bodied palate with crisp acidity. Rich, rounded finish. Clean and refreshing,
with a round character and no overt signs of oakiness. Drink now.

83 • Pillitteri (Canada) 1997 Chardonnay, Niagara Peninsula VQA. $7.77.
Deep old gold hue. Powerful butter and spice aromas belie generous wood treatment. A
soft attack leads to a full-bodied palate with adequate acidity through a lingering buttery
finish. Rather blowsy but tasty. Drink up.

83 • Mission Hill (Canada) 1997 Private Reserve, Bin 88, Chardonnay, Okanagan Valley. $6.

Brilliant golden yellow hue. Pleasant spice and vanilla aromas belie mild wood treatment. A firm attack leads to a full-bodied palate with aggressive acidity. Clean sharp finish. Well structured and youthful. Drink now or later. Can improve with more age.

81 • Magnotta (Canada) 1997 Limited Edition, Chardonnay, Ontario. $9.

Deep luminous golden-yellow hue. Subtle flint and mineral aromas. A crisp attack leads to a medium-bodied palate with a clipped clean finish. Lacking intensity, but sound. Drink now.

81 • Magnotta (Canada) 1997 Chile International Series, Chardonnay, Maipo Valley–Niagara. $5.

Luminous yellow-straw hue. Muted pear and mineral aromas. A firm attack leads to a medium-bodied palate with crisp acidity. Angular in character with a clipped clean finish. Subtle but tasty. Drink now.

81 • Cave Spring (Canada) 1997 Chardonnay, Niagara Peninsula. $11.99.

Pale brilliant greenish straw cast. Sound mineral and pear aromas. A firm attack leads to a moderately light-bodied palate with crisp acidity through a clipped buttery finish. Drink now.

Italian Chardonnays

91 • Stival (Italy) 1995 Le Rive, Chardonnay, Veneto. $11.99.

Bright gold. Moderately full-bodied. Full acidity. Highly extracted. Cheese, hazelnuts, tropical fruits. Extremely aromatic with a complex melange of aromas that follow through on the palate. Full and tightly wound on the palate with vibrant acidity through the finish.

91 • Fontanafredda (Italy) 1996 Ampelio, Chardonnay, Langhe. $15.

Pale straw hue. Moderately light-bodied. Full acidity. Moderately extracted. Moderately oaked. Vanilla, citrus, minerals. A light touch of wood is apparent on the nose. Racy and crisp in style with vibrant acidity. Well integrated and balanced, it is not unlike a wooded Chablis.

87 • Torresella (Italy) 1996 Chardonnay, Veneto. $7.99.

Deep straw cast. Moderately full-bodied. Balanced acidity. Moderately extracted. Lacquer, blanched almonds, oranges. Quite aromatic with a distinctive and complex array of flavors on the palate. Round and ripe with a linear note of acidity through the flavorful finish.

85 • Bollini (Italy) 1996 Barricato 40, Chardonnay, Trentino. $9.99.

Deep straw cast. Moderately full-bodied. Full acidity. Highly extracted. Minerals, citrus. Aromatically unyielding, with a full though lean palate feel. Linear acidity is the main feature of the finish.

85 • Antinori (Italy) 1996 Castello della Sala, Chardonnay, Umbria. $11.50.

Deep straw cast. Medium-bodied. Full acidity. Highly extracted. Citrus zest, minerals, yeast. Smoky, yeasty notes lead a firm and tightly wound palate. Zesty acidity makes for a crisp, assertive finish.

84 • Nozzole (Italy) 1997 Le Bruniche, Chardonnay, Toscana. $11.99.

Medium straw hue. Medium-bodied. Balanced acidity. Moderately extracted. Ripe, citric, smoky aromas lead a mouthful of rounded tropical flavors that taper through the finish. Easy-drinking style.

82 • Marega (Italy) 1996 Chardonnay, Collio. $12.99.

Bright gold. Medium-bodied. Full acidity. Highly extracted. Dried herbs, citrus, honey. Aromatic, with pungent and forceful flavors. Tightly wound in the mouth with firm acidity leading to a concentrated finish.

South African Chardonnays

88 • Stellenryck (South Africa) 1997 Chardonnay, Coastal Region. $12.
Deep yellow-straw color. Generous brown spice aromas show a hefty wood accent. A rich entry leads a moderately full-bodied palate with firm acidity. Clean, structured finish. Drink now.

88 • KWV (South Africa) 1997 Cathedral Cellar, Chardonnay, Coastal Region. $11.99.
Deep yellow-straw hue. Generous brown spice and citrus aromas show a hefty oak accent. A rich entry leads a moderately full-bodied palate with crisp acids. The finish is flavorful and well structured. Drink now.

86 • Chamonix (South Africa) 1997 Chardonnay, Franschhoek 1.73% rs. $15.
Bright pale gold. Fresh, tart aromas of passion fruit and citrus. A crisp entry is followed by a medium-bodied palate with toasty oak spice through the finish. Shows good fruit concentration.

84 • Boschendal (South Africa) 1997 Reserve, Chardonnay, South Africa. $14.99.
Bright straw hue. Powerful spicy aromas show a big wood accent. A firm entry leads a medium-bodied palate that shows angular acidity. Clean, wood-accented finish. Drink now.

83 • KWV (South Africa) 1997 Chardonnay, Western Cape. $7.99.
Deep straw hue. Restrained mineral and citrus aromas. A crisp entry is followed by a medium-bodied palate with angular acidity, and a lean, clean finish. Drink now.

83 • Backsberg (South Africa) 1997 Chardonnay, Paarl. $12.99.
Bright golden yellow. Forward citrus and vanilla aromas carry a gentle oak accent. A lush entry is followed by a moderately full-bodied palate with crisp acidity. Rounded banana-like overtones define the finish. Drink now.

82 • Villiera (South Africa) 1998 Chardonnay, Paarl. $12.
Pale green-straw hue. Subdued brown spice aromas. A rounded entry leads a medium-bodied palate with angular acidity. Soft banana flavors mark the finish. Drink now.

82 • Delheim (South Africa) 1998 Chardonnay, Stellenbosch. $13.
Bright straw hue. Herb and mineral aromas carry a slightly floral overtone. A brisk entry leads a medium-bodied palate with vibrant acidity and a big banana-flavored malolactic character. Crisp and clean through the finish. Drink now.

81 • L'Ormarins (South Africa) 1997 Chardonnay, Franschhoek Valley. $11.
Bright straw hue. Clean citrus, mineral, and bread overtones. A rich entry leads a moderately full-bodied palate with lean acidity through the finish. Angular. Drink now.

81 • De Wetshof (South Africa) 1997 Lesca, Chardonnay, Robertson. $11.99.
Pale straw hue. Citrus and mineral aromas have unusual overtones. A lean entry leads a medium-bodied palate with a touch of bitterness through the finish. Rather austere. Drink now.

81 • Baobab (South Africa) 1997 Chardonnay, Western Cape. $8.99.
Pale straw hue. Reserved mineral and citrus aromas. A rounded entry leads a moderately light-bodied palate with crisp acidity. Lacks real depth or grip, but decent.

South American Chardonnays

89 • Viu Manent (Chile) 1997 Reserve, Chardonnay, Colchagua Valley. $12.
Pale straw hue. Aromatically muted, with a note of citrus. Ripe, warm aromas show a vanilla note. Mildy viscous on the attack with a soft texture and rounded mouthfeel and good length. Smooth, though not hugely flavorful. Drink now.

87 • Calina (Chile) 1997 Selección de las Lomas, Chardonnay, Chile. $15.
Bright yellow-straw hue. Overtly oaky aromas with citrus zest. A lively attack leads a medium-bodied palate with bright citrus flavors and oak spice through the finish. Straightforward. Drink now.

86 • *La Palma (Chile) 1997 Gran Reserva, Chardonnay, Rapel. $14.*
Deep gold. Ripe aromas of butter and yellow apples. A crisp entry leads a medium-bodied palate with varietally expressive fruit flavors and subtle oak. Finishes with crisp fruit flavors. Drink now.

86 • *Concha y Toro (Chile) 1998 Casillero del Diablo, Chardonnay, Casablanca Valley. $10.*
Medium straw hue. Clean, fresh aromas of citrus and butter. A juicy entry leads a medium-bodied palate with bright varietal flavors that linger through the finish. Oak is very subtle. Drink now.

86 • *Casa Lapostolle (Chile) 1997 Chardonnay, Casablanca Valley. $10.*
Deep gold. Assertively aromatic with browned butter, yeast, and oak aromas. A rich attack leads a moderately full-bodied palate with generous mouthfeel and overtly buttery character through the finish. Drink now.

84 • *Walnut Crest (Chile) 1997 Estate Selection, Chardonnay, Casablanca Valley. $9.50.*
Deep golden yellow. Rather fat, buttery aromas show oak influences. A thick attack leads a moderately full-bodied palate with tart acids on the finish. Very buttery, and short on fruit flavors. Drink now.

84 • *Viña Tarapaca (Chile) 1998 Chardonnay, Maipo Valley. $7.*
Pale yellow. Weak aromas of tinned fruit. A weak attack leads a medium-bodied palate with sweet fruit flavors. A sweeter style that will please some. Cocktail for the masses.

84 • *Veramonte (Chile) 1997 Chardonnay, Alto de Casablanca. $10.*
Bright straw hue. Smoky, buttery aromas. A soft entry leads a medium-bodied palate with a nice mouthfeel and obvious oak accents. Finishes quickly. Drink now.

84 • *Caliterra (Chile) 1998 Chardonnay, Valle Central. $8.99.*
Bright golden yellow. Clean mild aromas of ripe citrus and apple. A crisp entry leads a medium-bodied palate with straightforward, clean varietal flavors. Shows little oak influence. Drink now.

84 • *Calina (Chile) 1998 Chardonnay, Valle de Itata. $9.*
Pale straw. Lean green apple aromas show no oak infuence. A crisp entry leads a moderately light-bodied palate with crisp flavors that finish quickly. Clean and quaffable. Drink now.

83 • *Vinterra (Argentina) 1997 Chardonnay, Mendoza. $6.99.*
Medium yellow-gold. Buttery, smoky aromas show a lanolin note. A warm entry leads a medium-bodied palate with a thick mouthfeel and ripe flavors through a somewhat short finish. A generous style. Drink now.

83 • *Trapiche (Argentina) 1997 Oak Cask, Chardonnay, Mendoza. $8.99.*
Bright golden yellow. Ripe buttery, yellow apple aromas. A ripe entry leads a medium-bodied palate with generous alcohol giving a round mouthfeel and a warm finish. Ripe, varietal fruit flavors are a plus.

83 • *Trapiche (Argentina) 1997 Fond de Cave, Chardonnay, Mendoza. $14.99.*
Bright yellow-gold. Oaky, mildly smoky aromas. A lean entry leads a medium-bodied palate with crisp flavors that finish quickly.

83 • *Santa Amelia (Chile) 1998 Reserve Selection, Chardonnay, Maule Valley. $7.50.*
Pale straw hue. Lean aromas. A crisp entry leads a medium-bodied palate with grassy, citrus flavors. More like a Sauvignon Blanc than a Chardonnay. Drink now.

82 • *La Playa (Chile) 1997 Estate Reserve, Chardonnay, Maipo Valley. $9.99.*
Bright golden yellow. Ripe buttery, warm aromas. A thick attack is followed by a moderately full-bodied palate with acids coming through on the finish. Nice mouthfeel, though not hugely flavorful. Drink now.

40

Scale: Superlative (96-100), Exceptional (90-95), Highly Recommended (85-89),
Recommended (80-84), Not Recommended (Under 80)

81 • Undurraga (Chile) 1998 Chardonnay, Maipo Valley. $7.99.

Pale straw hue. Aromatically muted with faint citrus zest notes. A lean entry leads a moderately light-bodied palate with crisp varietally expressive flavors that show a slight herbal note. Drink now.

81 • Santa Julia (Argentina) 1998 Chardonnay, Mendoza. $7.

Bright yellow-gold. Very aromatic with yellow apple and butter aromas. A flavorful entry leads a medium-bodied palate with bright, varietally pure flavors that finish with a note of alcohol warmth. Oak influence is restrained.

81 • Santa Ema (Chile) 1997 Reserve, Chardonnay, Maipo Valley. $12.

Medium yellow-gold. Tropical fruit aromas of peach. A soft juicy entry leads a medium-bodied palate with low acidity and mild fruit flavors that finish quickly. Undemanding. Drink soon.

81 • Santa Carolina (Chile) 1997 Reserva, Chardonnay, Maipo Valley. $9.

Pale straw hue. Mild crisp, grassy, apple aromas show no oak influence. A crisp entry leads a medium-bodied palate with bright citrus flavors. Finishes with a note of alcohol warmth. Drink now.

81 • Santa Alicia (Chile) 1996 El Cipres, Gran Riserva, Chardonnay, Maipo Valley. $9.99.

Full gold. Quite aromatic with oak and soft tropical accents. A plush entry is followed by a medium-bodied palate with a rounded, soft finish. This is an uncomplicated, easy-drinking style, though a touch bland.

81 • La Playa (Chile) 1998 Chardonnay, Maipo Valley. $6.99.

Bright pale yellow. Moderate aromas of tart citrus. A crisp entry leads a medium-bodied palate with good varietal flavors and no oak influence. Crisp and well balanced. Drink now.

80 • Santa Amelia (Chile) 1998 Chardonnay, Chile. $6.50.

Very pale straw hue. Lean, muted aromas of tartaric acid. Acid water. This has no Chardonnay character.

U.S. Chardonnays

92 • Zabaco (CA) 1996 Chardonnay, Russian River Valley. $14.

Rich gold. Aromatically lush with buttery, leesy, and oaky character showing. A lush attack leads a full-bodied palate with hedonistic texture and concentrated flavors. Finishes with an authoritative oaky accent.

91 • J. Lohr (CA) 1997 Riverstone, Chardonnay, Monterey. $14.

Medium golden yellow. Quite aromatic with butter and apple aromas marked by vanilla oak influence. A rich entry leads a moderately full-bodied palate with nutty oak flavors coming through on the persistent finish. Excellent match with lobster, crab, or any rich white fish. Drink now or later.

90 • Forest Glen (CA) 1997 Chardonnay, California. $9.99.

Rich golden yellow. Powerful toasted wood, citrus, and cream aromas show a hefty oak accent. A ripe attack leads a moderately full-bodied palate with juicy acidity. Flavorful, lengthy finish. Shows a lot of style. Drink now or later.

90 • Anapamu (CA) 1996 Chardonnay, Central Coast. $14.

Bright yellow-gold. Moderately full-bodied. Balanced acidity. Moderately extracted. Moderately oaked. Smoke, cream, tropical fruits. Aromatic and intense, with forward smoky flavors and a ripe creamy quality in the mouth. Shows fine balance through the lengthy finish.

89 • Treleaven (NY) 1997 Chardonnay, Cayuga Lake. $11.99.

Bright pale yellow. Interesting spicy, nutty aromas. A rich attack leads a medium-bodied palate with smooth texture and crisp apple flavors showing interesting spice through the finish. Rather distinctive.

89 • *Meridian (CA) 1996 Coastal Reserve, Chardonnay, Edna Valley. $15.*
Bright yellow-gold. Moderately full-bodied. Balanced acidity. Moderately extracted. Mildly oaked. Cream, minerals, citrus. Forward aromas feature a complex yeasty note. Big and ripe in the mouth with an opulent creamy texture. Lengthy flavorful finish.

89 • *Mark West (CA) 1996 Chardonnay, Russian River Valley. $15.*
Bright yellow-gold. Moderately full-bodied. Full acidity. Moderately extracted. Moderately oaked. Lemons, spice. Bright zesty aromas show a touch of spice. A crisp, lively mouthful of vibrant flavors grips the palate through the finish.

89 • *LinCourt (CA) 1997 Chardonnay, Santa Barbara County. $14.*
Deep gold. Rather developed oak spice aromas. Possibly a touch maderized. A rich entry leads a full-bodied palate with mature flavors and a thick alcoholic mouthfeel. Interesting now, but maybe not for cellaring.

89 • *Kestrel (WA) 1995 Chardonnay, Columbia Valley. $15.*
Deep gold. Rich, fat aromas of butter and ripe fruit. A juicy attack leads a full-bodied palate with opulent fruit flavors and a weighty mouthfeel. Smoky, toasty flavors persist well into the spicy finish. Impressively concentrated and flavorful. Drink now or later.

89 • *Jepson (CA) 1996 Chardonnay, Mendocino County. $15.*
Bright yellow-gold. Medium-bodied. Full acidity. Moderately extracted. Citrus, lemons, vanilla. Crisp and lively on the palate with a lemony firmness running through the finish that stands up to the buttery, oaky character. Flavorful and firm style.

89 • *Hess Collection (CA) 1996 Chardonnay, Napa Valley. $15.*
Bright yellow-gold. Medium-bodied. Balanced acidity. Moderately extracted. Mildly oaked. Yeast, citrus. Smooth, rounded mouthfeel has a ripe core of fruit flavors with restrained oak spice that does not overwhelm the ensemble. Very appealing and direct with a nice mouthfeel.

89 • *Henry Estate (OR) 1996 Chardonnay, Umpqua Valley. $15.*
Bright yellow-straw hue. Moderately full-bodied. Full acidity. Moderately oaked. Lime, vanilla, citrus. Spicy, oak-accented aromas lead a bright, racy palate with concentrated flavors and impressive persistence through the finish.

89 • *Daniel Lawrence (CA) 1996 Vineyard Reserve, Chardonnay, Santa Cruz Mountains. $15.*
Bright gold-yellow. Moderately full-bodied. Balanced acidity. Highly extracted. Moderately oaked. Green apples, vanilla, butter. Generously aromatic. A leesy, ripe character comes through on the deeply flavored palate, with opulent fruity flavors, texture, and length. Very stylish.

89 • *Beaucanon (CA) 1997 Reserve, Chardonnay, Napa Valley. $12.*
Pale straw cast. Moderately full-bodied. Balanced acidity. Moderately extracted. Minerals, melon, citrus. Forward aromas feature a subtle spicy accent. Rich and fruity on entry, with a weighty midpalate. Finishes with lingering zesty acids.

88 • *Willamette Valley Vineyards (OR) 1996 Founders' Reserve, Chardonnay, Oregon. $14.99.*
Deep straw hue. Opulent cream, butter, and toast aromas carry a generous oak accent. A lush entry leads a moderately full-bodied palate with firm acidity. Full and flavorful, with admirable balance between wood and fruit. Drink now.

88 • *Villa Mt. Eden (CA) 1997 Chardonnay, California. $10.*
Bright yellow-gold. Ripe smoky, browned butter aromas. A rich, flavorful entry leads a moderately full-bodied palate with impressively concentrated fruit flavors, juicy acids, and well-integrated oak character. Persistent fruity finish. Drink now or later.

88 • *Sterling (CA) 1997 Chardonnay, Napa Valley. $15.*
Bright straw hue. Moderately full-bodied. Balanced acidity. Moderately extracted. Mildly tannic. Citrus, butter, minerals. Creamy citric aromas lead a smooth-textured mouthful of butter and lemon flavors with fine persistence. Oak character is quite reserved and well integrated.

Scale: Superlative (96-100), Exceptional (90-95), Highly Recommended (85-89), Recommended (80-84), Not Recommended (Under 80)

88 • *Silver Ridge (CA) 1997 Chardonnay, California. $9.99.*
Brilliant yellow-straw hue. Generous vanilla and cream aromas carry an attractive oak accent. A rounded entry leads a medium-bodied palate with balanced acidity. Lengthy, flavorful finish. Drink now.

88 • *Pedroncelli (CA) 1997 F. Johnson Vineyard, Chardonnay, Dry Creek Valley. $13.*
Medium yellow-gold. Mild aromas of yellow apples and heavily charred oak. Crisp on the attack with a moderately full body and tart fruit flavors standing up to the alcohol. Rather angular through the finish. Drink now.

88 • *Macari (NY) 1996 Barrel Fermented, Chardonnay, North Fork of Long Island. $14.*
Deep yellow-straw hue. Forward spice, yeast, and banana aromas. A firm entry leads a moderately full-bodied palate. Full, lush, and complex with a persistent yeasty finish. Drink now.

88 • *Laurier (CA) 1996 Chardonnay, Sonoma County. $15.*
Bright yellow-gold. Generous citrus and vanilla aromas show an integrated wood accent. A lush entry is followed by a moderately full-bodied palate with creamy acidity and a soft, gentle finish. Stylish. Drink now.

88 • *Indigo Hills (CA) 1997 Chardonnay, Mendocino County. $11.*
Bright straw cast. Medium-bodied. Full acidity. Moderately extracted. Minerals, apples, citrus. Crisp, zesty aromas lead a firm mouthful of bright flavors that remain pure, vibrant, and crisp through the finish, with a subtle, lingering toasty accent.

88 • *Herzog (CA) 1997 Baron Herzog, Chardonnay, California. $12.95.*
Brilliant yellow-straw hue. Generous brown spice and pear aromas show a hefty oak accent. A rich entry leads a moderately full-bodied palate with rounded acidity. The finish is ripe and stylish. Drink now.

88 • *Gristina (NY) 1996 Chardonnay, North Fork of Long Island. $11.99.*
Rich yellow-straw hue. Forward tropical fruit and bread dough aromas. A supple entry leads a moderately full-bodied palate. Full yet crisp, with fine length. Drink now.

88 • *Gallo Sonoma (CA) 1997 Chardonnay, Russian River Valley. $14.*
Bright yellow-gold. Generous ripe citrus aromas with judicious oak and yeast accents. A generous, lush attack leads a moderately full-bodied palate with broad, full fruit flavors that persist through the finish. Hedonistic. Drink now.

88 • *Eola Hills (OR) 1996 Chardonnay, Oregon. $12.*
Medium green-straw hue. Medium-bodied. Balanced acidity. Moderately extracted. Green apples, citrus fruits. Bright, crisp aromas lead a rounded, fruity mouthful with clean flavors persisting through the finish.

88 • *Columbia Crest (WA) 1997 Estate Series, Chardonnay, Columbia Valley. $14.*
Full yellow-gold. Aromatically complex with butterscotch and vanilla character. A smoky entry leads a moderately full-bodied palate with assertive smoke and toasty oak flavors that are well integrated with fruity, buttery character. Acids are balanced through the oak-spiced finish. Very stylish, layered, and complex.

88 • *Canoe Ridge Vineyard (WA) 1997 Chardonnay, Columbia Valley. $14.*
Brilliant yellow-gold. Ripe but very subtle oaky aromas. A creamy attack leads a medium-bodied palate that has a lush, textured mouthfeel. Finishes with good fruit persistence. Drink now.

88 • *Barnard Griffin (WA) 1997 Chardonnay, Washington. $12.95.*
Bright gold. Moderately full-bodied. Full acidity. Moderately extracted. Moderately oaked. Brown spices, butter, citrus. Generous aromas carry a judicious oak accent. Crisp and zesty with a vibrant core of minerally, fruity flavors that remain refreshing through the finish.

87 • *Monthaven (CA) 1997 Chardonnay, Napa Valley. $9.99.*

Bright green-gold. Extravagent toasted coconut, smoke, and ripe fruit aromas. A sumptuous attack leads a full-bodied palate with impressive buttery richness and glycerous smoothness. Impressive depth of fruit flavors. Finishes with leesy complexity.

87 • *Glenora (NY) 1996 Chardonnay, Finger Lakes. $13.99.*

Bright pale gold. Vibrant citrus aromas. Brightly acidic on the attack, with a medium-bodied palate and tart lemon flavors following cleanly through the finish. Impressively concentrated. A zesty, refreshing style that will work well with seafood. Drink now.

87 • *Claar (WA) 1997 Chardonnay, Columbia Valley. $10.99.*

Brilliant yellow-gold. Heavy buttery aromas. A rich attack leads a full-bodied palate with broad, ripe apple flavors and full buttery qualities. This is a big, flavorful style with good acid balance. Very structured and tight, maybe further age will enhance it. Drink now or later.

86 • *Windsor (CA) 1996 Barrel Fermented, Private Reserve, Chardonnay, Russian River Valley. $15.*

Bright green-gold. Moderately full-bodied. Full acidity. Moderately extracted. Moderately oaked. Vanilla, spice, lemon zest. Bright lemony aromas show a spicy note that comes through well on the palate with bright citrus-accented flavors.

86 • *William Hill (CA) 1997 Chardonnay, Napa Valley. $14.50.*

Bright yellow-gold. Restrained yeasty and buttery aromas. A rich entry leads a moderately full-bodied palate with ripe, full fruit flavors and judicious oak. Generous alcohol gives this a degree of warmth on the finish.

86 • *Willamette Valley Vineyards (OR) 1997 Chardonnay, Oregon. $12.75.*

Pale straw hue. Elegant vanilla and lemon aromas show a judicious oak influence. A lean entry is followed by a medium-bodied palate with crisp acidity. Delicate and well balanced through the finish. Drink now.

86 • *W.B. Bridgman (WA) 1997 Chardonnay, Columbia Valley. $10.99.*

Yellow-straw hue. Aromas of yellow apples and butter. A soft entry leads a moderately full-bodied palate with fruit-centered flavors and soft acids that make for a quick finish. The mouthfeel shows a full buttery quality. Drink now.

86 • *Ste. Chapelle (ID) 1996 Chardonnay, Idaho. $9.*

Bright pale-straw cast. Medium-bodied. Full acidity. Moderately extracted. Toasted oak, citrus. Austere minerally aromas lead a lean, angular palate punctuated by tart acidity. Mouthfeel has a rounded character with a touch of smoky oak for complexity.

86 • *St. Supéry (CA) 1996 Dollarhide Ranch, Chardonnay, Napa Valley. $12.50.*

Bright straw cast. Moderately full-bodied. Full acidity. Moderately extracted. Citrus, melon, minerals. Quite aromatic with bright fruit flavors to the fore. Zesty and intense in the mouth with a clean, snappy finish.

86 • *Shale Ridge (CA) 1997 Chardonnay, Monterey. $9.99.*

Pale yellow-straw hue. Apple and pear aromas show no wood influence. A soft entry leads a medium-bodied palate with juicy fruit flavors that linger briefly through the finish. Very easy drinking and versatile. Drink now.

86 • *Rockbridge (VA) 1997 Reserve, Chardonnay, Virginia. $15.*

Deep yellow-gold. Ripe aromas show apple and butter. A bright entry leads a moderately full-bodied palate with a rounded buttery mouthfeel and concentrated flavors. Finishes with a note of alcohol warmth. A big, generous style. Drink now.

86 • *Raymond (CA) 1997 Chardonnay, Monterey. $13.*

Bright yellow-gold. Ripe buttery aromas. A vibrant entry leads a moderately full-bodied palate with a bright, lush, citrus center and full alcohol to match the acids. Finishes with lingering fruit acids. Very flavorful.

Scale: Superlative (96-100), Exceptional (90-95), Highly Recommended (85-89), Recommended (80-84), Not Recommended (Under 80)

86 • *Pellegrini (NY) 1996 Chardonnay, North Fork of Long Island. $12.99.*
Bright gold. Medium-bodied. Balanced acidity. Moderately extracted. Pears, minerals, cream. Ripe and intense with a rounded creamy impression on the palate. Firm and flavorful through the finish.

86 • *Oak Knoll (OR) 1996 Chardonnay, Willamette Valley. $14.*
Green-straw hue. Medium-bodied. Balanced acidity. Moderately extracted. Lemon, apples. Zesty aromas lead a full-flavored palate with bright fruity flavors that finish with a note of sourness, making for an assertive style.

86 • *Monterra (CA) 1997 San Bernabé Ranch, Chardonnay, Monterey County. $8.99.*
Pale straw hue. Yeasty, yellow apple aromas. A juicy entry leads a medium-bodied palate with judicious oak flavors and subtle yeasty notes. The subtle, lingering finish shows some juicy acidity. Drink now.

86 • *Lockwood (CA) 1997 Chardonnay, Monterey. $14.99.*
Medium-full yellow-gold. Generous aromas of sweet wood and tart fruits. A bright entry leads a moderately full-bodied palate with angular acids. Fruit flavors are generous and ripe with judicious oak accents through the finish.

86 • *Laurel Lake (NY) 1995 Reserve, Chardonnay, North Fork of Long Island. $13.99.*
Luminous straw hue. Generous citrus, yeast, and mineral aromas. A firm entry leads a moderately full-bodied palate with crisp acids. Firm and powerful, but restrained. Drink now.

86 • *Indian Creek (ID) 1997 Chardonnay, Idaho. $9.95.*
Pale green-gold. Aromatically restrained with subtle oak spice and citrus fruits. A juicy attack leads a medium-bodied palate with crisp, subtle fruit flavors well balanced by oak. A light, precise, cool-climate style. Drink now.

86 • *Hogue (WA) 1997 Chardonnay, Columbia Valley. $13.95.*
Brilliant green-gold. Very pure fruit-centered aromas of green apples. A smooth entry leads a moderately full-bodied palate with pure Chardonnay flavors and very restrained vanilla oak notes. Acids are markedly crisp through the finish. Well structured. Drink now or later.

86 • *Heartswood (CA) 1995 Private Reserve, Chardonnay, Monterey. $9.99.*
Deep yellow-straw cast. Moderately full-bodied. Balanced acidity. Moderately extracted. Flowers, spice. Forward, generous aromas show an opulent spicy accent. Lush, generous and rounded in the mouth with a note of viscosity.

86 • *Guglielmo (CA) 1997 Private Reserve, Chardonnay, Monterey County. $14.*
Emphatic deep gold. Butter and oak-spiced aromas show a subdued fruity character. A lean entry leads a moderately full-bodied palate with lush buttery qualities. Fruit flavors are faint through the finish. Drink now.

86 • *Franciscan (CA) 1997 Oakville Estste, Chardonnay, Napa Valley. $15.*
Bright gold. Moderate aromas of browned butter and tropical fruits. A rich entry leads a full-bodied palate with opulent texture, though the fruit flavors are somewhat restrained . The finish is clean. Drink now.

86 • *Foxridge (CA) 1997 Chardonnay, Carneros. $9.99.*
Pale straw hue. Medium-bodied. Balanced acidity. Moderately extracted. Citrus, apples. Clean, fruity aromas. Bright, lively, and juicy with a crisp finish that does not show much oak influence.

86 • *Domaine Laurier (CA) 1996 Reserve, Chardonnay, Sonoma County. $12.99.*
Deep straw cast. Medium-bodied. Full acidity. Moderately extracted. Ginger, tropical fruits, citrus. Unusual, forward aromas lead a lean and angular mouthfeel. Finishes with an angular citric bite.

86 • Deaver (CA) 1997 Chardonnay, Sierra Foothills. $11.99.

Pale straw hue with a greenish tint. Mild aromas show a muted green apple note. A crisp entry leads a medium-bodied palate with bright acids and juicy apple flavors. Oak influence is very subtle. Drink now.

86 • Concannon (CA) 1997 Selected Vineyard, Chardonnay, Central Coast. $10.95.

Pale yellow-straw hue. Mildly aromatic with apricot character. A smooth attack leads a medium-light body with subtle oak flavors. Clean, rather short finish. Very user friendly.

86 • Columbia Crest (WA) 1997 Chardonnay, Columbia Valley. $9.

Medium pale straw hue. Moderate aromas of butter, citrus and oak spice. A crisp entry leads a medium-bodied palate with tangy fruit and brown spice flavors that linger on the finish. Nice texture and mouthfeel. Drink now.

86 • Chateau Ste. Michelle (WA) 1996 Chardonnay, Columbia Valley. $14.

Bright yellow-straw cast. Moderately full-bodied. Balanced acidity. Moderately extracted. Mildly oaked. Minerals, citrus, cream. Aromatically reserved with a generous and rounded texture. Finishes with a sense of crispness.

86 • Chateau Morrisette (VA) 1997 "M," Meadows of Dan, Chardonnay, Virginia. $14.

Bright yellow-gold. Clean yellow-apple aromas. A bright entry leads a medium-bodied palate with crisp citrus flavors that persist through the finish. No sign of oak. A very refreshing style.

86 • Chateau Biltmore (NC) NV Chardonnay, American. $14.99.

Bright straw cast. Medium-bodied. Balanced acidity. Moderately extracted. Mildly oaked. Vanilla, minerals, nuts. Forward aromas show an enticing leesy accent. Finishes in a lush and generous manner.

86 • Caterina (WA) 1997 Chardonnay, Columbia Valley. $15.

Pale yellow-gold. Ripe aromas of butter and yellow apples, showing judicious oak influences. A rich attack leads a moderately full-bodied palate with a glycerous, smooth mouthfeel and juicy apple flavors through the clean finish. Drink now.

86 • Bookwalter (WA) 1997 Chardonnay, Columbia Valley. $8.

Bright straw cast. Medium-bodied. Full acidity. Moderately extracted. Minerals, citrus. Clean and focused, with pure fruit flavors. Zesty, angular, and refreshing through the finish.

86 • Beringer (CA) 1996 Chardonnay, Napa Valley. $15.

Bright yellow-gold. Medium-bodied. Balanced acidity. Moderately extracted. Green apples, brown spice, vanilla. Aromas of oak spice and butter follow through with a textured, rounded palate feel and a finish showing spicy persistence.

86 • Benziger (CA) 1996 Chardonnay, Carneros. $13.

Bright yellow-gold. Medium-bodied. Balanced acidity. Moderately extracted. Moderately oaked. Coconut, yeast, apples. Sweet oak aromas follow through on a ripe, juicy palate with a hint of dryness and spice on the finish.

86 • Bedell (NY) 1995 Reserve, Chardonnay, North Fork of Long Island. $14.99.

Deep yellow-straw hue. Complex, autolyzed, yeasty, smoky aromas. A firm attack leads a moderately full-bodied palate with crisp acids. Firm and concentrated with a phenolic edge to the finish. Drink now or later.

85 • Rutherford Vintners (CA) 1997 Chardonnay, Stanislaus County. $8.99.

Pale straw hue Faint melony aromas. A clean entry leads a medium-bodied palate with peach and apple flavors that linger on the medium-length finish. No oak influence. Drink now.

Scale: Superlative (96-100), Exceptional (90-95), Highly Recommended (85-89), Recommended (80-84), Not Recommended (Under 80)

**85 • *Lenz (NY) 1996 Vineyard Selection, Chardonnay,*
*North Fork of Long Island. $9.99.***
Rich yellow-straw hue. Subdued mineral, citrus, and butter aromas. A firm entry leads
a moderately full-bodied palate with crisp acids. Vibrant and restrained. Drink now.

85 • *Laurel Lake (NY) 1996 Chardonnay, North Fork of Long Island. $12.99.*
Brilliant straw hue. Pleasant citrus, vanilla, and herb aromas. An acidic entry leads a crisp,
moderately full-bodied palate. The finish is clipped and clean. Carries a bit of complexity
with a slight herbal edge. Drink now.

85 • *Harmony (CA) 1997 Chardonnay, San Luis Obispo County. $14.50.*
Deep yellow-straw hue. Opulent vanilla, citrus, and cream aromas show a hefty oak
accent. A firm entry leads a moderately full-bodied palate with rounded acidity.
Extremely lengthy buttery finish. Rather wood dominated, but hedonistically interesting.

**85 • *Hargrave (NY) 1995 Lattice Label, Chardonnay,*
*North Fork of Long Island. $14.99.***
Rich, saturated yellow-straw hue. Lean mineral and citrus aromas. A firm entry leads
a moderately full-bodied palate with crisp acidity. Firm and tight-fisted with a phenolic
edge to the finish. Drink now or later.

85 • *Cooper Mountain (OR) 1997 Chardonnay, Willamette Valley. $14.75.*
Pale straw cast. Medium-bodied. Full acidity. Moderately extracted. Apple, sweet lemon.
Apple aromas lead a lively, juicy mouthful of flavors with a clean, gripping finish. Fresh,
lively, and cleansing.

85 • *Charles Shaw (CA) 1997 Chardonnay, California. $8.99.*
Old gold hue. Muted mineral and spice aromas. A lean entry is followed by a medium-
bodied palate with angular acidity, and a clean finish. Not overly flavorful, but well
structured. Drink now.

85 • *Bedell (NY) 1995 Chardonnay, North Fork of Long Island. $11.99.*
Deep, saturated straw hue. Generous mineral and cream aromas show a mature nutty
accent. Supple and moderately full-bodied with shy acidity. Lush finish. Drink now.

Other Great Value Chardonnays

**87 • *Weingut Hermann Huber (Austria) 1997 Trocken, Strasser Chardonnay,*
*Kamptal. $13.30.***
Pale straw cast. Medium-bodied. Full acidity. Moderately extracted. Lemons, tart citrus
fruits. Eye-closing acidity and strong, austere citrus flavors make this assertive. Serious
purity and intensity of flavors are the keynotes.

**85 • *R. Zimmermann (Austria) 1997 Kabinett, Trocken, Chardonnay,*
*Wien. $10.***
Pale straw cast. Medium-bodied. Full acidity. Moderately extracted. Citrus, minerals,
slate. Aromatically reserved, but firm and concentrated on the palate, with a Chablis-like
intensity. Clean, racy acidity makes for a zesty finish. Should mature nicely.

84 • *Shingle Peak (New Zealand) 1997 Chardonnay, Marlborough. $14.*
Deep yellow-straw cast. Moderately full-bodied. Full acidity. Highly extracted. Tropical
fruits, minerals, cream. Shows subtle tropical nuances in the nose. Ripe and rich in the
mouth, but firmly structured and angular through the finish.

**84 • *Matthias Altenburger (Austria) 1997 Pannonischer Reigen Spatlese,*
*Altweibersommer, Chardonnay, Neusiedlersee 4.22% rs. $12.50.***
Bright pale yellow. Moderately full-bodied. Balanced acidity. Moderately extracted. Sweet
apples, grapes. Sweet, juicy fruit flavors linger through the finish. A soft, accessible style
with lower acids bringing out the sweetness.

**83 • *Saint Clair (New Zealand) 1998 Unoaked, Chardonnay,*
*Marlborough. $14.99.***
Pale straw cast. Moderately light-bodied. Full acidity. Subtly extracted. Dried herbs,
minerals. Lean herbal aromas lead a lighter-styled palate with a crisp mouthfeel. Finishes
with racy acidity. Tastes rather more like a varietal Sauvignon Blanc.

83 • House of Nobilo (New Zealand) 1998 Fall Harvest, Chardonnay, Gisborne. $9.99.

Bright straw cast. Medium-bodied. Full acidity. Moderately extracted. Minerals, citrus zest, dried herbs. Lean and subdued aromas have a subtle herbal quality. Angular and sharp with a crisp, pithy finish.

82 • Skouras (Greece) 1996 Chardonnay, Peloponnese. $14.

Deep straw hue with a greenish cast and brilliant clarity. Moderately full-bodied. Balanced acidity. Moderately extracted. Citrus, minerals, dried herbs. Has an herbal accent to the flavors, with a mouthfilling, vibrant quality to the palate. Fades a bit at the finish, but pleasant enough.

82 • Peters' Hill (Hungary) 1996 Chardonnay, Mocsenyi. $5.99.

Yellow-straw hue. Medium-bodied. Balanced acidity. Moderately extracted. Grape skins, apples, citrus. Phenolic aromas that are not unpleasant lead a rounded palate with some weight and persistence through the finish. Some malolactic character is a plus here. Quite modern.

82 • Carmel (Israel) 1997 Private Collection, Chardonnay, Galil. $11.

Pale straw color. Medium-bodied. Balanced acidity. Moderately extracted. Mildly oaked. Vanilla, dried herbs. Oak treatment is readily apparent in the nose. Light, crisp, and well balanced on the palate, with an herbal streak. Clean, somewhat clipped finish.

81 • Weingut Familie Maurer (Austria) 1997 Stoitzendorf-Sangerleiten, Trocken, Chardonnay, Weinviertel. $14.

Pale gold. Medium-bodied. Citrus, apples, minerals. Fresh Granny Smith apple aromas. Crisp and zesty, with juicy acids leaving the palate refreshed.

81 • Golan (Israel) 1994 Chardonnay, Galil. $12.75.

Bright gold. Medium-bodied. Balanced acidity. Subtly extracted. Mildly oaked. Vanilla, minerals. Oak accents present themselves in the nose and play out on a lean palate. Crisp and clean, this wine flattens out a bit on the finish.

81 • Bulgari (Bulgaria) 1996 Chardonnay, Pomorie. $5.99.

Pale straw. Moderately light-bodied. Full acidity. Moderately extracted. Mildly oaked. Flowers, kiwi fruit, chalk. Bright and racy, with crisp, tart citrusy flavors following through the finish. Refreshing style with minimal complexity.

three

≈

Sauvignon Blanc and White Bordeaux Varietal Blends

≈

Introduction	50
Reviews	52
White Bordeaux	52
Loire Sauvignon Blancs	53
Other French Sauvignon Blancs	53
New Zealand Sauvignon Blancs	54
Aussie Sauvignon Blancs	55
South American Sauvignon Blancs	55
U.S. Sauvignon Blancs	56
U.S. White Bordeaux Varietal Blends (Meritage)	60
Other Great Value Sauvignon Blancs	60

Introduction

Next to the ubiquitous Chardonnay, Sauvignon Blanc is the most recognized white wine variety in the United States, but it suffers from an acute identity crisis. Unlike most of the French varieties grown in the New World, Sauvignon Blanc has two distinct French role models. One style downplays the variety's inherent and distinctive herbal, grassy, and gooseberry-like aromas and flavors, while the other flaunts them. Coupled with this paradox is the steadfast popularity of Chardonnay. This prominence has led some producers to resort to a "if you can't beat them, join them" philosophy of winemaking that subjects Sauvignon Blanc to the same flavor-altering processes that Chardonnay regularly undergoes, such as oak aging and malolactic fermentation.

Perhaps it is the wine's distinctive and whetted flavors that prevent Sauvignon Blanc from becoming as fashionable as Chardonnay. For the most part, it is a variety that goes disturbingly unappreciated. However, the good news for the value seeker is that this lack of appreciation translates into relatively low prices. Well-made, inexpensive Sauvignon blanc comes from many wine regions of the world. Great examples can be found in the United States, South America, South Africa, and New Zealand. The latter produces the most provocative Sauvignon Blancs in the world.

Regions

As mentioned in the opening paragraph, Sauvignon Blanc has two distinct personalities in France. The first is Sauvignon Blanc from Bordeaux, a region which produces vast quantities of cheap Sauvignon Blanc labeled as Bordeaux Blanc. Many producers flout French appellation regulations and also use a varietal name, Sauvignon Blanc, on the label. In Bordeaux, the white wines are classically made with a blend of Sauvignon Blanc and a dash of Semillon. The addition of Semillon to Sauvignon Blanc softens the latter's acidity and herbaceous flavors, while adding richness and softening the palate. In Graves the whites are often oak aged, which offers further richness and toasty flavors.

Whites from Entre-Deux-Mers, a Bordeaux sub-region, are often a step up in quality from basic Bordeaux Blanc, and frequently cost less than $15. In particular, the Sauvignon Blanc-based wines of Entre-Deux-Mers offer a good deal of character for the money. During the 1990s, much investment and improvement of technique has been made in the region, resulting in cleaner, fresher wines. Occasionally some Entre-Deux-Mers contain a high proportion of Semillon, allowing them to age gracefully.

France's most famed Sauvignon Blancs come from the Loire. The Loire River is France's longest, and arguably its most picturesque. It stretches for 600 miles beginning west of Lyon and winding toward the Atlantic near the city of Nantes. This river is the lifeblood of a diverse viticultural region that is home to more than 40 distinct wine districts. Both red and white wines are made here although the region is most often known for its whites, which account for nearly two-thirds of Loire wines. Most notable of the dry white wines are Sancerre and Pouilly-Fumé, which are made entirely from Sauvignon Blanc. These two regions neighbor each other and are intersected by the Loire. Both wines are quite assertive and flavorful, exhibiting the classic Sauvignon Blanc characteristics of high acidity and herbal, grassy flavors. Sancerre and Pouilly-Fumé are more alike

Scale: Superlative (96-100), Exceptional (90-95), Highly Recommended (85-89), Recommended (80-84), Not Recommended (Under 80)

than different. Subtleties of distinction are often found in Pouilly-Fumé's smoky (fumé is French for smoked), minerally flavors, invoking thoughts of wet Loire river stone. Sancerre, at its best, exhibits flavors reminiscent of dried herbs and wet wool. It is still possible to find good examples for around $15, although many are closer to $20.

Vin de Pays from the Languedoc (Vin de Pays d'Oc) offer France's most consumer friendly varietally labeled Sauvignon Blancs, which invariably cost much less than $15. The Languedoc is a warmer region and these wines will rarely exhibit a classic herbal or leafy character, but rather a softer tropical one.

When shopping for Sauvignon from the Southern Hemisphere, don't forget the Kiwis. No other country features Sauvignon Blanc as its premier white wine varietal. When New Zealand Sauvignon Blanc burst onto the scene in the early 1990s, some thought that these wildly aggressive, intense wines must be flavored. In reality, the converse was true. These wines are the essence of Sauvignon Blanc. In a brief period of time, New Zealand Sauvignon Blanc has become recognized as one of the world's best examples of the variety. Some feel that they are in fact *the* best example of the varietal, though a Loire vigneron would argue the point.

As for U.S. Sauvignon Blanc, it started as a sweet style that often borrowed the name Sauternes, after the famed sweet wine appellation in Bordeaux, but by the early 1960s several dry examples were being produced. This led to much confusion among wine buyers who wondered which Sauvignon Blancs were sweet and which were dry. Later, Robert Mondavi coined the term "Fumé Blanc," evoking the name of Pouilly-Fumé, the renowned dry Sauvignon Blanc from France's Loire Valley. The name stuck and was used by producers throughout the state to describe Sauvignon Blanc made in the dry Loire style.

Today, the moniker Fumé Blanc is interchangeable with Sauvignon Blanc and has little meaning or suggestion of style. A majority of Sauvignon Blanc in America is being pro-

❦

Great Value Sauvignon Blanc and White Bordeaux Varietals at a Glance

Number of Wines
Recommended:

106

Countries
Represented:

11

duced in such a way as to suppress varietal character. In the past decade much of the wine industry was looking to Sauvignon Blanc as the heir apparent to Chardonnay. Producers found that many consumers were not ready for the variety's assertive flavors. Consequently, many winemakers began to produce Sauvignon Blanc in a more "acceptable" style. Not coincidentally, these modified versions have many of the characteristics of U.S. Chardonnay—woody, candied, fruity, and buttery.

Meritage is a name used by U.S. winemakers to describe wines, both red and white, made in the Bordeaux style with classic Bordeaux grape varieties. In the instance of White Meritage wines, the grape varieties are Sauvignon Blanc and Semillon. Many of the White Meritage producers made wines of this blend long before there was a name to market them under. These winemakers knew what their Bordeaux compatriots had learned; that Sauvignon Blanc is made softer, richer, and longer lived with the addition of Semillon.

When buying value Sauvignon Blanc, vintage is usually of little concern with New World examples; however, France is a completely different story. Fortunately, we are in the midst of a hot streak in the Loire, as the '95, '96, and '97 vintages are all excellent. Bordeaux has not been as blessed, although the same three vintages have been good for whites.

Sauvignon Blanc can be an excellent aperitif. Its natural acidity and crisp fresh fruit provide the perfect pre-meal stimulant. Examples from the United States, South America, and Bordeaux work best in this role as they will not shock your palate. New Zealand and Loire examples are a classic foil for smoked fish, seafood, and white meats. Both also require an appreciation for the true flavors of this noble grape.

Reviews

White Bordeaux

86 • Domaine de Montesquieu (France) 1994 M de Montesquieu, Sauvignon Blanc, Bordeaux. $9.99.
Medium golden straw. Medium-bodied. Moderately extracted. A beeswax-like, distinctive semillon character has taken a toasty lanolin note. Good mouthfeel and varietal typicity.

84 • Yvon Mau (France) 1996 Sauvignon Blanc, Bordeaux. $14.99.
Pale yellow straw. Moderately light-bodied. Moderately extracted. Grass, minerals, citrus. Fresh, fruity aromas follow through with clean flavors and a streak of acidity through the finish. A fresh aperitif style.

84 • Sichel (France) 1995 Sirius, Blanc, Bordeaux. $9.99.
Medium yellow straw. Medium-bodied. Moderately extracted. Mildly oaked. Citrus, spice, minerals. Hints of oak spice lead a rounded, spicy mouthful of flavors with the onset of maturity evident. This may have past its peak though is still drinking well.

84 • Ducla (France) 1996 Entre-Deux-Mers Blanc. $8.
Pale straw. Moderately light-bodied. Full acidity. Subtly extracted. Minerals, herbs, citrus. Clean, floral aromas lead a lively, tart mouthful of flavors through a mineral accented finish. Very refreshing.

Scale: Superlative (96-100), Exceptional (90-95), Highly Recommended (85-89), Recommended (80-84), Not Recommended (Under 80)

83 • Hostens-Picant (France) 1997 Cuvée des Demoiselles Blanc, Sainte-Foy Bordeaux. $12.99.
Bright yellow-gold luster. Medium-bodied. Moderately extracted. Mildly oaked. Vanilla, lime, lemon. Bright oak and yeast spiced aromas have a zesty backing that comes through on the palate. Nicely balanced with a piney oak accent throughout.

83 • Domaine de Montesquieu (France) 1994 Baron de Montesquieu, Reserve Blanc, Bordeaux. $11.99.
Pale straw. Moderately light-bodied. Moderately extracted. Minerals, citrus zest. Clean lime zest aromas follow through on a smooth easy-drinking palate, though the finish fades and the acidity does not follow through.

82 • Villa Bel-Air (France) 1995 Blanc, Graves. $14.99.
Bright straw. Medium-bodied. Moderately extracted. Mildly oaked. Minerals, honey, citrus. Mildly honeyed, mature aromas lead a softer, rounded palate with a mature character and a gentle finish. May have passed its peak.

81 • Michel Lynch (France) 1997 Sauvignon Blanc, Bordeaux. $8.99.
Yellow straw. Medium-bodied. Moderately extracted. Bitter lime, minerals, beeswax. Honeyed beeswax nose. Rounded and mature with bitter-lime flavors that persist through the finish. Fully mature now.

81 • Jean Michel Arcaute (France) 1996 "Comptes de Jonquegres," Bordeaux. $12.
Yellow straw. Medium-bodied. Moderately extracted. Floral, mature aromas follow through on the palate. This has some noble rot character. Mouthfeel is quite thick through the finish. Very unusual, and not for everyone.

Loire Sauvignon Blancs

89 • Clos Paradis (France) 1996 Sancerre. $14.
Bright yellow-gold. Moderately full-bodied. Balanced acidity. Moderately extracted. Gooseberries, herbs. Generous, fruit-laden aromas follow through on the palate, with rich flavors and glycerous texture. Very stylish, with color, weight and ripeness. Near-term drinking recommended.

88 • Jean Baptiste Thibault (France) 1997 La Duchesne, Sancerre. $14.99.
Medium straw hue. Medium-bodied. Full acidity. Moderately extracted. Citrus, minerals. Mineral-dominated nose follows through to a zesty, straightforward palate. Snappy style.

83 • Domaine de la Rossignole (France) 1997 Cuvée Vieilles Vignes, Sancerre. $13.99.
Pale platinum-straw hue. Medium-bodied. Balanced acidity. Moderately extracted. White fruits, minerals. Minerally aromas and flavors are not spectacular, though the rounded mouthfeel lends presence on the palate.

83 • Alain Cailbourdin (France) 1996 Les Cornets, Pouilly Fumé. $14.
Pale straw hue. Medium-bodied. Full acidity. Moderately extracted. Lemon, herbs. Brisk, zesty aromas. Tart, juicy citrus flavors persist through the finish. A clean, refreshing style.

Other French Sauvignon Blancs

84 • Georges Duboeuf (France) 1997 Sauvignon Blanc, Vin de Pays du Jardin de la France. $5.99.
Pale green-straw hue. Medium-bodied. Highly extracted. Grass, mineral, citrus. Clean, grassy aromas lead a crisp mouthful of citrus flavors, with vibrant acids leaving the palate refreshed. Very good varietal expression in a lighter frame.

83 • Jenard (France) 1996 Sauvignon Blanc, Vin de Pays d'Oc. $7.99.
Full yellow-gold. Medium-bodied. Highly extracted. Apples, lemons. Shows a certain oily note that works with the relatively thick texture and full flavors. Unusual for a Sauvignon Blanc, this sports plenty of character.

83 • Colour Volant (France) 1996 Sauvignon Blanc, Vin de Pays d'Oc. $8.
Pale green-straw hue. Medium-bodied. Moderately extracted. Tart melon, flowers. A
rather mild impression of clean Sauvignon Blanc aromas. Has simple follow-through
on the palate, with clean citrus flavors finishing quickly.

New Zealand Sauvignon Blancs

91 • Saint Clair (New Zealand) 1997 Sauvignon Blanc, Marlborough. $12.99.
Bright straw cast. Moderately full-bodied. Full acidity. Highly extracted. Asparagus,
tropical fruits, minerals. Expressive aromatics show both complexity and intensity. Rich
and ripe in the mouth with a generous texture buttressed by racy acidity. Flavorful and
zesty finish.

*90 • Spencer Hill (New Zealand) 1997 Tasman Bay, Nelson, Sauvignon Blanc,
Nelson. $12.*
Bright yellow-straw cast. Moderately full-bodied. Balanced acidity. Moderately extracted.
Moderately oaked. Vanilla, asparagus, spearmint. Attractive aromatics show a judicious
touch of wood and a core of very ripe Sauvignon Blanc flavors. Rounded and luxuriant
in the mouth, with both complexity and intensity.

*89 • Vavasour (New Zealand) 1997 Dashwood, Sauvignon Blanc,
Marlborough. $12.99.*
Brilliant platinum cast. Medium-bodied. Full acidity. Moderately extracted. Minerals, citrus zest, gooseberries. Attractive varietal aromas are forward and complex. Light in the
mouth with a crisp and racy palate feel. Zesty and angular through the finish.

*87 • Shingle Peak (New Zealand) 1998 Sauvignon Blanc,
Marlborough. $13.50.*
Bright straw cast. Medium-bodied. Full acidity. Moderately extracted. Minerals, citrus,
dried herbs. Shows attractive varietal aromas that lead to a racy and intense palate feel.
Ripe and full through the zesty finish.

87 • Nautilus (New Zealand) 1998 Sauvignon Blanc, Marlborough. $14.
Bright platinum cast. Moderately full-bodied. Full acidity. Highly extracted. Minerals,
citrus zest, dried herbs. Aromatically reserved with subtle herbal overtones. Clean and
intense in the mouth with a solid degree of ripeness. Powerful yet restrained, with a
pithy quality to the finish.

86 • Giesen (New Zealand) 1998 Sauvignon Blanc, Marlborough. $12.
Bright straw cast. Medium-bodied. Full acidity. Moderately extracted. Gooseberries,
minerals, dried herbs. Attractive varietal aromas lead a racy, crisp palate feel. Lean and
stylish, with a mildy phenolic finish.

*84 • Lawson's (New Zealand) 1998 Dry Hills, Sauvignon Blanc,
New Zealand. $12.99.*
Bright straw cast. Moderately full-bodied. Full acidity. Moderately extracted. Cream,
minerals, citrus. Rather subtle in flavor, but rich and ripe in the mouth. Supported
by an edgy streak of acidity that makes for a refreshing finish.

84 • Kim Crawford (New Zealand) 1997 Sauvignon Blanc, Marlborough. $15.
Deep straw cast. Moderately full-bodied. Balanced acidity. Moderately extracted.
Gooseberries, minerals, citrus zest. Generous varietal aromas lead a rounded palate
feel supported by edgy acidity through the finish. Shows an impressive mouthfeel.

*84 • Framingham (New Zealand) 1997 Sauvignon Blanc,
Marlborough. $13.50.*
Deep straw cast. Medium-bodied. Balanced acidity. Moderately extracted. Wool, citrus,
minerals. Shows a slightly funky Loire-like quality to the nose. Rounded and lush in
the mouth with a rush of acidity to the finish.

83 • *Matua (New Zealand) 1998 Sauvignon Blanc, Hawkes Bay. $14.*
Bright straw cast. Medium-bodied. Balanced acidity. Moderately extracted. Cream, minerals. Shows a creamy quality to the nose. Ripe and round in the mouth with a lush quality buoyed by zesty acidity in the finish. On the fat, lower-acid side of New Zealand Sauvignon Blanc.

83 • *House of Nobilo (New Zealand) 1998 Fall Harvest, Sauvignon Blanc, Marlborough $9.99.*
Deep straw cast. Moderately full-bodied. Full acidity. Highly extracted. Wool, earth, minerals. Has a slightly funky edge to the flavors that recalls the Loire. Big and intense in the mouth with a very racy palate feel. Tart and bracing through the finish.

Aussie Sauvignon Blancs

92 • *Abbey Vale (Australia) 1997 Sauvignon Blanc, Margaret River. $14.*
Pale straw cast. Moderately full-bodied. Balanced acidity. Moderately extracted. Asparagus, smoke, minerals. Quite aromatic, with an attractive and complex array of varietal flavors. Ripe and full in the mouth with an assertive, crisp finish. Impressively intense varietal character.

90 • *Taltarni (Australia) 1998 Sauvignon Blanc, Victoria. $13.*
Bright platinum hue. Moderately light-bodied. Balanced acidity. Subtly extracted. Gooseberries, dried herbs. Aggressive aromas are pure and varietally expressive. Surprisingly light in the mouth though wonderfully pure, flavorsome, and juicy. This is a stylish wine.

88 • *Katnook Estate (Australia) 1997 Sauvignon Blanc, Coonawarra. $9.*
Deep straw cast. Moderately full-bodied. Balanced acidity. Moderately extracted. Gooseberries, dried herbs, melon. Powerful, varietally expressive aromas lead a ripe and lush mouthfeel buttressed by crisp acidity. Generous and flavorful through the finish.

84 • *McGuigan (Australia) 1998 Cold Fermented, Bin 8000, Sauvignon Blanc, South Eastern Australia. $10.*
Very pale straw cast. Moderately light-bodied. Full acidity. Moderately extracted. Dried herbs, minerals. Clean, varietally correct aromas. Lean and fresh with a racy, lighter-styled palate feel. The finish is angular and vibrant.

83 • *Oxford Landing (Australia) 1998 Sauvignon Blanc, Australia. $8.*
Bright straw cast. Moderately light-bodied. Balanced acidity. Moderately extracted. Minerals, citrus zest. Rather subdued, with crisp, clean flavors and a lighter-styled mouthfeel. The finish is clean and zesty.

South American Sauvignon Blancs

86 • *Pionero (Chile) 1998 Sauvignon Blanc, Central Valley. $6.*
Bright green-straw hue. Varietally pure aromas with ripe lemon and herbal notes. A crisp entry leads a medium-bodied palate with bright lemony flavors through a clean, medium-length finish.

84 • *Viña Tarapaca (Chile) 1998 La Isla Vineyard, Sauvignon Blanc, Maipo Valley. $12.*
Medium pale straw hue. Muted, buttery aromas show a suggestion of grass. A thick attack leads a medium-bodied palate with broad texture though rather dull fruit flavors.

84 • *Casa Lapostolle (Chile) 1997 Sauvignon Blanc, Rapel Valley. $9.*
Pale straw hue. Aromatically muted with a mild buttery, tropical note. A flat entry leads a medium-bodied palate that shows soft acids and flavors.

83 • *Viña Tarapaca (Chile) 1998 Sauvignon Blanc, Maipo Valley. $7.*
Pale straw hue. Mild but clean aromas. A juicy entry leads a medium-bodied palate with clean, simple flavors of faint citrus fruits. Finishes quickly.

83 • *Santa Julia (Argentina) 1998 Sauvignon Blanc, Mendoza. $7.*
Deep straw hue. Unusual, high-toned mineral and herb aromas. A lean entry leads a medium-bodied palate with a creamy note to the acidity. The finish is rounded and flavorful. Well balanced. Drink now.

81 • Santa Amelia (Chile) 1998 Sauvignon Blanc, Maule Valley. $6.50.
Pale platinum-straw hue. Lean and simple aromas with a note of asparagus. A firm entry leads a moderately light-bodied palate with very muted flavors and a firm minerally finish. Not much character.

80 • Viña Undurraga (Chile) 1998 Sauvignon Blanc, Lontue Valley. $7.99.
Bright straw hue. Unusual aromas. A tart attack leads a moderately full-bodied palate with angular acids and citrus flavors through the dry finish. An assertive wine with brash, zesty citrus character.

80 • Caliterra (Chile) 1997 Sauvignon Blanc, Valle Central. $7.99.
Bright pale yellow-straw hue. Aromatically simple with mild citrus notes. A crisp entry leads a medium-bodied palate with juicy acids and mild fruit flavors. The somewhat short finish is fruity and clean.

U.S. Sauvignon Blancs

90 • Chateau St. Jean (CA) 1997 La Petite Etoile Vineyard, Fumé Blanc, Russian River Valley. $13.
Pale yellow-gold sheen. Complex aromas show a toasty oak accent with coconut and yeast notes. Rich on the attack with a moderately full body, concentrated flavors, and toasty, lemon pith notes on the finish. Warming alcohol is countered by fresh acids, though this is not exactly light on its feet. Drink now.

89 • Sierra Vista (CA) 1998 Herbert Vineyard, Fumé Blanc, El Dorado. $9.
Pale straw. Lovely aromas of melon, citrus, and sweet herbs. Crisp and vibrant on the attack, with a medium-bodied palate and concentrated, fruity flavors that follow from the aromas. Finishes cleanly and vibrantly. Drink now.

89 • Paradise Ridge (CA) 1998 Grandview Vineyard, Sauvignon Blanc, Sonoma County. $14.95.
Bright pale straw hue. Piercing, pure, fruity aromas. An intense, vibrant attack leads a medium bodied palate with impressive concentration of apple and citrus flavors. Finish is clean and persistent. Drink now.

89 • Lolonis (CA) 1997 Fumé Blanc, Redwood Valley. $12.
Bright yellow-straw hue. Very crisp citrus aromas show a nice herbal streak. Lively on the attack, with a medium-bodied palate and clean, citrusy, herbal flavors that show fine persistence. This features good varietal character with little oak influence. Drink now.

89 • Foley (CA) 1997 Sauvignon Blanc, Santa Barbara County. $14.
Brilliant green-gold sheen. Impressive aromas of ripe fruit with a buttery, oaky influence. Rich on the attack, with a moderately full-bodied palate, a fine oily texture, and very ripe, expressive, Sauvignon Blanc flavors that mingle with spicy oak notes on the finish. Drink now.

88 • Staton Hills (WA) 1997 Fumé Blanc, Yakima Valley. $9.95.
Pale straw hue. Fresh, grassy, citrus and herb aromas. Mouthwatering acids on the attack lead a medium-bodied palate with fresh flavors and a clean finish. This is a fresh, well-cut, unoaked style of Sauvignon.

88 • St. Clement (CA) 1997 Sauvignon Blanc, Napa Valley. $13.
Bright golden-yellow. Clean grapefruit and lime aromas. A crisp attack leads to a medium-bodied palate with very subtle oak flavors and modest fruit persistence. Acids are bright throughout and this is showing some varietal character. Drink now.

88 • Jamesport (NY) 1997 Sauvignon Blanc, North Fork of Long Island. $11.95.
Pale green-gold hue. Full citrus zest and herb aromas. A bright, zesty attack leads a medium-bodied palate with good intensity of fruit flavors and no oak influence. Finishes in a minerally, zesty manner. A good varietal expression with fine acid cut. Drink now.

**88 • *Davis Bynum (CA) 1998 Shone Farm, Fume Blanc,
Russian River Valley. $14.***
Brilliant pale metallic hue. Exotically pure citrus and herb-tinged aromas. Crisp and
lively on the attack, leading a medium-bodied palate with bright acids and piercing,
pure flavors. A fine expression of varietal character that will work with food in the same
manner as Loire Sauvignon. Drink now.

88 • *Covey Run (WA) 1997 Fumé Blanc, Washington. $8.*
Pale straw with a metallic sheen. Lovely aromas of vanilla, melon, herbs. Crisp on the
entry, with a medium-bodied palate and very pure, juicy fruit flavors and herbal notes,
concluding with well-judged oak spice nuances. Fresh and varietally expressive. Drink now.

88 • *Chateau Ste. Michelle (WA) 1997 Sauvignon Blanc, Columbia Valley. $10.*
Pale yellow-straw hue. Zesty citrus aromas. Bright and juicy acids on the attack, with a
medium-bodied palate and good concentration of fruit flavors complimented by buttery,
but subdued oak accents. Stylish. Drink now.

**87 • *Windsor (CA) 1998 Middle Ridge Vineyard, Private Reserve,
Fumé Blanc, Mendocino County. $12.***
Pale green-straw hue. Quite aromatic, with herb and pear character. Crisp on the attack,
leading a medium-bodied palate with good concentration of zesty fruit flavors and a
clean character through the finish. Drink now.

86 • *Raymond (CA) 1997 Reserve, Sauvignon Blanc, Napa Valley. $11.*
Pale golden hue. Bright citrus zest aromas. A crisp attack leads a medium-bodied palate
with zesty citrus flavors and acids that linger through the finish. Drink now.

**86 • *Justin (CA) 1997 Morrow Vineyard, Sauvingon Blanc,
Central Coast. $12.50.***
Bright yellow gold. Smoky, buttery aromas with a ripe citrus underlay. A bright attack
leads to a medium-bodied palate with fresh fruit flavors and subtle oak on the finish.
Drink now.

86 • *Columbia Crest (WA) 1997 Sauvignon Blanc, Columbia Valley. $8.*
Pale straw hue. Lean aromas show a minerally, citrus zest quality. Vibrant on the attack,
with a medium-bodied palate and clean lively citrus flavors. Finishes with a nice acidic
cut. Drink now.

86 • *Chateau St. Jean (CA) 1997 Fumé Blanc, Sonoma County. $9.*
Bright green-straw hue. Very aromatic with a big note of coconut and toasty oak. A zesty
entry leads to a moderately full-bodied palate with impressive concentration of flavors.
Finishes in a spicy manner. Drink now.

**86 • *Beringer (CA) 1997 Appellation Collection, Sauvignon Blanc,
Napa Valley. $11.***
Rich golden-yellow hue. Toasty oak and ripe tropical aromas. A spicy, buttery attack leads
a medium-bodied palate with a rounded mouthfeel and good persistence of fruit and
oak flavors. Drink now.

84 • *Windsor (CA) 1998 Fumé Blanc, North Coast. $10.*
Very pale straw hue. Fresh citrus aromas. Crisp and lively on the entry, with a medium-
bodied palate and a lively, zesty citrus character through the clean finish. Shows fine
acidic cut. Drink now.

84 • *Weinstock (CA) 1998 Sauvignon Blanc, California. $8.*
Pale straw hue. Faintly floral aromas. A light attack leads a moderately light-bodied palate
with rounded citrus fruit flavors and a quick finish. Drink now.

84 • *Van Roekel (CA) 1997 Fumé Blanc, Temecula. $8.95.*
Pale yellow-gold hue. Butter and ripe citrus aromas with a dash of oak. A crisp attack
leads a medium-bodied palate with clean, fresh, citrus fruit flavors and delicate oak spice
on the finish. Drink now.

84 • Topolos (CA) 1998 Harrison Vineyard, Sauvignon Blanc, Russian River Valley. $9.

Very pale straw hue. Crisp, clean, reserved, citrus and mineral aromas. Spritzy acids mark the attack. Medium-bodied, with vibrant, limey flavors making for a refreshing character throughout. This should work with shellfish. Drink now.

84 • Rodney Strong (CA) 1998 Charlotte's Home, Sauvignon Blanc, Alexander Valley. $10.

Pale green straw hue. Crisp, bright lemon aromas. Vibrant on the attack, leading a medium-bodied palate with bright lemon-citrus flavors and spritzy acids persisting through the finish. A clean, racy style with fine acidity. Drink now.

84 • Robert Mondavi (CA) 1997 Fumé Blanc, Napa Valley. $13.

Bright golden hue. Generous aromas show a toasty coconut accent. A smooth entry leads a medium-bodied palate with apple fruit, oak, and bright acids. Rather obvious but nicely done. Drink now.

84 • Paradise Ridge (CA) 1997 Grandview Vineyard, Sauvignon Blanc, Sonoma County. $12.95.

Bright green-gold hue. Richer, heavier aromas feature a bitter lemon quality. An angular, firm attack leads a medium-bodied palate with drying flavors coming through on the finish. Overall, a tad lean. Drink now.

84 • Macari (NY) 1998 Sauvignon Blanc, North Fork of Long Island. $14.

Bright yellow-gold hue. Herbal, zesty, minerally aromas. A bright attack leads a medium-bodied palate with zesty flavors, though the mouthfeel is smooth through the finish. A clean, lemony style. Drink now.

84 • Fetzer (CA) 1998 Echo Ridge, Sauvignon Blanc, California. $10.

Pale straw. Citrus and mineral aromas. A bright attack leads a moderately light-bodied palate with tart citrus fruit flavors that fade quickly. Drink now.

84 • Estancia (CA) 1997 Fumé Blanc, Monterey County. $14.

Medium golden hue. Ripe aromas of butter and vanilla with a tropical underlay. Juicy on the attack, leading a medium-bodied palate with light fruit flavors and a good glycerous mouthfeel. Finishes with a hint of oak. Drink now.

84 • Dry Creek Vineyard (CA) 1998 Fumé Blanc, Sonoma County. $11.50.

Bright pale-golden hue. Ripe melon and citrus aromas. A smooth entry leads a medium-bodied palate with clean fruit flavors, moderate acidity, and a hint of dryness on the finish. Drink now.

84 • Concannon (CA) 1997 Selected Vineyard, Sauvignon Blanc, Livermore Valley. $8.95.

Pale gold hue. Ripe aromas of honey and peach. Smooth on the attack, with a medium-bodied palate, a buttery texture, and moderate acids. Finishes in a floral manner. Drink now.

84 • Callaway (CA) 1998 Sauvignon Blanc, Temecula. $10.

Bright pale gold hue. Melon and floral aromas. A light attack leads a medium-bodied palate with juicy, floral flavors and a clean finish. A hint of fruit sweetness makes for an easy-drinking character. Drink now.

84 • Brophy Clark (CA) 1997 Sauvignon Blanc, 52% San Luis Obispo and 42% Santa Barbara Counties. $12.

Bright yellow-straw hue. Melon and herb aromas. A lean entry leads a medium-bodied palate with apple and melon flavors that finish quickly. Drink now.

83 • Waterbrook (WA) 1997 Sauvignon Blanc, Columbia Valley. $9.

Bright pale straw. Lean, reserved aromas show a mineral accent. A crisp attack leads to a medium-bodied palate with grassy, citrusy flavors and a quick minerally finish. Drink now.

Scale: Superlative (96-100), Exceptional (90-95), Highly Recommended (85-89), Recommended (80-84), Not Recommended (Under 80)

83 • *Taft Street (CA) 1998 Sauvignon Blanc, Russian River Valley. $9.*
Pale straw. Clean, floral aromas of melon and apples. A juicy attack leads a moderately light-bodied palate with a hint of fruit sweetness that lingers through the soft finish. An easy drinking, fruit-forward style. Drink now.

83 • *Napa Wine Co. (CA) 1997 Sauvignon Blanc, Napa Valley. $12.*
Pale straw hue. Bright citrus aromas have a minerally accent. A crisp attack leads a moderately light-bodied palate with crisp flavors and bright acids. Finishes quickly. Drink now.

83 • *Murphy-Goode (CA) 1998 Fumé Blanc, Sonoma County. $11.50.*
Pale straw hue. Clean, crisp aromas show a tart citrus accent. A zesty entry leads a moderately light-bodied palate with shy fruit flavors. Crisp through the finish. Drink now.

83 • *Maurice Carrie (CA) 1997 Sauvignon Blanc, Temecula. $7.95.*
Medium straw hue. Zesty, mildly smoky aromas. Crisp and juicy on the attack, with a medium-bodied palate featuring citrus zest and delicate oak accents. Drink now.

83 • *Macari (NY) 1997 Sauvignon Blanc, North Fork of Long Island. $14.*
Bright straw hue. Muted mineral and herb aromas. An acidic entry leads to a medium-bodied palate. Zesty and straightforward. Drink now.

83 • *Kendall-Jackson (CA) 1997 Vintner's Reserve, Sauvignon Blanc, California. $11.*
Pale straw hue. Generous aromas of bright citrus and butter. Juicy on the entry with a medium-bodied palate and a lingering citrusy finish showing fresh acidity. Drink now.

83 • *Joullian (CA) 1997 Sauvignon Blanc, Carmel Valley. $13.50.*
Medium golden hue. Sweet, tropical aromas show a honeyed character. Lively and juicy on the attack, with a medium-bodied palate and ripe citrus flavors. Round, soft finish. Drink now.

83 • *Husch (CA) 1998 La Ribera Vineyards, Sauvignon Blanc, Mendocino. $11.50.*
Pale metallic-straw hue. Mildy herbaceous, vanilla accented aromas. A light attack follows through to a medium-bodied palate with crisp appley and lively acids. Oak influence is restrained. Drink now.

83 • *Huntington (CA) 1997 Sauvignon Blanc, California. $7.99.*
Bright green-straw hue. Ripe citrus aromas. A rich attack leads a medium-bodied palate with tart lemon flavors and a degree of richness to the mouthfeel. Bright acids come though on the finish. Drink now.

83 • *Fall Creek (TX) 1998 Sauvignon Blanc, Texas. $9.*
Pale straw hue. Lean fruit aromas have an herbal twist. A firm entry leads a medium-bodied palate with crisp citrus flavors and a minerally finish. Drink now.

83 • *Dunnewood (CA) 1997 Sauvignon Blanc, Mendocino. $6.99.*
Pale straw hue. Straightforward aromas show a buttery, muted fruit character. A simple entry leads a medium-bodied palate with citrus cream flavors and crisp acids through the finish. Very drinkable, if not overly stylish.

83 • *Columbia Crest (WA) 1997 Estate Series, Sauvignon Blanc, Columbia Valley. $11.*
Pale yellow-straw hue. Vanilla-kissed aromas display a citrusy theme. A buttery entry leads a medium-bodied palate with clean fruity flavors and a soft texture. Oak spice lingers on the finish. Drink now.

83 • *Beringer (CA) 1997 Founders' Estate, Sauvignon Blanc, California. $9.*
Pale yellow-straw hue. Buttery aromas show a lick of new oak. A smooth entry leads a medium-bodied palate with subdued fruit nuances. Finishes quickly.

83 • *Beaulieu (CA) 1997 Sauvignon Blanc, Napa Valley. $12.*
Bright golden hue. Soft aromas of butter and citrus fruits. Lower in acidity, with a medium-bodied palate and a buttery, rounded mouthfeel. Nice texture, though rather subdued. Drink now.

81 • Ste. Genevieve (TX) NV Sauvignon Blanc, Texas. $3.99.

Pale straw hue. Apple and pear aromas. Fruity on the attack, with a moderately light-bodied palate and hints of sweetness. Finishes cleanly and quickly. Simple and highly drinkable, though not stylish. Drink now.

81 • Robert Mondavi (CA) 1997 Coastal, Sauvignon Blanc, North Coast. $9.

Pale straw hue. Lean, herbal aromas. Crisp, vibrant acids on the attack follow through to a medium-bodied palate with zesty citrus flavors that finish briefly. Drink now.

81 • Herzog (CA) 1998 Baron Herzog, Sauvignon Blanc, California. $8.95.

Pale straw hue. Grapefruit and butter aromas. Clean on the attack, with a medium-bodied palate showing hints of oak on a buttery frame. Drink now.

81 • Delicato (CA) 1998 Sauvignon Blanc, California. $4.99.

Very pale straw. Subdued, faintly floral aromas. A light attack leads to a light-bodied palate with subdued, faintly tropical flavors that finish quickly. Drink now.

80 • Firestone (CA) 1997 Sauvignon Blanc, Santa Ynez Valley. $8.50.

Bright yellow gold. Tart fruit aromas show smoke and oak spice accents. A bright attack leads to a medium-bodied palate with crisp acids and pure fruit flavors. Finishes quickly. Drink now.

U.S. White Bordeaux Varietal Blends

88 • Concannon (CA) 1997 Reserve Assemblage White, James Concannon Vineyard. $12.95.

Yellow gold hue. Interesting aromas of spice, honey, and herbs. Rich on the attack, with a moderately full-bodied palate, concentrated flavors, and moderate acids. Finishes in a grassy manner. More time might help to bring out the lanolin-like Semillon character. Drink now or later.

86 • de Lorimier (CA) 1997 Spectrum, Alexander Valley. $14.

Bright golden hue. Rich, fat, floral aromas have a glycerous character and a restrained oaky note. Very rounded on the attack, leading to a moderately full-bodied palate with peach, butter, and citrus flavors lingering on a smooth, mildly warm finish. Distinctive. Drink now or later.

81 • Ste. Genevieve (TX) NV Fumé-Chardonnay, Texas 1.2% rs. $8.99/1.5 L.

Bright pale straw hue. Mildly smoky, apple fruit aromas. Sweet juicy fruit on the entry with a medium body and a soft texture. An easy-drinking style. Drink now.

Other Great Value Sauvignon Blancs

88 • Boschendal (South Africa) 1998 Sauvignon Blanc, Coastal Region. $11.99.

Very pale straw hue. Generous herbal aromas are pure and varietally intense. A rounded attack leads a medium-bodied palate with lush acidity. Brimming with flavor. Drink now.

86 • Neil Ellis (South Africa) 1998 Sauvignon Blanc, Groenekloof. $11.99.

Very pale straw hue. Generous herb and mineral aromas. A lean entry is followed by a medium-bodied palate with angular acidity. Taut varietal finish with a hint of pithiness. Drink now.

85 • Calona (Canada) 1997 Private Reserve, Fumé Blanc, Okanagan Valley. $9.50.

Pale brilliant straw hue. Subtle, clean bread dough and citrus aromas. Subtle wood treatment is apparent. A soft attack leads to a medium-bodied palate with balanced acidity. Smooth in character. Lingering flavorful finish. An ideal match for sole or delicate fish. Drink now.

Scale: Superlative (96-100), Exceptional (90-95), Highly Recommended (85-89), Recommended (80-84), Not Recommended (Under 80)

84 • Weingut Familie Markowitsch (Austria) 1997 Trocken, Sauvignon Blanc, Carnuntum. $15.

Very pale straw cast. Medium-bodied. Full acidity. Moderately extracted. Tart tropical fruits, minerals, herbs. High-toned tropical Sauvignon Blanc aromas follow through on a very acidic palate, with intense flavors that fade quickly.

84 • Chamonix (South Africa) 1998 Sauvignon Blanc, Franschhoek 1.78% rs. $10.

Bright pale gold. Fresh, tart aromas of passion fruit and citrus. A crisp entry leads a medium-bodied palate with toasty oak spice through the finish. Shows good fruit concentration. The steely finish has nice grip.

83 • Yarden (Israel) 1995 Sauvignon Blanc, Galil. $13.

Pale gold. Medium-bodied. Full acidity. Moderately extracted. Lanolin, pine. Pleasantly aromatic with telltale lanolin aromas that point to the fact that this is blended with Semillon. Full and clean in the mouth with a brisk finish.

83 • Magnotta (Canada) 1996 Limited Edition, Sauvignon Blanc. $9.

Deep, brilliant yellow-straw hue. Intense powerful dried herb and citrus aromas. A firm attack leads to a moderately full-bodied palate with crisp acidity. Quite lively through a clipped clean finish. Shows excellent varietal character but lacks a bit for intensity. Drink now.

83 • Domaine Constantin Lazaridi (Greece) 1996 Amethystos Fumé, Sauvignon Blanc, Drama. $14.99.

Pale green-yellow. Medium-bodied. Low acidity. Moderately extracted. Vanilla, lemon cream, smoke. Warm aromas lead a soft, somewhat thick mouthfeel with some good varietal Sauvignon Blanc flavors that taper off quickly on the finish. Needs a little more acidity.

82 • Weingut Hermann Huber (Austria) 1997 Ried Grub, Trocken, Strasser Sauvignon Blanc, Kamptal. $14.

Very pale straw hue. Moderately light-bodied. Full acidity. Subtly extracted. Lemon, minerals. Simple, tart, and relatively dilute. Very clean and refreshing, with a distinct citrus zest accent.

81 • Magnotta (Canada) 1997 Chile International Series, Sauvignon Blanc, Niagara–Maipo Valley. $5.

Pale brilliant straw hue. Intense unusual foxy, herbal aromas. A firm attack leads to a moderately full-bodied palate with crisp acidity. Shows an angular character through a clipped phenolic finish. Rather ungenerous but sound. Drink now.

81 • KWV (South Africa) 1997 Sauvignon Blanc, Western Cape. $7.49.

Pale green-straw hue. Subdued wool and mineral aromas. A lean entry leads a moderately light-bodied palate with angular acidity and a pithy sensation. Rather austere but well structured. Drink now.

80 • Gamla (Israel) 1995 Sauvignon Blanc, Galil. $10.99.

Pale straw color. Moderately light-bodied. Full acidity. Highly extracted. Dried herbs, minerals. Clean and crisp with vibrant acidity and an herbal streak. Has a slight sense of bitterness on the finish.

four

White Rhône Varietals and Pinot Blanc

Introduction to White Rhônes	64
Reviews	65
Rhône Valley Originals	65
Other French Viogniers	65
U.S. White Rhônes	66
Other Great Value Viogniers	66
Introduction to Pinot Blanc	67
Reviews	67
Alsatian and Austrian Pinot Blanc	67
U.S. Pinot Blanc	68

Introduction to White Rhônes

The Rhône River Valley is a large wine-producing region located in southeastern France, running south from the city of Vienne, near Lyon, to Avignon, not far from the Mediterranean Sea. The region takes its name from the mighty Rhône River, which flows from the Swiss Alps to the Mediterranean. The Rhône Valley is typically known for its red wines rather than for its whites, as a majority of the Rhône's appellations produce only, or a disproportionate amount of, red wines. However, several excellent white wines, such as Condrieu, White Hermitage, and even Côtes du Rhône Blanc, do exist. Recently, New World and particularly U.S. winemakers have taken a fancy to the lesser-known white varieties of the Rhône Valley. The most popular whites are Marsanne, Roussanne, and Viognier. All are capable of producing lovely wines. However, Viognier stands alone both in terms of fame and reputation.

The Rhône Valley's most renowned whites are Condrieu and Chateau Grillet, whose lovely and fragrant wines are made from the Viognier grape. Lamentably, these wines are usually priced well over $20. However, varietally labeled Viogniers from vineyards outside the Rhône, most notably the Vin de Pays, offer tasty wines at equally tasty prices. One producer, Georges Duboeuf of Beaujolais fame, deserves a special mention as having the largest holdings—in the Languedoc—of Viognier vines in the world. Abundant volumes of stylish Viognier, bearing the Duboeuf name, can be purchased for as little as $9.

Other white wine values from the Rhône Valley exist most often in the form of Côtes du Rhône Blanc. Côtes du Rhône whites vary in flavor and composition, as every producer has its own blend of the permitted varieties, which include Grenache Blanc, Clairett, Bourboulenc, Marsanne, and Roussanne. Côtes du Rhône Blanc is dry and often earthy, with minerally notes on the finish. When young, these wines exude fresh fruit flavors and a floral bouquet. At times the wonderful and difficult-to-find Châteauneuf du Pape Blanc squeaks into the value range. This wine shares many of the same characteristics of Côtes du Rhône Blanc, albeit with more richness and fragrance.

U.S. Rhône varietal wines are the darlings of both the press and industry insiders alike. Despite this fact, most of these varieties are grown on such minuscule acreage that they don't even show up in California state statistics. Low supply coupled with high demand rarely results in bargains, and Rhône varietal whites are no exception. A majority of these wines fall into the $20-plus category, and precious few values exist.

In the United States, the so-called Rhône Rangers, an informal group of winemakers dedicated to Rhône-style wines, remain true to their Rhône model with a notable red bias. However, as in the Rhône, many quality white wines are produced in smaller quantities. Viognier leads the way; Marsanne and Roussanne lag well behind. Viognier was not seen in California vineyards until 1982. In the 1990s the variety gained somewhat of a cult following. Viognier vineyard acreage is on the rise, although it is still relatively insignificant at this time. The volume of Viognier should increase shortly as considerable Viognier acreage that has yet to bear fruit comes on line.

When purchasing wines from white Rhône varieties, freshness is key. Although many of these wines—Viognier in particular—are big and bold, their fruit and aromas fade quickly. As in its native France, wines made of Viognier are incredibly deep and complex, with flavors that can be likened to no other wine. It has the backbone to stand up to many rich dishes, trading on a rich, opulent, almost viscous texture.

Reviews

Rhône Valley Originals

86 • *Perrin (France) 1997 Blanc Réserve, Côtes du Rhône Blanc. $10.49.*
Bright straw cast. Moderately full-bodied. Full acidity. Moderately extracted. Tropical fruits, dough, minerals. Pleasant aromatics feature a note of complexity. Full and firm in the mouth, with a sense of richness and an angular finish.

86 • *Guigal (France) 1997 Blanc, Côtes du Rhône Blanc. $10.*
Bright straw cast. Moderately full-bodied. Full acidity. Highly extracted. Bread dough, minerals. Soft aromas, with a rounded and firm mouth feel. This has a sound palate presence, though the flavors tend to be neutral.

83 • *La Vieille Ferme (France) 1997 Rhone Valley Blanc. $7.49.*
Bright straw cast. Moderately full-bodied. Balanced acidity. Moderately extracted. Dried herbs, minerals. Steely aromatics carry a slight herbal overtone. Full but firm in the mouth, with an angular finish.

82 • *Reine Pédauque (France) 1997 Les Rigaudes, Côtes du Rhône Blanc. $9.*
Bright straw cast. Medium-bodied. Full acidity. Moderately extracted. Blanched almonds, minerals. Carries a slight hint of oxidation in the nose, with a subtle fino sherry-like quality on the palate. Unusual, but lean and snappy.

Other French Viogniers

90 • *Domaine de Triennes (France) 1996 Viognier, Vin de Pays du Var. $12.99.*
Deep yellow-straw cast. Full-bodied. Balanced acidity. Highly extracted. Tropical fruits, salmon, sweet herbs. Outrageously aromatic, with a wave of pure and varietally intense flavors. Rich and lush in the mouth, with fine length and intensity.

86 • *Henri Miquel (France) 1996 "Domaine Miquel," Viognier, Vin de Pays d'Oc. $12.99.*
Bright yellow-gold. Medium-bodied. Balanced acidity. Moderately extracted. Herbs, minerals, peach. Generous aromas show fine varietal character. Rounded texture is complemented by a good acid cut that leaves the mouth refreshed.

Great Value White Rhône Rangers Varietals at a Glance

Number of Wines Recommended:

17

Countries Represented:

4

Great Value Pinot Blanc at a Glance

Number of Wines Recommended:

14

Countries Represented:

3

86 • *Georges Duboeuf (France) 1997 Viognier, Vin de Pays de L'Ardeche. $9.*
Pale yellow-straw luster. Medium-bodied. Moderately extracted. Nutmeg, flowers, citrus oil. Floral, spicy aromas lead a rounded, glycerous palate with textural elegance and a spicy note on the finish. An excellent varietal expression for such a meager price.

83 • *Vichon (France) 1996 Viognier, Vin de Pays d'Oc. $10.*
Medium green-straw hue. Medium-bodied. Moderately extracted. Spice, lime, mineral. Zesty citrus nose with dry, taut flavors that show a firm, minerally backbone. Finishes with a spicy note.

83 • *Domaine La Chevalière (France) 1996 Viognier, Vin de Pays d'Oc. $12.99.*
Bright green-straw cast. Medium-bodied. Full acidity. Moderately extracted. Tropical fruits, minerals. Forward aromas feature a slight tropical cast and an earthy edge. Lean and racy through the finish, with spritzy acidity.

U.S. White Rhônes

91 • *Rosenblum (CA) 1997 Viognier, Santa Barbara County. $15.*
Bright straw cast. Moderately full-bodied. Full acidity. Moderately extracted. Tropical fruits, oranges, flowers. Quite aromatic, with an extremely ripe and complex fruit-centered flavor profile. Vibrant acidity balances the weightiness of the wine through a fine and intense finish.

84 • *McDowell (CA) 1996 Viognier, Mendocino. $15.*
Deep straw cast. Full-bodied. Full acidity. Moderately extracted. Minerals. Rather reserved aromatically, with a generous mouthfeel buttressed by vibrant and racy acidity. Well structured but neutral in the flavor department.

84 • *Concannon (CA) 1996 Marsanne, Santa Clara Valley. $13.95.*
Deep gold. Moderately full-bodied. Full acidity. Highly extracted. Oranges, blanched almonds, cream. Quite ripe aromatically with a viscous entry. Turns rather lean in the mouth with a sense of angularity and some mild bitterness to the finish.

82 • *Van Roekel (CA) 1996 Viognier, Temecula. $10.95.*
Bright straw cast. Medium-bodied. Full acidity. Highly extracted. Dried herbs, earth, zoo. Quite pungent, with a forceful, earthy flavor profile. Crisp, zesty, and well balanced on the palate, with a racy flavorful finish. Flavors may not appeal to everyone.

82 • *Sobon (CA) 1997 Roussanne, Shenandoah Valley. $15.*
Very deep old-gold cast. Full-bodied. Low acidity. Moderately extracted. Spiced pears. Dusty, spicy aromas lead a thick, richly textured mouthfeel. Flavors seem mature, so this is for near-term consumption.

81 • *Jepson (CA) 1997 Viognier, Mendocino County. $15.*
Gold with a copper cast. Full-bodied. Low acidity. Moderately extracted. Cream, citrus. Extremely fat and ripe with a viscous quality. Somewhat muddled in flavor, with a note of spritzy acidity on the tongue and a weighty finish.

Other Great Value Viogniers

91 • *Yalumba (Australia) 1997 Limited Release, Viognier, Barossa. $15.*
Bright yellow-straw hue. Moderately full-bodied. Balanced acidity. Moderately extracted. Stone fruits, honey. Elegant floral, honeyed aromas lead a sumptuous, thick mouthfeel with peachy flavors that linger through the finish. Very attractive and displays fine varietal character.

83 • *Bodegas Escorihuela (Argentina) 1997 Don Miguel Gascón, Viognier, Mendoza. $11.99.*
Deep straw hue. Subdued tropical fruit and mineral aromas. A lean entry leads a medium-bodied palate with a hint of bitterness. The finish is austere and angular. Drink now.

Introduction to Pinot Blanc

Pinot Blanc would never be described as flashy or chic. It is unlikely that it will ever become trendy or develop a cult following like Viognier and Gewürztraminer have. For fans of the variety, Pinot Blanc is useful for its simplicity, delicacy, and balanced flavors. Pinot Blanc is most often described as a fairly neutral variety, with moderate fruit and an austere finish—in other words, poor man's Chardonnay. However, in the hands of the right producer, Pinot Blanc can be delicate and refreshing, with flavors of peaches, apples, and meringue balanced by citrusy acidity.

Bargains abound, as Pinot Blancs from around the globe rarely exceed $15 per bottle. Some of the best examples come from the Alsace region of France, and fine and reasonably priced examples can be had from Germany, Austria, and Italy. Few wines from this variety are being produced in the United States today, but those that are can be quite agreeable.

In Alsace, Pinot Blanc is second only to Riesling in total acreage and is the work horse wine grape of the region. The wines of Pinot Blanc are not permitted Grand Cru status in Alsace, as are its more famous stablemates, Riesling, Gewürztraminer, Pinot Gris, and Muscat. Accordingly, Alsatian Pinot Blanc rarely exceeds $15 at retail, and most hover around the $10 mark. Pinot Blanc is cultivated elsewhere in Europe, most notably in Germany and Austria, where it is known as Weissburgunder, and Italy, where it is called Pinot Bianco.

Pinot Blanc plantings in California barely exceed 1,000 acres, with much of this being used in sparkling wine blends, but Monterey County in particular has adopted the varietal as its own and produces most of the best examples. Other examples of Pinot Blanc are being produced on Long Island in New York. They often show a charm similar to the cool-climate wines of Alsace.

Buy and consume Pinot Blanc when young, as the subtle flavors and crisp bite of acidity fade quickly. Vintages in Alsace, as in all cool growing regions, are often an important consideration, but vintages from 1995 to the present have all been very good to excellent. Pinot Blanc's best application is that of an aperitif. Heavy and aggressive dishes can overwhelm its flavors.

Reviews

Alsatian and Austrian Pinot Blanc

91 • Pfaffenheim (France) 1995 Schneckenberg, Pinot Blanc, Alsace. $11.
Dark luminous old-gold hue. Moderately full-bodied. Full acidity. Highly extracted. Honey, lacquer, lime. Pleasantly aromatic, with a reserved yet complex array of flavors. Full and well structured in the mouth, with a firm finish. This could withstand rich foods.

89 • Hopler (Austria) 1995 Privat Reserve, Halbtrocken, Pinot Blanc, Neusiedlersee. $12.
Deep golden straw hue. Moderately full-bodied. Balanced acidity. Highly extracted. Caramelized apples, spices. Rich, late harvest aromas. Juicy, luscious, and ripe, showing generous flavors. Somewhere between a dessert wine and a table wine.

89 • Ostertag (France) 1997 Barriques, Pinot Blanc, Alsace. $14.

Medium straw hue. Moderately full-bodied. Balanced acidity. Highly extracted. Butter, flint, green herbs. Pleasantly aromatic, with a complex array of flavors. Full and firm in the mouth, with a sense of leanness to the lengthy finish.

88 • Pierre Sparr (France) 1997 Réserve, Pinot Blanc, Alsace. $9.90.

Brilliant greenish straw hue. Medium-bodied. Full acidity. Moderately extracted. Minerals, citrus. Pleasantly aromatic, with a crisp and zesty mouthfeel. Lean and clean through the finish. An excellent shellfish wine.

86 • Jean-Marc Bernhard (France) 1997 Bouquet de Printemps, Pinot Blanc, Alsace. $9.

Brilliant yellow-straw hue. Moderately full-bodied. Full acidity. Highly extracted. Blanched almonds, flint, cream. Generous aromas are quite complex. Rounded and soft in the mouth, with enough acidity to lend a sense of balance. Drinking quite well now.

86 • Dopff & Irion (France) 1997 Pinot Blanc, Alsace. $11.

Medium straw hue. Medium-bodied. Full acidity. Moderately extracted. Butter, minerals, toast. Pleasantly aromatic, with a firm and lean palate feel. Features a lengthy, clean finish.

86 • Charles Baur (France) 1996 Pinot Blanc, Alsace. $8.50.

Brilliant yellow-straw hue. Moderately full-bodied. Full acidity. Highly extracted. Minerals, citrus zest. Aromatically reserved, with a lean, firm, zesty mouthfeel. Clean and weighty in the mouth, this would make a versatile table wine.

U.S. Pinot Blanc

86 • Saddleback (CA) 1997 Pinot Blanc, Napa Valley. $13.50.

Deep straw cast. Medium-bodied. Full acidity. Highly extracted. Mildly oaked. Butter, minerals, tropical fruits. Quite buttery in aroma and flavor with a lean and angular palate feel that still conveys a sense of ripeness. Good lengthy finish.

85 • Murphy-Goode (CA) 1996 Pinot Blanc, Sonoma County. $13.50.

Bright gold. Medium-bodied. Full acidity. Moderately extracted. Moderately oaked. Toasted coconut, minerals. Marked oak spice on the nose also dominates the flavors on the palate. Clean and brisk in structure with vibrant acidity making for a snappy finish.

84 • Martini & Prati (CA) 1996 Pinot Bianco, Monterey. $10.

Deep gold. Moderately full-bodied. Balanced acidity. Moderately extracted. Flowers, citrus, tropical fruits. Quite aromatic, with some complexity to the flavors. Full though angular on the palate, with steely acidity through the finish.

84 • Hargrave (NY) 1997 Pinot Blanc, North Fork of Long Island. $9.99.

Deep straw hue. Subdued melon, toast, and butter aromas. A supple entry leads a medium-bodied palate with a lingering buttery finish. Clean and stylish with Alsatian-type viscosity. Drink now.

82 • Palmer (NY) 1996 Estate, Pinot Blanc, North Fork of Long Island. $9.99.

Dull gold. Medium-bodied. Full acidity. Highly extracted. Earth, minerals, honey. Aromatically, a hint of overripeness with an earthy edge. Lean and quite angular in the mouth with some bitterness to the finish.

82 • Chimére (CA) 1996 Bien Nacido Vineyard, Pinot Blanc, Santa Barbara County. $13.

Very deep gold. Medium-bodied. Full acidity. Moderately extracted. Honey, vanilla, marzipan. Aromatically more indicative of a late harvest wine that has seen botrytis. Racy and angular in the mouth with linear acidity. Interesting, if rather unusual.

80 • Glenora (NY) 1996 Pinot Blanc, Finger Lakes. $11.99.

Very pale straw color. Moderately light-bodied. Full acidity. Subtly extracted. Minerals, citrus. Rather unusual in aromas with a slight earthy edge. Lean and light on the palate with extremely vibrant acidity through a bracing finish.

five

Riesling

Introduction	70
Reviews	72
German Riesling	72
Kabinett	73
Spätlese	74
Auslese	74
Alsatian Riesling	75
Australian Riesling	76
Austrian Riesling	77
U.S. Riesling	77
Other Great Value Rieslings	82

Introduction: Riesling

Why is it that a noble grape variety that is responsible for world-class white wines from three continents and five countries goes almost completely unappreciated by American wine consumers? Perhaps it is because most consumers continue to merrily don Chardonnay-colored goggles that blind them to other possibilities. As wine consumers become more educated and move into the world of dry wines, they reject off-dry and slightly sweet wines as being unsophisticated. Whatever the answer, the result is that a truly great white wine value is being seriously neglected. That wine is Riesling.

A native of Germany, Riesling prefers cool climates, although it has shown well in many areas in which it has been planted. Quality Riesling is pure essence of the variety, unadulterated by oak and flavor-altering techniques so often used with Chardonnay. Riesling displays fresh and vibrant fruit flavors that run the gamut from apples and pears to peaches and honey, beautifully balanced by racy natural acidity. A winemaker's greatest influence is to determine the amount of residual sugar to leave in the finished wine. Residual sugar is the measure of unfermented sugar present in finished wine, usually expressed as a percentage of volume. This is the major indicator of the wine's sweetness on the palate. Most cool climate Riesling benefits from residual sugar. Without it, these naturally high-acid wines may seem to be excessively thin or biting.

German Styles

In the cool growing regions along Germany's Rhine and Mosel rivers, the pursuit of ripeness is the grower's primary concern, because Germany's precise system of grading and classification is based upon ripeness. Indications of natural sugar levels are expressed on the wine's label. From lowest to highest sugar levels, the categories are *Kabinett, Spätlese, Auslese, Beerenauslese,* and *Trockenbeerenauslese.* Beerenauslese and Trockenbeerenauslese are intensely sweet wines; they are among the world's elite dessert wines and are prohibitively expensive. Auslese is usually fairly sweet, considered by most to be a dessert wine. It, too, is frequently beyond our $15 boundary, although some bargains still prevail.

Kabinett, Spätlese, and so on are indications of the sugar levels of ripe unfermented grapes, not the finished wine. The grapes' natural sugar levels at harvest translate to the subsequent body and alcohol of the wine. As a general rule, German Rieslings are low in alcohol; 8% to 11% by volume is normal. Also, the amount of residual sugar in a Kabinett may be equal to that of an Auslese, but the Auslese will be richer and more mouth filling, with a higher degree of natural alcohol.

If the word Trocken appears on the label, it indicates that the wine has been fermented completely dry. Halbtrocken, meaning half-dry, indicates a wine bottled with only a hint of residual sugar. Dry versions are excellent aperitifs, and off-dry versions complement a variety of foods. Rhine wines are richer and spicier than Mosel examples, and are sold in brown bottles. Mosel wine comes in green bottles and is generally a shade lighter and more minerally.

Alsace

In neighboring France, a few miles west of the Rhine, lies the famed viticultural region of Alsace. The vineyards extend for 70 miles along the slopes of the

Scale: Superlative (96-100), Exceptional (90-95), Highly Recommended (85-89), Recommended (80-84), Not Recommended (Under 80)

Vosges Mountains from Strasbourg in the north to Mulhouse in the south. The vineyards of Alsace lie south of the great vineyards of Germany. Although Alsace is a cool region, it is considerably warmer than Germany's Rhine and Mosel. As a result, Riesling from Alsace is fuller and richer with a higher degree of alcohol. Unlike much of France, here the wines are varietally named as they are in the United States. Riesling is the variety that leads the way in both vineyard acreage and reputation. In Alsace, Riesling is one of just four grapes permitted Grand Cru status and it is grown in the region's finest vineyard sites. Although Alsace Rieslings can be sweet, such wines are of the much pricier late harvest variety. Generally, Alsace Riesling is dry. Most Alsace producers have a thoroughly drinkable to very good basic Riesling for under $15.

U.S. Riesling

The United States has had a long and sometimes confusing history with Riesling. Until 1997, the name Riesling on the label was no guarantee that the wine contained any Riesling at all. Today most true Riesling is labeled as White Riesling or Johannisberg (a famed wine village in Germany) Riesling. In 1999 the rules changed again, forbidding use of the term Johannisberg. Confusion over nomenclature notwithstanding, the United States has produced some fine examples of true Riesling, and many are available at reasonable prices. In the United States, as in Europe, Riesling performs best in cool climates. This fact is punctuated by the quality of Rieslings available from relatively cool states such as Ohio, Michigan, New York, and Washington, and from California's cooler growing regions, such as Monterey.

U.S. Riesling is made in many different styles. Some—but not nearly enough—labels will disclose the residual sugar levels, and all will indicate the percentage of alcohol. Don't shirk wines with moderate sugar (2% to 3%), as this often perks up the fruit flavors, offering a needed counterbalance to high acidity levels. These wines make great quaffers in summer, pairing well with soft cheeses and fruits.

Great Value Riesling at a Glance

Number of Wines Recommended:

115

Countries Represented:

7

Australian Riesling

Riesling has long been the most widely planted white variety in Australia. For much of the past, Riesling was used to produce cheap box wines to be guzzled while trampling through the bush or skulled while taking in a footy match. Today Riesling is serious business, as producers, primarily in the state of South Australia, are crafting some of the world's best dry Rieslings.

Buying Riesling from German or U.S. producers can be tricky because it is often difficult to determine from the label if the wine is sweet or dry. Riesling from both Alsace and Australia is usually dry. Another important consideration is the vintage, as it is in all cool European growing regions. Happily, Germany has been blessed with a string of good to great vintages throughout the nineties and Alsace is on a great run from '95 to '97, with '98 looking reasonably good.

Reviews

German Riesling

(Note: "rs" indicates residual sweetness)

88 • Dr. Loosen (Germany) 1997 Riesling, Mosel-Saar-Ruwer. $10.
Bright straw cast. Medium-bodied. Balanced acidity. Moderately extracted. Minerals, earth, peaches. Generous mineral-accented aromas. Round and forward in the mouth, with a hint of sweetness balanced by crisp acidity. Shows some complexity.

86 • Weingut Heinrich Schmitges (Germany) 1997 Riesling, Mosel-Saar-Ruwer. $10.
Bright straw cast. Moderately full-bodied. Full acidity. Highly extracted. Talc, green apples, peaches. Pleasantly aromatic, with a full and rounded palate feel. A hint of sweetness is offset nicely by angular acidity. Should develop nicely with mid-term aging.

85 • Weingut Dr. H. Thanisch (Germany) 1997 Riesling, Mosel-Saar-Ruwer 3.6% rs. $14.99.
Bright pale straw cast. Medium-bodied. Full acidity. Moderately extracted. Citrus zest, minerals. Pleasantly aromatic, with an angular, crisp quality throughout. Flavorful and pure, with zesty acidity balancing a hint of sweetness for a refreshing finish.

84 • Sybille Kuntz (Germany) 1997 Trocken, Riesling, Mosel-Saar-Ruwer. $8.99.
Pale straw cast. Medium-bodied. Full acidity. Moderately extracted. Minerals, citrus zest. Lean and crisp, with solid structure evident in the minerally backbone and austere flavors. Straightforward and refreshing.

84 • Schloss Saarstein (Germany) 1997 Trocken, Riesling, Mosel-Saar-Ruwer. $12.
Bright straw cast. Medium-bodied. Full acidity. Highly extracted. Minerals. Aromatically muted, with a lighter-styled though well-structured palate feel. Clean, crisp, and rather lean.

83 • Baron zu Knyphausen (Germany) 1997 Riesling, Rheingau 1.53% rs. $9.95.
Pale platinum hue. Moderately light-bodied. Balanced acidity. Subtly extracted. Melon, citrus zest. Bright, floral aromas lead a juicy, crisp palate with light citrus flavors through a clean finish. Shows a mild touch of sweetness.

81 • Von Lade (Germany) 1996 Dry, Riesling, Rheingau. $9.99.
Bright pale gold. Moderately light-bodied. Full acidity. Moderately extracted. Minerals, citrus. Zesty aromas reveal a lean, steely palate with vibrance through the finish.

Scale: Superlative (96-100), Exceptional (90-95), Highly Recommended (85-89), Recommended (80-84), Not Recommended (Under 80)

81 • St. Ursula (Germany) 1997 Devil's Rock, Riesling, Pfalz. $6.99.
Very pale gold. Moderately light-bodied. Balanced acidity. Moderately extracted. Melon, apples. Minty nose. Juicy fruit acids play well on the palate, lifting the fruit flavors through a clean finish.

81 • Rudolf Muller (Germany) 1997 "The Bishop of Riesling", Bereich Bernkastel, Riesling, Mosel-Saar-Ruwer 2.8% rs. $6.49.
Bright platinum cast. Moderately full-bodied. Full acidity. Moderately extracted. Talc, minerals. Pleasantly aromatic, with a delicate, rounded quality tempered by angular acidity through the finish.

German Riesling: Kabinett

89 • Weingut Studert-Prum (Germany) 1997 Wehlener Sonnenuhr Kabinett, Riesling, Mosel-Saar-Ruwer 3.7% rs. $9.99.
Bright pale gold. Medium-bodied. Balanced acidity. Moderately extracted. Minerals, sweet citrus, peach. Floral, high-toned aromas. Mild residual sweetness is well balanced by bright acids that give a snappy finish, making for a very refreshing style.

86 • Weingut Johannishof (Germany) 1996 Johannisberger Goldatzel Kabinett, Riesling, Rheingau 3.29% rs. $12.50.
Very pale gold. Medium-bodied. Balanced acidity. Moderately extracted. Citrus, minerals. Lean, minerally flavors make for a refreshing style that has some grip and pairs easily with lighter foods.

86 • Weingut Heyl zu Herrnshelm (Germany) 1997 Niersteiner Oelberg Kabinett, Riesling, Rheinhessen 2.22% rs. $12.50.
Pale platinum cast. Moderately light-bodied. Full acidity. Subtly extracted. Apples, citrus. Mildly floral aromas. Lean, fresh character with clean, bright flavors and a sense of structure in a lighter frame.

86 • Weingut Dr. Bürklin-Wolf (Germany) 1997 Kabinett, Forster Riesling, Pfalz 2.08% rs. $11.50.
Bright medium gold. Medium-bodied. Balanced acidity. Moderately extracted. Citrus zest, minerals. Quite aromatic, with a rich, rounded entrance that is generous up front, though the finish turns lean and dry. This will show best with food.

86 • Prinz zu Salm-Dalberg'sches Weingut (Germany) 1997 Schloss Wallhausen Kabinett, Riesling, Nahe 3.62% rs. $14.
Very pale gold. Medium-bodied. Full acidity. Moderately extracted. Green apples, minerals. Crisp and snappy, with brisk flavors showing a very bright, clean character. An ideal, delicate aperitif style.

86 • Friedrich Wilhelm Gymnasium (Germany) 1996 Graacher Himmelreich Kabinett, Riesling, Mosel-Saar-Ruwer 3.6% rs. $12.
Brilliant platinum-straw hue. Medium-bodied. Full acidity. Moderately extracted. Citrus, white peach, minerals. Vibrant and juicy, with great balance between acids and sugars. This balance lends a piercing quality through the finish.

83 • Carl Graff (Germany) 1997 Graacher Himmelreich Kabinett, Riesling, Mosel-Saar-Ruwer 3.3% rs. $7.95.
Pale platinum cast. Medium-bodied. Full acidity. Moderately extracted. Minerals, herbs, citrus. Earthy, herbal aromas lead a broad, minerally palate with a touch of fruit sweetness lingering.

82 • Weingut Heinrich Schmitges (Germany) 1997 Erdener Treppchen Kabinett, Riesling, Mosel-Saar-Ruwer 4.5% rs. $13.50.
Bright pale straw hue. Moderately light-bodied. Balanced acidity. Grapefruit, minerals. Assertive, zesty aromas have distinct yeasty accents. Flavors seem muted through a brisk finish.

81 • Weinkellerei Leonard Kreusch (Germany) 1996 Piesportes Michelsberg Kabinett, Riesling, Mosel-Saar-Ruwer 3.2% rs. $9.99.

Pale gold. Medium-bodied. Balanced acidity. Moderately extracted. Peach skins, herbs, minerals. Very pronounced grassy, herbal aromas. Mild sweetness lifts the almost earthy palate.

81 • J.L. Wolf (Germany) 1996 Deidesheimer Herrgottsacker Kabinett, Riesling, Pfalz. $13.50.

Very pale gold. Moderately light-bodied. Full acidity. Moderately extracted. Grapefruit, lemons, minerals. Strong zesty, minerally aromas follow through on the palate. Not very refined, though it has presence.

81 • Carl Graff (Germany) 1997 Piesporter Goldtropfchen Kabinett, Riesling, Mosel-Saar-Ruwer 3.67% rs. $11.95.

Very pale gold. Medium-bodied. Full acidity. Moderately extracted. Minerals, apple skins. Youthful, awkward aromas. Angular, brisk palate has minerals and tart fruit flavors, and a hint of residual sugar.

81 • Baron zu Knyphausen (Germany) 1997 Kabinett, Riesling, Rheingau 2.42% rs. $12.50.

Very pale gold. Moderately light-bodied. Balanced acidity. Moderately extracted. Apples, minerals. Clean, lively, and fresh, with light, fruity flavors. Relatively soft style that is drinking well now.

German Riesling: Spätlese

86 • Carl Graff (Germany) 1997 Piesporter Michelsberg Spätlese, Riesling, Mosel-Saar-Ruwer 4.53% rs. $8.75.

Bright platinum cast. Moderately full-bodied. Full acidity. Highly extracted. Minerals, citrus, talc. Aromatic and complex, with a firm, racy palate feel. Crisp acidity is offset by a hint of sweetness in a juicy finish.

86 • Carl Graff (Germany) 1997 Graacher Himmelreich Spätlese, Riesling, Mosel-Saar-Ruwer 4.28% rs. $10.

Bright platinum cast. Moderately full-bodied. Full acidity. Moderately extracted. Talc, minerals. Quite fragrant, with a lean, clean, racy palate feel. Zesty acidity balances a hint of sweetness in the finish.

85 • Rothrock (Germany) 1997 Wormser Liebfrauenmorgen Spätlese, Riesling, Rheinhessen 2.2% rs. $10.99.

Bright platinum cast. Medium-bodied. Full acidity. Highly extracted. Citrus, minerals. Crisp and aromatic, with a straightforward, zesty structure. On the delicate side, with a slight hint of sweetness to the racy finish.

81 • Carl Graff (Germany) 1997 Wehlener Sonnenuhr Spätlese, Riesling, Mosel-Saar-Ruwer 4.22% rs. $10.35.

Bright platinum cast. Medium-bodied. Full acidity. Moderately extracted. Stone fruits, minerals. Full and ripe, with juicy acidity and a hint of sweetness. A note of bitterness emerges on the finish.

German Riesling: Auslese

84 • Weinkellerei Leonard Kreusch (Germany) 1996 Piesporter Michelsberg Auslese, Riesling, Mosel-Saar-Ruwer 4.5% rs. $11.99.

Pale straw hue. Medium-bodied. Full acidity. Highly extracted. Minerals, fusel, lemons. Assertive, mineral-accented aromas. Vibrant flavors have plenty of zesty character in a dry style.

Alsatian Riesling

93 • Pfaffenheim (France) 1995 Rebgarten Grand Cru, Gueberschwihr, Riesling, Alsace. $13.

Full golden luster. Medium-bodied. Balanced acidity. Fusel, minerals, apples. Complex tertiary aromas are evident, following through on an oily but dry palate with fine texture and concentration. Powerful now, time will only enhance the petrol qualities, as acids are still lively.

90 • Francois Schwach & Fils (France) 1997 Rosacker Grand Cru, Riesling, Alsace. $15.

Pale emerald-yellow. Medium-bodied. Balanced acidity. Flowers, sweet citrus. Attractive, ripe aromas lead a juicy mouthful of fruit flavors that finish cleanly. User-friendly, easy-drinking style with a faint hint of sweetness, though this has the structure to age further.

89 • Schlegel Boeglin (France) 1996 Zinnkoepfle Grand Cru, Riesling, Alsace. $12.50.

Deep yellow-gold. Moderately full-bodied. Full acidity. Highly extracted. Honey, pear skin, yeast, spice. Excessively aromatic, with a lush and exotic mouthfeel. Rich and ripe on the palate, with a full lengthy finish.

89 • Cave Vinicole de Kientzheim-Kayersberg (France) 1996 Schlossberg Grand Cru, Riesling, Alsace. $15.

Bright pale gold. Moderately full-bodied. Full acidity. Paraffin, green apples. Hints of tertiary aromas show intense varietal expression. Forceful concentration of flavors gives a long, lingering finish punctuated by acids. Structure and balance suggest that further aging will be rewarded.

89 • Bott Frères (France) 1996 Réserve Personelle, Riesling, Alsace. $12.

Bright yellow-straw. Medium-bodied. Full acidity. Petrol, mineral, tart peach. Fine, petrol-accented nose. Racy, elegant flavors show a degree of intensity and length.

88 • Pierre Sparr (France) 1997 Réserve, Riesling, Alsace. $12.99.

Pale straw. Medium-bodied. Full acidity. Lemon, minerals. Intense, citrus-dominated aromas. Generous on the midpalate, this finishes with a persistent bitter-lemon note. Further age may soften the acids.

88 • Charles Baur (France) 1997 Riesling, Alsace. $11.

Brilliant yellow-gold. Medium-bodied. Balanced acidity. Apple, melon. Juicy, pure aromas follow through on the palate. Sensational mouthfeel and textural elegance point to real class.

88 • Bott Frères (France) 1996 Cuvée Exceptionnelle, Riesling, Alsace. $10.

Bright yellow-gold. Medium-bodied. Full acidity. Citrus, fusel. Fine, petrol-edged aromas are youthful and vibrant. Palate follows through with citrus and mineral qualities that linger.

87 • Riefle (France) 1995 Côte de Rouffach, "Gaentzbrunnen de Pfaffenheim," Riesling, Alsace. $14.99.

Deep old-gold hue. Moderately full-bodied. Balanced acidity. Moderately extracted. Flowers, grappa, dried herbs. Outrageously aromatic, with a complex array of flavors. Full and firm on the palate, with an angular finish. Intense.

86 • Pfaffenheim (France) 1997 Riesling, Alsace. $9.

Brilliant yellow-gold. Medium-bodied. Full acidity. Moderately extracted. Peach, apples. Waxy tropical aromas are fully expressed on the palate, with a sense of concentration and purity that bodes well for the next few years.

85 • Boeckel (France) 1996 Réserve, Riesling, Alsace. $13.75.

Bright yellow-gold. Moderately full-bodied. Balanced acidity. Apple, minerals. Fine tertiary aromas are showing through. Textured, rounded mouthfeel, with a minerally intensity on the long finish.

84 • *Leon Beyer (France) 1997 Riesling, Alsace. $13.95.*

Bright pale straw. Medium-bodied. Balanced acidity. Lemon, mineral. Clean, pure, and focused by bright acids. This shows an austere, minerally character with citric acids as the keynote. Will be at its best with appropriate food.

84 • *Francois Schwach & Fils (France) 1997 Cuvée Clement, Riesling, Alsace. $12.50.*

Pale yellow-gold. Medium-bodied. Full acidity. Lemons, minerals. Aromas of glycerin suggest a roundness and texture that is observed on the palate. Flavors are dry and austere. This should gain more character with some further bottle age.

84 • *Bestheim (France) 1996 Rebgarten, Riesling, Alsace. $10.*

Brilliant greenish straw hue. Medium-bodied. Full acidity. Moderately extracted. Minerals, citrus. Beginning to open aromatically, with a lean, firm, crisp mouthfeel. Tight and linear through the finish.

83 • *Pierre Sparr (France) 1996 Réserve, Riesling, Alsace. $12.99.*

Pale emerald yellow. Medium-bodied. Full acidity. Lemon, apple. Crisp, herbal-edged aromas follow through on the palate with a sense of dryness and elegance.

83 • *Hartweg (France) 1996 Riesling, Alsace. $10.*

Bright pale emerald. Medium-bodied. Full acidity. Minerals, lemon skin. Mean, angular, and flat. Phenolic dryness comes through on the finish. Extremely young and awkward. Not much fun.

83 • *Francois Schwach & Fils (France) 1997 "Muehlforst," Riesling, Alsace. $11.50.*

Pale emerald straw. Moderately light-bodied. Full acidity. Lemons, minerals. Racy, crisp, and fresh, with a straightforward character and clean finish.

83 • *Fleith (France) 1997 Riesling, Alsace. $10.*

Bright straw cast. Moderately light-bodied. Full acidity. Subtly extracted. Citrus zest, talc, minerals. Pleasantly aromatic, with a light, zesty mouthfeel. Features a delicate wave of flavors through the finish.

83 • *Dopff & Irion (France) 1997 Riesling, Alsace. $12.*

Bright pale emerald sheen. Medium-bodied. Full acidity. Green apples, minerals. Crisp, cutting acids run through the palate with juicy fruit flavors persisting. Racy, fresh style.

81 • *Jean-Marc Bernhard (France) 1996 Riesling, Alsace. $12.*

Bright greenish straw cast. Medium-bodied. Full acidity. Moderately extracted. Minerals. Tart and bracing, with an unyielding structure. Features clipped flavors through the finish.

81 • *Charles Baur (France) 1996 Riesling, Alsace. $10.*

Brilliant pale gold. Medium-bodied. Full acidity. Lemons, minerals. Racy, clean and precise, with a decided accent on citric acids and minerals.

Australian Riesling

92 • *Gleeson's Ridge (Australia) 1996 Riesling, Clare Valley. $14.99.*

Bright gold-straw cast. Moderately full-bodied. Full acidity. Highly extracted. Petrol, lanolin, minerals. Exotically fragrant with an intense Riesling bouquet. Full and weighty in the mouth with an angular and vibrant character. This has all the classic elements for cellaring.

88 • *Orlando (Australia) 1998 St. Helga, Riesling, Eden Valley. $15.*

Pale straw hue with a greenish edge. Moderately full-bodied. Full acidity. Moderately extracted. Citrus zest, minerals, talc. Features a high-toned Germanic accent to the floral-edged flavors. Zesty and intense in the mouth with a very firm core of acidity. Lean and vibrant finish. Should open with age.

Scale: Superlative (96-100), Exceptional (90-95), Highly Recommended (85-89), Recommended (80-84), Not Recommended (Under 80)

86 • Leasingham (Australia) 1997 Bin 7, Riesling, Clare Valley. $7.99.
Bright straw cast. Medium-bodied. Full acidity. Moderately extracted. Minerals, citrus zest.
Aromatically reserved, with a tight and focused mouthfeel. Crisp and intense, if rather
unyielding through the finish.

86 • Jacob's Creek (Australia) 1998 Dry Riesling, Australia. $7.99.
Pale straw cast. Moderately light-bodied. Full acidity. Moderately extracted. Citrus,
flowers, minerals. Quite fragrant, with a high-toned range of fruity flavors. Light and
crisp in the mouth, with a zesty, drying finish.

Austrian Riesling

89 • Weingut R & A Pfaffl (Austria) 1997 Terrassen Sonnleiten, Lieblich, Riesling, Weinviertel. $15.
Brilliant yellow-gold. Moderately full-bodied. Full acidity. Highly extracted. Earth, citrus
oil, herbs. Aromatically deep. Broad, mouthfilling flavors show fine concentration and
persistence. This has an ageworthy structure.

89 • Peter Dolle (Austria) 1997 Strasser Gaisberg, Trocken, Riesling, Kamptal. $13.
Brilliant pale gold. Moderately full-bodied. Full acidity. Moderately extracted. Tart
pineapple, citrus, minerals. Exotic floral aromas lead a wonderfully concentrated,
pure palate with a lingering finish. This has the structure to age.

84 • Weingut Schildhof (Austria) 1997 Lieblich, Riesling, Langenloiser 1.8% rs. $11.50.
Yellow-gold. Medium-bodied. Full acidity. Moderately extracted. Apples, dried herbs.
Crisp, juicy aromas follow through convincingly on the palate. Drinking well now.

83 • Naturnaher Weinbau Alfred Deim (Austria) 1997 Schonberger, "Stoamandl" Trocken, Riesling, Kamptal. $15.
Bright pale gold. Medium-bodied. Full acidity. Moderately extracted. Minerals,
citrus. Bright, zesty aromas follow through convincingly on the palate. Lean, precise
and angular.

81 • Weingut Zull (Austria) 1997 Innere Bergen, Trocken, Riesling, Weinviertel. $14.
Bright pale gold. Medium-bodied. Full acidity. Moderately extracted. Citrus oil, dried
herbs, flint. Bright, minerally aromas. Piercing acidity makes this difficult to appreciate
at present. Flavors are intense. This wine will age well.

U.S. Riesling

90 • Paraiso Springs (CA) 1997 Riesling, Santa Lucia Highlands. $9.
Bright yellow-gold. Intense varietally pure aromas of petrol, minerals, and peach.
A flavorful attack leads a medium-bodied palate with mild sweetness and good acid
balance through the finish. Quite stylish. Drink now.

89 • Firestone (CA) 1997 Riesling, Santa Barbara County 1.67% rs. $7.
Medium green-gold hue. Exotic aromas of petrol and minerals. A rich entry leads a
medium-bodied palate with a glycerous mouthfeel, peach flavors, and an oily texture that
sets this apart. Lingering, rich finish. An excellent match with pork or other white meats.
Drink now or later.

88 • Good Harbor (MI) 1997 Semidry White Riesling, Leelanau Peninsula 2% rs. $8.
Rich gold. Deep, ripe tropical aromas. A rich entry leads a moderately full-bodied
palate with a glycerous mouthfeel, and a note of persistent fruit sweetness on the finish.
Drink now.

88 • Fetzer (CA) 1997 Johannisberg Riesling, California 2.93% rs. $6.99.
Medium yellow-straw hue. Rich aromas of ripe stone fruits and petrol are classic,
pure Riesling. A rich attack follows through well on the medium-bodied palate, with
oily flavors through the finish. Drink now.

88 • *Dr. Konstantin Frank (NY) NV Salmon Run, Johannisberg Riesling, New York. $8.95.*

Medium yellow-straw hue. Tropical, ripe peach aromas. A flavorful attack leads a medium-bodied palate with generous fruity flavors and a glycerous midpalate. Finishes smoothly with good persistence. Drink now.

86 • *Woodward Canyon (WA) 1997 Riesling, Walla Walla County. $9.*

Bright pale golden hue. Aromas show a tropical, pithy character. Sweet and juicy on entry, with a medium-bodied palate and an herbal note to the sweet flavors that linger on the finish. Features fine varietal character. Try with fresh fruit.

86 • *V. Sattui (CA) 1998 Dry Johannisberg Riesling, Napa Valley. $11.25.*

Medium gold. Very classic aromas of petrol with herbal and mineral nuances. A soft entry leads a medium-bodied palate with a rounded mouthfeel and deep, impressive, petrolly flavors. A streak of acid comes through on the finish. Very stylish. Drink now or later.

86 • *Ste. Chapelle (WA) 1998 Dry Johannisberg Riesling, Idaho. $6.*

Medium yellow-gold. Fresh aromas of crisp apples and herbs. A bright attack leads a medium-bodied palate with crisp fruit flavors persisting on the finish. Very refreshing. Drink now.

86 • *LaVelle (OR) 1997 Susan's Vineyard, Riesling, Willamette Valley 2.4% rs. $8.*

Medium gold. Classic Riesling aromas of petrol and tropical fruits. A lush entry leads a medium-bodied palate with a fine glycerous mouthfeel and generous sweet fruit flavors. The finish has an oily note. A soft, medium-sweet style. Drink now.

86 • *Kendall-Jackson (CA) 1997 Vintner's Reserve, Johannisberg Riesling, California 2.42% rs. $11.*

Deep yellow-gold. Aromatically generous with big ripe fruit character. A rich, moderately sweet entry leads a medium-bodied palate with pure green apple flavors that linger through the finish. A soft, juicy style. Drink now.

86 • *Henke (OH) NV Riesling, American 1.75% rs. $10.37.*

Bright pale gold. Oily, tropical aromas. A flavorful attack leads a medium-bodied palate with bright acids and classic, oily, minerally Riesling flavors that linger on the finish. Drink now.

86 • *Hagafen (CA) 1998 Johannisberg Riesling, Napa Valley 2.6% rs. $12.*

Pale straw hue. A lean attack leads a medium-bodied palate with stone fruit flavors and subtle herbal notes through the finish. Mildly off-dry style. Drink now.

85 • *Concannon (CA) 1997 Johannisberg Riesling, Arroyo Seco-Monterey 3% rs. $9.95.*

Bright yellow-gold. Distinctive minerally, mildly honeyed aromas seem to show a touch of botrytis. A heavy attack leads a moderately full-bodied palate with concentrated flavors and low acids. Mildly bitter notes through the finish. Interesting. Drink now.

84 • *Wollersheim (WI) NV White Riesling, American 2.5% rs. $7.*

Pale straw hue. Mild aromas of apples and minerals. A sweet fruit attack leads a moderately light-bodied palate with mild flavors finishing quickly. Leaves a subtle herbal impression. Drink now.

84 • *Wollersheim (WI) NV Dry Riesling, American. $8.*

Very pale straw hue. Clean, bright aromas of white peach and herbs. A juicy entry leads a medium-bodied palate with juicy acids lingering on the finish. Very refreshing. Drink now.

84 • *Swedish Hill (NY) 1997 Dry Riesling, Finger Lakes. $9.99/.*

Pale straw hue. Attractive aromas show peach and apricot character. A juicy, bright entry follows through on a medium-bodied palate. Tropical flavors are well balanced by a citrus zest character on the finish. Drink now.

Scale: Superlative (96-100), Exceptional (90-95), Highly Recommended (85-89), Recommended (80-84), Not Recommended (Under 80)

84 • Mirassou (CA) 1998 Family Selection, Riesling,
Monterey County 1.6% rs. $7.50.
Pale straw hue. Aromas of butter, flowers, and tart apple with an herbal twist. A soft entry leads a medium-bodied palate with juicy fruit flavors lingering on the finish. Drink now.

84 • Jekel (CA) 1998 Johannisberg Riesling, Monterey 1.4% rs. $10.
Bright pale gold. Generous apple and tropical fruit aromas. A juicy, moderately sweet attack leads a medium-bodied palate with clean, straightforward flavors through the finish. Drink now.

84 • Indian Creek (ID) 1998 White Riesling, Idaho 2.2% rs. $6.95.
Bright pale platinum hue. Ripe, sweet apple aromas. A juicy entry leads a medium-bodied palate with moderately sweet flavors of ripe apples and peaches. Finishes cleanly. A soft, sweet style. Drink now.

84 • Henry Estate (OR) 1998 White Riesling, Umpqua Valley 2% rs. $8.
Very pale straw hue. Yellow apple aromas. A juicy entry leads a moderately light-bodied palate with a good concentration of fruit flavors persisting through the finish. Drink now.

84 • Harmony (CA) 1997 Johannisberg Riesling, Paso Robles 2.1% rs. $9.
Medium gold. Classic aromas of petrol and green apples. A bright attack leads a medium-bodied palate with rich flavors and an oily note through the finish. Fine, pure Riesling character. Drink now.

84 • Glenora (NY) 1998 Dry Riesling, Finger Lakes 1.8% rs. $7.99.
Pale straw hue. Perfumed aromas of yellow apple and herbs. A soft entry leads a medium-bodied palate with crisp flavors and juicy acids through to the finish. Drink now.

84 • Dr. Konstantin Frank (NY) 1997 Semi-Dry Johannisberg Riesling,
New York 2.5% rs. $9.95.
Medium yellow-straw hue. Pleasant aromas of minerals, apples, and herbs. A juicy, sweet entry leads a medium-bodied palate with straightforward flavors and a hint of sour apple on the finish. An off-dry style. Drink now.

84 • Chateau Lafayette Reneau (NY) 1997 Dry Riesling,
Finger Lakes 1.2% rs. $9.99.
Very pale straw hue. Aromatically muted. A simple attack leads a moderately light-bodied palate with attractive tart peach and herb flavors that linger on a fairly lengthy finish. Drink now.

84 • Chateau Grand Traverse (MI) 1997 Select Harvest, Dry Johannisberg
Riesling, Old Mission Peninsula. $12.49.
Medium yellow-straw hue. Varietally pure aromas of wax and minerals. A crisp entry leads a medium-bodied palate with tart acids and an angular finish that shows good persistence of dry flavors. This would be a good foil for lighter foods. Drink now.

83 • V. Sattui (CA) 1998 Off-Dry Johannisberg Riesling,
Napa Valley 2% rs. $11.25.
Medium gold. Very aromatic with petrolly whiffs and tropical character. A sweet, tropical attack leads a medium-bodied palate with glycerous richness and off-dry sweetness through the finish. Drink now.

83 • Ste. Chapelle (WA) 1998 Johannisberg Riesling, Idaho 2.7% rs. $6.
Pale platinum-straw hue. Muted aromas of minerals and citrus zest. A crisp attack leads a medium-bodied palate with dry, zesty flavors and minerally firmness through the finish. Drink now.

83 • St. Julian (MI) 1997 Riesling, Michigan 1.5% rs. $11.99.
Pale green-straw hue. Crisp, tart fruit aromas. A vibrant entry leads a medium-bodied palate with white peach flavors and a note of glycerine on the mouthfeel. Finishes cleanly. Drink now.

83 • *Maurice Carrie (CA) 1998 Johannisberg Riesling, California 2.2% rs. $7.95.*
Bright pale straw. Ripe, tropical aromas have a note of zest and minerals. A lean attack leads a medium-bodied palate showing sweetish citrus flavors. Relatively low in acid, with a clipped finish. Drink now.

83 • *Heron Hill (NY) 1997 Ingle Vineyard, Johannisberg Riesling, Finger Lakes 2% rs. $8.49.*
Bright pale straw hue. Clean aromas of flowers and minerals. A juicy entry leads a medium-bodied palate with white peach flavors that give way to a minerally finish. Lighter aperitif style. Drink now.

83 • *Heron Hill (NY) 1996 Semi-Dry Riesling, Finger Lakes 1.75% rs. $8.49.*
Pale straw hue. Lighter aroma of flowers and grapes. A crisp entry leads a light-bodied palate with brief mineral-accented flavors that finish quickly. A good match with shellfish. Drink now.

83 • *Grand Cru (CA) 1996 Johannisberg Riesling, California 4.41% rs. $7.99.*
Gold-straw hue. Aromatically intense with petrol and mineral accents. Concentrated flavors on the attack, leading a moderately full-bodied palate with sweetness up front giving way to leaner, drier flavors on the finish. Rather unusual. Drink now.

83 • *Glenora (NY) 1998 Riesling, Finger Lakes 2.55% rs. $7.99.*
Pale straw hue. Mild aromas of minerals and stone fruits. A muted attack leads a moderately light-bodied palate with straightforward fruit flavors that finish quickly. An off-dry style. Drink now.

83 • *Gainey (CA) 1998 Riesling, Central Coast 1.7% rs. $10.*
Pale straw hue. Tart citrus aromas with a floral note. Crisp on entry, leading a medium-bodied palate with leaner citrus flavors lingering on the finish. Drink now.

83 • *Claar (WA) 1997 White Riesling, Columbia Valley 2.1% rs. $5.99.*
Pale straw hue. Clean aromas of citrus zest and minerals. An off-dry entry leads a medium-bodied palate with juicy acids and a quick finish. Drink now.

83 • *Chateau Grand Traverse (MI) 1997 Late Harvest Johannisberg Riesling, Michigan 4.2% rs. $12.49.*
Medium gold-straw hue. Pear and apple aromas have mild herbal overtones. A vibrant entry leads a medium-bodied palate with mild sweetness, stone fruit flavors, and a drying finish. Drink now.

83 • *Chalet DeBonné (OH) 1998 Reserve, Riesling, Grand River Valley 3.1% rs. $8.49.*
Bright pale straw hue. Crisp citrus zest aromas. A vibrant entry leads a moderately light-bodied palate with clean, mineral-edged flavors through the finish. Drink now.

83 • *Cedar Creek (WI) 1998 Semi-Dry Riesling, American 2.3% rs. $7.*
Very pale straw hue. Lean aromas show a minerally, floral note. A juicy entry leads a medium-bodied palate with bright apple flavors that linger on the finish. Decent flavor concentration. Drink now.

83 • *Cayuga Ridge (NY) NV Riesling, Cayuga Lake. $9.50.*
Very pale straw hue. Crisp aromas of tart peach and apple. A lively attack leads a medium-bodied palate with juicy, tart peach flavors and a dry minerally finish. Drink now.

82 • *Willamette Valley Vineyards (OR) 1997 Tualatin Estate, Riesling, Willamette Valley. $8.50.*
Very pale straw hue. Distinctive aromas of pears and herbs. A clean, juicy attack leads a medium-bodied palate with pure pear flavors and a clean, lingering finish. Not very typical for a Riesling, but interesting. Drink now.

82 • *Lamoreaux Landing (NY) 1997 Dry, Riesling, Finger Lakes. $9.*
Bright yellow-gold. Fresh aromas of green apples and citrus fruits. A flavorful attack leads a medium-bodied palate with crisp fruit flavors lingering on the finish. Good concentration and length on the finish. Drink now.

Scale: Superlative (96-100), Exceptional (90-95), Highly Recommended (85-89), Recommended (80-84), Not Recommended (Under 80)

82 • Dr. Konstantin Frank (NY) 1997 Dry, Johannisberg Riesling, New York. $9.95.

Medium yellow straw. Mildly oily, sweet fruit aromas. Juicy and mildly sweet on the attack, with a medium body and a dry, citrus zest finish. Drink now.

82 • Chateau Grand Traverse (MI) 1997 Semi-Dry Johannisberg Riesling, Michigan 2.4% rs. $9.99.

Medium gold. Aromatically lean with an herbal, minerally accent. A firm entry leads a moderately full-bodied palate that does not deliver much depth of flavors and finishes with an austere note. Drink now.

81 • Renaissance (CA) 1998 Demi-Sec, Riesling, North Yuba 2% rs. $11.99.

Pale straw hue. Clean aromas of green apple. A crisp entry leads a medium-bodied palate with juicy flavors though a short finish. Drink now.

81 • Osprey's Dominion (NY) 1997 Johannisberg Riesling, North Fork of Long Island. $11.99.

Brilliant yellow-straw hue. Lean citrus, apple, and mineral aromas. A crisp entry leads a moderately full-bodied palate with lively acids. Piercing and clean, but showing some weight. Drink now.

81 • Naked Mountain (VA) 1998 Riesling, Virginia 2.5% rs. $13.

Very pale platinum hue. Lean aromas of herbs and minerals. A juicy, appley attack leads a moderately light-bodied palate with an off-dry finish. Drink now.

81 • Hinman (OR) 1998 Riesling, Willamette Valley 3% rs. $6.99.

Pale straw hue. Bright aromas of citrus zest and flowers. A juicy, vibrant attack leads a medium-bodied palate with mouthwatering acidity and forward fruit flavors. The finish is clean. Drink now.

81 • Forest Ville (CA) 1996 Johannisberg Riesling, California 3.52% rs. $5.99.

Medium gold. Distinctive, minerally, medicinal aromas. A lean attack leads a medium-bodied palate with firm stone fruit flavors. Drink now.

81 • Elk Run (MD) 1998 Johannisberg Riesling, American 3% rs. $12.

Pale straw hue. Muted aromas. A mildly sweet attack leads a medium-bodied palate with low acids and rounded, sweet flavors through the finish. Drink now.

81 • Claar (WA) 1997 Dry Riesling, Columbia Valley. $5.99.

Pale straw hue. Reserved aromas of white peach and apples. A bright attack leads a moderately light-bodied palate with crisp citrus flavors and a clean, short finish. Drink now.

81 • Chateau Lafayette Reneau (NY) 1997 Johannisberg Riesling, Finger Lakes 2.5% rs. $9.99.

Very pale platinum appearance. Muted aromas of minerals and apples. A lean attack leads a moderately light-bodied palate with brief flavors that finish quickly. Drink now.

81 • Chateau Grand Traverse (MI) 1997 Dry Johannisberg Riesling, Michigan. $9.99.

Medium yellow-straw hue. Muted aromas of minerals and earth. A lean attack leads a medium-bodied palate with tart acids, though flavors fall short on the finish. Drink now.

81 • Chalet Debonné (OH) 1998 Riesling, Lake Erie 1.5% rs. $8.49.

Pale straw hue. Lean, fresh aromas show a grassy note. A crisp entry leads a moderately light-bodied palate with mineral and citrus flavors that finish cleanly. Drink now.

81 • Bookwalter (WA) 1998 Johannisberg Riesling, Washington 4.3% rs. $6.

Pale straw hue. Straightforward apple and mineral aromas. A sweet attack leads a moderately light-bodied palate with a very quick finish. Drink now.

81 • Bidwell (NY) 1996 Semi-Sweet Riesling, North Fork of Long Island. $9.99.

Deep, saturated yellow-straw hue. Sound melon and mineral aromas. A firm entry leads a moderately full-bodied palate with a hint of sweetness. Crisp and tasty. Drink now.

Other Great Value Rieslings

86 • Jackson-Triggs (Canada) 1996 Proprietors' Reserve, Dry Riesling, Okanagan Valley 1.26% rs. $6.90.

Luminous yellow-straw hue. Muted clean mineral and slate aromas. A firm attack leads to a medium-bodied palate with crisp acidity. Angular in character with a lingering flavorful finish. Showing the beginnings of a classic petrolly development. Drink now.

84 • Yarden (Israel) 1996 White Riesling, Galil. $10.99.

Bright gold. Medium-bodied. Full acidity. Highly extracted. Petrol, minerals, citrus peel. Clean and racy in a very full style for Riesling. Resembles an Australian example in flavor. Has an angular palate feel with a clipped but precise finish.

82 • Jackson-Triggs (Canada) 1997 Proprietors' Reserve, Dry Riesling, Okanagan Valley 1.12% rs. $6.90.

Brilliant green-gold hue. Powerful, pleasant pineapple and citrus aromas. A firm attack leads to a moderately light-bodied palate with sharp acidity and a hint of sweetness. Lively in character. Clipped phenolic finish. Drink now.

81 • Cave Spring (Canada) 1997 Off Dry, Riesling, Niagara Peninsula 1.5% rs. $7.99.

Deep luminous yellow-straw hue. Subtle clean citrus and floral aromas. An acidic attack leads to a medium-bodied palate with sharp acidity. Fresh in character, though this shows a clipped phenolic finish. Reserved but stylish. Drink now.

Scale: Superlative (96-100), Exceptional (90-95), Highly Recommended (85-89), Recommended (80-84), Not Recommended (Under 80)

six

Gewürztraminer

Introduction 84

Reviews 85

    Alsatian Gewürztraminer 85

    U.S. Gewürztraminer 86

    Other Great Value
Gewürztraminers 88

Introduction: Gewürztraminer

Gewürz is a German word meaning "spice." Anyone who has had the pleasure of enjoying a cool glass of Gewürztraminer would agree that the variety is aptly named. The grape is believed to have derived the second part of its name from a grape grown in the vicinity of the village of Tramin, which is located in what is now northern Italy. Gewürztraminer is a unique variety that is capable of producing some of the world's greatest and most memorable white wines. It has inspired flavor comparisons to lychee, rosewater, honeysuckle, mango, papaya, coconut, apricot, peach, and Jamaican allspice. To say that Gewürztraminer is deeply flavored and complex would be one of wine's biggest understatements. Further, its texture is entirely unique, with a richness and weight that often borders on viscosity.

Gewürztraminer can be a fickle variety to produce, preferring cooler regions that allow the grape to mature slowly. Too cold, and the grape will not develop its signature perfumed aromas. Too hot, and Gewürztraminer loses its opulent flavors and balance, becoming heavy, thick, or plodding.

One might assume that such exotic wines from a temperamental grape would naturally be expensive. Fortunately, the wine gods are smiling upon us, as Gewürztraminer is more often than not a bargain. Although Gewürztraminer has its origins outside of France, it is most often associated with France's province of Alsace, and Alsace in general is one of France's most value-friendly regions. In the United States, Gewürztraminer has never enjoyed great popularity, a fact that some attribute to its difficult name. Nonetheless, many fine examples are produced in the United States, and they rarely sell for more than $15.

Regions

Many zealous Gewürztraminer devotees believe that this variety's truest expression is attained solely in Alsace, which is one of the world's greatest white wine regions. Alsatian Gewürztraminer is unique in achieving great depth of flavors and ripeness while maintaining a sense of balance. Most acknowledge that the success of this variety in Alsace is due to the dry conditions caused by the Vosges Mountains, which block much of the rain coming from the west and retain the sun's heat, making Alsace one of Europe's driest wine regions. Dry growing conditions concentrate and intensify the grape's flavors, while excessive rains in other regions cause swelling of the fruit and diluted flavors.

Gewürztraminer has had a home in America for some time, having been introduced to California in 1862. The variety has always proved troublesome in the state, as arguments abound concerning clonal selection and vineyard locations. Many of the vineyards are clearly in regions that are too hot for the variety to reach its full potential. As with Riesling, states with cooler climates have had reasonable success with Gewürztraminer.

When buying Gewürztraminer produced in the United States, you need not worry too much about vintage. Alsace is a different story, although the 1990s have been very good to the region and all vintages from 1995 forward are very good to excellent in quality.

Gewürztraminer is an extremely versatile wine at the table, marrying well with a vast array of cuisines. Of course this variety is a wonderful choice with Alsatian kraut and sausages as well as the local cheese, Muenster. It is also excellent with spicy foods such as Indian curry, Szechwan, and Thai. Alsatian versions of Gewürztraminer range from dry to mildly sweet. American Gewürztraminer may indicate sweetness—residual sugar—on the label. Don't shy away from bottlings with some sweetness, roughly 2%, as they can be the best choices with spicy dishes.

Reviews

Alsatian Gewürztraminer

92 • Pfaffenheim (France) 1997 Gewürztraminer, Alsace. $10.

Brilliant gold. Moderately full-bodied with balanced acidity and accents of lychee and tropical fruits. Rich, glycerous spice aromas lead a thick, rounded palate with a streak of acid on the finish. A weighty, powerful style with a long, long finish.

88 • Schlegel Boeglin (France) 1996 Zinnkoepfle Grand Cru, Gewürztraminer, Alsace. $13.

Bright greenish gold. Moderately full-bodied with balanced acidity and highly extracted aromas and flavors of spice, citrus peel, and minerals. Quite aromatic, with a full but lean palate. Firm and flavorful through the spicy, drying finish.

88 • Charles Baur (France) 1997 Fronenberg, Gewürztraminer, Alsace. $14.

Brilliant emerald luster. Intensely spicy and pungent, with similar intensity in the flavors on a moderately full-bodied palate that shows balanced acidity. Very long and concentrated, with lychee nut and mineral accents. An extraordinary varietal expression.

87 • Pierre Sparr (France) 1996 Réserve, Gewürztraminer, Alsace. $11.99.

Bright yellow-gold. Moderately full-bodied with balanced acidity. Buttery, fat aromas follow through on the palate along with mineral and spice notes. Rich, round, and generous, it also shows some grip and structure.

86 • Pierre Sparr (France) 1997 Réserve, Gewürztraminer, Alsace. $13.99.

Brilliant yellow-gold. Moderately full-bodied with balanced acidity. Nutty, minerally, spicy accents. Sweet, juicy aromas have a fine varietal expression. Lush, textured mouthfeel has a fine acid balance.

Great Value Gewürztraminer at a Glance

Number of Wines Recommended:

48

Countries Represented:

5

84 • Jerome Geschickt & Fils (France) 1997 Kaefferkopf, Gewürztraminer, Alsace. $15.
Pale gold. Mineral and spice aromas. Straightforward varietal expression of aromas. Simple, unremarkable flavors finish quickly. Generous mouthfeel is a plus.

84 • Clos du Letzenberg (France) 1996 Gewürztraminer, Alsace. $12.
Pale straw hue. Notes of flowers and butter. Light, floral aromas lead a soft, medium-bodied, citrus-accented palate with spicy overtones and balanced acidity.

84 • Charles Baur (France) 1996 Pfersigberg Grand Cru, Gewürztraminer, Alsace. $15.
Bright emerald-straw hue. A medium-bodied palate with balanced acidity. Dried herbs and lychee accents. Juicy yet dry. Alcohol shows through in the finish. An austere style with faithful varietal character.

84 • Bestheim (France) 1997 Marckrain Grand Cru, Gewürztraminer, Alsace. $15.
Pale green-straw hue. Straightforward, juicy, and mildly sweet, with balanced acidity. A hint of spicy varietal character and melon notes show through on a medium-bodied palate.

83 • Leon Beyer (France) 1997 Gewürztraminer, Alsace. $14.95.
Bright straw cast. Accents of minerals and charred yeast. Lean, crisp, and minerally, with a firm, fully acidic palate feel that does not develop much spicy authority. Crisp, clipped finish.

83 • Jean-Pierre Bechtold (France) 1996 Collection Robert Beltz, Gewürztraminer, Alsace. $13.
Deep straw cast. Aromatically reserved, with a moderately full-bodied palate, a big but firm mouthfeel, and highly extracted mineral and citrus zest flavors. Crisp and angular, with balanced acidity through the finish.

83 • Charles Baur (France) 1995 Pfersigberg Grand Cru, Gewürztraminer, Alsace. $15.
Bright yellow-gold. Varietally expressive, high-toned aromas lead a medium-bodied, dry, severe palate with a minerally presence and lychee accents through the finish.

83 • Abarbanel (France) 1997 Gewürztraminer, Alsace. $12.99.
Bright yellow-gold. Aromatically reserved, with a moderately full-bodied, fat and rounded mouthfeel showing low acidity. Moderately extracted notes of minerals and bananas. Rather clipped, though the finish features some tropical notes.

U.S. Gewürztraminer

93 • Martinelli (CA) 1997 Gewürztraminer, Russian River Valley. $12.
Deep, saturated green-gold hue. Powerful, varietally intense lychee, spice, and sweet citrus aromas. A rich entry leads a full-bodied palate with crisp acidity and a hint of sweetness. Big, intense, and rich, with great power. Drink now.

92 • Adler Fels (CA) 1997 Gewürztraminer, Sonoma County. $11.
Deep yellow-gold. Penetrating, opulent lychee, spice, and melon aromas show great varietal intensity. A rich entry leads a full-bodied palate with vibrant acidity and a glycerous texture. Extremely lengthy, flavorful finish. Drink now.

89 • Thomas Fogarty (CA) 1997 Gewürztraminer, Monterey. $12.50.
Deep yellow-straw hue. Generous flower and spice aromas jump from the glass. A lush entry leads a moderately full-bodied palate with mild sweetness offset by vibrant acidity. Ripe, flavorful finish. Drink now.

88 • Lenz (NY) 1995 Gewürztraminer, North Fork of Long Island. $10.99.
Brilliant yellow-straw hue. Pleasant, classic lychee and flower aromas. A soft entry leads a moderately full-bodied palate. Convincingly varietal, with an oily texture. Drink now.

Scale: Superlative (96-100), Exceptional (90-95), Highly Recommended (85-89), Recommended (80-84), Not Recommended (Under 80)

87 • Paraiso Springs (CA) 1997 Gewürztraminer, Santa Lucia Highlands. $9.

Bright straw hue. Clean, intense mineral and honeyed tropical fruit aromas. A lean entry leads a medium-bodied palate with an assertive acidic edge. Firm through the dry finish. Taut and stylish. Drink now.

86 • Husch (CA) 1998 Gewürztraminer, Anderson Valley. $11.

Pale straw hue. Lean aromas are youthful and undeveloped, with a sulfurous note that should diminish with further bottle age. A crisp entry leads a medium-bodied palate with a touch of sweetness and vibrant acidity. Clean, crisp finish. Could use a few more months to come together. Drink now or later.

86 • Forest Ville (CA) 1997 Gewürztraminer, California. $5.99.

Deep yellow-straw hue. Generous spice, citrus, and orange-rind aromas. A lush entry leads a moderately full-bodied palate with marked sweetness offset by solid acidity. Flavorful and intense. Drink now.

86 • Columbia Winery (WA) 1998 Gewürztraminer, Yakima Valley. $6.

Bright straw hue. Generous spice and honeyed melon aromas. A rich entry leads a medium-bodied palate with marked sweetness offset by crisp acidity. Clean, well-balanced finish. Drink now.

85 • Covey Run (WA) 1997 Celilo Vineyard, Gewürztraminer, Washington. $12.

Bright straw hue. Lean minerally aromas show an edge of residual sulfur that should dissipate with a bit more bottle age. A lush entry leads a medium-bodied palate with a slight hint of sweetness offset by bright acidity. Spicy, flavorful finish. Clean. Drink now.

84 • Sakonnet (RI) 1997 Gewürztraminer, Southeastern New England. $14.95.

Bright yellow-straw hue. Aromatically subdued with clean, minerally citrus flavors in the mouth. Medium-bodied and crisp with vibrant acidity. Spicy, flavorful finish. Drink now.

84 • Henry Estate (OR) 1998 Gewürztraminer, Umpqua Valley. $10.

Brilliant platinum hue. Subdued mineral and citrus aromas. A racy entry leads a medium-bodied palate with aggressive acidity balancing ample richness. Clean, stylish finish. Drink now.

83 • V. Sattui (CA) 1998 Gewürztraminer, Sonoma County. $11.25.

Bright straw hue. Intense spice and banana aromas. A racy entry leads a medium-bodied palate with mild sweetness offset by crisp acidity. Refreshing finish. A quaffer. Drink now.

83 • Firelands (OH) 1998 Gewürztraminer, Lake Erie. $8.99.

Deep straw hue. Generous spicy aromas jump from the glass. A rich entry leads a fat, moderately full-bodied palate with a bit of acidity through the finish to lend a sense of balance. Straightforward, tasty finish with a touch of sweetness. Drink now.

83 • Concannon (CA) 1997 Limited Bottling, Gewürztraminer, Arroyo Seco-Monterey. $9.95.

Deep old-gold hue. Fat, overripe melon aromas show a slight herbal accent. A rich entry leads an oily, moderately full-bodied palate. Lean through the finish. Drink now.

82 • Firestone (CA) 1997 Carranza Mesa Vineyard, Gewürztraminer, Santa Ynez Valley. $9.

Deep old-gold hue. Assertive ripe pineapple and tropical fruit aromas. A rich entry leads a full-bodied palate with a lush texture. Lean through the finish. Drink now.

82 • Fetzer (CA) 1997 Gewürztraminer, California. $5.99.

Bright straw hue. Aromatically reserved with clean citric flavors in the mouth, enhanced by lean acidity. Medium-bodied with marked sweetness. A straightforward quaffer. Drink now.

82 • Covey Run (WA) 1998 Gewürztraminer, Washington. $6.

Deep straw hue. Generous spice and citrus aromas. A crisp entry leads a medium-bodied palate with a hint of sweetness. Flavorful, straightforward finish. Drink now.

82 • Carmenet (CA) 1997 Gewürztraminer, Sonoma Valley. $14.

Deep straw hue. Forward spicy, buttery aromas. A lush entry leads a medium-bodied palate with a touch of sweetness and lots of spice through the finish. Drink now.

81 • Prejean (NY) 1997 Semi Dry, Gewürztraminer, Finger Lakes. $12.

Deep straw hue. Aromatically unusual, with candied, talcy overtones and deep spicy flavors. Rich and full with a touch of sweetness through the finish. Lush. Drink now.

81 • Gundlach Bundschu (CA) 1997 Rhinefarm Vineyards, Gewürztraminer, Sonoma Valley. $12.

Bright yellow-straw hue. Aromatically reserved. A sharp entry leads a medium-bodied palate with vibrant, aggressive acidity. Lean through the finish. Drink now.

81 • Elk Run (MD) 1998 Gewürztraminer, American. $13.25.

Very pale straw hue. Subdued minerally aromas show an earthy, spicy edge. A lush entry leads a moderately full-bodied, fat palate. Rounded finish. Lacks somewhat for grip, with mild sweetness a prominent feature. Drink now.

81 • Dr. Konstantin Frank (NY) 1998 Limited Release, Gewürztraminer, Finger Lakes. $12.95.

Bright straw hue with a copper cast. Subdued spice and toast aromas. A lush entry leads a medium-bodied, rich palate with lean acidity through the finish. Soft and straightforward. Drink now.

80 • Washington Hills (WA) 1998 Gewürztraminer, Columbia Valley. $6.

Pale straw hue. Subdued citrus and tropical fruit aromas. A soft entry leads a medium-bodied palate with marked sweetness. Supple finish. Lacks a bit for grip. Drink now.

80 • Prejean (NY) 1997 Dry, Gewürztraminer, Finger Lakes. $12.

Bright platinum-straw hue. Forward spice aromas. A lush entry leads a medium-bodied palate with crisp acidity. Drying, subdued finish. Drink now.

80 • Grand Cru (CA) 1996 Gewürztraminer, California. $7.99.

Brilliant yellow-straw hue. Candied melon and very ripe fruit aromas. A fat entry leads a sweet palate with simple fruit flavors. Straightforward but decent. Drink now.

80 • Apex (WA) 1997 Barrel Fermented, Dry Gewürztraminer, Columbia Valley. $13.

Deep yellow-straw hue. Intense butter and vanilla aromas are rather unusual for a Gewürztraminer. A fat entry leads a full-bodied palate with a very buttery finish. Rich, to be sure, but one dimensional. Drink now.

Other Great Value Gewürztraminers

90 • Weingut Schreiber Zink (Germany) 1997 Dalsheimer Steig, Gewürztraminer, Rheinhessen. $7.

Medium straw hue. Medium-bodied. Balanced acidity. Lychee, pineapple. Sweet, nutty aromas are varietally pure. Glycerous, sweet fruit flavors fill the mouth, with a nutty note pervading through the finish.

88 • Hopler (Austria) 1996 Trocken, Gewürztraminer, Neusiedlersee. $13.

Bright yellow-gold. Medium-bodied. Balanced acidity. Moderately extracted. Nuts, lychee, citrus. Spicy, varietally expressive aromas show a touch of earth, leading a taut yet flavorsome palate with a bright acids lingering on the finish.

86 • Weinkellerei P.J. Valckenberg (Germany) 1997 Gewürztraminer, Pfalz. $8.95.

Pale straw hue. Medium-bodied. Balanced acidity. Moderately extracted. Glycerin, peach. Oily, rich aromas follow through to the palate, showing a glycerous presence. Not varietally intense, though still generous.

86 • *Magnotta (Canada) 1996 Medium-Dry, Limited Edition, Gewürztraminer, Ontario. $9.*
Brilliant green-gold hue. Clean and intense citrus zest and spice aromas. A soft attack leads to a moderately full-bodied palate with zesty acidity. Racy flavorful finish. Refreshing and varietally intense. Drink now.

86 • *Jackson-Triggs (Canada) 1997 Proprietors' Reserve, Gewürztraminer, Okanagan Valley. $6.89.*
Brilliant greenish-straw hue. Generous lychee, pineapple, and spice aromas. A brisk attack leads to a moderately light-bodied palate with crisp acidity. Persistent flavorful finish. Well balanced and racy in a lighter style. Drink now.

84 • *Weingut Geil (Germany) 1997 Mettenheimer Michelsberg Kabinett, Gewürztraminer, Rheinhessen. $14.99.*
Medium straw cast. Medium-bodied. Low acidity. Moderately extracted. Ripe apples. Ripe, fruity aromas lead a softer-styled palate, with rounded, mildly sweet flavors lingering on the finish.

83 • *Weingut Paul Braunstein (Austria) 1997 Trocken, Gewürztraminer, Neusiedlersee. $9.*
Pale platinum color. Moderately light-bodied. Balanced acidity. Moderately extracted. Flowers, lychees. Perfumed, delicate aromas lead a vibrant palate, with light flavors and a warm, alcoholic finish.

83 • *Magnotta (Canada) 1996 Limited Edition, Gewürztraminer, Ontario. $9.*
Brilliant yellow-straw hue. Subtle clean mineral and citrus zest aromas. A crisp attack leads to a medium-bodied palate with firm acidity through a vibrant phenolic finish. Well structured but lacks somewhat for flavor intensity. Drink now.

83 • *Bergstrasser Winzer (Germany) 1997 Bensheimer Paulus Spatlese, Gewürztraminer, Hessische Berstrasse. $14.99.*
Bright pale-straw hue. Moderately light-bodied. Balanced acidity. Subtly extracted. Wax, apples. Mildly sweet and juicy, though showing much varietal character. A tad bland and simple, but inoffensive.

seven

Pinot Grigio and Pinot Gris

Introduction	92
Reviews	93
Italian Pinot Grigio	93
Alsatian Pinot Gris	95
U.S. Pinot Gris	96
Other Great Value Pinot Gris	97

Introduction: Pinot Gris

Pinot Gris is a grape of many names. In Italy it is known as Pinot Grigio; in the Alsace region of France it is known as Tokay d'Alsace or Pinot Gris; in Germany and Austria it is known as Ruländer. Its variety of names is rivaled only by its variety of flavors, which can change dramatically if the wines are bottled with any residual sugar. However, Pinot Gris is usually dry, showing flavors of orange blossom, smoke, and minerals. Pinot Gris performs best in a cool climate where it can develop its subtle varietal flavors while retaining acidity to offset its naturally oily texture.

Regardless of where Pinot Gris is produced, it is almost always a value. Examples of great value Pinot Gris can come from France, Italy, and the United States. These wines, particularly examples from Alsace in France, and the U.S.'s premier region for Pinot Gris, Oregon, are not always easy to find, but do not be discouraged—seek them out.

In the 1980s, Pinot Grigio became the hottest white variety from Italy, a trend that did not slow much in the 1990s. When you think of Pinot Grigio in Italy, don't summon thoughts of sunny Mediterranean Italy but rather the cool Alpine Italy bordering Austria. Pinot Grigio is produced mainly in two regions, Trentino–Alto Adige and Friuli–Venezia. The northern half of Trentino–Alto Adige, known simply as Alto Adige, was once part of Austria's Tyrol. Most inhabitants still speak German and refer to themselves as *Südtirolers*. Here both grape and technique come together to produce wines unique from those of its neighbors. The nose is beautifully perfumed and quite assertive. The palate is full and firm with an earthy note. Neighboring Friuli produces Pinot Grigios that are more fleshy and fruity, with a hearty dose of alcohol enlivened by acidity on the finish.

Pinot Gris, native to France, is a variant of Pinot Noir. In Alsace, Pinot Gris is one of the four varieties afforded Grand Cru status, but production is dwarfed by that of Gewürztraminer, Riesling, and Pinot Blanc. Pinot Gris makes up less than 10% of Alsace's total acreage—barely more than Pinot Noir. In Alsace, Pinot Gris obtains a spicy and exotic character not found elsewhere. The wines tend to be highly perfumed and rich, but never cloying on the palate. As is the case with other Alsatian wines, many bargains may be found, although most Grand Cru wines reside in the $20 and up range.

In the United States, Oregon has shown the greatest success with Pinot Gris. The dry, cool vineyard lands of the Willamette Valley are at present the New World's most promising home for the variety. This should come as no surprise, as Pinot Gris's cousin, Pinot Noir, has already gained a world-class reputation here. Oregon's Pinot Gris is generally medium-bodied, flinty, and clean. Some 50 producers in Oregon offer Pinot Gris as part of their repertoire. Oregon Pinot Gris acreage outnumbers California's two to one, and it is the state's number three variety behind Chardonnay and Pinot Noir. It is a fantastic match with the fresh seafood of the Pacific Northwest.

Vintages often come into play when buying wine from cool growing regions. Fortunately, Alsace has been blessed as of late. All vintages from 1995 forward are very good to excellent. Northern Italy has also had three excellent recent vintages, '95, '96, and '97. These are excellent food wines, exhibiting substantial body with a clean note of acidity on the finish. Pinot Gris is wonderful with shellfish and salmon. It is also lively and refreshing enough to be served as an aperitif.

Run, don't walk, to your local wine merchant and get your hands on some Pinot Gris. Opportunities to experience some of the best wines of a given category for less than $15 seem to diminish with each new vintage.

Reviews

Italian Pinot Grigio

89 • *Terlano (Italy) 1995 Klaus, Pinot Grigio, Alto Adige. $14.99.*
Brilliant yellow-gold. Moderately full-bodied. Full acidity. Highly extracted. Citrus, herbs. Zesty, fragrant aromas have a smoky note. Sensational acidity and concentration of flavors play out on a long, long finish. Racy, generous style.

88 • *Villanova (Italy) 1996 Pinot Grigio, Collio. $14.99.*
Clear, bright yellow-gold. Medium-bodied. Full acidity. Moderately extracted. Citrus, minerals. Tart, zesty aromas follow through well on the palate. Clean minerally finish with bright acidity.

88 • *Villa Frattina (Italy) 1997 Pinot Grigio, Lison-Pramaggiore. $12.*
Bright straw cast. Moderately full-bodied. Full acidity. Highly extracted. Minerals, green apples. Rather subtle in aromatics, with an extremely focused and precise palate feel. Crisp and vibrant finish. Refreshing.

88 • *Terlano (Italy) 1996 Pinot Grigio, Alto Adige. $11.49.*
Bright gold. Moderately full-bodied. Full acidity. Highly extracted. Dried herbs, smoke, minerals. Subtle but complex aromas play out with great intensity on the firm palate. Firm acidity makes for a clean finish with a hint of dryness. Concentrated and tightly wound style.

86 • *Castello Banfi (Italy) 1997 San Angelo, Pinot Grigio, Toscana. $13.*
Bright yellow-gold. Medium-bodied. Balanced acidity. Moderately extracted. Mildly oaked. Citrus zest, vanilla. Well balanced, with a touch of oak evident in the nose and the finish.

Great Value Pinot Grigio and Pinot Gris at a Glance

Number of Wines Recommended:

50

Countries Represented:

8

85 • *Livio Felluga (Italy) 1996 Esperto, Pinot Grigio. $14.*

Bright straw cast. Moderately full-bodied. Full acidity. Moderately extracted. Green herbs, earth, minerals. Subtle aromas, yet the flavors are complex, with a nuanced character. Ripe and round in the mouth with a solid edge of acidity through the finish.

84 • *Campanile (Italy) 1997 Pinot Grigio, Friuli. $11.*

Deep straw cast. Moderately full-bodied. Full acidity. Moderately extracted. Cheese, earth, minerals. Forward aromatics are unusual but distinctive, with a rounded, earthy, flavorful palate feel. Concentrated and intense through the smoky finish.

83 • *Scarlatta (Italy) 1996 Pinot Grigio, Veneto. $4.75.*

Bright straw cast. Moderately full-bodied. Full acidity. Moderately extracted. Cheese, cream, slate. Distinctive aromatics. Flavorful and rounded in the mouth with a vibrant edge of acidity that makes for a refreshing finish. Fine length and intensity.

83 • *Moletto (Italy) 1997 Pinot Grigio, Piave. $9.99.*

Bright straw cast. Medium-bodied. Full acidity. Highly extracted. Tropical fruits, apricots, minerals. Extremely aromatic, with a pure, fruit-centered flavor profile. Expressive and quite crisp on the palate. The finish has a real snap. Intense.

83 • *Josef Brigl (Italy) 1997 Pinot Grigio, Alto Adige. $9.99.*

Bright straw cast. Medium-bodied. Full acidity. Moderately extracted. Minerals, citrus zest. Aromatically reserved, with a clean minerally palate. Rounded mouthfeel, with zesty acidity through the finish.

83 • *Albola (Italy) 1995 Pinot Grigio, Umbria. $10.*

Bright straw cast. Moderately full-bodied. Full acidity. Moderately extracted. Cheese, smoke. Forward, distinctive aromatics lead a lush, beautifully textured, supple palate. Round and ripe, with a great edge of acidity to the flavorful finish.

82 • *Cantine Mezzacorona (Italy) 1997 Pinot Grigio, Trentino. $7.99.*

Bright straw cast. Medium-bodied. Full acidity. Moderately extracted. Minerals. Reserved aromatically, with a steely, clean palate feel and a vibrant finish. Lean flavors, but refreshing.

81 • *Pighin (Italy) 1996 Pinot Grigio, Grave del Friuli. $11.99.*

Bright gold. Moderately full-bodied. Full acidity. Moderately extracted. Minerals. Unyielding aromatically, with a rounded palate feel that is buoyed by vibrant acidity. A tad shy of flavor, with some dry assertiveness on the finish.

81 • *Cielo (Italy) 1996 Pinot Grigio, Veneto. $5.99.*

Old-gold cast. Moderately full-bodied. Full acidity. Highly extracted. Maderization, blanched almonds. Nutty, full aromas. Weighty mouthfeel, though assertive flavors conclude with a mildly bitter note. May not appeal to all palates.

81 • *Bollini (Italy) 1996 Reserve Selection, Pinot Grigio, Grave del Friuli. $14.99.*

Bright straw cast. Medium-bodied. Full acidity. Moderately extracted. Minerals. Reserved aromatically, with a lighter-styled high-acid palate feel. Clean through the finish, but lacks a bit for flavor.

80 • *Marega (Italy) 1996 Pinot Grigio, Collio. $12.99.*

Bright straw cast. Moderately full-bodied. Full acidity. Highly extracted. Lacquer, blanched almonds, dried herbs. Quite aromatic, with a distinctive note of terroir and a flavorful though firm palate feel. Lean and crisp through the finish with a solid edge of acidity and a hint of bitterness.

80 • *La Colombaia (Italy) 1996 Pinot Grigio, Valdadige. $9.99.*

Bright straw cast. Moderately full-bodied. Full acidity. Moderately extracted. Cheese, toast, cream. Aromatic, with a forceful and unusual cheesy note. Full, ripe, and rounded in the mouth, with solid balancing acidity and a supple texture through the finish.

Scale: Superlative (96-100), Exceptional (90-95), Highly Recommended (85-89), Recommended (80-84), Not Recommended (Under 80)

Alsatian Pinot Gris

89 • *Fleith (France) 1996 Réserve, Tokay Pinot Gris, Alsace. $10.*
Deep yellow-gold. Moderately full-bodied. Full acidity. Moderately extracted. Oranges, spice, minerals. Pleasantly aromatic, with a rich and full mouthfeel balanced by vibrant acidity. Zesty through the finish.

89 • *Cave Vinicole de Kientzheim-Kayersberg (France) 1997 Réserve, Tokay Pinot Gris, Alsace. $14.*
Bright straw hue with a slight copper cast. Medium-bodied. Balanced acidity. Moderately extracted. Oranges, smoke, minerals. Aromatically reserved, but fat and ripe in the mouth, with a touch of sweetness and full flavors.

88 • *Marcel Deiss (France) 1996 Bergheim, Pinot Gris, Alsace. $15.*
Deep old-gold hue. Full-bodied. Full acidity. Highly extracted. Citrus peel, minerals, spice. Rather reserved aromatically, but full-throttled on the palate, with hearty extraction and very vibrant acidity. Finishes with marked sweetness. Built for long-term aging.

87 • *Marcel Deiss (France) 1995 Bergheim, Pinot Gris, Alsace. $14.*
Bright yellow-straw cast. Moderately full-bodied. Full acidity. Highly extracted. Minerals, citrus zest. Aromatically reserved, with a slight minerally oxidized note. Full but crisp through the finish.

87 • *Dopff & Irion (France) 1997 Tokay Pinot Gris, Alsace. $13.*
Pale straw cast. Medium-bodied. Balanced acidity. Moderately extracted. Minerals, citrus peel, yellow apple. Aromatically reserved, with a lean and crisp mouthfeel. Vibrant and angular through the finish.

86 • *Trimbach (France) 1995 Réserve, Pinot Gris, Alsace. $15.*
Deep straw cast. Moderately full-bodied. Balanced acidity. Moderately extracted. Minerals, apples. Aromatically reserved, with a full but angular mouthfeel. Lean and minerally through the finish.

86 • *Pierre Sparr (France) 1996 Réserve, Pinot Gris, Alsace. $11.99.*
Deep yellow-straw hue. Moderately full-bodied. Full acidity. Moderately extracted. Minerals, citrus. Aromatically reserved, with a ripe and full mouthfeel buttressed by racy acidity. Leaves a taut, firm, tightly wound impression.

86 • *Pfaffenheim (France) 1997 Cuvée Rabelais, Tokay Pinot Gris, Alsace. $14.50.*
Deep straw hue with a copper cast. Medium-bodied. Full acidity. Talc, smoke, orange blossom. Features full, forceful, high-toned aromatics. Ripe and full in the mouth, yet with a lean edge. Crisp through the lengthy finish.

86 • *Jean-Pierre Bechtold (France) 1996 "E," Tokay Pinot Gris, Alsace. $14.*
Bright straw cast. Medium-bodied. Full acidity. Moderately extracted. Minerals, smoke. Muted aromatics lead to a lean and brisk mouthfeel. Sharp and vigorous through the finish.

86 • *Bott Frères (France) 1996 Réserve Personnelle, Pinot Gris, Alsace. $13.*
Crystalline greenish straw cast. Moderately full-bodied. Full acidity. Highly extracted. Minerals, citrus peel. Precise and crisp aromas lead a firm and lean palate feel with piercing acidity. Taut and zesty through the finish.

84 • *Leon Beyer (France) 1997 Tokay Pinot Gris, Alsace. $13.95.*
Crystalline greenish straw cast. Medium-bodied. Full acidity. Highly extracted. Minerals. Crisp, lean, and firm—an edgy, mineral-dominated style. Crisp and rather tart through the finish.

83 • *Lucien Albrecht (France) 1997 Tokay Pinot Gris, Alsace. $14.*
Pale straw hue with a slight copper tinge. Moderately full-bodied. Balanced acidity. Moderately extracted. Minerals, slate, smoke. Aromatically reserved, with a rounded, oily mouthfeel. Features a firm, minerally backdrop throughout.

83 • *Jean-Pierre Bechtold (France) 1997 "E," Tokay Pinot Gris, Alsace. $15.*
Pale greenish straw cast. Medium-bodied. Full acidity. Moderately extracted. Smoke, citrus. Aromatically reserved, with a lean mouthfeel broadened by a hint of sweetness. Not very complex, but well balanced.

81 • *Clos du Letzenberg (France) 1997 Tokay Pinot Gris, Alsace. $12.*
Bright emerald gold. Medium-bodied. Balanced acidity. Herbs, sweet apples. Curiously herbal, sweet, and disjointed on the palate. The mouthfeel has some thickness and body.

U.S. Pinot Gris

90 • *King Estate (OR) 1996 Pinot Gris, Oregon. $13.*
Bright yellow-straw cast. Moderately full-bodied. Full acidity. Moderately extracted. Oranges, minerals, spice. Features a ripe nose with a spicy accent to the fruit flavors. Full and rich with vibrant acidity through the rounded, smoky finish.

88 • *Martini & Prati (CA) 1996 Vino Grigio, California. $12.50.*
Bright gold. Moderately full-bodied. Full acidity. Moderately extracted. Tropical fruits, spice, cream. Ripe aromas follow through with a sense of richness to the fruit-accented flavors. Full and lush on the palate with zesty acidity providing good grip.

87 • *Dos Cabezas (AZ) 1997 Pinot Gris, Cochise County. $14.95.*
Deep yellow-gold. Moderately full-bodied. Balanced acidity. Moderately extracted. Moderately oaked. Toasted coconut, minerals, smoke. Oak is readily apparent on the nose and is joined by an exotic spicy note on the palate. Full and ripe with richness tempered by acidity through a weighty, smoky finish.

87 • *Bargetto (CA) 1997 Pinot Grigio, Central Coast. $15.*
Bright platinum cast. Moderately full-bodied. Balanced acidity. Moderately extracted. Smoke, citrus, minerals. Aromatic and flavorful with a ripe melange of smoky flavors. Full in the mouth yet balanced by angular acidity. Shows fine grip and intensity on the finish.

86 • *Montinore (OR) 1997 Pinot Gris, Willamette Valley. $9.99.*
Platinum with a bright copper cast. Medium-bodied. Full acidity. Highly extracted. Blanched almonds, pears. Distinctive aromas lead an austere palate with taut acids through a dry finish. Quite an assertive style that should partner with foods.

86 • *LaVelle (OR) 1996 Winter's Hill Vineyard, Pinot Gris, Oregon. $13.*
Deep yellow-straw cast. Moderately full-bodied. Full acidity. Moderately extracted. Tropical fruits, cream, minerals. Quite ripe and aromatic with a sense of richness to the flavors. Vibrant acidity lends a cleansing note to the palate. Good grip with fine length on the finish.

86 • *Cooper Mountain (OR) 1997 Pinot Gris, Willamette Valley. $14.75.*
Bright straw hue. Medium-bodied. Full acidity. Moderately extracted. Minerals, flint. Lean, crisp, and racy, with a sharp and tangy mouthfeel. Fleshes out with a bit of richness through the finish. Will cut rich foods well.

86 • *Callaway (CA) 1997 Pinot Gris, Temecula. $12.*
Bright copper cast. Moderately full-bodied. Balanced acidity. Moderately extracted. Dried herbs, minerals, gooseberries. Distinctively aromatic with a big earthy, herbal streak. Full and rich in the mouth with some racy acidity through the smoky finish.

86 • *Bridgeview (OR) 1997 Pinot Gris, Oregon. $9.99.*
Dark straw color with a slight copper cast. Moderately full-bodied. Full acidity. Moderately extracted. Bananas, minerals. Quite aromatic with a very ripe nose. Full and rich on the palate with lean acidity lending vibrance to the rounded, smoky finish.

85 • *Columbia Winery (WA) 1996 Pinot Gris, Yakima Valley. $10.99.*
Bright gold. Medium-bodied. Full acidity. Highly extracted. Minerals, grapefruit zest. Rather unyielding in aromatics, with a clean, racy, mildly bitter palate feel. A buttery note emerges in the finish.

Scale: Superlative (96-100), Exceptional (90-95), Highly Recommended (85-89), Recommended (80-84), Not Recommended (Under 80)

84 • Silvan Ridge (OR) 1996 Pinot Gris, Oregon. $13.
Dull, pale gold. Moderately full-bodied. Balanced acidity. Highly extracted. Minerals, earth, blanched almonds. Aromatically reserved, with a rich though lean palate feel. Features a mild bitter note through the lengthy, nutty finish.

84 • Oak Knoll (OR) 1996 Pinot Gris, Willamette Valley. $13.
Bright straw cast. Medium-bodied. Full acidity. Moderately extracted. Citrus zest, minerals. Bright, fresh, and racy in style with zesty acidity. If a tad unyielding in flavors, it is clean and crisp and leaves the palate refreshed.

82 • Erath (OR) 1997 Pinot Gris, Willamette Valley. $12.
Bright platinum cast. Medium-bodied. Low acidity. Subtly extracted. Smoke, minerals. Smoky aromas reveal a soft style of Pinot Gris with minerally austerity and a dry finish.

81 • Barboursville (VA) 1997 Pinot Grigio, Monticello. $13.
Bright straw cast. Moderately full-bodied. Full acidity. Highly extracted. Minerals, citrus zest, earth. Rather unusual in aromatics with an earthy edge. Quite full in the mouth with zesty, spritzy acidity. Finishes on a rather flat note.

Other Great Value Pinot Gris

84 • Shingle Peak (New Zealand) 1997 Pinot Gris, Marlborough. $14.
Deep straw cast. Moderately full-bodied. Full acidity. Moderately extracted. Orange blossom, wool, minerals. Rather muted aromatically with subtle citrusy overtones. Full and extremely racy in the mouth. Clean, crisp finish.

84 • Erzherzog Johann Weine (Austria) 1997 Exklusiv, Steirischer, Kabinett, Trocken, Pinot Gris, Sudsteiermark. $15.
Bright pale gold. Medium-bodied. Balanced acidity. Moderately extracted. Apples, minerals. Crisp, juicy, and snappy. A lighthearted style, very appealing.

83 • Calona (Canada) 1997 Artist Series, Pinot Gris, Okanagan Valley. $6.97.
Very pale platinum-straw hue. Mild aromas show a hint of smoke and a note of citrus zest. Brightly acidic on the attack, leading a medium-bodied palate with clean flavors and minerally accent through the finish. Drink now.

80 • Weinkellerei P.J. Valckenberg (Germany) 1997 Pinot Gris, Pfalz. $8.95.
Very pale straw hue. Moderately light-bodied. Balanced acidity. Subtly extracted. Smoke, citrus. Zesty, mildly smoky nose. Mild flavors show a trace of Pinot Gris character, though this is otherwise very straightforward.

80 • Murfatlar (Romania) 1990 Pinot Gris, Murfatlar. $8.99.
Bright golden-yellow. Medium-bodied. Balanced acidity. Moderately extracted. Flowers, sweet apples, kerosene. Somewhat solventy and floral on the nose. Juicy and sweet, with a rounded mouthfeel and simple finish. This has some aromatic varietal character, though it lacks complexity.

eight

Stylish Italian Whites

Introduction 100

Reviews 102

  Arneis 102

  Gavi 103

  Orvieto 103

  Soave 103

  Tocai Friulano 103

  Vernaccia di San Gimignano 104

  Other Great Value
Italian Whites 104

Introduction: Italian Whites

When we were children, we never wanted to go to an ice cream parlor that had only a few flavors. We wanted 20, 30, or even 50 flavors to choose from. As children we understood that more choices is a good thing. Somehow we have misplaced our childhood wisdom. When looking for a white wine, we reflexively reach for Chardonnay, or perhaps in moments of uncontrolled spontaneity, Sauvignon Blanc. If this sounds like you, it's time to broaden your horizons and look to Italy.

Most often known for its red wines, Italy produces an amazing array of whites from all 20 of its provinces. No other nation can approach Italy's amazing assortment of varieties, both native and foreign. Many of the native varieties have been in use since the time of the Roman Empire. Don't be intimidated by new flavors and unfamiliar varieties. If you give them a try, you will be treated to some of the world's most interesting and food-friendly white wines.

Italy is a white wine value seeker's paradise. Most of Italy's unpretentious whites can be considered values. Prices for the nation's best whites rarely climb to levels seen for the top red wines. A few wines, such as Vernaccia di San Gimignano and Arneis, have gained in appreciation in recent years, causing prices to rise steadily. Values still remain among these wines, although it is probably just a matter of time before most eclipse the $20 plateau.

Arneis

Piedmont, a northern region dominated by red wine production, also features an attrative indigenous white variety, Arneis. In the hierarchy of Piemontese whites, Arneis is a distant third behind Moscato, which is responsible for Asti Spumante, and Cortese, the Gavi grape. Until recently, Arneis was largely ignored by producers. It was planted along prized Nebbiolo vineyards in order to sway bees from those vines. Arneis, which means "little difficult wine" in the local dialect, is considered to be fickle in the vineyard and prone to oxidation during vinification. When skillfully produced, however, Arneis exhibits a beautiful and distinctive bouquet of ripe pears and wild flowers. On the palate Arneis shows a fabulously crisp texture with a taut, refreshing mouthfeel. This is a wine on the rise that may one day be considered among Italy's finest whites. Some Arneis is capable of aging, but most is best when young. Serve it at a cool temperature, but not too cold, because this mutes the wine's subtle flavors. Try it with shellfish, or drink it to cut a rich, flavorful fish such as red snapper or halibut.

Gavi

Gavi is Piedmont's most recognized dry white wine, made entirely from the Cortese grape in and around the small village of Gavi. It is on the neutral side, with an inherent richness that often draws comparison to Chardonnay. In 1974, the wines were granted DOC status—that is, the nation's wine control organization classified Gavi as a distinct wine-producing area. Production skyrocketed, increasing by roughly tenfold in the first decade of classification. Wines labeled Gavi di Gavi come from the village of Gavi itself. No inference to quality should be made, as wines from neighboring villages entitled to the Gavi name often produce wines of equal quality. The Cortese variety is vulnerable to mold as it nears maturity, which creates a dilemma for growers who desire fully ripe fruit but fear devastation from mold. The wines of Gavi are often high in acid. Finer examples are a product of patient growers who allow the vines to develop sufficient fruit to balance this sometimes bracing acidity. Cortese should be drunk when young. It can be served with a wide range of dishes; however, it seems most comfortable supporting fish.

Orvieto

Orvieto is a blend of Trebbiano, Malvasia, and Grechetto grapes, made in central Italy's province of Umbria, near Rome. The wines are typically simple and clean with a faint earthy quality. Wines coming from the territory closest to the town of Orvieto are identified by the term Classico. Originally, Orvieto was produced in a slightly sweet style, known as *abboccato*, that emphasized ripe peach and tropical fruit flavors as well as a silky mouthfeel. Today most wines of Orvieto are dry, often carrying the word *secco* on the label to indicate this fact. Drink them cold, and serve the youngest examples available. These are great aperitifs.

Soave

Soave is perhaps the best-known white wine of Italy. Often it is maligned and misunderstood by wine drinkers outside of the country. To the Italians, Soave is meant to soothe, not provoke. It is an ideal sipping wine, excelling as a simple aperitif or accompaniment to food. Soave is produced in the northern Veneto, primarily on flat lands between the cities of Vicenza and Verona, from the Garganega and Trebbiano di Soave (lighter than the Trebbiano of Tuscany) varieties. In and around the town of Soave lies the original, hillier production zone. The wines of this area are permitted the Classico designation. Drink these wines while they are young. Excellent recent vintages include 1995, 1996, and 1997.

Great Value White Italian Varietals at a Glance

Number of Wines Recommended:

35

Countries Represented:

1

Tocai Friulano

Tocai Friulano is the Tocai variety from Friuli, a province in northeastern Italy. Tocai is a wonderful and complex wine demonstrating a unique merging of fruity, floral, and herbal aromas. The palate is washed with silky, soft tropical fruit flavors and sharp acidity, which maintains a sense of balance. Several regions produce Tocai Friulano and some top producers fetch a handsome price for their wines. At the moment, values exist and should be enjoyed whenever the opportunity presents itself. This wine can age, but it is best enjoyed with all of its youthful fruit intact. Be sure not to serve it too cold. Tocai Friulano is fantastic with veal, poultry, or fish in a rich sauce.

Vernaccia di San Gimignano

From the slopes and plains surrounding San Gimignano come the vigorous and aggressive wines of the Vernaccia variety. Vernaccia di San Gimignano is Tuscany's preeminent white wine. Traditionally, the wines were produced in a massive style that could be mellowed only by aging in wood barrels. Today, many lighter styles with little or no wood aging abound, creating a more flowery wine. Vernaccia di San Gimignano has gained much popularity outside of Italy in the past decade, driving prices up. Values do remain, albeit with less regularity than in years past. Much of today's Vernaccia di San Gimignano is best drunk young. These wines are wonderfully intense and balanced. They can be enjoyed on their own or with rich dishes.

Reviews

Arneis

90 • Deltetto (Italy) 1996 San Michelle, Arneis, Roero. $13.99.
Pale straw hue. Medium-bodied. Full acidity. Highly extracted. Green apples, minerals, cream. Extremely aromatic and well translated onto the palate with a purity to the flavors. Racy acidity lends a clean and intense finish. Well balanced and stylish.

88 • Azienda Agricola Cantine Del Castello Neive (Italy) 1996 Arneis, Langhe. $13.50.
Bright platinum hue. Moderately light-bodied. Full acidity. Moderately extracted. Cream, sweet herbs, yeast. Light, delicate, and racy in style, with an expansive array of champagne-like flavors on the palate. Crisp acidity makes for a clean finish.

81 • Cairel (Italy) 1996 Arneis, Langhe. $15.
Pale straw hue. Moderately full-bodied. Full acidity. Highly extracted. Mildly oaked. Citrus, minerals, cream. Soft hints of wood create a rounded mouthfeel. Features a bit of spritziness on the palate, however, creating a disjointed but not necessarily unpleasant wine.

80 • Tenuta Carretta (Italy) 1996 Vigna Canorei, Arneis, Roero. $15.
Deep straw hue. Moderately light-bodied. Full acidity. Moderately extracted. Flint, minerals. Aromatically restrained, with a crisp subtle character on the palate. Tart and angular, though refreshing. Shellfish, anyone?

Gavi

88 • *Villa Sparina (Italy) 1996 Gavi di Gavi. $15.*
Pale straw hue. Moderately light-bodied. Full acidity. Moderately extracted. Bananas, minerals, citrus. Pleasantly aromatic with delicate and pure flavors. Clean, racy, and vibrant, with some spritz. Well balanced and well made without the bitterness the varietal often acquires.

84 • *Batasiolo (Italy) 1995 Gavi . $11.*
Pale gold. Moderately full-bodied. Full acidity. Highly extracted. Green apples, lanolin, lacquer. Quite aromatic and not unlike a young Hunter Valley Semillon. Full in the mouth, with a firm structure and some bitterness toward the finish. A tad overextracted, but very interesting.

83 • *Banfi (Italy) 1996 Principessa Gavia, Gavi . $12.*
Pale straw color. Moderately light-bodied. Full acidity. Moderately extracted. Green apples, minerals. Light, crisp, and clean in a very modern style. Angular acidity on the palate rounds out toward the finish. Well balanced.

82 • *Villa Rosa (Italy) 1996 Black Label, Gavi di Gavi. $12.99.*
Pale straw hue. Medium-bodied. Full acidity. Moderately extracted. Citrus, minerals. Flavors are a little subdued, but it has a rounded mouthfeel and crisp, angular acidity. Clean, well-balanced finish.

Orvieto

84 • *Bigi (Italy) 1996 Secco, Orvieto Classico. $5.99.*
Pale green-straw hue. Medium-bodied. Balanced acidity. Moderately extracted. Citrus, pear. Muted aromas lead clean, fresh flavors on the palate. The finish is clean though short.

84 • *Antinori (Italy) 1996 Campogrande, Orvieto Classico. $9.*
Bright yellow-gold. Medium-bodied. Full acidity. Moderately extracted. Yeast, crabapple. Broad, zesty aromas have a yeasty note. Crisp, mildly tart flavors on the palate turn dry on the finish. A clean-tasting, refreshing wine.

81 • *Roccadoro (Italy) 1995 Secco, Orvieto Classico. $8.*
Medium straw hue. Medium-bodied. Low acidity. Moderately extracted. Butter, citrus zest. Soft and rounded with some glycerin and weight on the palate. This has a soft buttery character that is counterbalanced by nice acids, though flavors are mild.

Soave

87 • *Ca'Rugate (Italy) 1996 Monte Alto, Soave Classico. $13.99.*
Full gold-yellow. Moderately full-bodied. Balanced acidity. Moderately extracted. Cheese, asparagus, spice. Distinctive minerally, sweaty aromas show complexity. Rounded, fat, juicy flavors with a weighty mouthfeel. Light and quite clean on the finish with very subtle spicy notes.

83 • *Ca'Rugate (Italy) 1996 Soave Classico. $11.99.*
Full gold-yellow. Moderately full-bodied. Balanced acidity. Moderately extracted. Ripe citrus, minerals. Soft, rounded mouthfeel reveals ample, ripe flavors that give a weighty, fat sensation on the palate, with a crisp finish.

82 • *Bolla (Italy) 1996 Tufaie Castellaro, Soave Classico. $14.*
Brilliant pale straw hue. Medium-bodied. Balanced acidity. Moderately extracted. Bitter almond, lemons, flowers. Perfumed aromas show a varietal quality. Fresh tropical flavors unravel on a clean, juicy palate. Very attractive and exotic.

Tocai Friulano

89 • *Pra'di Pradis (Italy) 1994 Tocai Friulano, Collio. $13.99.*
Deep straw cast. Moderately full-bodied. Full acidity. Highly extracted. Flowers, citrus zest, green herbs. Extremely aromatic, with complex flavors. The mouthfeel is full and rounded yet well balanced by vibrant acidity. Shows fine length and concentration through the finish.

80 • *Marega (Italy) 1996 Collio, Tocai Friulano. $12.99.*
Bright straw cast. Moderately full-bodied. Low acidity. Moderately extracted. Earth, minerals. Distinctive earthy aromas lead a rounded mouthfeel that is a bit shy of acidity. Somewhat flat through the finish.

Vernaccia di San Gimignano

86 • *Spalletti (Italy) 1996 Vernaccia di San Gimignano. $9.99.*
Bright pale gold. Medium-bodied. Balanced acidity. Moderately extracted. Apples, peach skins. Fresh and fruity, with a clean, glycerous mouthfeel. Finishes with a touch of phenolic dryness. Very versatile style.

84 • *Riccardo Falchini (Italy) 1996 Ab Vinea Doni, Vernaccia di San Gimignano. $14.99.*
Bright yellow-gold. Medium-bodied. Full acidity. Moderately extracted. Pineapple, apples. Fresh, clean, and fruity, showing a good acidic cut that lingers through the finish.

83 • *Riccardo Falchini (Italy) 1997 Vigna a Solatio, Vernaccia di San Gimignano. $9.99.*
Bright yellow-gold. Moderately light-bodied. Balanced acidity. Moderately extracted. Citrus zest. Delicate aromas reveal a light, clean, refreshing palate.

Other Great Value Italian Whites

90 • *Mastroberardino (Italy) 1996 Bianco, Lacryma Christi del Vesuvio. $15.*
Bright yellow-gold. Moderately full-bodied. Balanced acidity. Moderately extracted. White melon, honey. Grassy, complex aromas. Rounded, weighty palate has a fine mouthfeel. Flavors develop through the long, long finish.

89 • *Umani Ronchi (Italy) 1996 Casal di Serra, Verdicchio Classico Superiore. $8.99.*
Bright gold-straw hue. Medium-bodied. Balanced acidity. Moderately extracted. Peaches, honey. Honeyed aromas have a late harvest character. The palate is dry, with the impression of sweetness in the flavors. Delicious juicy finish. Generous and weighty style.

86 • *Illuminati (Italy) 1997 Costalupo, Controguerra. $8.*
Pale green-straw hue. Medium-bodied. Balanced acidity. Moderately extracted. Zest, tropical fruits. Bright, clean fruit salad aromas follow through on the palate. Plenty of aromatic varietal character.

86 • *Casa di Pescatori (Italy) 1996 Sicilia. $5.99.*
Pale platinum-straw hue. Medium-bodied. Balanced acidity. Moderately extracted. Citrus, herbs, minerals. Oily, rich aromas lead a fine glycerous mouthfeel with a crisp citrusy, herbal edge through the finish. Clean.

86 • *Bigi (Italy) 1997 Graffiti, Est!Est!!Est!!! di Montefiascone. $5.99.*
Pale brilliant straw hue. Moderately light-bodied. Full acidity. Moderately extracted. Apples, grass. Grassy high-toned aromas lead a juicy, rounded palate with clean flavors and a touch of dryness on the finish. Intense and pure.

84 • *Michele Satta (Italy) 1997 Costa di Giulia, Toscana. $15.*
Pale yellow-gold. Medium-bodied. Full acidity. Moderately extracted. Citrus zest, smoke, minerals. Elegant smoky aromas. Zesty, angular style with good acidic cut and some glycerous mouthfeel.

84 • *Furlan (Italy) 1996 Castelcosa Grigio, Friuli Venezia Giulia. $12.99.*
Bright yellow-gold. Medium-bodied. Balanced acidity. Moderately extracted. Minerals, flowers. Minerally nose with a floral note. Weighty, firm palate has dry flavors through the finish. Quite full, structured, and austere, with acids accentuating the dryness.

84 • Contadi Castaldi (Italy) 1996 Terre di Franciacorta, Bianco, Franciacorta. $9.49.
Bright yellow-straw hue. Medium-bodied. Balanced acidity. Moderately extracted. Dried herbs, limes. Fresh Sauvignon Blanc-like aromas follow through on a clean, fruity palate with fresh acids. A very lively and refreshing style.

84 • Cocci Grifoni (Italy) 1996 Podere Colle Vecchio, Vino Bianco delle Marche. $12.99.
Bright gold-yellow. Medium-bodied. Balanced acidity. Moderately extracted. Flint, citrus. Minerally nose follows through on the focused palate. Lively acids and a minerally feel give good grip and length.

84 • Ca' Montini (Italy) 1997 Luna di Luna, Chardonnay-Pinot Grigio, Veneto. $10.
Very pale straw hue. Moderately light-bodied. Balanced acidity. Moderately extracted. Flowers, minerals, citrus. Elegant floral, citrusy nose follows through on a clean, juicy palate with delicious freshness through the finish.

83 • Ruffino (Italy) 1996 Libaio, Chardonnay-Pinot Grigio, Toscana. $12.
Bright golden yellow. Medium-bodied. Balanced acidity. Moderately extracted. Ripe, glycerous mouthfeel. Generous sweet fruit flavors on entry, with a minerally finish.

83 • Fontana Candida (Italy) 1996 Superiore, Frascati. $7.49.
Pale yellow-straw hue. Medium-bodied. Balanced acidity. Moderately extracted. Zest, white citrus. Fresh, zesty flavors follow through on the palate. Straightforward and pleasant with a hint of dryness on the finish.

82 • Scarlatta (Italy) 1995 Trebbiano d'Abruzzo. $4.25.
Pale straw cast. Moderately light-bodied. Balanced acidity. Moderately extracted. Cheese, earth, minerals. Marked aromas have a yeasty character. The lightly styled palate has a complex yeasty note with juicy acids. Interesting though distinctive.

80 • Tenuta di Caparzo (Italy) 1995 Le Crete, Chardonnay-Trebbiano, Toscana. $9.
Deep gold-straw cast. Moderately full-bodied. Balanced acidity. Highly extracted. Minerals, citrus. Rustic, zesty aromas lead a dry, austere palate showing some signs of age. Drink soon.

80 • Antinori (Italy) 1996 Castello della Sala, Sauvignon, Umbria. $11.50.
Pale straw hue. Medium-bodied. Full acidity. Moderately extracted. Citrus, limes. Old yeasty notes accent bright, juicy aromas that follow through on the palate. Quite herbal and crisp through the finish.

nine

Rosé

Introduction	108
Reviews	109
French Rosé	109
U.S. Rosé	110
Other Great Value Rosé	113

Introduction: Rosé

Rosé wines, or blush wines as they have come to be known in the United States, are made in most every wine-producing nation from a wide variety of grapes. The resulting wines may be dry or sweet, deep ruby hued or showing the faintest tinge of pink. Rosé is made by crushing red wine grapes, then allowing the skins to remain in contact with the juice just long enough to sufficiently color the wine pink. Hence the moniker, Rosé, which is actually French for pink, but has de facto become part of the English language.

Rosés—particularly those with a bit of sweetness—are often considered introductory wines, and have served as many a consumer's first wine experience. Unfortunately, these styles—especially White Zinfandel—have given poorly informed wine snobs the chance to dismiss Rosés entirely, despite the fact that the category offers an ever-increasing number of "serious" dry table wines. If you, too, have dismissed Rosé, take your next step in wine discovery and reintroduce yourself to the style, appreciating both its fresh and playful qualities as well as its more complex manifestations.

Rosés are generally good values. Rarely do they exceed $15, and they often don't even go beyond $10. They are rarely placed in expensive oak barrels and can be released soon after fermentation is complete. In strict business terms, Rosé is good cash flow, and the savings created by straightforward production methods and swift turnover are passed directly on to the consumer.

Regions

The Rosés of the Rhône Valley, and in particular France's most famous Rosé, Tavel, are distinctively earthy and complex with a unique pinkish orange color. Tavel all but disappeared from store shelves in the United States during the height of the White Zinfandel craze. Its return has been slow and troublesome, as many now sell for more than $15. Rosé from the general Côtes du Rhône appellation, and Rosé d'Anjou, a slightly sweet wine from the Loire, can be much easier to find and are almost always priced around $10. In recent years many Rosés have been introduced from Provence and other parts of the south of France. The latter often carry a Vin de Pays, or country wine, designation and both categories often represent terrific bargains.

As for the United States, White Zinfandel continues to lead the way, outselling all other American Rosé. This fact does not suggest that the Rosé category is slumbering. Quite the opposite is true, as many new styles are emerging, with drier, more flavorful versions being released. Today, most every conceivable red variety is being used to make Rosé in the United States. The trendiest of varieties such as Sangiovese, Nebbiolo, and Syrah have gotten into the Rosé act with pleasant and sometimes remarkable results. Perhaps the most promising trend is that of dry Rhône-style Rosé, often made primarily with Grenache, as it is in the Rhône Valley. These drier examples of Rosé show a good deal more character than the phalanx of bland or neutral Chardonnays currently filling the shelves, and they can be had for a fraction of the price.

When buying Rosés, buy young. The charm and attraction of Rosé is its freshness. Clean fruit flavors and crisp balancing acidity are prized in both dry and off-dry styles. Whether dry or sweet, Rosés are best served with a chill. Dry examples such as Rosé from the south of France or new-wave U.S. versions are excellent aperitifs, showing well with lighter summer hors d'oeuvres. Unfortunately, it is difficult to know if the French Vin de Pays or U.S. Rosé you eye on the store shelf is dry or contains a bit of sweetness. An indication of residual sugar (a measure of unfermented sugar present in finished wine, usually expressed as a percentage of volume) on wine labels is becoming a more common practice, but it is far from universal. This is where the tasting notes accompanying the reviews in this book become essential. Wines with a dose of residual sugar—at least those that are balanced by corresponding acidity—can be delightful, and are excellent with a wide range of foods. Mayonnaise-based cold salads are beautifully accented by an off-dry Rosé, and spicy foods such as Thai and Mexican are brilliantly counterbalanced by the refreshing properties of such wines.

In sum, it would be a mistake to think that you have "graduated" from Rosé. Ignoring Rosé is to deprive yourself of one of the wine world's most important and versatile styles. Besides, they're just plain fun, and how many wines can you really say that about?

Reviews

French Rosé

91 • Guigal (France) 1996 Rosé, Côtes du Rhône. $10.
Bright salmon cast. Moderately full-bodied. Balanced acidity. Highly extracted. Bread dough, cream, red fruits. Outrageously aromatic, with a complex and attractive set of flavors. Ripe and full in the mouth, with a rounded, generous quality. Lengthy and flavorful through the balanced finish.

86 • Mas de Gourgonnier (France) 1997 Rosé, Les Baux de Provence. $9.
Deep reddish pink. Full-bodied. Full acidity. Highly extracted. Bread dough, red fruits, minerals. Ripe and aromatic, with a complex and hearty array of flavors. Weighty in the mouth, yet clean and angular through the finish.

〜

Great Value Rosé at a Glance

Number of Wines Reviewed:
54

Countries: Represented
7

86 • Domaine de Triennes (France) 1996 Gris de Triennes,
Vin de Pays du Var. $6.99.

Bright copper cast. Moderately full-bodied. Balanced acidity. Highly extracted. Bread dough, yeast, minerals. Pleasantly aromatic, with a gentle yeasty accent and a firm, minerally backbone. Full and dry through the finish, with considerable weight.

85 • Domaine des Beates (France) 1996 "Les Matines," Rosé,
Coteaux d'Aix en Provence. $8.99.

Bright pinkish copper cast. Moderately full-bodied. Full acidity. Highly extracted. Toast, yeast. Aromatically reserved, with a full though very firm and direct mouthfeel. Finishes on an angular note, with lengthy, yeast-accented flavors.

82 • Domaine Tempier (France) 1996 Rosé, Bandol. $12.

Pale salmon cast. Moderately full-bodied. Full acidity. Highly extracted. Minerals. Aromatically reserved, with a firm, youthful mouthfeel. Lean and austere, yet full on the palate. Interesting, but severe.

82 • Abarbanel (France) 1997 White Grenache, Vin de Pays d'Oc. $6.

Deep king salmon color. Moderately full-bodied. Full acidity. Moderately extracted. Toast, minerals. Unusual toasty aromas lead a full but crisp mouthfeel. Lean and angular through the finish.

81 • Domaine Capion (France) 1996 Rosé, Vin de Pays de L'Hérault. $6.

Pale pink. Medium-bodied. Full acidity. Highly extracted. Minerals, citrus peel. Aromatically reserved, with a firm and drying mouthfeel. Rather austere without food.

81 • Abarbanel (France) 1997 White Merlot, Vin de Pays d'Oc. $6.

Pale salmon cast. Medium-bodied. Full acidity. Moderately extracted. Minerals, orange peel, candied red fruits. Unusual aromas lead a lean, crisp mouthfeel, with a hint of richness through the finish.

U.S. Rosés

92 • Pedroncelli (CA) 1998 Vintage Selection, Zinfandel Rosé,
Sonoma County. $8.

Very deep raspberry pink. Intense, grapey, red fruit aromas. A firm entry leads a medium-bodied palate with tons of flavor and great acidity. A powerful, stylish rosé. Drink now.

90 • Wollersheim (WI) 1998 Prarie Blush, White Marechal Foch,
Wisconsin 1.8% rs. $7.50.

Pale cherry hue with a slight fade and a gentle spritz. Generous berry, herb, and toast aromas. A crisp entry leads a medium-bodied palate with lots of flavor and lean, mouth-watering acidity. Snappy, tasty finish. Very refreshing. Drink now.

90 • Thornton (CA) 1998 Collins Ranch, Grenache Rosé,
Cucamonga Valley. $9.99.

Saturated, deep raspberry pink. Attractive, forward red fruit and licorice aromas. A rich entry leads a moderately full-bodied palate with rounded acidity. Generous and quite flavorful. Drink now.

88 • Sobon (CA) 1997 Rhone Rosé, Shenandoah Valley. $9.

Brilliant pale cherry hue. Forward red fruit and mineral aromas have a lean citric edge. A firm entry leads a moderately full-bodied palate with vibrant acidity. Flavorful, intense and refreshing. Drink now.

88 • Laurel Lake (NY) NV Lake Rosé, North Fork of Long Island. $9.99.

Rich, saturated raspberry pink. Intense blackberry, citrus, and bread dough aromas. A firm entry leads a moderately full-bodied palate with crisp acids and a dry finish. Shows some southern French overtones. Drink now.

Scale: Superlative (96-100), Exceptional (90-95), Highly Recommended (85-89),
Recommended (80-84), Not Recommended (Under 80)

88 • Curtis (CA) 1997 Syrah Rosé, Santa Ynez Valley. $8.
Pale cherry red. Intense briar fruit and herb aromas jump from the glass. A fat entry leads a weighty, moderately full-bodied palate with rounded acidity. A full, rich, flavorful rosé for the table. Drink now.

87 • Swanson (CA) 1998 Rosato, Sangiovese, Napa Valley. $14.
Deep cherry red. Attractive toasty aromas show a subtle oak accent. A lush entry leads a moderately full-bodied palate with crisp acids and ripe fruit flavors. Angular, edgy finish. Drink now.

87 • Cedar Creek (WI) NV Cranberry Blush, American 2.9% rs. $7.
Saturated, pale pinkish garnet hue. Intense sweet berry aromas jump from the glass. A crisp entry leads a zesty, medium-bodied palate with great acidic cut and a touch of sweetness. Juicy, flavorful finish. Drink now.

86 • Montevina (CA) 1997 Rosato, Nebbiolo, Amador County 1.7% rs. $7.50.
Bright pink. Medium-bodied. Full acidity. Moderately extracted. Minerals, citrus, red fruits. Pleasantly aromatic, with a clean, green edge. Ripe and full in the mouth, with an uplifting finish and a hint of sweetness.

86 • Macari (NY) 1997 Rosé d'Une Nuit, North Fork of Long Island. $11.
Bright raspberry pink. Generous bread and red fruit aromas. A firm entry leads a moderately full-bodied palate with a clean, lingering finish. Rich and rounded in a dry Tavel-like style. Drink now.

85 • Yakima River (WA) 1997 Sof Lem, Lemberger, Yakima Valley. $8.49.
Pale ruby purple. Attractive spice and red fruit aromas carry a Rhône-like herbal overtone. A crisp entry leads a peppery, medium-bodied palate with a snappy, flavorful character. Soft through the finish. Drink now.

85 • Gristina (NY) 1997 Rosé of Cabernet, North Fork of Long Island. $8.99.
Rich, brilliant raspberry pink. Reserved raspberry and bread dough aromas. A firm entry leads a full-bodied palate with sharp acidity. Fruit centered, with a big bready finish. Drink now.

85 • Chateau Lafayette Reneau (NY) 1998 Pinot Noir Blanc, Finger Lakes 2.5% rs. $6.99.
Pale cherry-garnet hue with a slight spritz. Forward, pleasant berry aromas. A zesty entry leads a flavorful, medium-bodied palate. Crisp acids balance mild sweetness. Lengthy, clean, refreshing finish. Drink now.

85 • Callahan Ridge (OR) 1998 White Zinfandel, Umpqua Valley 4% rs. $7.
Brilliant pale pink. Subdued mineral and candied berry aromas. A crisp entry leads a medium-bodied palate with mild sweetness and a firm acidic cut. Tart, juicy finish. Drink now.

84 • Weinstock (CA) 1998 White Zinfandel, California 3.2% rs. $6.95.
Pale pink. Subdued berry and mineral aromas. A crisp entry leads a medium-bodied palate with sharp fruit acidity balanced by mild sweetness. Very clean and refreshing. Vibrant. Drink now.

84 • Rutherford Vintners (CA) 1997 White Zinfandel, Lodi 3.83% rs. $5.99.
Saturated raspberry pink. Generous talc and berry aromas. A lush entry leads a medium-bodied palate with good flavor intensity. Decent acid/sugar balance through the finish. Drink now.

84 • Eberle (CA) 1997 Lauridsen Vineyard, Counoise Rosé, Paso Robles. $11.
Pale cherry-garnet hue. Forward spice and berry aromas. A rich entry leads a moderately full-bodied palate with a wave of exotic, smoky fruit flavors. Acidity is on the low side, making for a big, heavy rosé. Drink now.

84 • Bel Arbor (CA) 1997 White Zinfandel, California 2.88% rs. $5.99.
Very pale pink. Subdued citrus and berry aromas. A crisp entry leads a medium-bodied palate with a nice balance between sweetness and acidity. Shows decent intensity of flavor with a lengthy finish. Drink now.

84 • Beaulieu (CA) 1997 Signet Collection, Pinot Noir Vin Gris, Carneros. $8.
Very pale russet hue. Generous strawberry and herb aromas. A lush entry leads a medium-bodied palate with supple acidity. Flavorful, stylish finish. Quite light, but showing interesting flavors. Drink now.

83 • McDowell (CA) 1997 Grenache Rosé, Mendocino. $9.
Very pale pinkish salmon hue. Subdued berry and citrus aromas. A crisp entry leads a moderately light-bodied palate with vibrant acidity. Clean, flavorful finish. Taut. Drink now.

82 • V. Sattui (CA) 1997 White Zinfandel, California. $7.75.
Saturated pinkish copper hue. Candied bubble gum and herb aromas jump from the glass. A vibrant entry leads a crisp, racy palate with spritzy acidity and moderate sweetness. Full through the finish. Drink now.

82 • Ste. Genevieve (TX) NV White Zinfandel, American 2.5% rs. $4.99.
Very pale pink. Subdued herb and berry aromas. A crisp entry leads a light-bodied palate with a clean citric edge and a hint of acidity. Drink now.

82 • Preston Premium (WA) 1998 Gamay Beaujolais Rosé, Columbia Valley 1.5% rs. $8.
Brilliant pale cherry red. Forward herb and berry aromas. A lean entry leads a crisp, medium-bodied palate with firm acidity. Taut, with a mild green undertone. Drink now.

82 • M.G .Vallejo (CA) 1997 White Zinfandel, California 3% rs. $6.
Brilliant pale pink. Aromatically subdued. A crisp entry leads a medium-bodied palate with attractive berry flavors and moderate sweetness. Simple, but tasty. Drink now.

82 • Forest Ville (CA) 1998 White Merlot, California 3.7% rs. $5.99.
Brilliant pale pink. Subdued candied berry and talc aromas. A soft entry leads a sweet, medium-bodied palate. Lean acidity buoys the finish. Straightforward. Drink now.

81 • Windsor (CA) 1998 Rosé du Soleil, California. $12.
Pale salmon hue. Subdued herb and mineral aromas. A taut entry leads a lean, medium-bodied palate with a drying finish. Rather rustic and firm. Drink now.

81 • Santino (CA) 1997 White Harvest Zinfandel, Shenandoah Valley 2.39% rs. $4.95.
Pale pinkish copper hue. Unusual herb and rhubarb aromas. A crisp entry leads a flavorful, medium-bodied palate with marked sweetness and tart acidity. A bit off-center, but interesting. Drink now.

81 • Forest Ville (CA) 1997 White Zinfandel, California 3.79% rs. $4.99.
Very pale pinkish copper hue. Aromatically subdued. A crisp entry leads a lean, medium bodied-palate. Mild sweetness is offset by brisk acidity through the finish. Drink now.

81 • Beringer (CA) 1998 White Zinfandel, California 3.4% rs. $6.
Pale pink. Generous candied berry aromas. A ripe entry leads a medium-bodied palate with moderate sweetness offset by crisp acidity. Shows some richness. Commercial but tasty. Drink now.

80 • Van Roekel (Ca) 1997 Rosé of Syrah, Temecula 2.05% rs. $9.95.
Pale cherry hue with a slight fade. Unusual berry aromas have a very spicy overtone. A crisp entry leads a medium-bodied palate with a touch of sweetness and lots of acidity. Taut, herbal finish. Drink now.

80 • V. Sattui (CA) 1997 Gamay Rouge, California 1.5% rs. $13.75.
Very pale cherry-garnet hue. Unusual sweet tart and plum aromas. A crisp entry leads a medium-bodied palate with marked sweetness and tart acidity. Lean, pithy, phenolic finish. Drink now.

80 • Montpellier (CA) 1997 White Zinfandel, California 3.75% rs. $5.99.
Pale pinkish copper hue. Unusual herb and berry aromas. A soft entry leads a sweet, flat, medium-bodied palate. Turns lean on the finish, with some grip. Drink now.

80 • Mirassou (CA) 1998 Family Selection, White Zinfandel, California 2.19% rs. $6.95.
Very pale pink. Subdued mineral and talc aromas. A lean entry leads a moderately light-bodied, herbal palate. Lean, clean finish. Drink now.

80 • Marcus James (CA) NV Special Reserve, White Zinfandel 3.2% rs. $6.99.
Saturated pinkish copper hue. Muted earthy aromas. A crisp entry leads a medium-bodied palate with moderate sweetness balanced by crisp acidity. Very simple, but refreshing. Drink now.

80 • Lenz (NY) 1996 Blanc de Noir, North Fork of Long Island. $7.99.
Pale onion-skin hue. Herb and mineral aromas carry an unusual overtone. A firm entry leads a medium-bodied palate. Dry, flat finish. Drink now.

80 • Herzog (CA) 1998 Baron Herzog, White Zinfandel, California 2.1% rs. $6.95.
Pale pink. Restrained, lean aromas show a hint of sulfur that blows off with aeration. A crisp entry leads a moderately light-bodied palate with a hint of sweetness balanced by sharp acidity. Clean, but not overly flavorful. Drink now.

80 • Fetzer (CA) 1997 White Zinfandel, California 2.88% rs. $5.99.
Very pale pink. Aromatically subdued. A crisp entry leads a medium-bodied palate with mild sweetness and zesty acidity. Not overly flavorful, but clean. Drink now.

80 • Estrella (CA) 1998 White Zinfandel, California 3.74% rs. $4.99.
Saturated pinkish copper hue. Subdued berry aromas have a medicinal undertone. A rich entry leads a crisp, medium-bodied palate with marked sweetness. Refreshing finish. Drink now.

80 • Dunnewood (CA) 1997 White Zinfandel, California 1.6% rs. $5.99.
Very pale copper hue. Unusual candied berry aromas. A crisp entry leads a simple palate with a hint of sweetness and vibrant acidity. Clean finish. Drink now.

80 • Barefoot (CA) NV White Zinfandel, California 2.8% rs. $3.99.
Very pale pinkish copper hue. Lean herb and berry aromas. A crisp entry leads a medium-bodied palate with tart acidity and moderate sweetness. Simple but balanced. Drink now.

Other Great Value Rosé

86 • Jackson-Triggs (Canada) 1997 Proprietors' Reserve Blanc de Noir, Okanagan Valley 1.15% rs. $6.46.
Brilliant raspberry-pink hue. Clean berry and mineral aromas. A crisp attack leads to a moderately light-bodied palate with zesty acidity. Sharp flavorful finish. A stylish dry rosé. Drink now.

84 • Valdemar (Spain) 1997 Vino Rosado, Rioja. $8.
Pale pinkish red. Medium-bodied. Balanced acidity. Moderately extracted. Cherry skins, minerals. Cherry skin aromas lead a rounded mouthfeel, showing cherrylike fruit flavors that finish in a dry manner.

84 • Charles Melton (Australia) 1997 Rosé of Virginia, Barossa Valley. $12.
Brilliant pale ruby-purple hue. Medium-bodied. Full acidity. Moderately extracted. Red fruits, minerals. Bright, cheerful aromas lead a crisp and zesty palate feel. Shows rather substantial flavors on a lighter frame.

83 • Mastroberardino (Italy) 1995 Lacrimarosa, Dry Rosé, Irpinia. $14.99.
Bright orange. Medium-bodied. Balanced acidity. Moderately extracted. Butter, minerals. Austere in fruit flavors, but rounded, with a buttery mouthfeel. Burned butter flavors come through on the finish.

82 • Carmel (Israel) 1997 White Zinfandel, Samson. $5.

Bright pink. Moderately light-bodied. Balanced acidity. Subtly extracted. Cream, red fruits. Pleasantly aromatic with a subtle lactic note. Well balanced and flavorful on the palate, with a touch of fruit and the slightest hint of sweetness on the finish.

80 • Marques de Caceres (Spain) 1997 Dry Rosé, Rioja. $6.99.

Pale orange-red. Medium-bodied. Full acidity. Moderately extracted. Minerals. Austere, minerally aromas follow through to a dry, minerally palate. An austere style of rosé.

ten

Cabernet Sauvignon

Introduction   116
Reviews   118
  Aussie Cabernets   118
  French Cabernets   119
  South American Cabernets   120
  U.S. Cabernets   122
  Other Great Value
  Cabernets   126

Introduction: Cabernet Sauvignon

Cabernet Sauvignon is the undeniable master of all red wine grapes. No other red variety enjoys its popularity or success. Cabernet is cultivated and produced around the globe. From its native France to North America, South America, South Africa, Australia, and even Lebanon, wines made from Cabernet Sauvignon are often among that nation's very best. In the United States, Cabernet Sauvignon is so popular that it has become synonymous with red wine. Just try ordering a "glass of red" in any bar or restaurant—chances are you'll get Cabernet Sauvignon. Perhaps the most remarkable factor when considering this variety's popularity is that Cabernet Sauvignon is no lightweight. It can even be downright tough in youth. Even the softest and tamest examples of Cabernet are flavorful and distinctive. People in the industry like to call it "varietal character." What is Cabernet Sauvignon's varietal character? Full-bodied, with firm tannins and elegant, often minerally, black currant flavors.

Bargain Cabernet Sauvignon is easy to find because it is so widely produced. As with any popular variety, there are value hot spots and restrictions. In the variety's native Bordeaux, Cabernet Sauvignon is most often blended with other grapes and named for the estate (Chateau) that produces the wine. These wines can be expensive, and are among the finest in the world. Values do exist elsewhere in France, however, as the Vin de Pays designation comes to the rescue once again, offering quality varietally named wines at reasonable prices, usually less than $10 a bottle. The vast sea of Cabernet Sauvignon produced in the United States also offers many values. The same can be said of Australia, where Cabernet Sauvignon takes a backseat to the mighty Shiraz. One of the most reliable providers of value Cabernet Sauvignon is South America, particularly Chile. In recent years some wines have crept above the value zone, some to ridiculous levels, but the majority are still priced to please.

Regions

Finding value Cabernet Sauvignon in the United States is an easy task, as wineries across the nation compete aggressively in the lucrative "fighting varietal" market. As with many of the top varietals, value Cabernet Sauvignon can be found from nearly every wine producing state. Washington is a major player, as that state's most charmed variety is Merlot, which results in many undervalued Cabernets. Eastern states such as New York and Virginia provide Cabernet Sauvignon in virtually every segment of the market, including value wines. In terms of sheer numbers, California still leads the pack. The prestige districts of the Napa Valley are most definitely out-of-bounds for bargain seekers. California Cabernet Sauvignon priced at $15 or less is most often labeled with a broad "California" designation. Value seekers should not assume that these broadly named wines are second rate. While it is difficult to get California's very best for less than $15, it is an absolute certitude that many inexpensive Cabernet Sauvignons are as good as or better than some wines costing three to four times as much. When it comes to California Cabernet prices, image is everything.

South America is a virtual one-stop shopping center for those seeking inexpensive varietal wines. Among the familiar varieties, Cabernet Sauvignon has always been the most consistent and sought after wine. Traditionally, red wines were aged for long periods in old oak barrels, in the manner of Spanish wines. This

Scale: Superlative (96-100), Exceptional (90-95), Highly Recommended (85-89), Recommended (80-84), Not Recommended (Under 80)

gave the wines a soft, mellow character. Styles are on the move, however, as wineries retool to meet the demands of a new century. Tremendous foreign investment and involvement fuel much of the change. Chile is now a "who's who" of California and European winemakers who jump south across the equator while their vineyards lie dormant through the winter months. As a result of these flying winemakers, one is now more likely to find Cabernet in a technically correct, fruit-forward, accessible, and thoroughly international style. With such diverse talent and know-how mingling about with the many capable Chilean winemakers, questions of stylistic direction for the future remain unanswered. All that can be sure is that Chile's fabulous wine prices won't last forever. When buying value South American Cabernet Sauvignon, vintage is generally of little concern.

Australia's Cabernet Sauvignon has much in common with its counterparts in California. Styles run the gamut from grapey "session" wines to complex and sophisticated vintages worthy of cellaring. Regardless of style, Australian Cabernet Sauvignon is invariably luscious and inviting in its youth. Oz Cabs are uniquely styled with sweet vanilla flavors—often imparted by American Oak—and herbal notes that tend toward eucalyptus rather than the mint and cedar nuances more commonly experienced in French and California Cabernet. Echoing California, bargains are to be found in wines with broad designations such as South Australia or South Eastern Australia.

When buying value Cabernet Sauvignon you can reasonably assume that the wine you select will be ready to drink. Most of the heavily extracted and tannic, age-worthy wines can be quite expensive. Food pairings with Cabernet Sauvignon are endless. Steaks are good, but lamb or duck can be even better. Hard cheeses also work well, especially powerfully flavored examples such as Parmigiano Reggiano.

It is a safe bet that Cabernet Sauvignon will be the hottest red wine for many years to come. If you're stuck on Cabs, be sure to diversify by adding wines from several regions and nations to your shopping list.

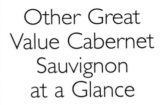

Other Great Value Cabernet Sauvignon at a Glance

Number of Wines Recommended:

107

Countries Represented:

13

Reviews

Aussie Cabernets

92 • *Hill of Content (Australia) 1996 Cabernet Sauvignon, McLaren Vale. $12.99.*

Deep blackish ruby cast. Moderately full-bodied. Balanced acidity. Moderately extracted. Moderately oaked. Moderately tannic. Cedar, chocolate, black fruits. Ripe, rich, and lush with an attractive spicy wood accent and a ripe core of fruit flavors that persist through the lingering, supple finish.

90 • *Lindemans (Australia) 1996 Special Selection, Cabernet Sauvignon, Coonawarra. $15.*

Opaque blackish purple cast. Full-bodied. Balanced acidity. Highly extracted. Heavily oaked. Quite tannic. Vanilla, briar fruits. A showy style with big, extracted color, flavor, and texture accented by a hefty dose of new oak. Packed and youthful, with tannic grip. Has the balance to take needed long-term cellaring.

89 • *Wolf Blass (Australia) 1997 Yellow Label, Cabernet Sauvignon, South Australia. $11.99.*

Deep ruby cast. Medium-bodied. Balanced acidity. Moderately extracted. Mildly oaked. Mildly tannic. Red fruits, brown spices, minerals. Generous aromas show an attractive spicy accent. Well balanced and well structured with a lean edge to the firm, flavorful finish.

86 • *Yalumba (Australia) 1996 Cabernet Sauvignon, South Australia. $15.*

Bright ruby red. Medium-bodied. Balanced acidity. Moderately extracted. Mildly oaked. Mildly tannic. Red fruits, dill pickle. Crisp and aromatic with a bright fruity quality in the mouth. Straightforward and lively through the finish.

86 • *Wynns (Australia) 1995 Cabernet Sauvignon, Coonawarra. $14.*

Opaque blackish ruby hue. Moderately full-bodied. Balanced acidity. Moderately extracted. Mildly tannic. Cassis, minerals, chocolate. Aromatically reserved, though rich and flavorful in the mouth with a focused dark fruit character. A lush, supple style.

86 • *McGuigan (Australia) 1998 Oak Aged, Bin 4000, Cabernet Sauvignon, South Eastern Australia. $12.*

Bright purple. Moderately light-bodied. Balanced acidity. Moderately extracted. Mildly tannic. Black fruits. Forward grapey aromas are effusive. A straightforward, generous quaffing style with a bright fruity center. Drinking well now.

86 • *Lindemans (Australia) 1997 Bin 45, Cabernet Sauvignon, South Eastern Australia. $9.*

Bright ruby cast. Medium-bodied. Balanced acidity. Moderately extracted. Mildly tannic. Black fruits, minerals. An austere, compact style that is rather reserved aromatically. Firm and dense through the finish with a solid, chewy midpalate.

86 • *Jacob's Creek (Australia) 1997 Cabernet Sauvignon, South Eastern Australia. $8.99.*

Bright ruby cast. Medium-bodied. Balanced acidity. Moderately extracted. Moderately oaked. Mildly tannic. Sweet herbs, red fruits, brown spices. Generous aromas carry a spicy, herbal tinge that adds a degree of complexity. Ripe and supple through the finish.

86 • *David Wynn (Australia) 1996 Cabernet Sauvignon, Eden Valley. $15.*

Deep blackish ruby cast. Moderately full-bodied. Balanced acidity. Moderately extracted. Moderately oaked. Mildly tannic. Chocolate, minerals, black fruits. Aromatically reserved, with a full palate feel showing ripe fruit flavors and velvety chocolatey notes that turn firm through the finish.

Scale: Superlative (96-100), Exceptional (90-95), Highly Recommended (85-89), Recommended (80-84), Not Recommended (Under 80)

85 • Seaview (Australia) 1996 Cabernet Sauvignon, South Australia. $10.
Opaque blackish ruby hue. Full-bodied. Balanced acidity. Highly extracted. Moderately tannic. Minerals, licorice, black fruit. Aromatically reserved, with a big, rich, chunky mouthfeel. Thick and intense through the finish, but rather unyielding due to big firm tannins.

84 • Wyndham (Australia) 1996 Bin 444, Cabernet Sauvignon, South Eastern Australia. $9.99.
Deep ruby hue. Medium-bodied. Balanced acidity. Moderately extracted. Mildly oaked. Mildly tannic. Cassis, minerals, chocolate. Firm and complex in flavor with a deep core of dark fruit flavors and a spicy herbal accent. Aromatic and generous through the finish.

84 • Seppelt (Australia) 1996 Black Label, Terrain Series, Cabernet Sauvignon, South Eastern Australia. $10.
Very dark ruby cast. Moderately full-bodied. Balanced acidity. Highly extracted. Moderately tannic. Black cherries, minerals. Generous aromas lead a concentrated, fruit-driven palate. Ripe and tasty through the finish with soft, lingering tannins.

83 • Marienberg (Australia) 1995 Reserve, Cabernet Sauvignon, South Australia. $12.
Bright ruby-garnet hue. Medium-bodied. Balanced acidity. Moderately extracted. Moderately oaked. Mildly tannic. Brown spices, red fruits, minerals. Crisp and racy in style, though showing no lack of substance. Finishes on a deep minerally note.

83 • Callara (Australia) 1996 Reserve Bin, Cabernet Sauvignon, South Eastern Australia. $7.
Bright ruby cast. Medium-bodied. Balanced acidity. Moderately extracted. Mildly oaked. Mildly tannic. Mint, red fruits, chocolate. Forward aromas carry a high-toned minty accent. Ripe and generous with a lean quality to the structure.

French Cabernets

88 • Michel Lynch (France) 1997 Cabernet Sauvignon, Bordeaux. $8.99.
Bright ruby purple cast. Medium-bodied. Balanced acidity. Moderately extracted. Mildly tannic. Dried herbs, minerals. Forward aromas show a distinctive herbal edge. Rounded and generous with some grip to the finish.

86 • Vichon (France) 1996 Mediterraean, Cabernet Sauvignon, Vin de Pays d'Oc. $10.
Bright ruby hue with a slight fade. Medium-bodied. Full acidity. Moderately extracted. Mildly tannic. Minerals, red fruits. Forward aromas lead a lighter-styled, angular mouthfeel. Crisp and lean, yet flavorful, with excellent grip through the finish.

84 • Gallerie (France) 1995 Cabernet Sauvignon, Vin de Pays de L'Hérault. $6.99.
Bright ruby cast. Medium-bodied. Full acidity. Moderately extracted. Mildly tannic. Red fruits, mint. High-toned, fruit-centered aromas lead a lean and crisp mouthfeel. Vibrant and linear, with a finish that has some grip.

84 • Domaine de Triennes (France) 1995 Cabernet Sauvignon, Vin de Pays du Var. $9.99.
Deep blackish ruby cast. Moderately full-bodied. Balanced acidity. Highly extracted. Mildly tannic. Minerals, licorice, black fruits. Aromatically reserved, with a lean, firmly structured, Bordeaux-like quality. Firm through the finish, with angular acidity. Should work well with food.

82 • Michel Picard (France) 1996 Cabernet Sauvignon, Languedoc-Roussillon, Vin de Pays. $9.99.
Deep ruby with a slight fade. Medium-bodied. Balanced acidity. Moderately extracted. Mildly tannic. Dried herbs, red fruits, wood. Unusual earthy aromatics lead a lighter-styled mouthfeel. Crisp, linear finish.

82 • La Baume (France) 1995 Cabernet Sauvignon,
Vin de Pays d'Oc. $6.99.

Deep ruby cast. Moderately full-bodied. Balanced acidity. Highly extracted. Mildly tannic. Cassis, minerals, herbs. A fruit-centered style, with deep flavors and a lean texture. Mildly green finish.

82 • Jenard (France) 1996 Caves des Papes, Cabernet Sauvignon,
Vin de Pays d'Oc. $7.99.

Bright pale ruby cast. Medium-bodied. Balanced acidity. Moderately extracted. Mildly tannic. Minerals, dried herbs. Aromatically reserved, with a firm and austere mouthfeel. Finishes on a lean, minerally note.

South American Cabernets

89 • La Playa (Chile) 1996 Cabernet Sauvignon, Maipo Valley. $6.99.

Deep, saturated ruby red with purple highlights. Forward wood spice, black fruit, and mineral aromas. A lush entry leads a medium-bodied palate with ripe, rounded tannins. Flavorful, generous finish. Drink now.

88 • Veramonte (Chile) 1997 Cabernet Sauvignon, Alto de Casablanca. $10.

Deep, saturated ruby red. Forward black fruit and spice aromas carry a hefty wood accent. A lush entry leads a medium-bodied palate that shows firm tannins. Ripe, rounded finish. Drink now.

88 • Los Vascos (Chile) 1997 Cabernet Sauvignon, Colchagua. $8.99.

Bright ruby purple. Complex mineral, lead pencil, and red fruit aromas. A lean entry leads a firm, medium-bodied palate with lean tannins. Structured, flavorful finish. Drink now or later.

88 • La Palma (Chile) 1997 Cabernet Sauvignon, Rapel Valley. $7.

Deep ruby hue. Aromatically subdued with ripe black fruit overtones. A lush entry is followed by a moderately full-bodied palate with ripe, rounded tannins. Chewy, flavorful finish. Drink now.

86 • Undurraga (Chile) 1997 Cabernet Sauvignon, Colchagua Valley. $7.99.

Bright ruby red. Forward grapey, red fruit aromas. A lush entry leads a medium-bodied palate with ripe, fruit-centered flavors and supple tannins. The finish is ripe and rounded. A stylish quaffer. Drink now.

86 • Trumpeter (Argentina) 1996 Cabernet Sauvignon, Maipu. $10.

Bright ruby red. Forward dill pickle and spice aromas show a strong oak influence. A lush entry leads a medium-bodied palate with soft tannins. The finish is flavorful and harmonious. Well balanced with a stylish mouthfeel. Drink now.

86 • La Palma (Chile) 1997 Reserve, Cabernet Sauvignon, Rapel. $11.

Deep, saturated ruby hue. Generous red fruit and brown spice aromas show a big oak accent. A lush attack leads a medium-bodied palate with supple tannins. Rounded, flavorful finish. Drink now.

86 • Cousiño Macul (Chile) 1996 Antiguas Reservas, Cabernet Sauvignon,
Valle del Maipo. $14.

Bright cherry red with a slight fade. Forward cedar, red fruit, and mineral aromas. A lean entry leads a medium-bodied palate with firm tannins and some grip. Complex, flavorful finish. Very stylish in an unusual rustic way. Drink now.

86 • Concha y Toro (Chile) 1997 Casillero del Diablo, Cabernet Sauvignon,
Maipo Valley. $10.

Bright ruby hue. Generous red fruit and mineral aromas. A lush entry leads a medium-bodied palate with velvety tannins. Shows complexity and fruit persistence through the finish. Stylish. Drink now.

86 • Casa Lapostolle (Chile) 1996 Cabernet Sauvignon, Rapel Valley. $10.

Bright ruby hue. Generous overripe red fruit, spice, and plum aromas. A lush entry leads a very ripe, medium-bodied palate with subtle tannins. Delicate, flavorful finish. Drink now.

Scale: Superlative (96-100), Exceptional (90-95), Highly Recommended (85-89), Recommended (80-84), Not Recommended (Under 80)

85 • *Trapiche (Argentina) 1995 Oak Cask, Cabernet Sauvignon, Mendoza. $8.99.*
Deep ruby red. Generous spice and mineral aromas show a hefty oak accent. A lush entry leads a moderately full-bodied palate with lean, firm tannins that carry through the finish. Drink now.

84 • *Santa Ema (Chile) 1995 Reserve, Cabernet Sauvignon, Maipo Valley. $12.*
Bright ruby with with subtle purple highlights. Quite aromatic with oaky accents. A spicy entry leads a medium-bodied palate with good cassis flavors and vanilla notes coming through on the finish. Has a note of tannic grip, though it is drinking well now.

84 • *Santa Amelia (Chile) 1997 Reserve Selection, Cabernet Sauvignon, Maule Valley. $7.50.*
Deep ruby purple. Forward grapey aromas show a touch of overripeness and a gentle wood accent. A lush entry leads a medium-bodied palate with firm tannins. Structured, flavorful finish. Drink now.

84 • *Pionero (Chile) 1998 Cabernet Sauvignon, Central Valley. $7.*
Bright purple. Muted aromas carry gentle red fruit and herb undertones. A firm entry leads a moderately light-bodied palate. Tannins have some grip. The finish is fruity and straightforward. A quaffer. Drink now.

84 • *La Playa (Chile) 1995 Estate Reserve, Cabernet Sauvignon, Maipo Valley. $9.99.*
Deep ruby hue. Forward anise and spice aromas show a big woody influence. A lush entry leads a medium-bodied palate with firm tannins. Fades toward the finish. Drink now.

84 • *Caliterra (Chile) 1996 Cabernet Sauvignon, Valle Central. $8.99.*
Bright garnet hue with a slight fade. Forward brown spice and mineral aromas. A lean entry leads a medium-bodied palate with firm tannins that have some grip. Intense, flavorful finish. Drink now.

84 • *Calina (Chile) 1997 Valle del Rapel, Cabernet Sauvignon, Chile. $9.*
Deep, saturated ruby purple. Subdued black fruit and mineral aromas. A firm attack leads a full-bodied palate with big chewy tannins. Rich, weighty finish. Though it shows good fruit intensity, it is just a touch monolithic. Drink now or later.

83 • *Viña Santa Carolina (Chile) 1996 Reserva, Cabernet Sauvignon, Maipo Valley. $9.*
Pale cherry red. Forward herb and mineral aromas. A lush entry is followed by a light-bodied palate with lean tannins that show some grip. Subdued finish. A straightforward quaffer. Drink now.

83 • *Santa Julia (Argentina) 1996 Oak Reserve, Cabernet Sauvignon, Mendoza. $10.*
Fading garnet-ruby hue. Mature aromas of brown spice and dusty red fruits. A lean attack leads a medium-bodied palate with mature, austere flavors. The acids are crisp through the finish, with mild, dry tannins giving some grip. Drink now.

83 • *Santa Amelia (Chile) 1997 Cabernet Sauvignon, Maule Valley. $6.50.*
Bright ruby hue. Forward herb, red fruit, and mineral aromas. A lean entry leads a light-bodied palate with mildly astringent tannins. Clipped, clean finish. Drink now.

82 • *Doña Consuelo (Chile) 1997 Reserve, Viña Segú Ollé, Cabernet Sauvignon, Maule Valley. $10.*
Bright purple. Subdued red fruit and mineral aromas. A lush entry leads a medium-bodied palate with lean tannins that have grip. Ripe, edgy finish. Drink now.

81 • *Viña Tarapaca (Chile) 1996 Reserva, Cabernet Sauvignon, Maipo Valley. $11.*
Bright garnet hue with a fading rim. Intense, unusual herb and mineral aromas. A lush attack leads a medium-bodied palate with ripe flavors and subtle tannins. Lacks somewhat in structure through the finish. Drink now.

81 • Undurraga (Chile) 1995 Reserva, Cabernet Sauvignon,
Maipo Valley. $11.99.
Bright garnet hue. Mature forest, spice, and earth aromas carry a big oak accent.
A lush entry leads a medium-bodied palate with grainy tannins. Woody, mature finish.
Drink now.

81 • Trapiche (Argentina) 1996 Fond de Cave, Cabernet Sauvignon,
Mendoza. $14.99.
Deep ruby hue. Mellow spicy aromas carry a gentle wood accent. A lush entry is followed
by a medium-bodied palate with firm tannins. Ripe but structured finish. Drink now.

80 • Santa Monica (Chile) 1996 Cabernet Sauvignon, Rapel Valley. $7.99.
Bright garnet with a fading rim. Forward spice and wood aromas show maturity and
a hefty wood accent. A lean entry is followed by a medium-bodied palate with firm
tannins. Fades toward the finish. Lacks depth. Drink now.

U.S. Cabernets

89 • Stone Creek (CA) 1995 Cabernet Sauvignon, California. $6.89.
Bright cherry red. Medium-bodied. Subtly extracted. Mildly tannic. Berry fruits, vanilla.
Jammy, ripe aromas lead soft fruity flavors, with a very ripe accent and quick finish. An
open-knit style, this is soft and easy-drinking, and will be best in its youth.

89 • Ste. Chapelle (ID) 1995 Cabernet Sauvignon, Washington. $8.
Brick red. Medium-bodied. Moderately extracted. Moderately oaked. Moderately tannic.
Candied red fruits, vanilla. Lean and taut, with elegant fruit flavors and drying tannins.
A tougher style that is not built for cellaring. Will show best with food.

89 • Osprey's Dominion (NY) 1995 Cabernet Sauvignon,
North Fork of Long Island. $13.99.
Deep, saturated ruby red. Generous dried herb, mineral, and cassis aromas show mild
oak influences. A soft entry leads a moderately full-bodied, supple palate with velvety tannins. Varietal character with fine length. Drink now.

89 • Napa Ridge (CA) 1996 Cabernet Sauvignon, Central Coast. $10.
Bright crimson red hue. Generous aromas show black cherry fruit and sweet oak accents.
A flavorful, fruity entry leads a medium-bodied palate with fleshy, ripe fruit flavors and
rounded tannins. Finishes with lingering fruit persistence and well-integrated oak flavors.
Drink now or later.

89 • Frey (CA) 1997 Butow Vineyards, Cabernet Sauvignon,
Redwood Valley. $10.50.
Bright purple red hue. Intense black fruit and vanilla aromas show a sweet oak accent.
A ripe attack leads to a moderately full-bodied palate with juicy acidity and lush tannins.
Flavorful, lengthy finish. Shows excellent cut and integration. Well balanced and stylish.
Drink now or later.

89 • Cloninger (CA) 1996 Quinn Vineyard, Cabernet Sauvignon,
Carmel Valley. $14.
Opaque violet red. Moderately full-bodied. Moderately extracted. Moderately oaked.
Mildly tannic. Dill, menthol, black fruits. Strong, oak-accented aromas lead a crisp
mouthful of tart fruit flavors, with spice emerging on the finish. Tannins are marginal.

89 • Casa Larga (NY) 1995 Cabernet Sauvignon, Finger Lakes. $13.99.
Saturated red-purple. Moderately full-bodied. Highly extracted. Quite tannic. Ripe
cherries, mineral, brown spice. Hints of overripe black fruits lead a firm palate of black
fruit flavors with strong oak influences apparent. Hard-edged tannins clamp down
on the finish.

88 • *Seven Peaks (CA) 1996 Cabernet Sauvignon, Central Coast. $11.*
Saturated violet-purple hue. Very rich aromas show a ripe cassis and toasted oak accent. A rich entry leads a full-bodied palate with fleshy flavors with significant new oak character. Very youthful and structured, with dry gripping tannins clamping on the finish. Drink now or later.

88 • *Pedroncelli (CA) 1996 Three Vineyards, Cabernet Sauvignon, Dry Creek Valley. $12.*
Bright red-purple. Medium-bodied. Highly extracted. Moderately tannic. Mineral and red fruit aromas lead a dry palate, with fine-grained tannins showing on the finish. Youthful, vibrant style.

88 • *Mystic Cliffs (CA) 1995 Cabernet Sauvignon, California. $6.99.*
Bright cherry red. Medium-bodied. Moderately extracted. Mildly tannic. Toasted oak, vanilla, red fruits. Bright, fruity nose leads a juicy, open-knit palate with a hint of oak spice and astringency on the finish.

88 • *Columbia Winery (WA) 1995 Reserve, Cabernet Sauvignon, Yakima Valley. $15.*
Deep ruby-violet hue with a subtle fade. Richly fruited aromas show classic cassis notes with generous oak accents. A rich entry leads a full-bodied palate with chewy fruit flavors and chunky, rich tannins. This is a very big wines with plenty of stuffing through a long flavorful finish. Drink within five years.

88 • *Bogle (CA) 1997 Cabernet Sauvignon, California. $10.*
Saturated purple hue. Generous cassis and vanilla aromas with a judicious oak accent. A supple attack leads to a moderately full-bodied palate with lush tannins on the finish. Very fruit centered and well structured. Drink now or later.

87 • *Monterra (CA) 1996 Promise, Cabernet Sauvignon, Monterey County. $9.99.*
Deep purple-red hue. Generous black fruit and vanilla aromas show a judicious oak component. A lush attack leads to a medium-bodied palate with soft, velvety tannins. Supple, harmonious finish. Rather shy of acidity, but very tasty in the near term. Drink now.

87 • *Gallo Sonoma (CA) 1994 Cabernet Sauvignon, Sonoma County. $12.*
Deep garnet hue. Generous cedar and brown spice aromas show a mellow oak accent. A rich entry leads to a full-bodied palate with silky tannins and excellent acidic structure. Firm, flavorful finish. A harmonious and very elegant wine. Drink now or later.

87 • *Fetzer (CA) 1995 Barrel Select, Cabernet Sauvignon, North Coast. $14.99.*
Saturated dark ruby hue. Elegant aromas of lavish oak and rich cassis and plum. A lush entry leads to a moderately full-bodied palate with velvety, abundant tannins and sweet cedary oak flavors that persist through the finish. Very supple and mouthfilling. Drink now.

87 • *E.B. Foote (WA) 1995 Cabernet Sauvignon, Columbia Valley. $15.*
Brick-ruby red. Medium-bodied. Moderately extracted. Moderately tannic. Black pepper, dried herbs, black fruits. Jammy, herbal aromas lead a thick mouthfeel, with mineral and herb flavors persisting.

87 • *Dunnewood (CA) 1994 Dry Silk, Cabernet Sauvignon, Napa Valley. $9.99.*
Brilliant violet-red hue. Generously aromatic with a spicy, pickle note and well-defined crisp fruits. A bright entry leads to a medium-bodied palate with sensational bright acids and deep black cherry flavors that finish cleanly with a lingering note of oak subtlety. Solid, in a more reserved, classical style. Drink now or later.

87 • *Arbor Crest (WA) 1995 Cameo Reserve, Cabernet Sauvignon, Washington. $13.*
Blood red with violet highlights. Moderately full-bodied. Highly extracted. Moderately tannic. Dried herbs, red fruits. Subtle, mildly herbal aromas lead a gently fruity palate. A lean style with mild tannins showing on the finish.

86 • Washington Hills (WA) 1995 Cabernet Sauvignon, Columbia Valley. $9.99.
Cherry-brick red with a slight fade on the rim. Medium-bodied. Moderately extracted. Moderately tannic. Berry fruits, minerals. Bright and juicy aromas follow through on the palate, with a fruit-forward entry that builds through the midpalate. Drier mineral and spice notes persist on the finish.

86 • W.B. Bridgman (WA) 1996 Cabernet Sauvignon, Columbia Valley. $14.
Brick red with a fading rim. Aromatically reserved with tertiary, mature character. A lean entry leads a moderately full-bodied palate with muted fruit flavors and tart acidity. Drink now.

86 • Ste. Chapelle (ID) 1995 Sagemoor's Dionysus Vineyard, Cabernet Sauvignon, Washington. $12.99.
Deep brick red. Medium-bodied. Moderately extracted. Moderately tannic. Black tea, earth, coconut. Dry and austere, this features drying tannins through the finish, with much primary fruit sensation.

86 • Shenandoah Vineyards (CA) 1996 Cabernet Sauvignon, Amador County. $11.95.
Deep ruby-red hue to the rim. Generous brown spice, licorice, and black fruit aromas show a hefty oak accent. A firm entry leads to a moderately full-bodied mouthfeel with big grippy tannins and shy acidity. Big, tannic finish. A flashy style, but without the acidity to age well for the long term. Drink within five years.

86 • Sea Ridge Coastal (CA) 1995 Cabernet Sauvignon, California. $10.
Saturated purple-red hue. Vibrant fruity, cassis aromas with judicious vanilla oak notes. A crisp entry leads to a moderately full-bodied palate with bright fruit-centered character and grainy, gripping tannins. Well structured and varietally expressive.

86 • Powers (WA) 1996 Cabernet Sauvignon, Washington. $12.
Medium dark violet red. Medium-bodied. Moderately extracted. Moderately tannic. Cassis, mineral. Fleshy, black fruit aromas. Wonderfully wrought, with plump fruit flavors and generous, fine-grained tannins that do not mask the pleasure.

86 • Pesenti (CA) 1996 Cabernet Sauvignon, Paso Robles. $15.
Deep ruby-purple hue. Moderate aromas show a sweet oak accent and ripe berry fruits. A fruity entry leads a medium-bodied palate with broad cherry fruit flavors and soft tannins lingering on the finish. Generously fruity with some underlying structure. Drink now.

86 • Pedroncelli (CA) 1995 Morris Fay Vineyard, Cabernet Sauvignon, Alexander Valley. $13.
Bright ruby cast. Medium-bodied. Balanced acidity. Moderately extracted. Mildly tannic. Minerals, dried herbs. Lighter in style, with a slight herbal character. Lean flavors linger through the finish.

86 • Paul Thomas (WA) 1995 Reserve, Cabernet Sauvignon, Washington. $14.99.
Bright violet-ruby color. Medium-bodied. Moderately extracted. Mildly tannic. Red fruits, minerals, dried herbs. Well balanced, with bright, juicy acids and supple yet dry tannins lingering on the finish.

86 • Parducci (CA) 1996 Vineyard Select, Cabernet Sauvignon, North Coast. $10.
Bright purple-red hue. Attractive toasted oak and cassis aromas. A smooth entry leads to a moderately full-bodied palate with lively, bright fruit flavors and very fine grippy tannins on the finish. Well balanced and flavorsome. Drink now or later.

86 • Oakencroft (VA) 1995 Cabernet Sauvignon, Monticello. $14.
Deep ruby red with a brightening rim. Medium-bodied. Moderately extracted. Mildly tannic. Red fruits, brown spices, peanut. Spicy, aromatic nose leads an elegant palate with a cedary, minerally profile and juicy acids. Mature claret style.

86 • *Naked Mountain (VA) 1996 Cabernet Sauvignon, Virginia. $15.*
Dark ruby with a subtle fade on the rim. Medium-bodied. Moderately extracted. Moderately oaked. Mildly tannic. Vanilla, brown spice, black fruits. Rounded, soft, sweet fruit-centered palate with a cedary, spicy overlay. Mineral dryness emerges on the finish. Well balanced, and drinking well now.

86 • *Monthaven (CA) 1995 Cabernet Sauvignon, Napa Valley. $9.99.*
Blood red. Medium-bodied. Moderately extracted. Moderately tannic. Black fruits, earth. Reserved aromas lead a chunky, broad palate of flavors with powdery tannins. Pleasantly rustic, with a spicy finish.

86 • *Meridian (CA) 1995 Cabernet Sauvignon, California. $12.*
Bright ruby red to the rim. Moderately full-bodied. Balanced acidity. Moderately extracted. Moderately oaked. Mildly tannic. Cedar, red fruits. Pleasantly aromatic, with a well-integrated oak accent and a core of ripe fruit flavors. Understated, elegant and well balanced.

86 • *Herzog (CA) 1996 Baron Herzog, Cabernet Sauvignon, California. $13.99.*
Bright cherry red. Medium-bodied. Moderately extracted. Mildly tannic. Vanilla, cassis. Clean, fruity accents follow through on the palate, with a supple character and a mild note of minerally astringency through the finish.

86 • *Hacienda (CA) 1996 Clair de Lune, Cabernet Sauvignon, California. $6.99.*
Bright cherry-red hue. Attractive cedar, vanilla, and cassis aromas. A rich entry leads to a moderately full-bodied palate with lush, velvety tannins and generous cassis fruit flavors. Drink now.

86 • *Fredericksburg Winery (TX) 1997 Winecup, Cabernet Sauvignon, Texas. $14.95.*
Saturated dark ruby hue. Medium-bodied. Moderately extracted. Heavily oaked. Mildly tannic. Chocolate, spice, black fruits. Exotic, toasted oak aromas show spicy complexity that comes through on the palate. Velvety, rich flavors are harmonious. Despite the hefty oak accent, this does not turn too dry.

86 • *Fox Hollow (CA) 1995 Cabernet Sauvignon, California. $8.99.*
Bright cherry red with subtle purple cast. Ripe fruit-centered aromas show cassis and subtle oak influence. A lush entry leads to a medium-bodied palate with lush, supple tannins and generous, ripe fruit flavors that linger on the finish. Drink now.

86 • *Elk Run (MD) 1997 Cabernet Sauvignon, Maryland. $15.*
Saturated ruby-red hue. Intense, unusual anise and brown spice aromas show a big oak accent. A lean entry leads to a medium-bodied palate with firm grippy tannins and crisp acidity. Angular, flavorful finish. Drink now or later.

86 • *Covey Run (WA) 1996 Cabernet Sauvignon, Columbia Valley. $12.99.*
Bright ruby-violet hue. Generously aromatic with a heavy oak accent and vibrant cabernet fruits. A bright entry leads a moderately full-bodied palate with notes of bitterness and astringency lingering on the finish.

86 • *Charles Shaw (CA) 1996 Cabernet Sauvignon, California. $8.99.*
Bright crimson hue. Herbs and black fruit aromas with mild oak accents. A crisp attack leads to a medium-bodied palate with fine grained grippy tannins through the finish. Drink now.

86 • *Castoro (CA) 1996 Cabernet Sauvignon, Paso Robles. $15.*
Bright purple hue. Markedly ripe, jammy aromas. A fat entry leads a moderately full-bodied palate with a ripe core of fleshy fruit flavors and firm tannins clamping down on the medium length finish. Rich and thick, though acids are rather soft. This should be better in a few years. Drink now or later.

86 • *Bonterra (CA) 1996 Cabernet Sauvignon, North Coast. $13.*
Saturated ruby-blood red hue. Lean, crisp aromas of tart black fruits and vanilla. A lean attack leads to a moderately full-bodied palate with vibrant acids and crisp, leaner fruit flavors. Finishes cleanly and quickly. A little ungenerous. Drink now or later.

86 • Biltmore (NC) Cabernet Sauvignon, American. $12.99.

Saturated brilliant red-purple. Medium-bodied. Highly extracted. Moderately oaked. Moderately tannic. Black cherries, minerals. Very expressive primary fruit aromas follow through on a lush entry that turns minerally and dry through the finish. Drinkable.

86 • Beaucanon (CA) 1996 Reserve, Cabernet Sauvignon, Napa Valley. $14.

Bright crimson-red hue with a subtle fade to the rim. Muted aromas show oak spice and dark fruits. A crisp entry leads a medium-bodied palate with moderate cassis fruit flavors and a minerally, tannic grip through the finish. A lighter style with lively acids. Drink now.

86 • Beaucanon (CA) 1995 Cabernet Sauvignon, Napa Valley. $14.

Bright ruby-violet hue. Medium-bodied. Highly extracted. Moderately tannic. Black fruits, brown spice. Light and crisp, showing a hint of very dry tannin on the finish. Fruit-centered, supple style that shows Cabernet flavors in a very balanced package. Suited to current drinking.

86 • Barboursville (VA) 1995 Cabernet Sauvignon, Monticello. $15.

Blood red with an even fade to the rim. Medium-bodied. Moderately extracted. Moderately tannic. Mineral, vanilla, red fruits. Juicy, generous mouthfeel shows ripeness and a deference to tertiary flavors that are seamlessly woven with bright red fruits. Has a nice acidic cut. Drinking well now.

85 • Stonehedge (CA) 1995 Cabernet Sauvignon, Napa Valley. $12.99.

Bright cherry red. Medium-bodied. Moderately extracted. Moderately tannic. Minerals, black fruits. Angular, mineral-dominant style with a dry finish. Straightforward, with enough flesh to carry the tougher structural elements. Subtle oak influence.

85 • Corbett Canyon (CA) 1995 Reserve, Cabernet Sauvignon, Sonoma County. $10.

Medium ruby-red hue. Moderately aromatic with dusty, soft cherry accents. A supple attack leads a medium-bodied palate with bright, soft fruity flavors showing development. Tannins are evolved and supple. Drink now.

Other Great Value Cabernets

90 • Weingut Familie Prieler (Austria) 1995 Cabernet Sauvignon, Neusiedlersee. $13.

Full bright ruby red. Medium-bodied. Moderately extracted. Mildly tannic. Lead pencil, red fruits, minerals. Very aromatic, with high-toned fruity notes. Ripe, generous flavors and supple mouthfeel, with soft, balanced tannins lingering on the finish. Stylish, with acids providing grip and structure.

89 • Delheim (South Africa) 1996 Cabernet Sauvignon, Stellenbosch. $15.

Bright garnet hue. Intense lead pencil and game aromas show complexity. A firm entry is followed by a moderately full-bodied palate with exotic flavors, sharp acidity, and firm tannins. Supple, flavorful finish. Drink now.

88 • Torre Rosazza (Italy) 1995 Ronco della Torre, Cabernet Sauvignon, Colli Orientali del Friuli. $14.99.

Deep blackish ruby cast. Moderately full-bodied. Balanced acidity. Highly extracted. Moderately oaked. Moderately tannic. Minerals, cassis. Youthful and tightly wound, with a firm and austere palate feel. Well balanced, with a lean finish. Mid-term cellaring should coax out the underlying core of flavors.

86 • Scarlatta (Italy) 1996 Cabernet, Veneto. $4.75.

Bright blackish ruby cast. Medium-bodied. Full acidity. Moderately extracted. Mildly tannic. Dried herbs, red fruits. Pleasantly aromatic with a distinctive herbal bent to the core of fruit flavors. A light style with a lean and intense finish.

Scale: Superlative (96-100), Exceptional (90-95), Highly Recommended (85-89), Recommended (80-84), Not Recommended (Under 80)

86 • KWV (South Africa) 1995 Cathedral Cellar, Cabernet Sauvignon, Coastal Region. $12.99.
Deep, saturated purple-red. High-toned anise and mineral aromas carry a subtle wood accent. A lush entry leads a medium-bodied palate that shows fine-grained tannins. Integrated and harmonious with a mellow woody quality through the finish. Drink now.

86 • Joan Raventos Rosell (Spain) 1997 Heretat Vall-Ventos, Cabernet Sauvignon, Penedes. $15.
Bright ruby purple. Medium-bodied. Moderately extracted. Moderately oaked. Moderately tannic. Vanilla, cedar, black currants. Crisp, aromatic fruity nose with vanilla oak accents. Aromas follow through on the palate with nice primary fruit flavors lingering through the vanilla finish.

86 • Gamla (Israel) 1995 Cabernet Sauvignon, Galil. $13.99.
Deep ruby with a slight purple cast. Medium-bodied. Balanced acidity. Moderately extracted. Mildly oaked. Mildly tannic. Mint, dried herbs, red fruits. Pleasantly aromatic with a juicy, fruit-driven palate feel. A slight herbal streak adds a measure of complexity to the firmly structured angular finish. Well balanced with good length.

86 • Chamonix (South Africa) 1996 Cabernet Sauvignon, Franschhoek 1.63% rs. $15.
Bright ruby hue with a fading rim. Nice minerally, somewhat lean aromas. A bright entry leads a medium-bodied palate with clean cherry fruit flavors and wiry, flavorful tannins that linger on the finish. Fine acids and grip. Drink now or later.

86 • Bodegas Piedemonte (Spain) 1995 Crianza, Cabernet Sauvignon, Navarra. $10.50.
Deep ruby cast. Medium-bodied. Balanced acidity. Moderately extracted. Mildly tannic. Minerals, red fruits. Unusual high-toned aromas carry a berryish quality. Full though lean in the mouth, with an angular spicy finish.

83 • Vini Winery (Bulgaria) 1994 Reserve, Cabernet Sauvignon, Sliven. $8.
Brightly saturated ruby purple. Moderately light-bodied. Balanced acidity. Highly extract-ed. Heavily oaked. Mildly tannic. Vanilla extract, minerals. Forcefully aromatic with a big veneer of oak flavors. Lean on the palate with a mildly astringent finish. Seems a little artificial, but tasty nonetheless.

83 • Golan (Israel) 1994 Cabernet Sauvignon, Galil. $9.99.
Deep ruby hue with a slight fade. Medium-bodied. Balanced acidity. Subtly extracted. Mildly tannic. Currants, minerals. Pleasantly aromatic featuring pure and typical Cabernet flavors. Somewhat light in style and lacking a little grip on the palate. Turns angular toward the clean finish.

82 • Magnotta (Canada) 1996 Limited Edition, Cabernet Sauvignon, Ontario. $13.
Hazy, opaque ruby-red hue. Forward overripe red fruit and spice aromas show a marked wood accent. A firm attack leads to a moderately full-bodied palate with drying tannins giving a clipped, tannic finish. Seems to be drying out.

81 • Magnotta (Canada) 1997 Chile International Series, Cabernet Sauvignon, Maipo Valley–Niagara. $5.
Bright pale purple-red hue. Subdued herb, red fruit, and mineral aromas. A firm attack leads to a moderately light-bodied palate with grippy tannins through a solid and flavor-ful finish. Drink now.

80 • Chateau Dalina (Bulgaria) 1997 Cabernet Sauvignon, Russe Region. $3.99.
Bright crimson with a lightening rim. Moderately light-bodied. Moderately extracted. Mildly tannic. Fleshy, berry fruit aromas lead a crisp palate with balanced tannins and acids, though fruity flavors not abundant. Herbal finish. Quite quaffable.

eleven

Merlot

Introduction	130
Reviews	131
Aussie Merlot	131
French Merlot	132
Italian Merlot	133
South American Merlot	134
Spanish Merlot	136
U.S. Merlot	136
Other Great Value Merlots	140

Introduction: Merlot

Meet Merlot, a classic overnight success story more than a hundred years in the making. After decades of playing a supportive role to Cabernet Sauvignon, both in terms of blending and market share, Merlot has earned its individual standing in the spotlight. In the 1990s, winemakers and restaurateurs have been telling us of Merlot's merits as a soft and supple wine, less tannic and more inviting in its youth than Cabernet Sauvignon. The campaigning seems to have worked, as Merlot has become one of the world's favorite grapes in record time.

Value Merlot is widely available from both Europe and the New World. By no means is this to suggest that Merlot is a bargain in general terms, for it is not. The wines of Bordeaux, as well as the elite districts and wineries of the United States, demand a handsome sum, but South America, particularly Chile, is a bargain hunter's paradise for Merlot, with few bottlings exceeding $15 and a great number of wines under $10. Merlot from Italy has seen price increases in recent years, with several wines exceeding $20 a bottle. However, many of the top wines are still available for less than $15 and are often overlooked by U.S. Merlot drinkers. Also, Australian Merlots are often good values.

Merlot is native to Bordeaux, where it offers precious few values. Typically, the wines of Bordeaux are a proprietary blend of Cabernet Sauvignon, Merlot, and Cabernet Franc, with lesser amounts of Malbec and Petite Verdot. Merlot plays both supporting and starring roles in Bordeaux.

In the districts of the Médoc and Graves, Merlot adds much-needed fruit to the tannic Cabernet Sauvignon. In the districts of St. Émilion and Pomerol, Merlot assumes a primary role in many wines. In fact, Pomerol's most renowned and expensive wine, Pétrus, is nearly 100% Merlot. Some varietally labeled wines, with a general Bordeaux designation, are available at reasonable prices. However, in France, value Merlot is most often found from the "Vin de Pays," or country wine, designation. More specifically, the Vin de Pays d'Oc, an expansive wine-producing zone along the Mediterranean coast, is producing a great number of reliable and fruity Merlots at reasonable prices.

The cool regions of northern Italy produce some of the world's most silky and charming Merlots. In fact, this French varietal is the most widely planted red in the Veneto region. Unlike Merlots from France and much of the New World, Italian Merlot is not heavily wooded. The resulting wines tend to be more perfumed, exhibiting fleshy, fruity, berry-like flavors balanced with classic Italian acidity.

With regard to Merlot, California is put in the unfamiliar role of sharing the spotlight with Washington. In the past decade, Washington's Merlots have gained great notoriety. In favorable vintages, Merlots from the cool growing regions of Washington develop deep and complex flavors unmatched elsewhere in the United States, and they are among the very best in the world. Cool California regions such as Napa Valley's Stag's Leap District and the Sonoma Valley are responsible for some of that state's best Merlot. Lamentably, these elite growing regions fetch elite dollars, leaving bargain chasers to look elsewhere. As is the case with many of the top California varieties, one must look to broader appellations such as Central Coast, North Coast, or simply California when value shopping. Eastern states such as New York and Virginia have also been producing quality wines for some time and should not be forgotten.

Purchasing Merlot from California, Australia, or South America can be done with very little vintage consideration. This is not the case for Italy and Bordeaux, as vintages can vary greatly. Generally speaking, the years of 1995 and 1997 are excellent ones for Italy's northern Merlot regions. In Bordeaux, the 1995 and 1996 vintages were excellent. Washington State's vintages are fairly consistent, although they have greater variance than California's. The best recent vintage is 1994, and all subsequent vintages have been at least good in quality. Remember that vintage evaluations are extremely vague, and your best resource is a trusted wine merchant.

Merlot's popularity is on the rise due in large part to its soft tannins and generous fruit. Merlot is generally medium-bodied with moderate acidity and tannin. The flavors have been described as black cherry, plum, herbs, chocolate, and black olives. Merlot in the value price range is often lighter and more fruit accentuated than the meaty, ageworthy bottles that also carry ample price tags. Merlot is versatile, complementing a wide range of dishes, and thus is often an ideal choice at the restaurant table, as it allows a group of diners to order a variety of menu selections. You may wish to shock your friends by serving red wine with fish, especially grilled tuna.

Reviews

Aussie Merlot

86 • Lindemans (Australia) 1997 Bin 40, Merlot, South Eastern Australia. $9.
Bright ruby red with a slight fade. Medium-bodied. Balanced acidity. Moderately extracted. Mildly tannic. Red cherries, minerals. Ripe, fruity aromas lead a lighter-styled palate. Crisp and lively through a finish that is framed with bright acidity.

Great Value Merlot at a Glance

Number of Wines Reviewed:
124

Countries Represented:
11

85 • *Diamond Ridge (Australia) 1997 Merlot, South Eastern Australia. $9.*
Deep ruby cast. Moderately full-bodied. Full acidity. Highly extracted. Moderately oaked. Quite tannic. Cocoa, minerals. Lean chocolatey aromas lead a firm and intense palate given some clout by big, aggressive tannins that bite down on the finish.

84 • *McGuigan (Australia) 1998 Bin 3000, Merlot, South Eastern Australia. $12.*
Deep ruby purple. Medium-bodied. Balanced acidity. Moderately extracted. Mildly tannic. Black fruits, raspberries. Bright grapey aromas portend a ripe and fruity style. Lighter in the mouth than the nose suggests. Bright primary fruit flavors and slight tannins show on the finish. Very user friendly.

83 • *Sheldrake (Australia) 1996 Stirling Estate, Merlot, Western Australia. $13.*
Bright ruby purple. Moderately full-bodied. Balanced acidity. Moderately extracted. Heavily oaked. Mildly tannic. Overripe red fruits, spice cabinet. Pungent aromas are forward and generous, showing a slightly portlike, jammy quality and a wave of spice flavors. Light in the mouth, but crisp and well balanced.

83 • *Jacob's Creek (Australia) 1997 Merlot, South Eastern Australia. $8.99.*
Bright ruby-garnet with a gentle fade. Moderately light-bodied. Balanced acidity. Subtly extracted. Mildly tannic. Minerals, red fruits. Aromatically reserved with a light palate feel. The red fruit flavors on the finish show a touch of bitterness.

French Merlot

88 • *Colour Volant (France) 1996 Merlot, Vin de Pays d'Oc. $8.*
Deep blackish ruby hue. Moderately full-bodied. Full acidity. Moderately extracted. Mildly oaked. Mildly tannic. Red fruits, minerals, cedar. Pleasantly aromatic, with a taut, linear palate feel. Clean and well defined on the palate, with bright acidity through the finish.

86 • *Michel Lynch (France) 1996 Merlot, Bordeaux. $8.99.*
Bright ruby purple cast. Moderately full-bodied. Balanced acidity. Moderately extracted. Mildly oaked. Mildly tannic. Spice, minerals. Forward aromas carry a pleasant wood influence. Lighter in the mouth with a core of fruit-accented flavors. Well balanced and angular through the finish.

86 • *Georges Duboeuf (France) 1997 Merlot, Vin de Pays d'Oc. $5.99.*
Bright ruby purple to the rim. Moderately full-bodied. Balanced acidity. Moderately extracted. Mildly oaked. Mildly tannic. Red fruits, vanilla, minerals. Pleasantly aromatic, with a firm yet generous palate feel. Shows excellent grip and fine length through the finish.

85 • *Richemont (France) 1995 Réserve, Merlot, Vin de Pays d'Oc. $7.*
Deep blackish ruby cast. Moderately full-bodied. Balanced acidity. Highly extracted. Mildly oaked. Moderately tannic. Plums, chocolate. Seriously made, with a ripe and extracted personality. Firm and full in the mouth, with excellent grip to the finish.

85 • *Bonverre (CA) 1995 Merlot, Vin de Pays d'Oc. $10.*
Deep blackish ruby cast. Moderately full-bodied. Balanced acidity. Moderately extracted. Mildly oaked. Mildly tannic. Cedar, black fruits. Quite aromatic, with a full and lush palate feel. Flavorful and intense, with fine depth.

84 • *Michel Picard (France) 1996 Merlot, Vin de Pays d'Oc. $9.99.*
Bright blackish ruby cast. Moderately full-bodied. Full acidity. Highly extracted. Mildly oaked. Mildly tannic. Brown spices, horse, black fruits. Quite aromatic, with a decided earthy edge. Rides the funky fence without falling off. Full and lush in the mouth, with solid intensity through the finish.

84 • *La Baume (France) 1995 Merlot, Vin de Pays d'Oc. $6.99.*
Bright ruby cast. Medium-bodied. Full acidity. Moderately extracted. Mildly tannic. Red fruits, dried herbs, minerals. Features a distinctive leafy streak throughout. Firm and lean in the mouth, with a flavorful, well-defined finish.

Scale: Superlative (96-100), Exceptional (90-95), Highly Recommended (85-89), Recommended (80-84), Not Recommended (Under 80)

84 • Gallerie (France) 1995 Merlot, Vin de Pays de L'Hérault. $6.99.
Bright blackish ruby cast. Medium-bodied. Balanced acidity. Highly extracted. Mildly tannic. Red fruits, cedar, dried herbs. Features a distinctive herbal streak, a core of fruit flavors, and a subtle oak overlay—all on a firm and angular frame. Lean and clean through the finish.

84 • Abarbanel (France) 1997 Merlot, Vin de Pays d'Oc. $9.
Bright ruby purple. Moderately full-bodied. Balanced acidity. Highly extracted. Mildly oaked. Mildly tannic. Black fruits, vanilla, minerals. Pleasantly aromatic, with a well-defined and flavorful palate feel. Firm and angular through the finish.

83 • Woodbridge (France) 1996 Merlot, Vin de Pays d'Oc. $7.
Bright pale ruby cast. Medium-bodied. Full acidity. Moderately extracted. Mildly tannic. Red fruits, dried herbs. Carries a green accent throughout, but also features a core of red fruit flavors. Lean, vibrant, and angular through the finish.

83 • Jenard (France) 1996 Caves des Papes, Merlot, Vin de Pays d'Oc. $7.99.
Bright ruby cast. Medium-bodied. Full acidity. Moderately extracted. Mildly tannic. Red fruits, minerals, lead pencil. Pleasantly aromatic, with some real complexity to the range of flavors. Full, though well defined, with a crisp and lengthy finish.

83 • Delas (France) 1996 Merlot, Vin de Pays d'Oc. $7.
Bright ruby cast. Medium-bodied. Full acidity. Moderately extracted. Mildly tannic. Minerals, red fruits. Bright, high-toned aromas lead a crisp, well-defined palate. Clean and angular through the finish, with a pleasant berry accent.

83 • Borie-Manoux (France) 1997 Le Birdie, Merlot, Vin de Pays d'Oc. $10.
Bright ruby cast. Medium-bodied. Full acidity. Highly extracted. Mildly tannic. Minerals, cassis, dried herbs. Pleasantly aromatic, with a firm and intense palate feel. Lean and focused through the finish, with a hint of bitterness.

82 • l'Orval (France) 1996 Merlot, Vin de Pays d'Oc. $5.99.
Bright ruby cast. Medium-bodied. Full acidity. Highly extracted. Mildly tannic. Cranberries, black tea, minerals. Pleasantly aromatic, with a bright, fruit-accented palate feel. Straightforward, with a zesty finish.

Italian Merlot

89 • Bollini (Italy) 1994 Reserve Selection, Merlot, Trentino. $14.99.
Bright cherry red. Medium-bodied. Balanced acidity. Moderately extracted. Dried herbs, cherries, lead pencil. Bright and juicy, with a fruit-centered palate and a clean finish. Very drinkable, with commendable concentration of flavors.

89 • Barone Fini (Italy) 1996 Merlot, Trentino. $8.99.
Bright cherry red. Medium-bodied. Balanced acidity. Moderately extracted. Mildly tannic. Black cherries, herbs, earth. Herbaceous cherry notes follow through on the palate. Generous, but showing grip through the finish. Classic cool-climate Merlot character.

88 • Bolla (Italy) 1996 Colforte, Merlot delle Venezia. $14.
Deep ruby red. Medium-bodied. Balanced acidity. Moderately extracted. Mildly oaked. Red plums, sweet herbs. Generous fleshy aromas do not disappoint on the palate. Rich and supple, with ripe flavors and sweet herbal overtones through the finish. Drinking nicely now.

86 • Villa Frattina (Italy) 1996 Vigneto Quartarezza, Merlot, Lison-Pramaggiore. $12.
Deep cherry red. Medium-bodied. Balanced acidity. Moderately extracted. Black cherries, pencil shavings. Seductively generous fruit flavors with supporting vanilla oak notes. Bright and modern, with good concentration of flavors and supple tannins on the finish.

86 • La Colombaia (Italy) 1996 Merlot, Veneto. $9.99.
Solid cherry red. Medium-bodied. Balanced acidity. Moderately extracted. Heavily oaked. Brown spice, vanilla, red fruits. Pronounced toasted oak aromas. Soft fleshy fruit defers to a huge dose of toasted oak flavors. Good mouthfeel and soft finish suggest that this is not for keeping.

86 • *Cantine Mezzacorona (Italy) 1996 Merlot, Trentino. $7.99.*
Deep cherry red. Medium-bodied. Balanced acidity. Highly extracted. Plums, sweet herbs. Dark plummy nose. Rich, textured mouthfeel has broad chewy tannins that give a sense of ripeness and depth to this straightforward, hedonistic quaffer.

82 • *Scarlatta (Italy) 1996 Merlot, Veneto. $4.75.*
Bright cherry red. Medium-bodied. Balanced acidity. Moderately extracted. Red berry fruits, dried herbs. High toned, juicy and bright, with sweet/tart red fruit flavor. Very vibrant and fruity. Highly quaffable.

82 • *Josef Brigl (Italy) 1995 Merlot, Alto Adige. $9.99.*
Garnet red with a fading rim. Medium-bodied. Balanced acidity. Moderately extracted. Earth, minerals, red fruits. Austere, leafy nose. Wonderful mouthfeel, with smooth glycerin and a firm base of minerals that persist through the finish. Drinking nicely now, though not for those seeking fruit-centered wines.

82 • *Bagnoli (Italy) 1996 Merlot, Friuli. $10.99.*
Bright cherry red with a lightening rim. Moderately light-bodied. Balanced acidity. Moderately extracted. Cherries, red fruits, herbs. A crisp herbaceous nose leads a firm, minerally palate with red currant flavors and acidity. Fine-grained tannins do not impede early drinking.

80 • *Furlan (Italy) 1994 Castelcosa, Merlot, Friuli Venezia Giulia. $14.99.*
Garnet hue with a fading rim. Moderately light-bodied. Balanced acidity. Moderately extracted. Mildly tannic. Minerals, tart red fruits. Dusty, minerally nose seems already mature. Brisk and racy with a minerally feel through the finish.

South American Merlot

90 • *Santa Marvista (Chile) 1998 Reserva, Merlot, Central Valley. $6.*
Saturated deep violet red. Very aromatic with a ripe, plummy character. Rich on the entry, with a moderately full-bodied palate and lush tannins with juicy acids to complement the generous plummy fruit flavors. Drink now.

89 • *Concha y Toro (Chile) 1996 Marques de Casa Concha, Peumo Vineyard, Merlot, Rapel Valley. $14.*
Saturated blood red. Austere earthy aromas. A solid entry leads a moderately full-bodied palate with dry, minerally flavors and a lingering austere finish. There is little fruit generosity, but it shows nice "terroir" notes. Drink now.

87 • *Viña Santa Carolina (Chile) 1996 Reserva, Merlot, Maule Valley. $9.*
Bright red-pink color. Candied berry aromas with a note of vanilla. A crisp entry leads a medium-bodied palate with bright, mildly candied berry flavors and soft tannins on the finish. Shows some depth of flavor. Drink now.

87 • *Veramonte (Chile) 1997 Merlot, Alto de Casablanca. $10.*
Deep ruby-brick red. Rich, complex aromas show mature fruit character with complex cedar notes. An elegant attack leads a moderately full-bodied palate with harmonious flavors of cedar and fruits that linger through the finish. Drink now.

87 • *Doña Consuelo (Chile) 1998 Viña Segú Ollé, Merlot, Maule Valley. $7.*
Bright neon violet hue. Muted floral aromas. A crisp entry leads a medium-bodied palate with crisp fruit flavors and drying tannins. Well structured and classic, if not overly flavorful.

86 • *La Palma (Chile) 1997 Reserva, Merlot, Rapel. $11.*
Bright purple-red. Vanilla and black fruit aromas show a youthful character. Crisp on the attack with a moderately full-bodied palate and solid tannins. Fruit flavors are generous and rich throughout. Nice now, though it will keep a few years.

86 • *Caliterra (Chile) 1998 Merlot, Valle Central. $8.99.*
Deep violet red. Moderately aromatic with crisp red fruit character. A bright entry leads a medium-bodied palate with high-toned flavors and light, drying tannins. Youthful and straightforward. Drink now.

84 • Santa Amelia (Chile) 1998 Merlot, Maule Valley. $6.50.
Saturated purple. Ungenerous aromas have pommace-like note. A firm entry leads a moderately full-bodied palate with tannic grip and cherry flavors. The style is rather rustic.

84 • Santa Alicia (Chile) 1995 El Pimiento, Gran Reserva, Merlot, Maipo Valley. $9.99.
Bright ruby red. Fruit forward, plummy aromas. A fruity entry leads a medium-bodied palate with nice varietally correct fruit flavors and supple tannins, with good acidity working on the finish. Drink now.

84 • Pionero (Chile) 1998 Merlot, Central Valley. $8.
Bright ruby hue with a pink rim. Aromatically lean with tart berry fruit aromas. A crisp attack leads a medium-bodied palate with bright acids and a lean minerally finish. Drink now.

84 • La Palma (Chile) 1997 Merlot, Rapel. $7.
Bright neon violet-pink hue. Youthful aromas show dark, ripe fruits and a floral note. Bright and juicy on the attack, followed by a medium-bodied palate with light but dry tannins giving some grip. Drink now.

83 • Montes (Chile) 1998 Special Cuvée, Merlot, Curico Valley. $10.
Bright purple-red. Mildly herbal aromas with cherry and vanilla notes. A tart entry leads a medium-bodied palate with mild tannins gripping the finish. Rather youthful and bright, nice to drink now.

83 • Concha y Toro (Chile) 1997 Casillero del Diablo, Merlot, Rapel Valley. $10.
Saturated blood red. Very ripe aromas show a plummy, chocolatey note. A rich attack leads a moderataly full-bodied palate with soft acids and alcohol on the finish. Tannins are soft and powdery. Drink now.

83 • Casa Lapostolle (Chile) 1997 Merlot, Rapel Valley. $10.
Saturated purple-red. Richly aromatic with deep fruity notes. A firm entry leads a moderately full-bodied palate with concentrated but austere flavors well supported by tannins and fine acids. Fruit flavors are slightly muted.

81 • Walnut Crest (Chile) 1996 Estate Selection, Merlot, Maipo Valley. $9.50.
Ruby-crimson hue with a subtly fading rim. Markedly herbal aromas. A lean attack leads a medium-bodied palate with crisp acids and tart red fruit flavors. There is a big herbal kick on the finish. This one is not structured for keeping. Drink up.

81 • Santa Monica (Chile) 1996 Merlot, Rancagua. $7.99.
Bright ruby red with a fading rim. Oak-accented aromas. A light entry leads a medium-bodied palate with rather vapid flavors and a hollow finish, though it does show good acids and some grip. Drink now.

81 • Santa Julia (Argentina) 1997 Merlot, Mendoza. $7.
Pale red. Dusty, minerally aromas. A lean entry leads a medium-bodied palate with dusty cherry flavors that persist on the finish. Rather elegant. Drink now.

81 • Mariposa (Argentina) 1997 Merlot, Mendoza. $9.
Deep ruby hue. Earthy, austere aromas. Firm on the attack, with a moderately full-bodied palate where tough tannins provide some grip. Rather structured and rustic in nature, it will be best with food.

81 • La Playa (Chile) 1996 Merlot, Maipo Valley. $6.99.
Bright pinkish red. Floral and candied aromas are quite unusual. A high-toned attack leads a medium-bodied palate with brief candied flavors and a note of green tannins on the short finish.

Spanish Merlot

89 • *Torres (Spain) 1997 Las Torres, Merlot, Penedes. $11.49.*
Bright purple. Medium-bodied. Moderately extracted. Vanilla, cassis. Floral, black fruit aromas lead oaky, bright cherry flavors that have a direct, simple appeal. Highly quaffable.

86 • *Joan Raventos Rosell (Spain) 1997 Heretat Vall-Ventos, Merlot, Penedes. $13.50.*
Pale fading ruby hue. Medium-bodied. Moderately extracted. Mildly tannic. Leather, red fruits. Perfumed, leathery aromas follow through on the crisp palate with subtle berry fruit flavors and a lean finish.

86 • *Bodegas Nekeas (Spain) 1996 Vega Sindoa, Merlot, Navarra. $9.*
Deep ruby purple. Medium-bodied. Full acidity. Moderately extracted. Mildly oaked. Mildly tannic. Vanilla, minerals, red fruits. Forward aromas show a core of lean fruit flavors and an oak accent. Clean, crisp, and linear in the mouth. Angular finish has grip.

83 • *Bodegas Marco Real (Spain) 1996 Homenaje, Merlot, Navarra. $9.*
Pale ruby cast. Medium-bodied. Full acidity. Moderately extracted. Mildly tannic. Red fruits, minerals, citrus. Forward fruity aromas carry a slight earthy edge. Bright and zesty in the mouth with a crisp finish.

82 • *Bodegas Piedemonte (Spain) 1997 Merlot, Navarra. $7.50.*
Pale ruby purple. Light-bodied. Balanced acidity. Moderately extracted. Mildly tannic. Black fruits, minerals. Deep fruity aromas show an earthy edge. Lean in the mouth with gripping tannins. Angular through the finish.

U.S. Merlot

89 • *Quatro (CA) 1996 Merlot, Sonoma County. $12.*
Brilliant violet red. Generous cherry fruit and vanilla aromas. A vibrant attack leads a medium-bodied palate with balanced fine-grained tannins. Finishes with juicy, fruity persistence. This is a concentrated, stylish wine to be consumed now or later. Can improve with more age.

88 • *Estancia (CA) 1996 Merlot, Sonoma County. $14.*
Bright violet-ruby hue. Black fruit and herb aromas. A supple attack leads a moderately full-bodied palate with firm, dry tannins. Finishes with an angular tannic grip. Drink now or later. Can improve with more age.

88 • *Charles Shaw (CA) 1997 Merlot, California. $8.99.*
Full violet red. Cherry fruit aromas lead a bright, crisp, moderately light-bodied palate with powdery tannins dominating the finish. Good structure and grip, with generous fruit flavors.

87 • *Grande River (CO) 1996 Merlot, Grand Valley. $11.99.*
Bright ruby red to the rim. Powerful cedar, herb, and red fruit aromas show a big oak accent. A firm attack leads a medium-bodied palate with solid tannins. Mouthwatering, buoyant, flavorful finish. Well balanced and showing classic Merlot flavor complexities. Drink within five years.

87 • *Gallo Sonoma (CA) 1996 Merlot, Sonoma County. $11.*
Deep, saturated purple-red. Subdued overripe red fruit aromas. A firm attack followed by a medium-bodied palate with robust tannins. The finish is lean and flavorful. Overall, on the firm side. Drink now.

86 • *Reliz Canyon (CA) 1996 Merlot, Monterey. $13.95.*
Violet red. Lean aromas of minerals, red fruits, and herbs. A bright attack, a medium-bodied palate, vibrant acids, and light, gripping tannins. Drink now.

86 • *Osprey's Dominion (NY) 1996 Merlot, North Fork of Long Island. $14.99.*
Rich ruby hue with a slight fade. Generous raspberry and spice aromas. Medium-bodied with silky tannins. Soft, smooth, and supple, with a lingering note of oak spice. Drink now.

Scale: Superlative (96-100), Exceptional (90-95), Highly Recommended (85-89), Recommended (80-84), Not Recommended (Under 80)

86 • Ingleside Plantation (VA) 1997 Merlot, Virginia. $14.99.
Bright violet hue. Generous aromas of vanilla and raspberries. A crisp attack leads a medium-bodied palate that is fleshy and fruit centered and shows velvety tannins. A forward, supple style with good varietal character. Drink now.

86 • Haywood (CA) 1997 Merlot, California. $7.99.
Bright violet-ruby red. Perfumed, fruity aromas have a berry fruit quality. Medium-bodied, lush on the attack with velvety tannins and juicy berry fruit flavors. Finishes with soft, lush tannins. Well stuffed and flavorsome. Drink now.

86 • Grand Cru (CA) 1997 Merlot, California. $7.99.
Violet purple with a bright cast. Bright fruity aromas have cherry and vanilla accents. Medium-bodied, flavorful, and fruity on the attack, showing fine grip and grainy tannins through the finish. Drink now or later. Can improve with more age.

86 • Fox Hollow (CA) 1997 Merlot, California. $8.99.
Bright violet red. Faintly fleshy aromas lead a soft attack with vanilla oak and black fruit flavors on a medium-bodied palate. Finishes with mild, grainy tannins. A soft, lush easy-drinking style. Drink now.

86 • Forest Ville (CA) 1997 Merlot, California. $5.99.
Bright violet red. Attractive vanilla and cherry fruit aromas. Medium-bodied, open-knit style with generous red fruit and oak accents through the clean finish. Very user friendly and supple.

86 • Chateau Julien (CA) 1996 Grand Reserve, Merlot,
Monterey County. $9.99.
Pale violet hue. Clean aromas of herbs, berry fruit, and vanilla. A soft entry leads a light-bodied palate with very gentle tannins. Easily quaffable. Drink now.

86 • Bella Vigna (CA) 1997 Twin Creeks Vineyard, Merlot, Lodi. $12.
Full ruby red with a subtle fade. Generously spicy aromas show a toasty oak accent with ripe fruity notes. A soft entry lead a medium-bodied palate with powdery, elegant tannins. Finishes with notably fine oak spice and fruit persistence. Very well balanced and varietally expressive. Drink now.

85 • Laurel Lake (NY) 1996 Merlot, North Fork of Long Island. $12.99.
Bright cherry red with a slight fade. Subdued black cherry, dried herb, and mineral aromas. A firm entry leads a crisp, medium-bodied palate with drying tannins. Light but stylish and not overmade. Drink now.

85 • Gristina (NY) 1995 Merlot, North Fork of Long Island. $14.99.
Dark, saturated ruby red. Black fruit and mineral aromas show a subtle oak accent. A firm entry leads a moderately full-bodied palate with drying tannins. Sturdy and rich with a tough finish. Drink now or later.

85 • Fetzer (CA) 1996 Merlot, North Coast. $14.99.
Bright ruby red to the rim. Clean cherry and mineral aromas. A lean attack leads a medium-bodied palate with firm tannins and juicy acidity, and a crisp, clipped finish. Racy and refreshing. Drink now.

84 • Rutherford Vintners (CA) 1997 Merlot, Stanislaus County. $8.99.
Light violet hue. Light fruit-scented, floral aromas are quite fragrant. A juicy attack reveals a lighter-bodied palate with crisp acidity and a clean finish. Drink now.

84 • Robert Mondavi (CA) 1997 Coastal, Merlot, Central Coast. $14.
Bright crimson red. Clean aromas of minerals and herbs. A crisp attack leads a medium-bodied palate with light drying tannins and lively acids that provide some grip. There are nice fruit accents throughout. The finish is clean and quick. Drink now.

84 • Montpellier (CA) 1997 Merlot, California. $6.99.
Bright violet hue with a fading rim. Floral, vanilla oak aromas. Jammy flavors on the attack with a soft, fruity character through the finish. A lighter-bodied wine with easy drinkability.

84 • *Monterra (CA) 1996 Promise, Merlot, Monterey. $9.99.*
Bright crimson-violet hue, well saturated. Ripe, jammy black fruit aromas. The medium-bodied palate shows low acidity, and thick tannins come forward on an earthy finish. Drink now.

84 • *Jekel (CA) 1996 Merlot, California. $12.*
Brickish ruby hue with a subtle fade. Spicy, woody aromas. A crisp attack followed by mildy astringent tannins on the medium-bodied palate. Well gripped by tannins and acids on the finish. Drink now.

84 • *Huntington (CA) 1996 Merlot, California. $10.*
Bright ruby red. Attractive red fruit aromas. A crisp attack is followed by a moderately light-bodied palate with juicy acidity and modest tannins. Lean finish. A bright quaffer to be consumed in the near term.

84 • *Hogue (WA) 1996 Barrel Select, Merlot, Columbia Valley. $14.95.*
Bright, pale ruby red. Generous red fruit, mineral, and vanilla aromas show a slight oak accent. A ripe attack leads a medium-bodied palate with lean tannins and a lush, flavorful finish. Eminently drinkable, with ripe flavors and a clean, precise structure. Drink within five years.

84 • *Hacienda (CA) 1997 Clair de Lune, Merlot, California. $6.99.*
Deep, dark violet hue. Brambly, ripe fleshy aromas. Medium-bodied, with bright blackberry and cherry flavors up front, and subtle velvety tannins and obvious vanilla oak flavors lingering on the finish. Drink now.

84 • *Blackstone (CA) 1997 Merlot, California. $10.*
Pale ruby red with a bright cast. Sweet berry aromas follow through to a medium-bodied palate with sweet fruit and oak flavors. Acids are quite low and tannins are soft through the finish. An easy-drinking quaffer for near-term consumption.

83 • *White Hall Vineyards (VA) NV Lot 97, Merlot, Virginia. $12.99.*
Medium ruby red with a subtle fade on the rim. Generous minerally, wood spice aromas. A supple attack leads a medium-bodied palate that has crisp acids and moderate, soft tannins. Drink now.

83 • *Van Asperen (CA) 1996 Merlot, Napa Valley. $15.*
Bright violet hue with a pale cast. Mildly floral aromas. Medium-bodied, with a soft attack and rounded, lighter flavors and a clean finish. Drink now.

83 • *Shale Ridge (CA) 1997 Merlot, Monterey. $9.99.*
Violet-ruby hue with a subtle fade. Unusual aromas of herbs and black fruits. A supple attack, with a moderately full-bodied palate that remains supple despite the chewy tannins. Drink now.

83 • *Forest Glen (CA) 1997 Merlot, California. $9.99.*
Full violet-ruby hue. Oak-accented aromas follow through on the medium-bodied palate with up-front brambly fruit flavors and an earthy dry note coming through on the finish.

83 • *Fetzer (CA) 1997 Eagle Peak, Merlot, California. $8.99.*
Bright violet-ruby hue. Moderately aromatic with weedy and oak accents and plummy fruit. A supple entry leads a medium-bodied palate with berry fruit flavors matched by supple tannins and lingering oak flavors. Well balanced with fine acidity and good grip on the finish. Drink now.

83 • *Delicato (CA) 1997 Merlot, California. $4.99.*
Bright violet hue. Herbal, berry fruit aromas have a vanilla accent. Medium-bodied, lush, and smooth through the finish with mild velvety tannins lingering. Straightforward and unchallenging. Drink now.

83 • *Daniel Lawrence (CA) 1997 Kathleen's Cuvée, Merlot, Alexander Valley. $11.99.*
Bright purple-red. Lean mineral and red fruit aromas. A crisp attack leads a light-bodied palate with gentle tannins. The finish is light and fruity. A quaffer. Drink now.

Scale: Superlative (96-100), Exceptional (90-95), Highly Recommended (85-89), Recommended (80-84), Not Recommended (Under 80)

83 • Bogle (CA) 1997 Merlot, California. $9.

Brilliant violet with a bright cast. Aromas of cordials and vanilla oak. Medium-bodied, with clean black fruit flavors and sweet oak and juicy acids through the finish. Drink now.

83 • Beaucanon (CA) 1996 Reserve, Merlot, Napa Valley. $15.

Full ruby-violet hue with a subtle fade. Crisp, fragrant aromas show red fruits and vanilla. Smooth on the attack, with a moderately full body and lush black cherry flavors. Finishes with fine-grained tannins and vanilla oak. Drink now or later. Can improve with more age.

82 • Maddalena (CA) 1996 San Simeon Reserve, Merlot, Central Coast. $14.95.

Saturated dark crimson red. Unusual earthy and floral aromas with faint fruity notes. A firm attack is followed by a moderately full-bodied palate that shows firm, grainy tannins and crisp acids.

82 • Henry Estate (OR) 1997 Merlot, Umpqua Valley. $15.

Deep purple-red. Muted mineral and red fruit aromas carry a subtle oak overtone. A firm attack leads a medium-bodied palate with lean, firm tannins. Angular, flavorful finish. Rather tight, but well structured and showing fine grip. Drink within five years.

82 • Bommarito (CA) 1997 Merlot, Napa Valley. $12.

Dark ruby red. Blackberry and earth aromas. Medium-bodied, with a soft attack that leads a rounded, crushed-fruit mouthful of flavors with a charred finish. Drink now.

81 • Woodbridge (CA) 1997 Merlot, California. $10.

Ruby red with a fading rim. Very ripe cherry fruit aromas. Moderately full-bodied with a thick attack and generous black fruit flavors. Finishes with robust tannins.

81 • Washington Hills (WA) 1997 Varietal Select, Merlot, Columbia Valley. $11.

Bright ruby red to the rim. Generous berry and mineral aromas carry a slight reductive note. A lush attack leads a medium-bodied palate with crisp tannins. The finish is lush and flavorful. A lighter-styled quaffer that is tasty, but it has a rather unusual note to the flavors. Drink now.

81 • Turning Leaf (CA) 1996 Winemaker's Choice Reserve, Merlot, Sonoma County. $12.

Saturated dark violet red. Very ripe oak and fleshy black cherry aromas. A solid entry leads a moderately full-bodied palate with thick, rich tannins. Drink now.

81 • Silver Ridge (CA) 1997 Merlot, California. $9.99.

Bright violet hue with a brilliant cast. Ripe raspberry and cherry aromas. Medium-bodied, and smooth on the attack with lush powdery tannins giving some grip through the finish.

81 • Silver Lake (WA) 1995 Merlot, Columbia Valley. $12.99.

Rich ruby red with a slight fade. Lean anise and mineral aromas. A crisp attack leads a light-bodied palate with angular tannins. Austere finish. Drink within five years.

81 • Round Hill (CA) 1996 Merlot, California. $8.

Bright violet-ruby hue. Generous aromas show black fruit and vanilla. A smooth attack reveals a moderately full-bodied wine with fleshy flavors and chunky, smooth tannins through the finish. Substantial, well-stuffed style. Drink now.

81 • Perry Creek (CA) 1996 Merlot, El Dorado. $12.

Medium ruby hue. Muted, minerally, floral aromas. A soft attack leads a moderately light-bodied palate with slight tannins and minerally grip through the finish. Rather light in the flavor department, though clean on the finish. Drink now.

81 • Pepperwood Grove (CA) 1997 Merlot, California. $7.

Pale ruby hue. Muted aromas. Medium-bodied, with a crisp, lean attack that does not develop any generosity on the midpalate. Finishes quickly with mild, cedary tannins. Drink now.

81 • *Peirano (CA) 1997 Six Clones, Merlot, Lodi. $9.99.*

Bright violet hue. Jammy, raisiny aromas with vanilla accents. A crisp entry is followed by a medium-bodied palate with smooth tannins and juicy acids. Rather flabby and overripe. Drink now.

81 • *Parducci (CA) 1997 Merlot, California. $10.*

Bright violet hue with a pale cast. Muted candied aromas. Medium-bodied, with a juicy, fresh attack leading to crisp berry flavors. The finish is clean, with mild astringency. Drink now or later. Can improve with more age.

81 • *Mission View (CA) 1996 Midnight Mischievous, Merlot, Paso Robles. $15.*

Bright pale ruby hue. Subdued candied strawberry aromas. A rounded attack is followed by a light-bodied palate with juicy acidity and candied flavors. Carries a sweet note to the finish. This one's a quaffer. Drink now.

81 • *Hoodsport (WA) 1997 Merlot, Yakima Valley. $14.99.*

Pale, brilliant cherry red. Lean sweet herb and mineral aromas. A soft attack leads a light-bodied palate with subtle tannins. The finish is sweet, lean, and crisp. Lacks somewhat for grip and intensity, but interesting. Drink now.

81 • *Dunnewood (CA) 1996 Merlot, North Coast. $8.99.*

Bright cherry red. Subdued mineral and herb aromas. A crisp attack leads a moderately light-bodied palate with lean tannins and a clipped finish. Refreshing, but not overly flavorful. Drink now.

81 • *Biltmore (NC) NV Merlot, American. $13.99.*

Medium brick-ruby red with a subtle fade. Muted minerally aromas. A firm entry leads a medium-bodied palate with rustic, dry tannins. Finishes with rough tannic grip. Not much underlying depth or fruit generosity. Drink now.

81 • *Bel Arbor (CA) 1997 Merlot, California. $6.99.*

Bright ruby red. Soft cherry and berry aromas. Medium-bodied with a juicy attack and clean acids giving a clean, lightly tannic finish. The finish is firm, with good grip. Has the acidity to work well with food. Drink now.

81 • *Bandiera (CA) 1996 Merlot, California. $9.*

Saturated violet hue. Deep, ripe aromas. Light in body with weak fruit flavors giving way to a lean minerally finish.

80 • *Pugliese (NY) 1995 Reserve, Merlot, North Fork of Long Island. $13.99.*

Light ruby red with a slight fade. Sound mineral, herb, and spice aromas. A firm entry leads a medium-bodied palate with drying tannins. Clipped finish. Tasty, if rather dilute. Drink now.

80 • *Napa Creek (CA) 1996 Merlot, Lodi. $8.99.*

Light ruby red. Minerally, slightly herbal aromas. A crisp attack leads a medium-bodied palate with slight, supple tannins. Flavors show a jammy quality throughout. Drink now.

80 • *Deer Valley (CA) 1996 Merlot, California. $5.99.*

Pale ruby red with a fading rim. Lean, herbal aromas. Moderately light-bodied with a crisp attack and lean flavors through to a minerally finish. Drink now.

Other Great Value Merlots

89 • *Baobab (South Africa) 1997 Merlot, Western Cape. $8.99.*

Deep, saturated ruby hue. Intense lead pencil, iron, and red fruit aromas show character and style. A firm entry leads a moderately full-bodied palate with lean tannins and outstanding flavor intensity. The finish is lengthy and complex. Drink now or later.

86 • Jackson-Triggs (Canada) 1996 Proprietors' Reserve, Merlot, Okanagan Valley. $11.30.
Brilliant ruby red hue to the rim. Generous red fruit and mineral aromas carry a spicy oak accent. A firm attack leads to a medium-bodied palate with grippy, lean tannins. Angular, flavorful finish. A focused, well-cut style. Drink now or later. Can improve with more age.

85 • Haskovo Winery (Bulgaria) 1996 Special Selection, Merlot, Stambolovo. $12.
Deep blackish ruby hue. Medium-bodied. Balanced acidity. Highly extracted. Moderately oaked. Mildly tannic. Brown spices, cherry cordial. Toasty barrel influences pop out on the nose and combine with a core of fruit flavor. Relatively lean and firmly structured through the finish with some astringent bitterness.

84 • Magnotta (Canada) 1997 Chile International Series, Merlot, Maipo Valley–Niagara. $5.
Pale ruby red hue with a fade to the rim. Unusual earth, herb, and mineral aromas. A firm attack leads to a moderately light-bodied palate with drying tannins through a clipped, crisp finish. Shows a particular (sulfur?) note to the nose that seems to blow off with aeration.

84 • Haskovo Winery (Bulgaria) 1996 Special Selection, Merlot, Sakar. $12.
Deep blackish ruby hue. Medium-bodied. Balanced acidity. Highly extracted. Heavily oaked. Mildly tannic. Brown spices, minerals. Aromas and flavors of oak with a highly toasted personality. Lean and angular on the palate with some slight bitterness to the finish. Well flavored and intense, but perhaps a tad overextracted.

83 • Valley of the Monks (Romania) 1996 Merlot, Dealu Mare. $4.50.
Pale cherry red. Moderately light-bodied. Subtly extracted. Beets, herbs, red fruits. Pleasant lightly herbal aromas lead a clean, light-framed palate with a lingering berry fruit finish. A quaffing style.

83 • Pillitteri (Canada) 1997 Merlot, Niagara Peninsula VQA. $11.97.
Bright ruby red hue to the rim. Forward dried herb and mineral aromas. A crisp attack leads to a medium-bodied palate with lean tannins through a crisp, angular finish. Rather ungenerous, but refreshing. Drink now.

83 • Bulgari (Bulgaria) 1996 Merlot, Pomorie. $5.99.
Opaque center, bright purple rim. Moderately light-bodied. Moderately extracted. Mildly tannic. Black cherry, vanilla. Inviting black cherry aromas lead a straightforward but balanced palate with black fruit flavors and fine-grained tannins supplying some grip.

82 • Premiat (Romania) 1995 Merlot, Dealul Mare. $4.99.
Pale cherry red. Moderately light-bodied. Balanced acidity. Subtly extracted. Mildly tannic. Red fruits, spice. Crisp red fruit aromas follow through on a simple, straightforward, clean palate. Although not complex, this is very drinkable.

82 • Magnotta (Canada) 1995 Limited Edition, Merlot, Ontario. $11.
Dark opaque ruby red hue. Unusual earth and mineral aromas. A hard attack leads to a moderately full-bodied palate with rough, astringent tannins. Clipped, lean finish. Rather structured with a tough character. Bottle age might improve this.

82 • KWV (South Africa) 1995 Cathedral Cellar, Merlot, Coastal Region. $12.99.
Dark, saturated garnet red. Generous brown spice and red fruit aromas carry a hefty oak accent. A firm entry leads a medium-bodied palate with angular, firm tannins. Rather wood dominated, but decent. Drink now.

82 • Hester Creek (Canada) 1997 Merlot, Okanagan Valley. $15.
Deep ruby-red hue. Intense, unusual anise and herb aromas. A soft attack leads to a medium-bodied palate with subtle tannins through a subdued, crisp finish. A lighter style of merlot. Drink now.

82 • *Haskovo Winery (Bulgaria) 1996 Merlot, Haskovo. $6.*

Bright blackish ruby hue. Moderately light-bodied. Balanced acidity. Moderately extracted. Mildly oaked. Mildly tannic. Red fruits, minerals. Pleasantly aromatic with a lean and angular presence on the palate. Clean through the finish with a hint of bitterness. Solid grip.

80 • *Chateau Dalina (Bulgaria) 1997 Merlot, Russe Region. $3.99.*

Pale purple-red. Moderately light-bodied. Moderately extracted. Moderately tannic. Red currants, flowers. Brash red fruit and floral aromas lead a dry palate with thin fruit flavors.

Scale: Superlative (96-100), Exceptional (90-95), Highly Recommended (85-89), Recommended (80-84), Not Recommended (Under 80)

twelve

❧

Bordeaux Blends, Cabernet Franc, and Malbec

❧

Introduction	144
Reviews	146
Red Bordeaux: The French Original	146
U.S. Red Bordeaux Varietal Blends	147
Aussie Red Bordeaux Varietal Blends	149
U.S. Cabernet Franc	149
Argentine Malbec	151
U.S. Malbec	152
Other Great Value Bordeaux Varietals	152

Introduction: Bordeaux Blends, Cabernet Franc, and Malbec

The red wines of Bordeaux are a careful blend of up to five different grape varieties. The blend varies from one chateau to another and is determined by a combination of winemaker, house style, and vineyard variables such as soil type and sun exposure. Two red Bordeaux varieties—Cabernet Sauvignon and Merlot—are familiar to most wine drinkers, as wines are now produced from these grapes grown in regions all over the world. The lesser-known performers are Cabernet Franc, Malbec, and Petite Verdot. Of these three, Cabernet Franc is by far the most important in Bordeaux, playing the role of the primary variety in several noteworthy wines. Cabernet Franc is softer and less tannic than Cabernet Sauvignon, showing a leafy, chocolatey, herbaceous character as opposed to Cabernet Sauvignon's taut, minerally, black currant flavors. Malbec and Petite Verdot are minor contributors, with Petite Verdot declining steadily even though it was once the dominant red grape of the region. In the New World, these varieties are grown and produced as both varietal wines and Bordeaux-inspired blends. In the United States, there is even a name for these Bordeaux-style blends—Meritage (rhymes with heritage).

As a general rule, the wines of Bordeaux are not considered to be great values. However, values do exist if one looks to lesser-known districts such as Côtes de Bourg and Côtes de Blaye, as well as broader designations such as Médoc or even simply Bordeaux. The Bordeaux-inspired U.S. Meritage wines are often a winery's preeminent bottling, which generally means it is also their most expensive wine. Varietally named Cabernet Franc is becoming a common part of the repertoire of wineries in the eastern United States, yet it remains a minor player in both Washington and California. These wines can be good values, offering an education regarding the variety's flavor contributions to traditional Bordeaux blends. If this should stir your curiosity, venture down to Argentina, the world's best supplier of Malbec after France. Malbec plays a major role in Argentina and has done so for decades. Fabulous bottles of Malbec produced from 50-year-old-plus vines can sell for as little as $10. These are not to be missed.

Staying in France but venturing outside of Bordeaux, we find Cabernet Franc and Malbec shedding their status as supporting players and taking on the starring role. Cabernet Franc is featured in parts of the Loire Valley, where it produces lean, crisp wines, most notably in the appellation of Chinon. Chinon is an attractive medium-bodied wine, showing red cherry fruit balanced with earth, licorice, and a bit of oak.

Malbec achieves its glory in the region of Cahors in southwestern France. This legendary wine was considered to be one of that nation's finest until *Phylloxera*, a tiny vine louse, destroyed all the vineyards in the late 19th century. The region was very slow to recover; significant vineyard plantings did not take place until the 1970s. The new style of Cahors is light and fruity, although small privately owned firms continue to produce Cahors in its traditional, tannic style that may not appeal to modern tastes. (There was good reason that these wines were once referred to as the "black wines of Cahors.") Prices have gone up in recent years, but bargains still remain.

Scale: Superlative (96-100), Exceptional (90-95), Highly Recommended (85-89), Recommended (80-84), Not Recommended (Under 80)

Wines from some of Bordeaux's lesser-known regions are showing increased availability, as merchants clamor for value wines to offer their customers, but wines such as Chinon and Cahors are most likely to be seen in only the most serious wine shops and restaurants. Don't be afraid to ask your wine store to order these wines for you, as most reputable merchants are eager to please.

Vintages in Bordeaux vary considerably. The value wines from 1995 and 1996 are generally excellent and should be drinking beautifully already. Although Bordeaux is known as one the world's most ageworthy wines, these secondary districts often produce wines to be drunk within a few years of release. If you are seeking Malbec from Argentina, you are in luck, as all recent vintages—1993 to the present—are excellent. These wines have a variety of uses, as styles range from light to full bodied. Here again is where the tasting notes will be invaluable.

Meritage is the name used to describe U.S. red and white wines made with blends of traditional Bordeaux varieties. The name became necessary when in 1983 the Bureau of Alcohol, Tobacco, and Firearms changed the required minimum of a named variety from 51% to 75%. This meant that lovely wines containing 65% Cabernet Sauvignon blended with Merlot and Cabernet Franc could one year call themselves Cabernet Sauvignon and the next year have to be labeled simply as "red table wines." In 1988, a number of winemakers who were producing Bordeaux-style blends formed an association, and the name Meritage (a blend of "merit" and "heritage") was chosen via a national contest. It should be noted that only members of the association may use the term Meritage, and many producers have their own proprietary names for these blends. (Yes, it is confusing.) As previously mentioned, a Meritage is often a winery's flagship red, fetching upwards of $100 a bottle. A few value-priced wines remain, however, being produced mainly in Washington and eastern states such as New York and Virginia.

❧

Great Value Red Bordeaux Varietal Blends, Malbec, and Cabernet Franc at a Glance

Number of Wines Reviewed:

91

Countries Represented:

8

Reviews

Red Bordeaux: The French Original

89 • Sichel (France) 1995 Sirius, Rouge, Bordeaux. $9.99.

Deep ruby cast. Moderately full-bodied. Balanced acidity. Moderately extracted. Mildly oaked. Mildly tannic. Cherry cordial, spice, minerals. Forward and attractive aromas carry a gentle oak accent to a core of cordial fruit flavors. Ripe and generous through the finish.

88 • Lagrange les Tours (France) 1995 Bordeaux Supérieur. $7.99.

Ruby garnet with a slight fade. Medium-bodied. Balanced acidity. Moderately extracted. Mildly tannic. Minerals, earth, chocolate. Shows a slight herbal overtone, with a solid four-square character. Chunky and firm through the finish. Well balanced.

87 • de La Tour (France) 1996 Bordeaux. $9.99.

Deep ruby purple cast. Moderately full-bodied. Balanced acidity. Moderately extracted. Mildly tannic. Licorice, minerals. Dark aromas portend a degree of depth on the palate. Ripe yet firm through the finish.

86 • Ginestet (France) 1996 1er, "Chateau La Croix de Guillot," Cotes de Blaye. $9.75.

Deep ruby garnet cast. Moderately full-bodied. Balanced acidity. Moderately extracted. Mildly tannic. Minerals, earth. Aromatically reserved with a firm minerally core of flavors. Angular, though well balanced through the finish.

85 • Villa Bel-Air (France) 1994 Rouge, Graves. $14.99.

Bright ruby garnet cast. Moderately full-bodied. Balanced acidity. Highly extracted. Moderately tannic. Minerals. Aromatically reserved with a rather tough, chunky character in the mouth. Firm and unyielding through the finish.

84 • Tour Grand Colombier (France) 1995 Lalande de Pomerol Contrôlée. $12.99.

Bright ruby garnet cast. Medium-bodied. Balanced acidity. Moderately extracted. Mildly tannic. Dried herbs, minerals. Shows a decided leafy accent, though quite ripe and generous in the mouth. Lush through the finish.

84 • Maison Blanche (France) 1994 Montagne-Saint Emilion. $12.99.

Bright ruby garnet cast. Medium-bodied. Balanced acidity. Moderately extracted. Mildly tannic. Spice, minerals. Generous aromas carry an attractive spicy accent. Lean and intense in the mouth with an angular finish.

84 • Les Graves de Viaud (France) 1996 Cotes de Bourg. $11.

Deep ruby cast. Medium-bodied. Balanced acidity. Moderately extracted. Mildly oaked. Mildly tannic. Vanilla, anise, minerals. Shows a judicious wood accent to the nose and a firm core of minerally flavors. Features some mild astringence to the finish.

84 • Labegorce Zede (France) 1996 Z de Zede, Bordeaux Supérieur. $11.99.

Deep ruby cast. Moderately full-bodied. Balanced acidity. Moderately extracted. Mildly tannic. Dried herbs, minerals, earth. Forward complex aromas carry a distinctive herbal edge. Ripe but angular through the finish. Shows solid grip.

84 • Hostens-Picant (France) 1996 Rouge, Sainte-Foy Bordeaux. $12.99.

Medium ruby-brick red. Medium-bodied. Lead pencil, black fruits. Spicy, well-developed aromas lead a leaner, well-textured mouthful of reserved flavors that conclude in a dry spicy manner.

83 • Tour du Pas St. Georges (France) 1994 St. Georges–St. Emilion. $14.99.

Bright ruby garnet cast. Moderately full-bodied. Balanced acidity. Moderately extracted. Mildly tannic. Minerals, dried herbs. Reserved and elegant in style with a firm minerally backbone. Angular through the finish.

Scale: Superlative (96-100), Exceptional (90-95), Highly Recommended (85-89), Recommended (80-84), Not Recommended (Under 80)

83 • *Lagrange les Tours (France) 1996 Bordeaux Supérieur. $8.99.*
Pale ruby garnet with a slight fade. Medium-bodied. Balanced acidity. Moderately extracted. Mildly tannic. Dried herbs, minerals. Aromatically muted with a lighter-styled, straightforward palate. Lean and structured though rounds out a bit on the finish.

83 • *Labegorce Zede (France) 1995 Z de Zede, Bordeaux. $9.99.*
Bright ruby purple cast. Moderately full-bodied. Balanced acidity. Highly extracted. Mildly tannic. Flowers, minerals. Unusual high-toned aromas lead to an extracted, though oddly hollow mid-palate. Firm, chunky finish.

83 • *l'Eglise Vieille (France) 1996 Haut-Medoc. $12.99.*
Bright ruby purple cast. Medium-bodied. Balanced acidity. Moderately extracted. Mildly tannic. Minerals, red fruits. Reined-in aromatically with an austere range of minerally flavors in the mouth. Lighter in style with a sense of angularity to the finish.

82 • *La Grande Clotte (France) 1996 Lussac-St. Emilion. $11.99.*
Bright ruby garnet cast. Medium-bodied. Balanced acidity. Moderately extracted. Mildly tannic. Minerals, red fruits. Aromatically reserved with some green overtones and a sense of lightness on the palate. Fades at the finish.

82 • *La Grande Clotte (France) 1995 Lussac-St. Emilion. $9.99.*
Bright ruby garnet cast. Medium-bodied. Balanced acidity. Moderately extracted. Mildly tannic. Dried herbs, minerals. Light in style with an herbal overtone throughout. Crisp, angular finish.

81 • *Saint Sulpice (France) 1995 Bordeaux. $11.*
Pale ruby-garnet hue with a fading rim. Dried herb and red fruit aromas show a decided green edge. Medium-bodied, with a soft, supple, lighter-styled finish. Drink now.

81 • *Pitray (France) 1996 Cotes de Castillon. $10.99.*
Bright ruby purple cast. Moderately full-bodied. Balanced acidity. Moderately extracted. Mildly tannic. Minerals, black fruits. Tight and reined-in with a firm and linear impression in the mouth. Angular and lean through the finish.

81 • *Ginestet (France) 1996 "Chateau Les Moiselles," Cotes de Bourg. $9.99.*
Bright ruby purple cast. Moderately full-bodied. Balanced acidity. Highly extracted. Mildly oaked. Quite tannic. Minerals, vanilla. Shows a hint of wood treatment, but seems rather overextracted, with a harsh astringent palate.

81 • *Ginestet (France) 1996 "Chateau Fonfroide," Bordeaux. $9.25.*
Bright ruby red cast. Medium-bodied. Balanced acidity. Moderately extracted. Moderately tannic. Minerals. Aromatically reserved with a core of minerally flavors on a surprisingly light palate. Finishes with some astringent tannins.

81 • *Cote Montpezat (France) 1995 Cotes de Castillon. $14.99.*
Deep ruby cast. Moderately full-bodied. Balanced acidity. Highly extracted. Mildly tannic. Earth, minerals, anise. Forward aromas carry an unusual earthy anise note. Ripe and lush in the mouth with a sense of thickness. Lacks a bit for grip.

U.S. Red Bordeaux Varietal Blends

87 • *Hahn Estates (CA) 1996 Red Meritage, Santa Lucia Highlands. $15.*
Saturated dark ruby red hue. Very ripe fruit with an herbal streak. A tart entry leads a moderately full-bodied palate with bright fruit flavors and racy tart acids that give this great cut through the finish. Finishes very cleanly. Drink now.

86 • *Powers (WA) 1996 Cabernet-Merlot, Washington. $12.*
Deep red-purple. Moderately full-bodied. Highly extracted. Moderately tannic. Black fruits. Big-shouldered and generous, with fleshy, dark fruit flavors and chunky tannins. No wallflower here. Firm tannins will need some meaty accompaniment.

86 • *Madroña (CA) 1993 Quintet, El Dorado. $15.*
Deep ruby-violet hue. Moderately full-bodied. Highly extracted. Quite tannic. Leather, earth, minerals. Austere, dark fruit aromas lead a dry, minerally mouthful of flavors with an earthy finish. Tannins are quite demanding and tough at present.

86 • Grande River (CO) 1996 Meritage, Grand Valley. $12.99.
Bright cherry-red hue. Perfumed spice, mineral, and red fruit aromas. A lean attack leads to a medium-bodied palate with angular, grippy tannins and sturdy acidity. Crisp, stylish finish. Drink now or later.

84 • Covey Run (WA) 1996 Cabernet-Merlot, Washington. $10.
Bright red-violet. Moderately light-bodied. Moderately extracted. Mildly tannic. Ripe berry fruits, vanilla. Bright berry fruit aromas lead a simple, crisp mouthful of similar flavors, with a hint of tannic bite for balance.

83 • Rockbridge (VA) 1995 Cabernet, Virginia. $14.
Bright violet-ruby. Medium-bodied. Moderately extracted. Mildly tannic. Spice, minerals. Dusty, minerally aromas. Plenty of oak spice flavors emerge on the palate, with lighter fruit flavors and a lean finish making for a more reserved style.

83 • Kiona (WA) 1997 Cabernet-Merlot, Columbia Valley. $9.99.
Bright violet-red. Moderately light-bodied. Moderately extracted. Mildly tannic. Flowers, dried herbs. Engaging floral aromas lead a light-framed palate with bright, floral flavors. Finishes with a hint of dry tannins.

83 • Dr. Konstantin Frank (NY) NV Cabernet, New York. $14.95.
Bright violet-red. Medium-bodied. Moderately extracted. Mildly tannic. Violets, red berries, minerals. Bright floral aromas lead a high-toned, fruity palate, with nice texture and a crisp, mineral-accented finish. Well balanced, and drinking well now.

83 • Bookwalter (WA) NV Red, Washington. $10.
Full brick red with a garnet cast. Medium-bodied. Moderately extracted. Moderately tannic. Dried herbs, earth. Herbal, mature aromas follow through on the palate, with dusty, dry tannins making for a lean finish.

82 • Norman (CA) 1996 No Nonsense Red, Claret, Paso Robles. $15.
Bright ruby red with a pale violet rim. Medium-bodied. Moderately extracted. Mildly tannic. Dried herbs, minerals, berries. Distinctive herbal aromas lead a brisk, tart, berry fruit palate with a minerally theme through the finish. Straightforward, appealing, and very quaffable, with enough acidity to be flexible at the table.

82 • E.B. Foote (WA) 1996 Cabernet-Merlot, Columbia Valley. $15.
Bright garnet hue. Reserved spice and licorice aromas. A crisp entry leads to a moderately light-bodied palate with racy acidity and lean tannins. Crisp, racy finish. A spicy quaffer. Drink now.

81 • Yakima River (WA) 1997 Cabernet-Merlot, Yakima Valley. $9.49.
Bright cherry-red hue. Forward candied berry and mineral aromas. A soft entry leads to a medium-bodied palate with crisp acidity and lean tannins. Zesty, fruity finish. A lighter-styled quaffer. Drink now.

81 • Washington Hills (WA) 1997 Cabernet-Merlot, Columbia Valley. $10.
Bright cherry-red hue. Light red fruit and herb aromas. A soft entry leads to a moderately light-bodied palate with mild tannins and grippy acidity. Quick, light finish. A quaffer, lacking real intensity. Drink now.

81 • Hedges (WA) 1997 Cabernet-Merlot, Washington. $10.
Bright purple-red hue. Generous red fruit and mineral aromas. A crisp attack leads to a medium-bodied palate with angular, grippy tannins. Firm, austere finish. Comes across as being a touch flat. Drink now.

81 • Grande River (CO) 1995 Meritage, Grand Valley. $12.99.
Pale garnet hue. Forward, mature earth and cedar aromas. A soft entry leads to a light-bodied palate with gentle tannins and crisp acidity. Quick crisp finish. Drink now.

81 • Duckhorn (CA) 1996 Decoy Migration, Napa Valley. $15.
Bright ruby hue. Forward leather and berry aromas. A supple entry leads to a lush, medium-bodied palate with silky tannins. Soft, earthy finish. Light and approachable. Drink now.

80 • *Hogue (WA) 1997 Cabernet-Merlot, Columbia Valley. $8.95.*
Pale cherry-red hue. Forward herb and candied cherry aromas. A crisp entry leads to a light-bodied, fruity palate with mild tannins. Lean finish. A quaffer.

Aussie Red Bordeaux Varietal Blends

86 • *Lindemans (Australia) 1996 Cabernet-Merlot, Padthaway. $15.*
Opaque blackish purple. Full-bodied. Balanced acidity. Highly extracted. Mildly oaked. Moderately tannic. Black fruits, minerals, pipe tobacco. Forward aromas lead a full and intense palate feel. Quite firm in the mouth, with gripping tannins biting into the finish.

85 • *Chateau Reynella (Australia) 1995 Basket Pressed, Cabernet-Merlot, McLaren Vale. $15.*
Opaque blackish ruby cast. Moderately full-bodied. Balanced acidity. Highly extracted. Moderately oaked. Moderately tannic. Black fruits, mint, minerals. Austere aromatics lead a rich but severe mouthfeel. Rather monolithic and a tad tough, with drying tannins biting into the core of dark flavors.

84 • *Tyrrell's (Australia) 1997 Old Winery, Cabernet-Merlot, South Australia. $10.99.*
Deep ruby cast. Moderately full-bodied. Balanced acidity. Highly extracted. Mildly oaked. Moderately tannic. Vanilla, black fruits. Quite youthful, with a firm and extracted structure and reserved flavors. Lean through the lengthy cassis-accented finish.

84 • *Abbey Vale (Australia) 1995 Cabernet-Merlot, Margaret River. $15.*
Bright ruby red with a slight fade. Medium-bodied. Balanced acidity. Moderately extracted. Mildly tannic. Dried herbs, minerals, red fruits, earth. Shows a distinct herbal/earthy note in the nose. Light in style and lean in the mouth, with a peppery quality to the finish.

83 • *Cassegrain (Australia) 1996 78% Cabernet Sauvignon-22% Merlot, Hastings River. $14.99.*
Pale ruby-garnet hue with a slight fade. Medium-bodied. Balanced acidity. Subtly extracted. Mildly oaked. Mildly tannic. Cedar, minerals, spice. Maturing aromas show a spicy wood influence. Light in the mouth with drying tannins through the finish. Pleasant, but for near-term drinking.

82 • *Cockatoo Ridge (Australia) 1997 Cabernet Sauvignon-Merlot, Australia. $10.*
Pale ruby red with a fade to the rim. Moderately light-bodied. Balanced acidity. Subtly extracted. Mildly tannic. Green pepper, dried herbs. Quite aromatic, with a distinctive green edge to the flavors. Very light in the mouth, showing mild fruity flavors. A decent quaffer.

82 • *Black Opal (Australia) 1997 82% Cabernet-18% Merlot, South Eastern Australia. $10.50.*
Bright ruby cast. Medium-bodied. Balanced acidity. Moderately extracted. Mildly tannic. Red fruits, minerals. High-toned fruity aromas lead a lean palate. Light in the mouth with a green edge to the flavors. Rather astringent through the finish.

U.S. Cabernet Franc

89 • *Pindar (NY) 1994 Cabernet Franc, North Fork of Long Island. $12.99.*
Light cherry red. Pleasant, perfumed sweet herb and spice aromas. A firm entry leads to a medium-bodied palate with drying tannins. Flavorful and angular with good bite. Drink now or later.

87 • *Midnight Cellars (CA) 1995 Crescent, Cabernet Franc, Paso Robles. $15.*
Bright ruby purple. Medium-bodied. Balanced acidity. Moderately extracted. Mildly oaked. Mildly tannic. Red fruits, brown spices, minerals. Aromatic, with a flavorful palate. Lean and angular through the finish, with a firm structure on a lighter frame.

86 • Yorkville (CA) 1996 Rennie Vineyard, Cabernet Franc, Mendocino County. $14.

Bright ruby purple. Moderately light-bodied. Full acidity. Subtly extracted. Moderately oaked. Mildly tannic. Cherries, vanilla. Tart and crisp, with bright, vanilla-accented fruit flavors. Lean and zesty through the brisk finish.

86 • Hargrave (NY) 1997 Cabernet Franc, North Fork of Long Island. $14.99.

Bright cherry red hue with a slight fade. Generous herb, red fruit and mineral aromas. A firm entry leads a medium-bodied palate with drying tannins and a clipped, leafy finish. A lean Chinon style. Drink now.

85 • W.B. Bridgman (WA) 1995 Cabernet Franc, Yakima Valley. $13.99.

Bright ruby-garnet cast. Medium-bodied. Balanced acidity. Moderately extracted. Moderately tannic. Minerals, wood. Lighter in style, with elegant and supple flavors. Features a judicious oak accent throughout. Well balanced.

85 • Mission View (CA) 1995 Cabernet Franc, Paso Robles. $13.50.

Bright ruby purple. Medium-bodied. Balanced acidity. Highly extracted. Moderately oaked. Mildly tannic. Bacon fat, vanilla, minerals. Oak-driven flavors play out on a lighter-styled palate. Lean and drying through the finish.

85 • Hogue (WA) 1994 Genesis, Cabernet Franc, Columbia Valley. $15.

Bright ruby red with a fade to the rim. Moderately full-bodied. Full acidity. Highly extracted. Moderately tannic. Minerals, red fruits. Lean and austere in style, with a firm structure. Finishes on a vibrant, earthy note.

85 • Autumn Hill (VA) 1997 Flarepath Vineyard, Cabernet Franc, Monticello. $15.

Bright ruby cast. Moderately light-bodied. Full acidity. Moderately extracted. Moderately oaked. Mildly tannic. Vanilla, cherries. Generous aromas reveal an interplay between fruit and wood nuances. Lean and very angular in the mouth, with a crisp, tart finish. Shows excellent grip.

84 • Pugliese (NY) 1997 Cabernet Franc, North Fork of Long Island. $13.99.

Bright ruby-garnet hue. Subdued mineral, red fruit, and herb aromas. A supple entry leads a medium-bodied palate with velvety tannins. Flavorful and straightforward. Drink now.

84 • Ingleside Plantation (VA) 1995 Cabernet Franc, Virginia. $11.99.

Bright ruby with a garnet rim. Medium-bodied. Full acidity. Moderately extracted. Mildly oaked. Mildly tannic. Vanilla, cherries, minerals. Aromatically reserved, but juicy and flavorful on the palate, with a lean and angular finish.

84 • Arciero (CA) 1995 Cabernet Franc, Paso Robles. $10.50.

Pale ruby red with a slight fade. Moderately light-bodied. Full acidity. Subtly extracted. Mildly oaked. Mildly tannic. Vanilla, citrus, red fruits. Lean and angular, with tart acidity through the finish. Flavors are wood driven and drying.

83 • Horton (VA) 1996 Cabernet Franc, Virginia. $12.

Pale ruby-garnet hue. Moderately light-bodied. Full acidity. Moderately extracted. Moderately oaked. Mildly tannic. Brown spices, cedar, minerals. Shows an obvious oak influence in the nose. Light and crisp in the mouth, with an angular finish.

83 • Hahn Estates (CA) 1996 Cabernet Franc, Santa Lucia Highlands. $10.

Bright ruby cast. Moderately light-bodied. Balanced acidity. Subtly extracted. Mildly tannic. Vegetables, minerals. Shows a green streak throughout. Light, though firmly structured in the mouth, with a lean finish.

83 • Clos du Lac (CA) 1996 Cabernet Franc, Sierra Foothills–Amador County. $15.

Bright ruby purple. Medium-bodied. Full acidity. Moderately extracted. Moderately oaked. Moderately tannic. Minerals, cassis, chocolate. Generous aromas lead a ripe and flavorful palate that shows complexity. Toughens a bit on the finish, where the tannins rear up.

Scale: Superlative (96-100), Exceptional (90-95), Highly Recommended (85-89), Recommended (80-84), Not Recommended (Under 80)

82 • *Naked Mountain (VA) 1997 Cabernet Franc, Virginia.* $12.

Bright ruby-purple hue. Generous berry and mineral aromas. A lean attack leads to a medium-bodied palate. Flavorful, fruit-accented finish. Shows fine intensity and solid grip with a firm minerally edge. Drink now.

82 • *Monthaven (CA) 1996 Cabernet Franc, Napa Valley.* $9.99.

Bright saturated ruby cast. Moderately full-bodied. Balanced acidity. Moderately extracted. Mildly tannic. Minerals, red fruits. Restrained aromas lead a core of minerally fruit flavors. Firm but ripe in the mouth, with an angular finish.

82 • *Lamoreaux Landing (NY) 1996 Cabernet Franc, Finger Lakes.* $14.

Deep ruby cast. Moderately full-bodied. Full acidity. Highly extracted. Heavily oaked. Moderately tannic. Mint, brown spices, cherry cordial. Quite aromatic, with a big, spicy oak overlay and a ripe, cordial-like quality to the fruit flavors. Still quite lean and firm, with a drying, angular finish.

82 • *Elk Run (MD) 1997 Cabernet Franc, Maryland.* $15.

Deep ruby hue. Unusual earth, smoke, and licorice aromas. A lean attack leads to a medium-bodied palate with shy acidity. Firm minerally finish. Drink now.

81 • *Tarara (VA) 1997 Cabernet Franc, Virginia.* $13.99.

Pale garnet hue. Forward cedar and herb aromas. A lean attack leads to a moderately light-bodied palate. Flavorful, lengthy finish. An interesting, mature, herbal style. Drink now.

81 • *Jefferson (VA) 1997 Cabernet Franc, Monticello.* $15.

Pale ruby hue. Unusual herb and earth aromas. A crisp attack leads to a medium-bodied palate with crisp acidity. Shows depth and intensity in the mouth. Firm, extracted finish. Drink now.

81 • *Fenestra (CA) 1995 Cabernet Franc, Santa Lucia Highlands.* $12.50.

Bright ruby cast. Moderately light-bodied. Balanced acidity. Subtly extracted. Moderately oaked. Mildly tannic. Vanilla, red fruits. Features a sweet oak accent throughout. Light, clean, and crisp on the palate, with a juicy finish.

80 • *Seth Ryan (WA) 1996 Cabernet Franc, Yakima Valley.* $14.81.

Pale ruby-garnet cast. Medium-bodied. Full acidity. Highly extracted. Mildly oaked. Quite tannic. Cedar, minerals. Heavily oak-accented aromas dominate the palate, with faint varietal flavors fighting through the dry finish.

80 • *Palmer (NY) 1995 Proprietor's Reserve, Cabernet Franc, North Fork of Long Island.* $15.

Bright ruby purple. Medium-bodied. Full acidity. Highly extracted. Moderately tannic. Black cherries, minerals. Aromatically reserved, with a lean and firm palate feel. Hearty extract leaves a slight astringent note on the finish, while the midpalate is a touch brittle.

Argentine Malbec

90 • *Bodegas Escorihuela (Argentina) 1997 Don Miguel Gascón, Malbec, Mendoza.* $11.99.

Saturated dark purple. Brooding anise and blackberry aromas. A rich attack leads a moderately full-bodied palate with fine-grained, rich tannins and concentrated flavors. Acids are rather soft. This wine will be best drunk in youth with rich foods.

86 • *Mariposa (Argentina) 1997 Tapiz Reserve, Malbec, Mendoza.* $15.

Saturated purple-pink. Deep black fruit aromas. A firm entry leads a moderately full-bodied palate with dark fruit flavors and moderate tannic grip through the finish. Shows good varietal character. Try with rich foods.

84 • *Trapiche (Argentina) 1995 Oak Cask, Malbec, Mendoza.* $8.99.

Bright ruby red. Very aromatic with a fleshy toasted-oak accent. A bright attack leads a medium-bodied palate with light cherry-berry flavors and soft tannins. Finishes with attractive toasted-oak notes. Drink now.

84 • Santa Julia (Argentina) 1996 Oak Reserve, Malbec, Mendoza. $10.
Pale ruby red. Attractively spiced aromas lead a moderately light-bodied palate with plenty of oak spice and subtle fruit flavors. Acids are crisp through the finish. A quaffer.

84 • Bodega Norton (Argentina) 1996 Malbec, Mendoza. $9.
Pale ruby red. Fennel aromas, with medicinal aromas that are very distinctive. A crisp entry leads a tart, moderately light-bodied palate that has crisp red fruit flavors and a distinct herbal accent. Drink now.

84 • Balbi (Argentina) 1997 Malbec, Mendoza. $12.
Bright ruby red. Moderately aromatic with subtle oak spice. Crisp on the entry, with a medium-bodied palate showing bright acids and clean black fruit flavors through the crisp finish. Very direct and appealing.

83 • Tri Vento (Argentina) 1997 Malbec, Mendoza. $7.
Bright red-purple. Muted reductive aromas that develop more fruity character with aeration. Crisp cherry flavors on the attack, with a medium-bodied palate and good flavor intensity. Tannins are light, giving a degree of grip. Very well balanced. Drink now.

83 • Alamos Ridge (Argentina) 1996 Malbec, Mendoza. $10.
Medium ruby-purple with a subtle fade. Jammy, warm aromas. A jammy attack leads a medium-bodied palate with a thick mouthfeel and a crisp acids. Finishes quickly, with very slight tannins.

82 • Santa Julia (Argentina) 1997 Malbec, Mendoza. $7.
Ruby red with a fading rim. Muted aromas. A lean entry followed by a medium-bodied palate with bright, faint berry flavors that finish quickly. A very simple wine in a lighter style.

80 • Vinterra (Argentina) 1997 Malbec, Mendoza. $6.99.
Bright ruby pink. Flawed aromas. Medium bodied, with jammy, tart flavors and a vapid finish. This wine seems both over- and underripe.

80 • Mariposa (Argentina) 1997 Malbec, Mendoza. $9.
Saturated dark crimson-purple. Dirty aromas. A dull entry leads a medium-bodied palate with poorly defined, earthy flavors.

U.S. Malbec

83 • Stonehedge (CA) 1994 Malbec, Napa Valley. $12.99.
Deep purple with a lightening rim. Moderately light-bodied. Moderately extracted. Moderately tannic. Vanilla, flowers, red fruit. Solid black fruit aromas follow through on the palate, with licorice-like intensity through the finish. Tannins are ripe and chewy. Tends toward the bland.

83 • Monthaven (CA) 1996 Malbec, Napa Valley. $9.99.
Bright violet-red. Medium-bodied. Moderately extracted. Mildly tannic. Black cherries, vanilla. Cheerful, fruity aromas follow through on the palate, with a dusting of fine-grained tannins providing some grip on the finish.

81 • Horton (VA) 1995 Malbec, Virginia. $15.
Pale ruby hue. Moderately light-bodied. Subtly extracted. Mildly tannic. Dill, sage, minerals. Very pronounced American oak aromas. The savory herb-filled palate has a lighter frame and a supple finish. Drinking well now, though it may not appeal to everyone. Very unusual style.

Other Great Value Bordeaux Varietals

93 • Bouwland (South Africa) 1997 Cabernet Sauvignon–Merlot, Stellenbosch. $10.99.
Deep purple-red. Generous red fruit and mineral aromas show a gentle oak overlay. A lush entry leads a medium-bodied palate with ripe tannins and excellent flavor intensity that are persistent and harmonious through the finish. Drink now.

88 • Viu Manent (Chile) 1997 Reserve, Oak Aged, Malbec, Colchagua Valley. $12.

Deep purple. Fantastically aromatic, with chocolate and blueberry aromas showing a toasty oak influence. A rich attack leads a moderately full body with forward chocolate and fleshy fruit flavors that finish with firm tannins and a long toasty note. Probably best drunk in its youth for its seductive, vivid flavors.

85 • Moulin des Sablons (France) 1996 Chinon. $9.99.

Bright red-purple. Medium-bodied. Balanced acidity. Moderately extracted. Violets, red fruits. Ripe, fruity aromas lead a lively palate with red fruit flavors. Smooth tannins linger through the finish.

84 • Jaja de Jau (France) 1996 Cabernet-Merlot, Vin de Pays d'Oc. $6.

Bright ruby purple. Medium-bodied. Full acidity. Subtly extracted. Mildly tannic. Red fruits. Quite aromatic, with a wave of fruit-accented aromas. Light and crisp in style, with a zesty finish. A Beaujolais-like style.

84 • Hester Creek (Canada) 1997 Cabernet-Merlot, Okanagan Valley. $14.

Deep garnet red hue. Forward iron, red fruit, and spice aromas show a generous oak accent. A crisp attack leads to a medium bodied palate with grippy tannins and zesty acidity through a clean flavorful finish. A lively, clean, fruit-forward style.

84 • Hester Creek (Canada) 1997 Cabernet Franc, Okanagan Valley. $13.

Bright pale brick-red hue. Forward herb and wood aromas show a marked oak influence. A firm attack leads to a medium-bodied palate with lean, drying tannins. Finish is rather oaky and tannic. Interesting flavors but seems to be drying out. Drink within five years.

83 • Schlumberger (Austria) 1994 Privatkeller, Cabernet Sauvignon/ Merlot, Thermenregion. $11.66.

Saturated blood red. Moderately full-bodied. Highly extracted. Moderately tannic. Black fruits. Chewy and well structured, with a thick mouthfeel. Flavors are austere, making for a tough, muted style.

81 • Santa Ema (Chile) 1996 Cabernet-Merlot, Maipo Valley. $10.

Bright ruby red with a fading rim. Mild aromas of tobacco and black fruits. A jammy entry leads a medium-bodied palate with ripe fruit flavors that fall short on the bland finish. Drink now.

81 • Magnotta (Canada) 1995 Limited Edition, Cabernet-Merlot, Ontario. $12.

Deep ruby red hue to the rim. Unusual earth and mineral aromas. A firm attack leads to a medium-bodied palate with lean, astringent tannins giving a short, mildly bitter finish. Rather tough and ungenerous.

thirteen

❧

Pinot Noir

❧

Introduction	156
Reviews	157
U.S. Pinot Noir	157
Other Great Value Pinot Noirs	160

Introduction: Pinot Noir

A handful of the world's wines, such as Sherry from Jerez, Beaujolais from France, and Riesling from many places, offer a bounty of choice to value-conscious consumers. Even the best of these wines often come to us at very modest prices. The same cannot be said of Burgundy's Pinot Noir. Pinot Noir is the unkept promise, the chronic underachiever, and it most often comes with a hefty price tag. To be fair, Pinot Noir is an exceedingly difficult and fragile grape. The entire production affair is fraught with danger from the spring's first bud-break through the vinification process. Pinot Noir is, perhaps, the wine world's most challenging variety. However, Pinot Noir is capable of achieving lush and incredibly complex wines that are perfectly proportioned and defy description.

If you are seeking Pinot Noir values from its native France, you may just as well be searching for the Holy Grail. Pinot Noir is the singular red grape from which the famed red wines of Burgundy are produced. Today, the simplest reds from Burgundy fetch a king's ransom, even in the poorest of vintages. Often a thin and disappointing bottle of Burgundy will cost as much as a case (12 bottles) of a simple but satisfying wine from an underappreciated region or variety. The notable exception to expensive Pinot Noir in France is varietally labeled Pinot Noir from Alsace. Alsatian Pinot Noir is pale in color, often looking like a deep Rosé. The aromas and flavors are fresh and lean, and the wines show a silky texture. These Pinots are almost always unoaked.

Value Pinot Noirs can be found from U.S. producers, primarily in California. U.S. value-priced Pinot Noirs tend to be simple, fruit oriented, and well balanced. Oregon has been proclaimed by connoisseurs to be the best hope that the United States has to capture the fleeting Burgundian magic. In good vintages Oregon has produced Pinot Noir showing incredible depth and balance, with refined and restrained, complex flavors rarely achieved in California. Staying true to the Burgundian model, the quality of Oregon Pinot Noirs is spotty, varying greatly from vintage to vintage; they are also rising rapidly in price. Cool growing regions in California, including the Russian River Valley, Carneros, the South Central Coast (Santa Barbara and San Luis Obispo counties), and parts of Monterey, are considered among the very best sites in the United States outside of Oregon. Sadly, these wines, too, are regularly priced beyond value considerations. Thus, as when hunting for any value wine from California, stick to the general appellations, and don't overlook wines from other states. Consumers buying value California wines rarely need to concern themselves with vintages, but Pinot Noir is the exception to this rule. Furthermore, you can't generalize about the state as a whole. Pinot Noir may be fabulous in Carneros and only acceptable in Santa Barbara or vise versa. As always, your best resource is a reputable wine merchant. In favorable vintages, value Pinot Noir will still be best before its fifth birthday.

Value Pinot Noir is most often medium- to light-bodied with moderate acidity. Flavors of black cherry, plum, violet, and spice are common. These wines can be charming and accessible to all, but will not appeal to the Burgundy snob. Just as well—you don't want to hang about that sort anyway. These wines are very versatile, giving much pleasure on their own or paired with food. Slow-roasted full-bodied meats marry well, as the textures meld and the fresh fruit perks up the food's flavors. They can work equally well with fish and grilled poultry.

Scale: Superlative (96-100), Exceptional (90-95), Highly Recommended (85-89), Recommended (80-84), Not Recommended (Under 80)

Reviews

U.S. Pinot Noir

88 • Belvedere (CA) 1996 Pinot Noir, Anderson Valley. $12.
Bright pale ruby cast. Medium-bodied. Full acidity. Moderately extracted. Mildly tannic. Iron, red fruits. Fragrant and intense, with an exotic minerally quality. Angular and zesty in the mouth with bright flavors and a clean finish.

86 • Hacienda (CA) 1996 Clair de Lune, Pinot Noir, California. $6.99.
Pale violet-red. Moderately light-bodied. Moderately extracted. Mildly tannic. Vanilla, red berries. Perfumed, sweetish aromas lead a bright and fruity palate with lively acids providing solid grip.

86 • Beringer (CA) 1996 Founders Estate, Pinot Noir, California. $9.99.
Brilliant red-violet. Medium-bodied. Moderately extracted. Mildly tannic. Red fruits, vanilla. Generous and vibrant floral, fruity flavors explode on the palate and are supported by restrained, soft tannins. A fine, easy-drinking style.

85 • Meridian (CA) 1997 Pinot Noir, Santa Barbara. $14.
Bright pale ruby cast. Moderately light-bodied. Full acidity. Moderately extracted. Moderately tannic. Minerals, red fruits. Lean minerally aromas lead a firm and tightly wound palate. Angular through the finish with a hint of bitterness.

84 • Wollersheim (WI) 1997 Cuvée 961, Pinot Noir, American. $12.
Pale cherry red. Moderately light-bodied. Subtly extracted. Mildly tannic. Crisp fruits, minerals. Subtle tart berry aromas follow through to a crisp yet flavorful palate with hints of oak spice lingering.

84 • Silver Ridge (CA) 1996 Pinot Noir, California. $9.99.
Pale violet. Moderately light-bodied. Subtly extracted. Mildly tannic. Red fruits, vanilla. Smooth yet crisp, with berry fruit flavors and balanced oak notes through the finish. Easy drinking.

84 • Robert Mondavi (CA) 1996 Coastal, Pinot Noir, Central Coast. $10.95.
Bright red-violet. Medium-bodied. Moderately extracted. Mildly tannic. Vanilla, butter, red fruits. Sweet red fruit aromas show an oak accent and crisp flavors through the finish. A straightforward, easy-drinking style.

Great Value Pinot Noir at a Glance

Number of Wines Reviewed:
51

Countries Represented:
8

84 • Lenz (NY) 1995 Estate, Pinot Noir, North Fork of Long Island. $14.99.
Bright ruby hue. Spice, mineral, and sour cherry aromas. A soft entry leads a moderately light-bodied palate with drying tannins. Snappy finish. Light and crisp in style, with faint Pinot perfume. Drink now.

84 • Indigo Hills (CA) 1996 Pinot Noir, Mendocino County. $12.
Full cherry red. Medium-bodied. Moderately extracted. Mildly tannic. Red fruits, minerals, brown spices. Jammy fruit aromas lead a fleshy, rounded palate with soft tannins lingering on the finish.

84 • Gallo Sonoma (CA) 1996 Pinot Noir, Russian River Valley. $11.99.
Light ruby hue with a slight fade. Moderately full-bodied. Balanced acidity. Moderately extracted. Mildly tannic. Minerals, chocolate. Aromatically reserved, with a weighty impression on the palate. Tasty, but a bit lacking in finesse.

84 • Fetzer (CA) 1996 Pinot Noir, California. $12.99.
Bright ruby cast. Medium-bodied. Balanced acidity. Moderately extracted. Mildly tannic. Minerals, red fruits. Lean aromas lead a firm mouthfeel with a lot of grip. Full yet lean through the finish.

84 • Estancia (CA) 1997 Pinot Noir, Monterey. $12.
Pale cherry red. Medium-bodied. Moderately extracted. Mildly tannic. Fruit cordial, vanilla. Ripe, cordial-like aromas follow through on the palate with a range of jammy flavors. Finishes with soft tannins.

84 • Charles Shaw (CA) 1996 Pinot Noir, California. $8.99.
Cherry red with violet highlights. Medium-bodied. Moderately extracted. Mildly tannic. Red fruits, vanilla. Berryish, oak-accented aromas follow through on the palate, with tart fruit flavors and mild astringency lingering on the finish.

83 • Ste. Genevieve (TX) NV Pinot Noir, Texas. $8.99/1.5 L.
Bright violet-red. Medium-bodied. Moderately extracted. Mildly tannic. Sweet cherries, blueberries. Attractive candied fruit aromas follow to a ripe fruity mouthful with the softest of tannins on the finish. Easy drinking, attractive.

83 • Pepperwood Grove (CA) 1997 Pinot Noir, California. $6.99.
Very pale violet. Moderately light-bodied. Subtly extracted. Mildly tannic. Cherries, vanilla. Vibrant, sweet, fruity aromas follow through on the palate, with a crisp finish that makes for a fresh style.

83 • Pedroncelli (CA) 1996 F. Johnson Vineyard, Pinot Noir, Dry Creek Valley. $13.
Pale ruby cast. Moderately light-bodied. Full acidity. Subtly extracted. Mildly tannic. Sweet herbs, minerals, meat. Unusual aromas lead a very light palate. Crisp through the finish.

83 • Mirassou (CA) 1996 Family Selection, Pinot Noir, Monterey County. $10.95.
Very pale red. Moderately light-bodied. Subtly extracted. Red fruits, dried herbs, minerals. Crisp fruity aromas lead a lightly framed palate with lean, bright flavors and a clean finish.

83 • Jekel (CA) 1996 Gravelstone, Pinot Noir, Monterey. $13.
Pale cherry red. Medium-bodied. Moderately extracted. Mildly tannic. Red berry fruits, minerals. Perfumed aromas follow through with lean flavors showing a mineral edge on the finish.

83 • Fox Hollow (CA) 1997 Pinot Noir, Monterey County. $8.99.
Bright violet-red. Cherries, vanilla. Crisp, vibrant, fruity aromas follow through on a supple palate with precise black cherry flavors.

83 • Dunnewood (CA) 1996 Pinot Noir, North Coast. $7.99.
Medium-dark ruby red. Medium-bodied. Moderately extracted. Moderately tannic. Minerals, earth. Austere earthy aromas lead a tight, somewhat lean mouthful of flavors with a touch of fruit generosity.

83 • Anapamu (CA) 1996 Pinot Noir, Central Coast. $14.
Pale cherry red. Moderately light-bodied. Subtly extracted. Mildly tannic. Red fruits, herbs, vanilla. Light, high-toned fruit aromas follow through on a lightly framed palate with subtle flavors that finish quickly.

82 • Turning Leaf (CA) 1996 Winemaker's Choice Reserve, Pinot Noir, California. $12.
Deep ruby cast. Medium-bodied. Balanced acidity. Moderately extracted. Mildly tannic. Overripe red fruits, minerals. Unusual aromas carry a slight hint of overripeness. Firm and lean in the mouth with a drying finish.

82 • Siduri (OR) 1997 Pinot Noir, Oregon. $14.99.
Pale ruby-garnet cast. Light-bodied. Full acidity. Subtly extracted. Moderately oaked. Mildly tannic. Minerals, tart cherries, sweet wood. Forward aromas feature bright, high-toned, fruity flavors. Light and crisp in the mouth. A quaffer.

82 • M.G. Vallejo (CA) 1996 Pinot Noir, California. $6.99.
Pale cherry red with a fading subtly garnet rim. Medium-bodied. Moderately extracted. Mildly oaked. Minerals, vanilla, red fruits. Mild leathery aromas lead a smooth fruity palate that finishes with soft tannins.

82 • Carneros Creek (CA) 1997 Fleur de Carneros, Pinot Noir, Carneros. $12.
Pale violet-rimmed ruby hue. Moderately light-bodied. Subtly extracted. Mildly tannic. Red fruits, minerals, spice. Mildly perfumed aromas lead a delicate yet smooth mouthful of flavors. The finish shows well-balanced tannic grip. Straightforward, yet a good expression of Pinot Noir.

81 • Willamette Valley Vineyards (OR) 1997 Whole Cluster Fermented, Pinot Noir, Oregon. $14.99.
Deep ruby cast. Light-bodied. Full acidity. Subtly extracted. Moderately tannic. Black fruits, pepper. Forward, primary, grapey aromas lead a ripe and supple mouthfeel. Lean through the finish with a hint of astringence.

81 • Sea Ridge Coastal (CA) 1996 Pinot Noir, California. $10.
Pale cherry red with a fading rim. Moderately light-bodied. Subtly extracted. Mildly tannic. Oak spice, butter, red fruits. Very up-front oak accents dominate the flavors on the palate, though bright acids make for a zesty mouthfeel.

81 • Sakonnet (RI) 1995 Pinot Noir, Southeastern New England. $14.99.
Pale, fading garnet red. Moderately light-bodied. Subtly extracted. Mildly tannic. Tart cherries, minerals. A delicate oak-spiced nose leads a crisp, flavorful palate with gentle tannins and a clean finish.

81 • Lorane Valley (OR) 1996 Pinot Noir, Oregon. $10.
Pale ruby-garnet cast. Moderately light-bodied. Full acidity. Subtly extracted. Mildly tannic. Minerals, red fruits, citrus. Lean aromas feature an austere minerally quality and subdued red fruit overtones. Crisp and zesty in the mouth with a vibrant finish.

81 • Henry Estate (OR) 1997 Umpqua Cuvée, Pinot Noir, Umpqua Valley. $11.
Very pale ruby-purple cast. Light-bodied. Full acidity. Subtly extracted. Mildly tannic. Cherries, minerals. Crisp and lively, with a fruit-centered palate. Angular and zesty through the finish. A quaffing style.

81 • Eyrie (OR) 1996 Pinot Noir, Willamette Valley. $14.
Pale garnet cast. Medium-bodied. Full acidity. Moderately extracted. Moderately oaked. Mildly tannic. Cedar, minerals, brown spices. Aromatic and complex, with an unusual range of herb and wood flavors. Light in the mouth, with a lingering finish.

81 • Estrella (CA) 1996 Proprietor's Reserve, Pinot Noir, California. $9.99/1.5 L.
Bright red-violet. Moderately light-bodied. Subtly extracted. Mildly tannic. Red berries, vanilla. Aromatic, though not perfumed. Smooth red fruit flavors finish cleanly. An easy-drinking style.

81 • Columbia Winery (WA) 1997 Pinot Noir, Washington. $12.
Pale garnet cast. Moderately light-bodied. Low acidity. Subtly extracted. Moderately tannic. Minerals, forest. Early-maturing aromas lead a lean and drying palate feel. Austere through the finish.

81 • Bridgeview (OR) 1997 Pinot Noir, Oregon. $9.99.
Bright cherry red. Moderately light-bodied. Balanced acidity. Subtly extracted. Mildly tannic. Berries, minerals, sweet herbs. Forward aromas feature a simple fruity note and an herbal accent. Light and crisp in the mouth with a zesty finish. A quaffer.

80 • Joseph Swan (CA) 1997 Lone Redwood Ranch, Pinot Noir, Russian River Valley. $10.
Pale garnet hue with a fading rim. Unusual caramel and herb aromas. A lean entry leads a light-bodied palate with drying tannins. Quite light and crisp. A bit off-center. Drink now.

80 • Grand Cru (CA) 1995 Premium Selection, Pinot Noir, California. $7.99.
Deep cherry red with a garnet cast. Medium-bodied. Moderately extracted. Moderately tannic. Leather, earth. Earthy, cooked fruit aromas follow through on the palate with leathery tannins playing out on the drying finish.

80 • Buena Vista (CA) 1996 Pinot Noir, Sonoma Valley, Carneros. $14.
Pale ruby red. Medium-bodied. Subtly extracted. Red fruits, vanilla. Lean, vague fruity aromas lead a soft mouthful of red fruit flavors with low acids, though this has some tannic bite. Austere through the finish.

Other Great Value Pinot Noirs

86 • Premiat (Romania) 1995 Pinot Noir, Dealul Mare. $4.99.
Pale garnet red. Medium-bodied. Moderately extracted. Mildly tannic. Leather, earth, red fruits. Nice, faintly leathery aromas lead a delicate palate, with a dry, lingering berry fruit and earth finish. Very drinkable, with some faithful varietal accents.

86 • Pfaffenheim (France) 1997 Pinot Noir, Alsace. $10.
Light cherry red with a slight fade. A moderately full-bodied palate with balanced acidity. Moderately extracted, mildly oaked, and mildly tannic. Plums, spice, and dried herbs are the keynotes. Pleasantly aromatic, with a surprisingly full and structured mouthfeel. Rich and zesty through the finish.

86 • Mission Hill (Canada) 1997 Private Reserve, Pinot Noir, Okanagan Valley. $7.
Bright garnet red hue to the rim. Subdued berry and mineral aromas. A firm attack leads to a medium-bodied palate with lean, drying tannins. Clipped, clean finish. Rather ungenerous, but refreshing. Drink now.

85 • Weingut Norbert Bauer (Austria) 1993 Trocken, Blauer Burgunder, Weinviertel. $9.
Dark ruby purple. Moderately full-bodied. Balanced acidity. Moderately extracted. Mildly tannic. Blueberries, chocolate. Extraordinarily aromatic, with deep, dark flavors that feature a haunting blueberry quality. Rich and supple in the mouth, with fantastic concentration. Seductive.

85 • Tyrrell's (Australia) 1997 Old Winery, Pinot Noir, South Eastern Australia. $10.99.
Pale ruby-garnet cast. Moderately light-bodied. Balanced acidity. Moderately extracted. Moderately oaked. Quite tannic. Sweet oak, overripe red fruits. Shows a jammy quality to the nose. Straightforward and tasty flavors play out until firm tannins take over on the finish.

84 • Yarra Ridge (Australia) 1998 Pinot Noir, Yarra Valley. $11.99.
Pale ruby purple. Moderately full-bodied. Balanced acidity. Highly extracted. Moderately tannic. Briar fruits, minerals. Jammy fruit flavors lead a light palate with light varietal fruit flavors that taper to a mildly astringent finish. A ripe manifestation of Pinot Noir.

Scale: Superlative (96-100), Exceptional (90-95), Highly Recommended (85-89), Recommended (80-84), Not Recommended (Under 80)

84 • Shingle Peak (New Zealand) 1997 Pinot Noir, Marlborough. $13.50.
Pale ruby hue with a slight fade. Medium-bodied. Full acidity. Subtly extracted. Mildly oaked. Mildly tannic. Minerals, red fruits, spice. Quite light in style, with subtle herb-tinged aromatics. Lean and angular through the finish with slight but dry tannins.

83 • Undurraga (Chile) 1998 Pinot Noir, Maipo Valley. $9.99.
Bright pinkish red. Candied berry aromas are attractive. A bright, juicy entry leads a medium-light body with candied red fruit flavors that finish with very light supple tannins. A fruity quaffer; drink it now.

83 • Magnotta (Canada) 1995 Limited Edition, Pinot Noir, Ontario. $13.
Medium garnet red hue with a slight fade. Restrained herb and red fruit aromas. A firm attack leads to a moderately light-bodied palate with lean tannins and crisp acidity through the sharp, clean finish. On the green side of the pinot noir spectrum, but refreshing. Drink now.

82 • Rosemount (Australia) 1997 Diamond, Pinot Noir,
South Eastern Australia. $9.99.
Pale ruby cast. Medium-bodied. Balanced acidity. Moderately extracted. Quite tannic. Minerals, red fruits. Lean, minerally, herbal aromas lead a firm and edgy palate feel. Finishes with a drying note of green tannins.

82 • Mission Hill (Canada) 1996 Grand Reserve, Pinot Noir,
Okanagan Valley. $11.
Bright brick-red hue with a slight fade. Generous sandalwood and spice aromas carry a forward oak accent. A hard attack leads to a medium-bodied palate with green astringent tannins through a firm finish. Rather tough, though some bottle age should help. Drink now.

81 • Wyndham (Australia) 1998 Bin 333, Pinot Noir,
South Eastern Australia. $9.99.
Bright ruby purple. Medium-bodied. Balanced acidity. Moderately extracted. Mildly oaked. Quite tannic. Vanilla, red fruits. Clean, fruit-driven aromas with a dash of oak. Ripe in the mouth, but turns lean and angular with aggressive astringent tannins on the finish.

81 • Weingut Umathum (Austria) 1996 Junger Berg, Trocken, Blauburgunder,
Donauland. $15.
Bright ruby purple. Medium-bodied. Moderately extracted. Red fruits, herbs, minerals. Fresh, lively, and straightforward, with a hint of tannic grip on the finish.

81 • Charles de Valliere (France) 1994 Brulottes, Pinot Noir,
Bourgogne. $11.99.
Pale cherry red with a weak rim. Medium-bodied. Balanced acidity. Moderately extracted. Sour cherry. A suggestion of brettanomyces on the nose. Nice, rather soft mouthfeel with some decent flavors that finish quickly.

fourteen

❧

Gamay

❧

Introduction	164
Reviews	166
Beaujolais	166
Other Great Value Gamays	168

Introduction: Gamay

The Gamay is a grape known for its fresh cherry and plum-like flavors enhanced by lively acidity. It is the sole grape varietal for the red wines of Beaujolais. This seductive, fruity, French wine is best known for its "Nouveau" style, released to the world on the third Thursday of every November. It is widely anticipated as the first wine in the world to be produced from that very year's vintage. The fruity, festive nature of Nouveau is cause for some to dismiss Beaujolais as a serious wine. This would be a mistake, as Beaujolais rarely fails to please both the palate and the pocketbook. Both Beaujolais and U.S. versions of Gamay are a bargain hunter's friend. Like Sherry, Beaujolais offers the wine buyer an opportunity to enjoy the best that this category has to offer without breaking the bank, while U.S. versions are almost always a bargain as well.

The Beaujolais district lies just north of Lyon, stretching 34 miles toward the Rhône Valley, running parallel to the Saône River. Beaujolais is recognized in three general categories:

- A wine labeled simply as Beaujolais is the most general designation.

- Beaujolais-Villages wines come from a select group of 39 villages in the northern half of the region, which have been recognized as producing superior wines.

- The top designations are cru Beaujolais, which come from one of ten individual villages within the Beaujolais-Villages zone whose wines merit special distinction. These cru Beaujolais are permitted to label their wines with the village name alone. One would have to examine the label to find the word Beaujolais. Each of these crus has a unique character, although for the purpose of this discussion we can group them into four general categories. The lightest of the crus are Brouilly, Chiroubles, Fleurie, and Regnie (the newest cru), which are best consumed in youth. The wines of Cote de Brouilly and Saint Amour are a bit more intense and structured. Morgon, Julienas, and Chenas are robust and lively wines that are often shocking to those only familiar with Beaujolais-Villages. The last category is reserved for a wine like no other, Moulin à Vent. This sturdy, full-bodied wine is lovely in its youth and is often capable of aging surprisingly well.

When discussing Beaujolais, it is difficult not to mention the name of Georges Duboeuf, the great ambassador for Beaujolais. Duboeuf was born in the region of Pouilly-Fuissé, just north of Beaujolais, into a family that had been cultivating vineyards since the 18th century. At the age of 19 Georges had bottled a wine of his own and sold it to restaurants in his local village. Soon Duboeuf earned a reputation as a supplier of quality wines, and in 1964 he launched his own company. In 1968 an international exhibition in Montreal brought Duboeuf's wines global recognition and acclaim. Today, both colleagues and wine admirers respectfully regard him as the "King of Beaujolais."

Duboeuf's Beaujolais, from the broadly labeled Beaujolais to the crus, differ stylistically from most other wines of the region. His fruit-oriented wines are created by use of a vinification technique known as carbonic maceration. Instead of crushing the grapes and allowing the fermentation to commence in the presence of air, whole clusters are placed in cool tanks filled with carbon dioxide. A partial fermentation occurs within the uncrushed grape. This also serves to weaken the skins causing grape clusters at the bottom to burst from the weight above. The juice then comes in contact with yeast, which begins the cycle of a normal alcoholic fermentation. As a consequence of this process, Duboeuf's wines are unabashedly grapey, with a bright purple color, beautiful aromas, and very little tannin. In nearly all cases they are best consumed while young. Wines made in a more customary method tend to be weightier and rather more tannic.

Gamay in the United States, especially California, has been troublesome. Most of what is labeled Gamay is not the same variety responsible for Beaujolais. U.S. Wines labeled "Gamay Beaujolais" are not Gamay at all, but actually a variant of Pinot Noir. In the past decade and a half, acreage of Gamay and Gamay Beaujolais has declined by over 75% in California. It would be a great loss to see these varieties disappear. Those that remain share many characteristics with Beaujolais—being soft, fruity, and shy of tannin, while showing a bit more weight and body overall.

Beaujolais has had a string of good to excellent vintages in the '90s, topped by the fabulous 1997 vintage. Beaujolais is widely available in both supermarkets and serious wine shops across the country. Restaurants, to a large degree, have been slow to include cru Beaujolais on their wine lists. This is unfortunate considering that Beaujolais is wonderful at the table, marrying well with a variety of dishes. Beaujolais and U.S. Gamay should be served at a cool room temperature. Beaujolais-Villages and lighter-styled crus can benefit from a slight chill.

With wide availability and fantastic prices there is ample reason to enjoy Beaujolais year round, not just in Nouveau season. You may wish to spark conversation at your next dinner party by offering two differing crus, such as the light Regnie and a richer style like Chenas. You and your guests will be amazed by the contrast in wines produced just miles apart—one of the least expensive and most convincing studies of the French concept of terroir that can be easily organized.

Great Value Gamay at a Glance

Number of Wines Reviewed:

41

Countries Represented:

3

Reviews

Beaujolais

90 • Georges Duboeuf (France) 1998 "Jean Descombes," Morgon. $9.99.
Brilliant ruby-pink hue. Outrageously pure, fruity aromas of cassis and blackberry preserves make this a standout wine. Concentrated jammy fruit flavors run through the opulent, medium-bodied palate with soft acids and tannins. Very lush, textured, and distinctive. Drink now.

90 • Georges Duboeuf (France) 1998 Domaine des Quatre Vents, Fleurie. $11.99.
Rich purple-pink hue. Attractive dark berry-laden aromas with floral flourishes. Concentrated and berry centered on the attack, leading a medium-bodied palate and a lingering, zesty, fruity finish. Stylish and delicious. Drink now or later.

89 • Louis Jadot (France) 1997 Domaine du Monnet, Brouilly. $12.
Pale ruby-red hue. Complex aromas of smoke, herbs, and red cherries follow through on the medium-bodied palate with spicy fruit flavors and a wisp of angular tannins. Unmistakably Gamay, but this has some of the traits of a good Bourgogne Rouge. Drink now or later.

89 • Louis Jadot (France) 1997 Chateau de Bellevue, Morgon. $12.
Pale ruby hue. Ripe, smoky aromas lead a medium-bodied palate with a smooth texture and a spicy, supple finish. This is remarkably complex and elegant, in a Burgundian manner. Drink now.

89 • Georges Duboeuf (France) 1998 Domaine de la Tour du Bief, Moulin-a-Vent. $11.49.
Deep reddish-pink hue. Smoky, oak-accented aromas show fleshy dark fruits. Concentrated and ripe on the entry, with a moderately full-bodied palate and a spiced finish. Well gripped. Drink now or later.

89 • Georges Duboeuf (France) 1998 Château des Déduits, Fleurie. $11.99.
Brilliant pink-purple hue. Lavish floral aromas. Juicy and bright on the attack, with a medium-bodied palate, a silky character, and lingering berry flavors. Very stylish and well balanced. Drink now or later.

89 • Georges Duboeuf (France) 1997 Oak-Aged, Moulin-a-Vent. $12.99.
Ruby, with a fading pink rim. Spicy, oak-accented aromas. Lively and juicy on the entry leading a medium-bodied palate with velvety, supple tannins and smoky berryish flavors. Lingering finish. Drink now.

88 • Georges Duboeuf (France) Domaine des Rosiers, Moulin-a-Vent. $11.49.
Full pinkish-red hue. Dark fruit aromas of plum and blackberry come though on a medium-bodied palate with substance and mouthfeel. Flavors show good concentration and linger through the finish. Drink now or later.

88 • Georges Duboeuf (France) 1998 Juliénas. $9.59.
Ruby-purple hue. Bright violet and ripe berry aromas follow through on the moderately light-bodied palate with generous flavor concentration and a lingering finish. Very supple and attractive. Drink now.

88 • Georges Duboeuf (France) 1998 Grande Cuvée, Brouilly. $9.69.
Bright pink-red hue. Ripe dark fruit and floral, grapey aromas follow through with black cherry flavors. Medium-bodied, with supple tannins that give this a textured mouthfeel. Very hedonistic. Drink now or later.

88 • Georges Duboeuf (France) 1998 Fleurie. $11.49.
Deep pink-purple hue. Wildflowers and dark berry fruit aromas. Crisp on the attack, leading a medium-bodied palate with dark berry flavors and very supple light tannins. Stylish, well-concentrated flavors. This would stand up to food. Drink now.

Scale: Superlative (96-100), Exceptional (90-95), Highly Recommended (85-89),
Recommended (80-84), Not Recommended (Under 80)

166

88 • Georges Duboeuf (France) 1998 Château de Javernand, Chiroubles. $9.69.
Pale pinkish red hue. Very aromatic with gamey, smokey notes to the berry fruit.
Generous currant fruit flavors on a medium-bodied palate with supple tannins
give this a hedonistic edge, yet finishes with some grip. Drink now.

86 • Louis Jadot (France) 1997 Beaujolais-Villages. $10.
Pale ruby-purple hue. Ripe red fruit centered aromas. Fleshy, fruity flavors on entry lead
a medium-bodied palate with supple, slight tannins supporting the ripe fruit. Drink now.

86 • Georges Duboeuf (France) 1998 Régnié. $8.49.
Pale pink-purple hue. Very floral, high-toned aromas have a sweet fruity accent. Shows
pure, candied, berry fruits on the moderately light-bodied palate with a very supple,
lingering, floral finish. Very hedonistic—almost delicate in style. Drink now.

86 • Georges Duboeuf (France) 1998 Morgon. $9.69.
Bright pinkish red hue. Fruit-centered aromas of blackberry and raspberry follow
through on a medium-bodied palate with bright acids and a hint of tannic grip.
Drink now or later.

**86 • Georges Duboeuf (France) 1998 "Domaine de la Feuillée,"
Cote-de-Brouilly. $9.69.**
Pink-purple hue. Lightly floral, warm, alcoholic aromas. Crisply fruity on the attack
with a moderately light-bodied palate and grapey flavors that finish cleanly. Drink now.

86 • Georges Duboeuf (France) 1998 Chateau de Nervers, Brouilly. $9.89.
Full pinkish red hue. Generously ripe, fruit-centered aromas. Concentrated, ripe berry
flavors come through on a medium-bodied palate. A dry, tannic finish supplies some
grip. Drink now or later.

85 • Louis Latour (France) 1996 Morgon "Les Charmes." $12.
Deep garnet hue. Exotic spice and earth aromas jump from the glass with a slight gamey
accent. A lean entry leads to a moderately light-bodied palate with grippy tannins.
Flavorful and stylish. Drink now.

84 • Georges Duboeuf (France) 1998 Moulin-a-Vent. $11.
Deep purple with pink highlights. Blackberry and floral aromas lead a medium-bodied,
chunky, fruit-centered palate that finishes quickly with some mildy grippy tannins. This
will be better in six months. Drink now or later.

84 • Georges Duboeuf (France) 1998 Domaine du Potet, Régnié. $8.49.
Bright pink-purple hue. Fruity, candied berry aromas. Supple and juicy on the attack,
with a moderately light-bodied palate and a clean finish. Drink now.

**84 • Georges Duboeuf (France) 1998 "Domaine de la Pirolette,"
Saint-Amour. $11.99.**
Pale purple-ruby hue. Minerally, floral, candied berry aromas follow through on a
medium-bodied palate with a degree of minerally grip through the finish. Showing
a degree of leanness and firmness that will appeal to some. Drink now or later.

84 • Georges Duboeuf (France) 1998 Domaine Bellevue, Morgon. $9.99.
Deep neon-pink hue. Very aromatic with a floral, grapey accent. Vibrant red fruit flavors
on the entry lead to a medium-bodied palate with a clean, minerally finish. Showing nice
grip. Drink now.

84 • Georges Duboeuf (France) 1998 Chiroubles. $9.69.
Pale pink-red hue. Warm, ripe aromas of black grapes lead a moderately light-bodied
palate with grapey flavors and a clean, quick finish. Drink now.

84 • Georges Duboeuf (France) 1998 Chénas. $9.49.
Bright neon-purple hue. Ripe, candied berry aromas. Bright and tart flavors on entry
lead a medium-bodied palate with a quick, lean finish. Drink now.

84 • Georges Duboeuf (France) 1998 Château des Poupets, Juliénas. $9.99.
Purple, with a pale, lightening rim. Tart black fruit aromas. Crisp on the attack with a
medium-bodied palate and plummy flavors that finish with mild tannic grip that will
allow this to stand up to food. Drink now.

**84 • Georges Duboeuf (France) 1998 "Chateau de Varennes,"
Beaujolais-Villages. $7.99.**

Bright neon purple hue. Citrus and red berry aromas. Bright acidity etches the pure
berry fruit flavors on the medium-bodied palate with very slight tannic grip on the finish.
Drink now.

84 • Georges Duboeuf (France) 1998 Beaujolais-Villages. $7.99.

Brilliant pale purple hue. Very floral, grapey aromas. Bright and lively on the attack with
a moderately light body and very slight tannins giving a hint of grip on the finish. Drink
now.

83 • Louis Latour (France) 1997 "Les Charmes," Morgon. $12.

Very pale ruby hue. Subtle, faintly smoky aromas. Soft and juicy on the attack, leading a
moderately light-bodied palate with red berry fruit and savory herbal notes. Drink now.

83 • Louis Jadot (France) 1998 Beaujolais. $10.

Pale pink-purple hue. Bright citrus and floral aromas. Crisp and snappy with a
light-bodied palate, vibrant acids, and a brief finish. Refreshing, with light red fruit
flavors. Drink now.

83 • Georges Duboeuf (France) 1998 Saint-Amour. $11.89.

Pale pink-purple hue. Minerally, floral aromas lead a medium-bodied palate with crisp
acids and a hint of tannic grip on the finish. More structure than generosity at present.
Drink now or later.

83 • Georges Duboeuf (France) 1998 Beaujolais. $7.49.

Pale neon-purple hue. Pure, candied berries and flowers on the nose. Juicy and supple
on the entry leading a moderately light body with succulent red fruit flavors and very
slight tannins. Drink now.

81 • Louis Latour (France) 1997 Chamero y, Beaujolais-Villages. $9.

Pale ruby with a light fading rim. Aromas suggest herbs and berries. Broad berry fruit
impression on entry with a moderately light-bodied palate and red berry flavors through
the soft finish. This is a more restrained, vinous style. Drink now.

81 • Georges Duboeuf (France) 1998 Côte-de-Brouilly. $9.49.

Pale pink-ruby hue. Restrained, warm aromas have a floral accent. Tart on entry with
a moderately light-bodied palate and a clipped finish. Drink now.

Other Gamays

**89 • Gallo Sonoma (CA) 1994 Barrelli Creek Vineyard, Valdigue,
Alexander Valley. $13.**

Deep cherry red. Medium-bodied. Moderately extracted. Mildly tannic. Briar fruit,
chocolate. Mature, earthy aromas lead a deeply flavored, fleshy mouthful of mature-
tasting fruit with dark chocolatey notes through the finish.

85 • Pindar (NY) 1997 Gamay, North Fork of Long Island. $8.99.

Light cherry red with a slight fade. Sound mineral and red fruit aromas. A soft entry
leads a moderately light-bodied palate with crisp acids. Ripe, fruity, and generous.
Drink now.

84 • Weinstock (CA) 1997 Gamay, Paso Robles. $7.49.

Bright neon-violet hue. Medium-bodied. Moderately extracted. Mildly tannic. Black
fruits. Grapey and fresh on the nose and through the palate, with clean, lightly astringent
notes on the finish. Very tasty and balanced.

84 • Cave Spring (Canada) 1997 Gamay, Niagara Peninsula. $8.99.

Bright purple-red hue to the rim. Lean mineral and cranberry aromas. A sharp attack
leads to a light-bodied palate with vibrant acidity. Clean, snappy finish. A refreshing
quaffer. Drink now.

Scale: Superlative (96-100), Exceptional (90-95), Highly Recommended (85-89),
Recommended (80-84), Not Recommended (Under 80)

*83 • **Wild Horse (CA) 1997 Valdigue, Paso Robles. $13.***
Full purple-red. Medium-bodied. Moderately extracted. Mildly tannic. Jammy red fruits, candied berries. Jammy, ripe aromas lead a mildly overripe mouthful of flavors with very soft tannins on the finish.

*83 • **Herzog (CA) 1997 Baron Herzog, Gamay, Paso Robles. $7.95.***
Pinkish red. Moderately light-bodied. Subtly extracted. Mildly tannic. Herbs, flowers, citrus. Crisp herbaceous aromas lead a taut, vibrant palate with a cleansing finish.

*81 • **Glen Ellen (CA) 1997 Proprietor's Reserve, Gamay Beaujolais, California. $5.***
Pale cherry red. Moderately light-bodied. Subtly extracted. Mildly tannic. Candied berries, herbs. Sweet, simple aromas follow through on the lightly framed palate. The finish is clean and simple.

*81 • **Beringer (CA) 1996 Gamay Beaujolais, California. $7.***
Bright cherry red. Moderately light-bodied. Moderately extracted. Red berries, herbs. Light, fragrant, and cheerful, with some sweet fruit flavors and a clean finish. Thick mouthfeel with a low acid level.

fifteen

Zinfandel

Introduction   172
Reviews   175
   Zinfandel   175

Introduction: Zinfandel

Baseball, hot dogs, apple pie, and Zinfandel. Wait a minute-Zinfandel? Yes, because Zinfandel is one of the most American of the red wine grape varieties. American vintners may have to suffer through comparisons of their Cabernets with top Bordeaux reds, and their Chardonnays with Burgundian whites, but Zinfandel is free of comparisons. It has no real Old World counterparts.

To many, Zinfandel conjures an image of a sweet pink wine—White Zinfandel. But Zinfandel is a red grape that can produce deeply colored and richly flavored wines, ranging from intense blackberry to spice and cedar flavors reminiscent of Spanish and Italian reds. Rarely a shy wine, Zinfandel is one of the world's most powerful reds.

Zinfandel is truly one of America's greatest bargains. Today, as it was 100 years ago, Zinfandel is the most widely planted red wine grape in California. Cabernet Sauvignon prices have reached staggering levels while Zinfandel has remained relatively humble. Many great values remain, as a majority of Zinfandels still sell for $15 a bottle or less, and rarely do they exceed $30. This is remarkable when you consider that Zinfandel has more "old vine" vineyards (some are better than 100 years old) than any other variety. Old vines translate into low vineyard yields and richer wines that, theoretically, should sell for higher prices. When California Cabernet Sauvignon vineyards age to 100 years, you can rest assured that the wines will sell for the price of your child's college tuition.

Zinfandel is pure hedonic pleasure. It is the perfect accompaniment to rich dishes, as the wine's natural acidity and explosive fruit flavors provide the ideal foil. Zinfandel's bold and spicy flavors marry well with grilled meats and vegetables. When choosing a Zinfandel, take note of the alcohol percentage indicated on the label. If the alcohol exceeds 13%, it is a good indication that the wine is full-bodied and intense. When young, these aggressive examples often show better with a very slight chill, which helps neutralize the wine's inherent heat. The indication of "Old Vines" on the label indicates that the wine is likely to be rich, concentrated, and full bodied, with firm, complex flavors.

The Ups and Downs of Zinfandel

Zinfandel's history in the United States began two decades before the grape was introduced to California. It is believed that Zinfandel first came to New York in 1829. The vines arrived untagged and unnamed on the manifest. This was not uncommon, but in the case of Zinfandel it would later spark a vehement debate regarding the grape's origins. Zinfandel spread to other nurseries in the Northeast, becoming a popular table grape in the New England states. In the late 1840s Americans were struck with gold rush fever and flocked to California. Few discovered gold, and perhaps fewer went back to the East. Many turned to agriculture as a means of survival, and in the early 1850s importation of horticulture stock into California became a big industry. Vast numbers of trees and vines were shipped westward, including Zinfandel, or Black St. Peter's, as it was also known.

Scale: Superlative (96-100), Exceptional (90-95), Highly Recommended (85-89), Recommended (80-84), Not Recommended (Under 80)

A milestone year for Zinfandel in California came in 1859. A San Jose nursery owner, Antoine Delmas, produced a wine from Black St. Peter's that captured top honors for red wines at the California State Fair. Later that same year, California suffered a bitterly cold winter. Zinfandel was one of the few new plantings of New England nursery stock to survive. In the 1880s, when America's first wine boom hit, Zinfandel was California's most widely planted grape. Unfortunately, as we have seen in more recent industry planting frenzies, Zinfandel was often planted without regard to where it might produce the best wine. Much of the new planting was done in the ultra-hot Central Valley. The wines were excessively pruney and alcoholic, and lacked any semblance of balance. Inevitably, quality suffered and Zinfandel's reputation as an alternative to claret (red Bordeaux) turned to one of a wine suitable for jug blends.

The arrival of National Prohibition in 1920 made it illegal to commercially produce alcohol. This effectively abolished the California wine industry. However, the grape industry flourished and California acreage actually grew. It was not illegal for households to produce wine for their own consumption. Red varieties were preferred and Zinfandel was one of the most popular. Much of the "old vine" Zinfandel vineyards in vogue today were Prohibition-era plantings. After repeal in 1933, Zinfandel returned to its pre-Prohibition role as a bulk wine component and as an increasingly popular variety for Port. Over the next three decades, few varietally labeled Zinfandels were produced.

The 1960s saw a renewed interest in wine. Zinfandel had maintained name recognition during the gloomy years and was now becoming a favorite among novice wine drinkers. Zinfandel grew in popularity and once again received critical acclaim. Zinfandel was bold and forward, and in many cases so were the men who made it. Without a European model, Zinfandel was free to be invented or to invent itself. Many styles emerged, ranging from restrained claret-like wines to dark,

Great Value Zinfandel at a Glance

Number of Wines Reviewed:
76

Countries Represented:
1

purple, and incredibly intense late harvest bottlings. The multitude of styles confused consumers. Writers criticized Zinfandel, claiming that the variety produced wines so deep and brooding that they would never favorably mature. Furthermore, some Zinfandel producers had the "audacity" to ask Cabernet-like prices.

During the late 1970s and early 1980s the variety that had earned the right to be considered the darling of the California wine industry was about to face its greatest challenge yet: White Zinfandel. In the mid-1970s, Napa Valley's Sutter Home had experimented with a small production of a dry rosé wine made from Zinfandel. In 1975 the fermentation stuck, meaning that much of the wine's fermentable sugar remained. Attempts to remedy the situation were of no avail, so the White Zinfandel was bottled in its off-dry state. The response to the "mistake" was phenomenal. Sutter Home had bridged the gap between wine coolers and varietal bottlings. The success of the wine grew throughout the 1980s, spawning many successful copycats. Wineries were finding it increasingly difficult to sell Zinfandel. White Zinfandel is made quickly, requires no oak, and can be sold months, rather than years, following the harvest. It was becoming economically unviable to produce traditional red Zinfandel, so many simply stopped. In 1989 Sutter Home sold over 3.5 million case of White Zinfandel, making it the best-selling wine in America. Zinfandel was dead, or was it?

Zinfandel Strikes Back

A band of vintners stuck with Zinfandel, believing that it was a unique part of California's viticultural heritage, producing wines like no other variety. Two pivotal characters emerged in the fight to keep Zinfandel alive: Paul Draper of Ridge, and Joel Petersen of Ravenswood. They were not alone. As well as other dedicated winemakers, many equally dedicated wine drinkers across America were preaching the Zinfandel gospel. A gospel indeed; Zinfandel had practically become a religion. By the mid-1990s Zinfandel was again on solid ground. The White Zinfandel fad had tempered, prompting several wineries to dedicate great old vineyards, recently used for White Zinfandel, to red wine production, often with smashing results.

Origins

The most common debate among Zinfandel enthusiasts has always surrounded the variety's mysterious lineage. Vintners knew that the grape had come to them from the East Coast. It was also known that the Long Island nursery sourced the vines from Vienna. Complicating matters further, there has never been a grape in Europe known as Zinfandel. In the 1880s Arpad Haraszthy claimed that his father, Agoston Haraszthy, had introduced Zinfandel to California. However, the facts contradicted his claim. In 1967 a breakthrough was made when a U.S. plant pathologist noticed a vine named Primitivo in southern Italy that looked identical to Zinfandel. He sent cuttings to the University of California at Davis, where it was later proved through isozyme fingerprinting and DNA tests to be the same as Zinfandel. Scientific proof notwithstanding, some still believe that Zinfandel came to California via an alien craft, and other recent findings have even pointed to Croatia, leading to a Balkanization of current opinion.

Scale: Superlative (96-100), Exceptional (90-95), Highly Recommended (85-89), Recommended (80-84), Not Recommended (Under 80)

Reviews

Zinfandel

93 • *Sierra Vista (CA) 1996 Reeves Vineyard, Zinfandel, El Dorado. $15.*
Deep blackish purple. Moderately full-bodied. Balanced acidity. Moderately extracted. Moderately oaked. Mildly tannic. Black fruits, vanilla. Quite aromatic, with a generous, vanilla-accented core of fruit flavors. Rich and full, though extremely well balanced. It carries its weight effortlessly through the lengthy finish.

91 • *David Bruce (CA) 1995 Ranchita Canyon Vineyard, Zinfandel, Paso Robles. $15.*
Deep blackish purple. Moderately full-bodied. Balanced acidity. Highly extracted. Moderately oaked. Mildly tannic. Vanilla, black fruits, mint. Quite aromatic, with a very full, focused palate feel. Firmly structured, intense, and lengthy, with a vibrant finish. Great grip and depth.

90 • *Pedroncelli (CA) 1996 Mother Clone, Special Vineyard Selection, Zinfandel, Dry Creek Valley. $12.*
Deep blackish ruby with a brilliant cast. Moderately full-bodied. Low acidity. Moderately extracted. Mildly oaked. Mildly tannic. Briar fruits, minerals, chocolate. Quite aromatic, with a flavorful palate feel. Soft and generous in the mouth, with low acidity. Finishes with mild astringence.

89 • *Deaver (CA) 1994 Old Vines, Zinfandel, Amador County. $12.99.*
Deep blackish purple. Full-bodied. Balanced acidity. Highly extracted. Heavily oaked. Moderately tannic. Port, vanilla. Carries a slightly overripe, portlike note to the nose. Extremely full and rich on the palate, with a firm structure and hefty oak accents. The overall impression is that of drinking a dry port.

88 • *David Bruce (CA) 1996 Ranchita Canyon Vineyard, Zinfandel, Paso Robles. $15.*
Deep blackish purple. Full-bodied. Balanced acidity. Highly extracted. Heavily oaked. Mildly tannic. Brown spices, cedar, black fruits. Quite aromatic, with a hefty overlay of wood spice and a deep core of fruit flavors. Full and rich on the palate, with enough acidity to maintain a sense of balance.

88 • *Bogle (CA) 1995 Old Vine Cuvée, Zinfandel, California. $11.*
Bright blackish ruby hue. Moderately full-bodied. Full acidity. Moderately extracted. Mildly oaked. Mildly tannic. Vanilla, black fruits. Pleasant spicy oak nuances combine with a solid core of dark fruit flavors on the palate. Approachable, but showing solid concentration through the finish.

87 • *Zayante (CA) 1995 Zinfandel, Santa Cruz Mountains. $14.*
Deep blackish ruby color. Full-bodied. Full acidity. Highly extracted. Mildly oaked. Quite tannic. A pungent tobacco-tinged nose leads a full-throttle, tannic, acidic mouthfeel. Tough, bracing finish.

87 • *Stonehedge (CA) 1995 Zinfandel, Napa Valley. $14.99.*
Opaque dark red. Medium-bodied. Balanced acidity. Highly extracted. Mildly oaked. Moderately tannic. Blackberries. Quite tough and solid, with heavily wrought flavors that don't show a fruity center. The tannins are rather dry and fine-grained.

87 • *Monthaven (CA) 1995 Zinfandel, Napa Valley. $9.99.*
Full dark cherry red. Medium-bodied. Balanced acidity. Moderately extracted. Mildly oaked. Mildly tannic. Black fruits. Very straightforward; a burst of solid black fruit flavors tapers off with indecent haste. Quite generous.

87 • *Gallo Sonoma (CA) 1995 Barrelli Creek Vineyard, Zinfandel, Alexander Valley. $14.*
Opaque blackish cast. Full-bodied. Balanced acidity. Moderately extracted. Moderately oaked. Mildly tannic. Chocolate, black fruits. Quite aromatic, with a deep, brooding quality. Lush, rich, and flavorful on the palate, with a thick, velvety quality. Supple and well balanced through the finish.

86 • *Windsor (CA) 1996 Shelton Signature Series, Zinfandel, Alexander Valley. $14.50.*

Bright blackish ruby cast. Medium-bodied. Balanced acidity. Moderately extracted. Mildly oaked. Mildly tannic. Black fruits, brown spices, minerals. Somewhat reserved in style, with a firm, balanced mouthfeel. Made in more of a claret style, with elegant interplay between fruit and oak nuances. Shows solid grip through the finish.

86 • *Wildhurst (CA) 1996 Zinfandel, Clear Lake. $13.50.*

Bright blackish ruby cast. Moderately full-bodied. Balanced acidity. Moderately extracted. Mildly oaked. Mildly tannic. Black fruits. Fruit-centered and aromatic, with a rich, ripe, lush palate feel. Quite flavorful, with solid length and velvety tannins. Oak nuances come through in the finish.

86 • *Sierra Vista (CA) 1996 Herbert Vineyard, Zinfandel, El Dorado. $15.*

Deep blackish purple. Moderately full-bodied. Balanced acidity. Moderately extracted. Mildly oaked. Moderately tannic. Brown spices, briar fruits. Aromatic and fruit-centered, with a big, flavorful palate feel. A little rugged through the finish.

86 • *Shenandoah Vineyards (CA) 1996 Vintners Selection, Zinfandel, Shenandoah Valley. $15.*

Bright blackish ruby cast. Moderately full-bodied. Balanced acidity. Highly extracted. Heavily oaked. Moderately tannic. Vanilla, red fruits. Quite aromatic, with a hefty wood component and a sturdy core of red fruit flavors. Firm and well structured on the palate, with a tannic, lengthy, flavorful finish.

86 • *Pedroncelli (CA) 1996 Pedroni-Bushnell Vineyard, Single Vineyard Selection, Zinfandel, Dry Creek Valley. $13.*

Deep blackish ruby with a purple edge. Moderately full-bodied. Balanced acidity. Moderately extracted. Mildly tannic. Black fruits, earth, chocolate. Aromatic and quite deeply flavored, with brooding dark fruit notes. Surprisingly soft and supple on entry, with some mild astringency through the finish.

86 • *Mission View (CA) 1996 Eastside Ecstasy, Zinfandel, Paso Robles. $13.50.*

Bright ruby cast. Moderately full-bodied. Balanced acidity. Highly extracted. Moderately tannic. Briar fruits. There is a slight sense of overripeness in the generous fruit flavors. Firm and compact on the palate, with an overtone of sweetness and hefty tannins through the finish.

86 • *Meridian (CA) 1996 Zinfandel, Paso Robles. $12.*

Deep blackish ruby cast. Medium-bodied. Balanced acidity. Moderately extracted. Heavily oaked. Mildly tannic. Vanilla, black fruits. A fragrant oak influence is readily apparent on the nose, and joins a restrained core of fruit flavors in the mouth. Well balanced and elegant, in a sturdy claret style.

86 • *Louis Martini (CA) 1993 Heritage Collection, Zinfandel, Sonoma Valley. $12.*

Bright ruby cast. Moderately full-bodied. Balanced acidity. Moderately extracted. Mildly tannic. Minerals, red fruits. Reserved aromatically, with distinctive minerally nuances. Features an elegant, balanced character with a firm, focused finish. Artfully crafted for those who tire of "Zin monsters."

86 • *Kenwood (CA) 1995 Zinfandel, Sonoma Valley. $15.*

Bright blackish ruby cast. Medium-bodied. Balanced acidity. Moderately extracted. Mildly tannic. Black fruits, minerals. Reserved aromatically, with a firm, well-structured palate feel. Though tightly wound, a core of dark fruit flavors emerges here and there. Shows fine grip to the finish. Well balanced; should open up in the near term.

86 • *Herzog (CA) 1996 Baron Herzog, Zinfandel, California. $12.99.*

Bright ruby purple. Medium-bodied. Full acidity. Moderately extracted. Moderately oaked. Mildly tannic. Vanilla, briar fruits. Toasty oak nuances come out in the nose and join a wave of bright, fruit-centered flavors in the mouth. Somewhat light in style, with a sense of liveliness brought forth by buoyant acidity.

Scale: Superlative (96-100), Exceptional (90-95), Highly Recommended (85-89), Recommended (80-84), Not Recommended (Under 80)

86 • Guenoc (CA) 1996 Zinfandel, California. $11.
Deep blackish purple. Medium-bodied. Full acidity. Highly extracted. Moderately tannic.
Black fruits, minerals. Rather unyielding aromatically, with a firm, highly structured,
intense palate feel. Features a core of brooding black fruit flavors, and finishes with
solid tannins.

86 • Granite Springs (CA) 1995 Zinfandel, El Dorado. $11.50.
Bright blackish ruby cast. Moderately full-bodied. Balanced acidity. Moderately extracted.
Moderately oaked. Mildly tannic. Chocolate, black fruits. Quite aromatic, with a firm and
flavorful mouthfeel. Well balanced and deep through the finish.

86 • Edgewood (CA) 1995 Zinfandel, Napa Valley. $14.
Opaque dark red. Medium-bodied. Balanced acidity. Highly extracted. Moderately oaked.
Ripe black fruits, vanilla. Ripe nose suggests port. Solid and compact palate with dry,
dusty tannins on the finish. Rather structured, though lacking midpalate stuffing.

86 • Deaver (CA) 1995 Zinfandel, Amador County. $15.
Deep blackish ruby cast. Moderately full-bodied. Balanced acidity. Highly extracted.
Mildly oaked. Mildly tannic. Black fruits, chocolate, minerals. Somewhat reserved
aromatically, but rich, ripe, and concentrated on the palate. Full and intensely flavored,
with a thick, well-balanced finish.

86 • Castoro (CA) 1996 Zinfandel, Paso Robles. $12.95.
Deep blackish purple. Moderately full-bodied. Full acidity. Moderately extracted.
Moderately oaked. Mildly tannic. Black fruits, chocolate. Quite aromatic, with a full,
flavorful palate feel. Lush and supple in the mouth, with vibrant acidity making for
a bright finish. Big but well balanced.

85 • Zabaco (CA) 1994 Zinfandel, Sonoma County. $9.
Deep blackish ruby cast. Moderately full-bodied. Balanced acidity. Moderately extracted.
Mildly oaked. Mildly tannic. Black fruits, wood. Pleasantly aromatic, with a distinct woody
note throughout. Firm, lean, and angular through the finish. Features some drying
wood tannins.

85 • Rosenblum (CA) NV Vintners Cuvée XVI, Zinfandel, California. $9.50.
Deep ruby purple. Moderately full-bodied. Balanced acidity. Moderately extracted. Mildly
tannic. Red berries, minerals. Bright, fruit-centered aromatics lead a lighter-styled, lively
palate feel. Precocious and tasty, with good grip to the finish. Well balanced.

*85 • Monterey Peninsula Winery (CA) 1995 Naraghi Vineyard, Zinfandel,
Monterey County. $14.99.*
Bright ruby-garnet cast. Medium-bodied. Low acidity. Moderately extracted. Mildly
tannic. Cherry tomatoes, stewed fruits. Engaging, mildly overripe notes in the nose.
Relatively light on the palate, with low acidity through the finish. A distinctive style,
though very quaffable.

85 • Clos du Val (CA) 1995 Zinfandel, California. $15.
Bright ruby-garnet cast. Medium-bodied. Balanced acidity. Moderately extracted. Mildly
tannic. Tea, minerals. An interesting melange of earthy aromas plays out well on the firm,
well-structured palate. A rather reserved claret style, though it has fine grip and intensity.

84 • Windsor (CA) 1996 Zinfandel, Sonoma County. $9.75.
Bright ruby hue. Medium-bodied. Balanced acidity. Subtly extracted. Mildly oaked.
Mildly tannic. Black fruits, spice. Fairly aromatic, with a lighter-styled palate feel. Crisp
and flavorful through the finish. Good grip.

*84 • Windsor (CA) 1996 Old Vines Private Reserve, Zinfandel,
Russian River Valley. $13.50.*
Bright ruby with a slight garnet cast. Medium-bodied. Balanced acidity. Subtly extracted.
Mildly oaked. Mildly tannic. Stewed fruits, vanilla. Carries a slightly overripe note in the
aromatics and through the palate. Lighter in style, with a soft character. Tasty, but lacks
intensity.

84 • Villa Mt. Eden (CA) 1996 Zinfandel, California. $12.

Bright blackish ruby hue. Moderately full-bodied. Balanced acidity. Highly extracted. Moderately oaked. Moderately tannic. Brown spices, black fruits. Pleasantly aromatic, with a flavorful palate feel. Firm and well structured, with dusty tannins through the finish. Nicely balanced and lengthy.

84 • Vigil (CA) 1996 Tres Conados, Zinfandel, California. $12.99.

Bright blackish purple. Moderately full-bodied. Balanced acidity. Moderately extracted. Mildly tannic. Black fruits, minerals. Reserved aromatically, but there is a solid core of brooding, dark fruit flavors. Well structured and firm, with good grip to the finish.

84 • Sobon (CA) 1996 Lubenko Vineyard, Zinfandel, Fiddletown. $15.

Bright blackish ruby cast. Moderately full-bodied. Full acidity. Moderately extracted. Mildly oaked. Mildly tannic. Briar fruits, minerals. Quite aromatic, with a full though angular palate feel. Vibrant acidity provides a juicy finish.

84 • Sobon (CA) 1996 Cougar Hill, Zinfandel, Shenandoah Valley. $15.

Bright ruby-garnet cast. Medium-bodied. Balanced acidity. Moderately extracted. Mildly oaked. Mildly tannic. Black fruits, minerals, vanilla. Reserved aromatically, with gentle, spicy oak overtones. Lush and generous through the finish. Well balanced.

84 • Shenandoah Vineyards (CA) 1996 Special Reserve, Zinfandel, Amador County. $9.

Deep blackish ruby cast. Moderately full-bodied. Balanced acidity. Moderately extracted. Mildly oaked. Mildly tannic. Chocolate, black fruits. Pleasantly aromatic, with a core of deep fruit flavors and toasty oak overtones. Thick and rich in the mouth, with a generous, chunky finish.

84 • Seghesio (CA) 1996 Zinfandel, Sonoma County. $11.

Deep blackish purple. Moderately full-bodied. Low acidity. Highly extracted. Mildly oaked. Moderately tannic. Minerals, black fruits, pepper. Rather reserved aromatically, with a lean, firm palate feel. Deeply flavored, with a minerally, austere finish.

84 • Schuetz Oles (CA) 1996 Zinfandel, Napa Valley. $12.

Deep blackish ruby cast. Moderately full-bodied. Balanced acidity. Highly extracted. Moderately oaked. Moderately tannic. Tea, brown spices, minerals. Complex in aromatics, with a firm, austere palate feel. Astringent tannins clamp down on the finish, but the flavor keeps going. Needs a bit of time.

84 • Santino (CA) 1995 Zinfandel, California. $10.

Deep blackish ruby hue. Full-bodied. Full acidity. Highly extracted. Mildly oaked. Mildly tannic. Brown spices, chocolate. Oak overtones are readily apparent on the nose, and play out on the palate. Thick and chunky, with a drying, dusty finish. A tad rustic.

84 • Rutherford Vintners (CA) 1996 Zinfandel, Lodi. $8.99.

Bright red-purple. Medium-bodied. Balanced acidity. Moderately extracted. Mildly tannic. Red berries. Superripe, fleshy, berry aromas follow through on the palate. Generous and round, with soft tannins. Easy drinking.

84 • Peterson (CA) 1995 Zinfandel, Dry Creek Valley. $14.

Deep blackish ruby cast. Moderately full-bodied. Balanced acidity. Highly extracted. Moderately oaked. Moderately tannic. Spice, chocolate, dried herbs. Somewhat reined in aromatically, with a firm, austere palate feel. Rather lean through the finish.

84 • Latcham Vineyards (CA) 1995 Special Reserve, Zinfandel, El Dorado. $14.

Deep blackish purple. Moderately full-bodied. Balanced acidity. Highly extracted. Mildly oaked. Moderately tannic. Plums, minerals. Quite aromatic, with a decided minerally note. Firm and dense on the palate, though well structured. The finish is precise and focused.

84 • Grand Cru (CA) 1996 Premium Selection, Zinfandel, California. $7.99.
Deep blackish purple. Medium-bodied. Balanced acidity. Moderately extracted. Heavily oaked. Moderately tannic. Vanilla, black fruits. Hefty oak notes dominate the nose and join ripe berry flavors on the palate. Rather light in style and relatively soft, with a pleasant, lingering finish.

84 • Gallo Sonoma (CA) 1995 Frei Ranch Vineyard, Zinfandel, Dry Creek Valley. $14.
Deep blackish purple. Medium-bodied. Balanced acidity. Moderately extracted. Mildly oaked. Mildly tannic. Black fruits, minerals. Somewhat reserved aromatically, with a lighter-styled, minerally palate feel. Firm and compact through the finish, with solid grip. A lean and elegant style.

84 • Frick (CA) 1994 Zinfandel, Dry Creek Valley. $15.
Bright blackish purple. Medium-bodied. Full acidity. Highly extracted. Mildly tannic. Briar fruits, minerals. Quite aromatic, with a high-toned quality. Light in the mouth, with a juicy, angular quality. Finishes on a tart note.

84 • Cedar Brook (CA) 1995 Zinfandel, California. $8.99.
Bright blackish ruby color. Medium-bodied. Balanced acidity. Moderately extracted. Moderately oaked. Mildly tannic. Brown spices, coffee, black fruits. Oak nuances dominate the aromas and play out on the palate. Soft, supple, and velvety in the mouth, with a lingering finish.

84 • Brutocao (CA) 1995 Hopland Ranch, Zinfandel, Mendocino. $14.
Bright ruby-garnet cast. Moderately full-bodied. Balanced acidity. Moderately extracted. Moderately oaked. Mildly tannic. Chocolate, minerals. Pleasantly aromatic, with a soft, supple palate feel. Finishes on a generous note, with velvety tannins and fine length.

84 • Beringer (CA) 1995 Appellation Collection, Zinfandel, North Coast. $12.
Dark cherry red. Moderately light-bodied. Balanced acidity. Moderately extracted. Mildly oaked. Mildly tannic. Minerals, black fruits, pepper. Toasty nose with tarlike notes, revealing a light, black fruit-centered palate with a firm, minerally undernote that comes through on the finish.

84 • Belvedere (CA) 1995 Zinfandel, Dry Creek Valley. $12.
Bright ruby purple to rim. Medium-bodied. Balanced acidity. Highly extracted. Moderately tannic. Briar fruits, chocolate, dried herbs. Fairly aromatic, with a firm and somewhat angular mouthfeel. Showing solid grip, but a little ungenerous.

84 • Beaulieu (CA) 1996 BV, Zinfandel, Napa Valley. $14.
Bright cherry red. Medium-bodied. Balanced acidity. Moderately extracted. Mildly oaked. Moderately tannic. Vanilla, black fruits. Ripe berry aromas lead a rounded palate with aggressive tannins drying the finish.

83 • Latcham Vineyards (CA) 1995 Zinfandel, El Dorado. $10.
Deep blackish ruby cast. Moderately full-bodied. Balanced acidity. Moderately extracted. Mildly oaked. Mildly tannic. Minerals, black fruits. Rather reserved aromatically, with a firm, well-structured palate feel. Compact and flavorful, with a bit of tannic bite to the finish.

83 • Geyser Peak (CA) 1995 Zinfandel, Sonoma County. $15.
Bright blackish purple. Moderately full-bodied. Full acidity. Moderately extracted. Mildly oaked. Mildly tannic. Red fruits, minerals. Fruit-centered and relatively high-toned aromas. Full but quite lively on the palate, with balanced acidity.

83 • Creston (CA) 1995 Zinfandel, Paso Robles. $13.
Bright ruby cast. Medium-bodied. Full acidity. Moderately extracted. Mildly tannic. Briar fruits. Quite aromatic, with a fruit-centered quality. Light in the mouth, with juicy acidity making for a vibrant finish.

83 • Clos du Bois (CA) 1995 Zinfandel, Sonoma County. $14.
Bright ruby-garnet cast. Medium-bodied. Balanced acidity. Subtly extracted. Mildly oaked. Mildly tannic. Dried herbs, vanilla. Quite aromatic, with distinctive herbal overtones. Soft and lush on the palate, with a supple finish.

82 • *York Mountain Winery (CA) 1996 Zinfandel, San Luis Obispo County. $14.*

Bright reddish purple. Medium-bodied. Full acidity. Highly extracted. Moderately tannic. Herbs, red fruits. Herbal aromas lead a minerally palate that has some grip, with sweet red fruit flavors overlaid. Tannins are rather mean and unripe, giving a disjointed note to the finish.

82 • *Van Asperen (CA) 1995 Zinfandel, Napa Valley. $10.*

Rusty red. Moderately light-bodied. Balanced acidity. Moderately extracted. Mildly tannic. Brown spice, cocoa, red fruits. Very spicy aromas have red fruit character that follows through on the palate. Seems to be showing some maturity.

82 • *Rosenblum (CA) 1996 Zinfandel, Contra Costa County. $15.*

Deep blackish ruby cast. Medium-bodied. Balanced acidity. Moderately extracted. Mildly tannic. Briar fruits. An outrageously fruit-centered bouquet leads a lighter-styled palate. Extremely flavorful and well balanced, with a linear quality to the finish.

82 • *Milano (CA) 1995 Sanel Valley Vineyard, Zinfandel, Mendocino County. $12.*

Very deep blackish ruby cast. Moderately full-bodied. Full acidity. Highly extracted. Mildly tannic. Overripe red fruits. Features a rather portlike aromatic note, and carries a distinct impression of sweetness on the palate. Deeply flavored, with some tannic grip through the finish.

82 • *Martini & Prati (CA) 1995 Zinfandel, California. $15.*

Bright ruby with a slight garnet cast. Moderately full-bodied. Balanced acidity. Moderately extracted. Mildly tannic. Red fruits, minerals. Reserved aromatically, but ripe, generous, and forward on the palate, with a fruit-centered quality. Fine intensity.

82 • *Estrella (CA) 1996 Proprietor's Reserve, Zinfandel, California. $9.99/1.5 L.*

Deep blackish purple. Moderately full-bodied. Balanced acidity. Moderately extracted. Mildly tannic. Black fruits. Reserved aromatically, with a soft, fruit-centered palate feel. Features a firm, minerally finish.

82 • *Angeline (CA) 1996 Old Vine Cuvée, Zinfandel, Mendocino County. $11.*

Bright ruby-garnet cast. Medium-bodied. Low acidity. Subtly extracted. Mildly tannic. Red fruits. Reserved aromatically, with a lighter-styled, soft palate feel. Lacks intensity through the finish.

81 • *Windsor (CA) 1996 Private Reserve, Zinfandel, Mendocino County. $13.50.*

Bright ruby cast. Medium-bodied. Balanced acidity. Moderately extracted. Moderately oaked. Mildly tannic. Red fruits, spice. Pleasantly aromatic, with a spicy quality throughout. Light on the palate, with a lean, focused finish.

81 • *Stevenot (CA) 1996 Zinfandel, Sierra Foothills. $12.*

Bright ruby cast. Medium-bodied. Balanced acidity. Moderately extracted. Mildly oaked. Mildly tannic. Minerals, red fruits. Reserved aromatically, with a firm, focused palate feel. Finishes on an angular, minerally note.

81 • *Sea Ridge Coastal (CA) 1996 Zinfandel, California. $10.*

Bright blackish ruby hue. Moderately light-bodied. Balanced acidity. Subtly extracted. Moderately tannic. Minerals. Somewhat reserved aromatically, with a lighter-styled mouthfeel. Finishes with a tannic kick.

81 • *Robert Mondavi (CA) 1995 Coastal, Zinfandel, North Coast. $10.*

Bright ruby-garnet cast. Moderately light-bodied. Low acidity. Moderately extracted. Mildly tannic. Stewed fruits, minerals. The aromas have a slightly overripe note. Soft and ripe on the palate, with a firm finish.

81 • Perry Creek (CA) 1996 Zin Man, Zinfandel, Sierra Foothills. $12.
Bright blackish ruby hue. Medium-bodied. Balanced acidity. Moderately extracted.
Mildly oaked. Mildly tannic. Pickle barrel, black fruits. Aromatic, with forward oak
accents. Lean and firm in the mouth, with some mild astringency through the finish.

81 • Pepperwood Grove (CA) 1996 Zinfandel, California. $6.99.
Bright ruby with a slight garnet cast. Medium-bodied. Balanced acidity. Moderately
extracted. Mildly tannic. Beets, pepper. Carries some slight vegetal overtones to the
nose. Falls flat on the palate, with a rather dilute sensation.

81 • CK Mondavi (CA) 1996 Zinfandel, California. $7.
Bright blackish purple. Medium-bodied. Full acidity. Moderately extracted. Mildly tannic.
Black cherries. Forward, fruit-centered aromas lead a bright, lively palate feel. Crisp and
vibrant through the finish.

81 • Charles Krug (CA) 1995 Zinfandel, Napa Valley. $11.
Dark blood red. Medium-bodied. Balanced acidity. Moderately extracted. Moderately
tannic. Brown spice, earth, black fruits. Rustic aroma. Rather lean and unfleshy, with
powdery, earthy tannins on the finish.

81 • Castoro (CA) 1996 Vineyard Tribute, Zinfandel, Paso Robles. $15.
Deep blackish ruby cast. Medium-bodied. Full acidity. Highly extracted. Mildly tannic.
Overripe red fruits. Carries a slightly portlike note to the nose, and features an acidic,
highly extracted palate feel. Austere finish.

80 • Van Roekel (CA) 1996 Zinfandel, Temecula. $13.95.
Deep blackish ruby cast. Full-bodied. Low acidity. Moderately extracted. Moderately
tannic. Dried herbs, earth. Unyielding aromatically, with a firm, earthy palate feel.
Comes across as oddly flat, with a real kick of astringent tannins through the finish.

80 • Twin Hills (CA) 1994 Zinfandel, Paso Robles. $15.
Deep blackish ruby cast. Moderately full-bodied. Balanced acidity. Highly extracted.
Moderately oaked. Quite tannic. Wood, minerals. Somewhat reserved in flavor, with a
firm, woody character. Compact and lean on the palate, with an aggressive tannic finish.

80 • Sobon (CA) 1996 Rocky Top, Zinfandel, Shenandoah Valley. $15.
Blackish ruby hue with a slight garnet cast. Moderately full-bodied. Balanced acidity.
Moderately extracted. Mildly tannic. Dark berries, minerals. Earthy aromas reveal a rustic
style with smoky accents.

80 • Montpellier (CA) 1996 Zinfandel, California. $6.99.
Dark blackish purple. Moderately full-bodied. Balanced acidity. Moderately extracted.
Mildly oaked. Mildly tannic. Black fruits, brown spices. Spicy aromatics lead a ripe core
of black fruit flavors. Soft and lush in the mouth, with a flavorful, velvety finish.

80 • Monthaven (CA) 1996 Zinfandel, California. $9.99.
Bright blackish ruby hue. Medium-bodied. Subtly extracted. Quite tannic. Black fruits,
minerals. Rather ungenerous on the nose, with a firm, unyielding palate feel. Finishes
with a big kick of tannins. Tough.

80 • Lang (CA) 1995 Twin Rivers Vineyards, Zinfandel, El Dorado. $14.
Bright blackish ruby cast. Full-bodied. Balanced acidity. Highly extracted. Quite tannic.
Pepper, green herbs. Seemingly unripe in aromatics, with a lean, mean, austere palate
feel. Finishes with a kick of bitterness.

sixteen

Red Rhône
Varietals

Introduction   184
Reviews   187
   Northern Rhône Originals   187
   Southern Rhône Originals   188
   Other French "Rhônes"   189
   Aussie Shiraz   189
   Other Aussie "Rhônes"   191
   U.S. Syrah   192
   U.S. Petite Sirah   194
   Other U.S. "Rhônes"   195
   Other Great Value "Rhônes"   196

Introduction: Red Rhône Varietals

Much ado has been made in the past decade or so concerning Rhône varietals and America's near-mythic Rhône Rangers. The Rhône is an important and extensive wine region in the southeastern quarter of France. Historically, the Rhône was considered to be a second-class region behind the commercially powerful wines of Bordeaux and Burgundy. This is not the case today.

New World wine-producing nations have undeniably taken their lead from France. The New World wine scene is dominated by two French wine appellations: Bordeaux, which gives us Cabernet Sauvignon, Merlot, and Sauvignon Blanc; and Burgundy, which contributes Chardonnay and Pinot Noir. The grape varieties of the Rhône have been largely ignored, with one major exception: Shiraz in Australia. Shiraz, identical to France's Syrah, is Australia's most widely planted and important red grape, responsible for some of the world's greatest red wines. Generalizations of flavor and style in regards to Rhône varietals and blends are futile.

Despite their popularity, many values remain among New World red Rhône wines, as well as the French originals. In France's Rhône Valley, wines of the South generally offer greater value than do those of the North, notably those broadly designated as Côtes du Rhône. Value seekers are also blessed with a number of good quality moderately priced Vin de Pays Syrah. These wines rarely exceed $10 a bottle and are among France's best wine buys. In the United States, no Rhône varietal is absent from the value category. Many varietally labeled Syrahs and Rhône styled blends are quite costly, but many others are bargains. Australia's Shiraz and Shiraz blends have been rapidly climbing out of value consideration, although many still represent excellent value.

France

It is useful to understand the French originals before tackling the New World's interpretation of Rhône wines. A common misconception of the Rhône is that it is a single, hot growing region. The Rhône should be considered as two distinct growing regions, divided into north and south districts. The Rhône Valley begins in the town of Vienne, south of Lyon, and stretches 125 miles south to Avignon. Northern appellations, such as Côte Rôtie, lie at a latitude north of top Bordeaux chateaus in what is described as a "Continental" climate. The southern Rhône, home of Châteauneuf du Pape, features a Mediterranean climate, as it is less than 40 miles from the sea.

In the north, Syrah is the only permitted red varietal. This is home to the great wines of Côte Rôtie and Hermitage, but unfortunately they are on the pricier side. Several lesser-known appellations are capable of producing excellent wines, especially in good vintages. The small appellation of Cornas, about a dozen miles from Hermitage, produces one of France's most sturdy and robust wines. Cornas is also one of France's most undervalued wines. St. Joseph, across the river from Hermitage, is significantly different from the wine of Cornas. It is often soft, supple, and fruity, though being the largest appellation in the Northern Rhône, differences can be quite marked. St. Joseph produces nearly 10 times the volume of Cornas. Crozes-Hermitage, which surrounds the appellation of Hermitage, has often been referred to as "poor mans Hermitage." Styles vary from one producer to the next, ranging from light and fruity to hard

Scale: Superlative (96-100), Exceptional (90-95), Highly Recommended (85-89), Recommended (80-84), Not Recommended (Under 80)

and tannic. Follow the top producers, especially in the best vintages. Vintages to keep an eye out for include '89, '90, and '91, which may be difficult to find, as they are not current, but they are among the best vintages in the past 20 years. Recently, vintages from '94 to the present have all been very good to excellent, led by 1995 and 1997.

In addition to the obvious climatic changes from north to south, Southern Rhône wines are not produced from a single variety, but rather, a blend of several of the region's permitted grapes. The most famous wine of the Southern Rhône is Châteauneuf du Pape. Unfortunately, fame translates to higher prices, as few real bargains from this appellation are available today. However, many neighboring appellations such as Gigondas, Cairanne, and Vacqueyras offer tremendous values. These wines tend to be rustic and generous with rich, roasted, dried fruit flavors balanced by cedar, pepper, and truffle notes. These wines are often approachable and enjoyable in their youth, while offering five to 15 years of aging potential. Wines labeled as simply "Côtes du Rhône" make up about 75% of the area's total production. The quality of Côtes du Rhône varies widely although most are quite acceptable, if not exceptional. Much improvement and modernization has taken place in the past two decades, eliminating many of the dirty and oxidized wines of the past. Côtes du Rhône is almost always a good value. Additional values may also be found in the esoteric districts of Côtes du Vivarais, Coteaux du Tricastin, and Côtes du Ventoux. These wines are not as commonplace as Côtes du Rhône but almost always offer great value.

Australia

Australian Shiraz comes in a variety of styles and falls into virtually every segment of the market, from $9 to $100 and up. Sadly, more are creeping toward the top of the price scale, as Australian Shiraz is quickly becoming one of the worlds most respected and sought after red wines. An Australian winery making Shiraz is at least as common as a U.S. winery producing Cabernet Sauvignon (or Pinot

Great Value Red Rhône Varietals at a Glance

Number of Wines Reviewed:
104

Countries Represented:
6

Noir if you are of the Oregonian persuasion). The wines are medium- to full-bodied, deeply colored, and explosively fragrant. On the palate one is likely to encounter notes of black cherry and plum with elements of earth, pepper, and the sweet vanilla sensations of American oak. Australian Shiraz is inviting and pleasurable in its youth, while many are capable of aging for a decade or more, which softens the forward grapey fruit flavors and brings about a seamless integration of earth, pepper, and oak. If you have not ventured into the world of Aussie Shiraz you should do so. When buying Aussie Shiraz keep in mind that there are vintage variations between the nation's largest growing regions. Rarely do the major Australian regions (with the possible exception of the Hunter Valley) have a truly bad Shiraz vintage, but it doesn't hurt to consult your favorite wine merchant. These wines demand rich and flavorful foods. Roasted or grilled meats are the obvious accompaniments.

The U.S.

In the recent past, the varietals of France's Rhône Valley were virtually unknown in the United States. Today, U.S. winemakers produce both varietal wines and Rhône-inspired blends from Carignane, Cinsault, Grenache, Mourvédre, and most notably, Syrah. Varietals of the Rhône have been slow to catch on relative to those from Bordeaux or Burgundy. However, it appears that the future is positive, as Rhône varietals possess three keys that point to a successful movement: a grassroots effort and organization among producers, a cult following among wine drinkers, and a catchy moniker—"Rhône Rangers."

Among the Rhône varietals, Mourvèdre has the longest history in the United States. The variety was widely planted in California in the late 1800s, through Prohibition in the 1930s. At this time the variety was known by its Spanish name, Mataro. At its height, in terms of acreage, Mourvèdre was most often used as a blending variety. It was also a popular grape among California home winemakers. Today less than 500 acres of vines exist in California, as compared to more than 8,000 in the late 1930s. However, many of the existing Mourvèdre plantings are "old vine" vineyards in Contra Costa County that produce wines with incredible depth and richness.

Carignane, which is the most planted red variety in France, came to California about a decade or so after Mourvèdre. It has a similar history of use as a blending variety and a popular grape for home winemakers. Large numbers of Carignane vines were planted, as California had nearly 30,000 acres at one point. Significant acreage remains today, albeit predominately in the hot Central Valley where it is destined for generic red blends. However, more than 1,000 acres of old-vine vineyards remain in various premium regions. Wines made from Carignane are medium- to full-bodied, with rich fruit flavors reminiscent of plum, cherry, and raspberry, balanced with notes of anise and earth.

Petite Sirah is a variety cloaked in mystery and confusion concerning its origin and true identity. Some vines are believed to actually be Syrah, while much of it is likely to be Durif—a hybrid developed in France whose lineage is half Syrah. It is unclear why the name Petite Sirah was given in California. Until the recent rise in popularity of Rhône varietals, Petite Sirah was rarely sold for more than $10. Today, about half of all Petite Sirah sells for $15 or less. Styles vary greatly, as some emphasize soft blueberry-like fruit and little tannin, while others are deep, concentrated wines with rich black fruit and earthy flavors. Consult the tasting notes provided in this section in order to find one to your liking.

Syrah is the most recognized and accepted of all the Rhône varietals. This varietal has seen a dramatic increase in planting over the past decade. In 1987 California had fewer than 125 acres of Syrah. Today there are roughly 4,500 acres and this is expected to rise dramatically in the coming years. U.S. growers are finding out what Aussie wineries have known for years, that Syrah is a bit of a chameleon, adapting well to both cool and hot regions. Cool regions such as Monterey, Mendocino, and Washington tend to produce wines with tremendous balance and austere fruit. Hot regions produce Syrah that is unbelievably purple in color with rich, jammy, berry fruit flavors. Old vines tend to produce more complex wines while younger vines offer precise peppery flavors. Some Syrahs have reached the luxury price range in the United States, though many fine examples remain affordable.

U.S. Rhône Rangers vary significantly in style and flavor. Uses also vary, although many are enjoyable young and work well without food. Wines exhibiting forward fruit are typically great accompaniments to stews and roasted meat, as Rhône flavors tend to add vibrancy to slow cooked dishes. Shiraz, or Syrah, is often a great match with lamb. Grenache is great with poultry and spiced fish dishes. Vintages have been fairly consistent in the United States, especially in California.

Reviews

Northern Rhône Originals

92 • Alain Graillot (France) 1996 Crozes-Hermitage Rouge. $15.
Saturated red-purple. Moderately full-bodied. Highly extracted. Moderately tannic. Coal tar, black fruits, minerals. Impressive, dense aromas lead a solid, tight palate with some tough edges, yet underlying generosity shows through. This will be better in a few years.

89 • Reine Pédauque (France) 1995 Chantoiselle, Crozes-Hermitage Rouge. $12.
Ruby red with a lightening rim. Medium-bodied. Balanced acidity. Moderately extracted. Moderately tannic. Black fruit, bacon fat, minerals. Smoky aromas. Clean, mineral-accented palate with an austere character and grainy tannins through the finish. A lighter style, but very individual and drinkable.

89 • du Colombier (France) 1996 Crozes-Hermitage Rouge. $15.
Bright purple-red. Medium-bodied. Balanced acidity. Moderately extracted. Mildly tannic. Coal tar, black fruits. Fruit-laden aromas do not disappoint, with mouth-filling primary fruit flavors showing fine medicinal Syrah character. Softer tannins are apparent on the finish.

89 • Caves des Papes (France) 1995 Les Reillots, Cornas. $15.
Bright ruby purple. Full-bodied. Balanced acidity. Highly extracted. Mildly oaked. Moderately tannic. Brown spices, earth, red fruits. Aromatic, with a full and grainy palate feel characterized by a rich, ripe mouthfeel and firm tannins through the finish.

87 • du Colombier (France) 1996 Cuvée Gaby, Crozes-Hermitage Rouge. $15.
Bright purple. Medium-bodied. Balanced acidity. Moderately extracted. Mildly tannic. Dried herbs, red fruits. Bright, vigorously youthful aromas follow through on the palate. Minerally yet supple through the finish, this will be best appreciated in its youth.

84 • Thomas Moillard (France) 1996 Crozes-Hermitage Rouge. $11.99.
Bright ruby hue. Medium-bodied. Moderately extracted. Mildly tannic. Minerals, herbs, red fruits. A lighter style, showing herbal notes and a minerally backbone. This is drinking well now.

83 • Cave de Tain l'Hermitage (France) 1996 Les Nobles Rives, St. Joseph Rouge. $15.

Bright ruby purple. Moderately full-bodied. Balanced acidity. Highly extracted. Moderately tannic. Dried herbs, minerals. Quite aromatic, with a decided herbal streak throughout. Firm and lean through the finish, showing a hint of unripe tannins.

Southern Rhône Originals

86 • Guigal (France) 1995 Côtes du Rhône. $10.

Deep ruby cast. Medium-bodied. Balanced acidity. Moderately extracted. Mildly tannic. Spice, minerals. Aromatically reserved, with a firm and lean mouthfeel. Tightly wound and angular, though flavorful through the finish.

86 • Delas (France) 1997 "Val Muzols," Côtes du Ventoux. $7.

Bright purple. Medium-bodied. Balanced acidity. Moderately extracted. Mildly tannic. Black fruits, minerals. Pleasantly aromatic, with a fruit-centered quality. Firm and well structured on the palate, though this has a lighter frame.

86 • Domaine Saint Benoit (France) 1995 Châteauneuf du Pape Rouge. $15.

Saturated dark ruby red. Moderately full-bodied. Highly extracted. Moderately tannic. Earth, red fruits. Impressive earthy aromas. Rich, sumptuous mouthfeel has a degree of fruity softness and ripeness that make for a hedonistic style.

84 • Perrin (France) 1996 Rouge Réserve, Côtes du Rhône Rouge. $10.49.

Bright ruby purple. Medium-bodied. Balanced acidity. Moderately extracted. Mildly oaked. Mildly tannic. Vanilla, minerals, black fruits. Quite aromatic, with a full and flavorful palate showing a fruity center, and a focused, lean finish with good persistence.

84 • La Vieille Ferme (France) 1996 Rhône Valley Rouge. $7.49.

Brilliant bright purple. Moderately full-bodied. Balanced acidity. Moderately extracted. Mildly tannic. Black fruits, flowers. Grapey aromas, with a wave of forward, primary aromas. A lighter, quaffing style, but shows respectable weight on the palate, with a fine intensity of flavor.

84 • J.C. Chassagne (France) 1995 Domaine du Pourra, Gigondas. $12.

Deep ruby cast. Moderately full-bodied. Balanced acidity. Moderately extracted. Mildly tannic. Brown spices, earth. Aromatic and full, with a lean and intense mouthfeel. Flavorful and crisp through the finish.

84 • Gabriel Liogier (France) 1996 Domaine de la Taladette, Côtes du Rhône Rouge. $8.99.

Bright ruby cast with a slight fade. Medium-bodied. Balanced acidity. Subtly extracted. Mildly tannic. Minerals, red fruits. Generous aromas feature a distinctive peppery accent. Light in style, though lively and flavorful. A quaffer.

84 • Delas (France) 1997 Saint Esprit Rouge, Côtes du Rhône. $8.

Bright ruby purple. Medium-bodied. Balanced acidity. Moderately extracted. Mildly tannic. Flowers, spice, earth. Floral aromas lead a rounded, ripe mouthfeel that shows bright, tart fruit flavors and a degree of spice on the finish.

83 • Thomas Moillard (France) 1997 Les Violettes, Côtes du Rhône Rouge. $8.99.

Pale ruby hue with a slight purple overtone. Medium-bodied. Balanced acidity. Subtly extracted. Mildly tannic. Vanilla, red fruits, minerals. Vanilla-scented aromas, but lean, with a taut and linear palate feel. Crisp and flavorful finish makes for a brash style.

82 • Lucien Deschaux (France) 1994 Le Vieux Abbe, Châteauneuf du Pape Rouge. $14.99.

Bright ruby hue with a garnet edge. Medium-bodied. Balanced acidity. Moderately extracted. Mildly oaked. Mildly tannic. Brown spices, red fruits, leather. Pleasantly aromatic, with a lighter-styled, mature palate feel. Lean and crisp through the finish.

Scale: Superlative (96-100), Exceptional (90-95), Highly Recommended (85-89), Recommended (80-84), Not Recommended (Under 80)

81 • *Mommessin (France) 1997 Château de Domazan,*
Côtes du Rhône Rouge. $7.99.
Pale ruby cast. Light-bodied. Balanced acidity. Subtly extracted. Mildly tannic. Minerals, red fruits. Crisp and light, with brief, bright fruity flavors and a simple, minerally finish. Unchallenging but quaffable.

Other French "Rhônes"

88 • *Richemont (France) 1995 Réserve, Syrah, Vin de Pays d'Oc. $7.*
Deep blackish ruby hue. Moderately full-bodied. Full acidity. Highly extracted. Mildly oaked. Moderately tannic. Black fruits, chocolate. Pleasantly aromatic, with a subtle oak overlay. Flavorful and crisp in the mouth, with a racy edge to the finish.

88 • *Michel Picard (France) 1996 Syrah, Vin de Pays d'Oc. $9.99.*
Bright ruby purple. Moderately full-bodied. Balanced acidity. Moderately extracted. Mildly oaked. Mildly tannic. Minerals, black fruits, spice. Pleasantly aromatic, with a full and forceful mouthfeel. Shows fine intensity through the lingering finish.

86 • *La Baume (France) 1996 Syrah, Vin de Pays d'Oc. $6.99.*
Deep ruby purple. Moderately full-bodied. Balanced acidity. Moderately extracted. Mildly tannic. Black fruits, minerals, tar. Pleasantly aromatic, with a pure presentation of varietal flavors. Lighter in style, but shows flavor intensity in a sturdy, angular finish.

86 • *Abarbanel (France) 1997 Syrah, Vin de Pays d'Oc. $9.*
Deep blackish purple. Moderately full-bodied. Balanced acidity. Highly extracted. Mildly oaked. Mildly tannic. Cherry cordial, chocolate, mint. Ripe and generous, with sound intensity to the firm, dark flavors. Weighty but well structured, with an angular finish. Shows a slight medicinal note often associated with old-vine Syrah. Impressive.

85 • *Domaine de Triennes (France) 1995 Syrah, Vin de Pays du Var. $9.99.*
Bright ruby purple. Medium-bodied. Full acidity. Highly extracted. Mildly tannic. Red fruits, minerals. Pleasantly aromatic, with a lighter-styled, crisp, delicate palate feel. Finishes with lively acidity.

84 • *Jaja de Jau (France) 1996 Syrah-Grenache, Vin de Pays d'Oc. $6.*
Bright ruby purple. Medium-bodied. Balanced acidity. Highly extracted. Mildly tannic. Minerals, black fruits. Aromatically reserved, with a firm and minerally palate feel. Lean, firm, and angular through the finish.

82 • *Domaine Borie de Maurel (France) 1997 Syrah, Minervois. $8.*
Bright ruby purple. Medium-bodied. Balanced acidity. Highly extracted. Mildly tannic. Minerals, chocolate, red fruits. Aromatically reserved, with a full but firm palate feel. Finishes on a solid linear note.

81 • *Lucien Deschaux (France) 1996 Syrah, Vin de Pays d'Oc. $6.99.*
Bright pale ruby cast. Medium-bodied. Balanced acidity. Highly extracted. Mildly tannic. Red fruits, earth, sweet herbs. Aromatically unusual, with a complex array of flavors. High-toned and crisp in the mouth, with a very lean and vibrant finish.

81 • *Georges Duboeuf (France) 1997 Syrah, Vin de Pays d'Oc. $5.99.*
Bright ruby purple. Medium-bodied. Full acidity. Subtly extracted. Red fruits. Forward, grapey fruit aromas are indicative of carbonic maceration. Lean, high-toned, and crisp on the palate. A quaffer.

Aussie Shiraz

92 • *Peter Lehmann (Australia) 1996 Shiraz, Barossa. $15.*
Deep blackish ruby hue. Moderately full-bodied. Balanced acidity. Moderately extracted. Moderately oaked. Mildly tannic. Game, chocolate, black fruits. Exotic aromas are generous and complex. Lush and supple in the mouth, with a seamless velvety quality. Rich and intense, with a lengthy chocolatey finish. Drinking well now.

89 • *Yalumba (Australia) 1996 Shiraz, Barossa. $15.*

Deep ruby purple. Moderately full-bodied. Balanced acidity. Moderately extracted. Moderately oaked. Mildly tannic. Dusty red fruits, minerals, spice. Pleasantly aromatic with a sweet, spicy quality to the nose. Full but crisp in structure, with an edge providing balance toward the well-gripped and intense finish.

88 • Riddoch (Australia) 1996 Shiraz, Coonawarra. $9.

Bright ruby cast. Medium-bodied. Full acidity. Moderately extracted. Mildly oaked. Mildly tannic. Red fruits, vanilla. Fruit centered and light in style with a crisp character. Tasty and lush through the attractive finish.

88 • Redbank (Australia) 1997 Long Paddock, Shiraz, Victoria. $9.

Deep ruby purple. Moderately full-bodied. Balanced acidity. Moderately extracted. Moderately oaked. Mildly tannic. Black fruits, mint, tar. Ripe aromas show complexity and depth. Full and rich in the mouth, yet well balanced, with acidity lending an attractive edge to the finish.

88 • Leasingham (Australia) 1996 Bin 61, Shiraz, Clare Valley. $14.99.

Bright dark purple. Moderately full-bodied. Balanced acidity. Moderately extracted. Moderately oaked. Mildly tannic. Vanilla, red fruits. Features a hefty oak overlay and a core of ripe fruit flavors. Full but lean in structure with an edgy, flavorful finish.

87 • Sheldrake (Australia) 1995 Shiraz, Western Australia. $13.

Deep ruby hue with a slight fade. Moderately full-bodied. Full acidity. Moderately extracted. Mildly oaked. Moderately tannic. Game, roasted meat, earth. Generous aromas feature a distinctive roasted, gamey quality. Ripe and full in the mouth, with juicy acidity buoying the finish. Intense, well balanced, and fairly concentrated.

86 • Tatachilla (Australia) 1997 Wattle Park, Shiraz, South Australia. $9.99.

Bright ruby cast. Medium-bodied. Balanced acidity. Moderately extracted. Mildly tannic. Red fruits, minerals. Ripe and fruity, with a generous array of flavors. Light in the mouth, with an edgy, minerally quality through the finish.

86 • Taltarni (Australia) 1996 Shiraz, Victoria. $15.

Deep ruby cast. Medium-bodied. Balanced acidity. Moderately extracted. Mildly tannic. Black pepper, minerals. Forward peppery aromas are present throughout. Lean and angular in style, with gripping tannins through the finish.

86 • d'Arenberg (Australia) 1996 The Footbolt, Old Vine Shiraz, McLaren Vale. $14.

Deep purple. Moderately full-bodied. Balanced acidity. Moderately extracted. Mildly oaked. Mildly tannic. Earth, red fruits. Shows a rather unusual rubbery quality in the nose that seems to blow off with aeration. Light in the mouth with a lean structure. Intense and deeply fruited finish.

86 • Cassegrain (Australia) 1997 Shiraz, Hastings River. $14.99.

Bright purple. Medium-bodied. Balanced acidity. Moderately extracted. Moderately tannic. Black fruits, minerals. Aromatically reserved, with a firm and angular palate feel. Youthful and powerful, but rather unyielding. Perhaps time will help.

85 • Wyndham (Australia) 1996 Bin 555, Shiraz, Australia. $9.99.

Bright ruby-garnet cast. Moderately full-bodied. Low acidity. Moderately extracted. Moderately tannic. Stewed fruits, sweet herbs, pine. Spicy aromatics, with a rich, ripe, stewed quality. Shows a touch of heat on the palate that cuts the finish a bit short.

84 • Wynns (Australia) 1996 Coonawarra Estate, Shiraz, Coonawarra. $13.

Deep ruby purple. Medium-bodied. Full acidity. Moderately extracted. Mildly tannic. Black pepper, dried herbs. Shows a distinctive peppery quality throughout. Light in the mouth with a sense of crispness through the finish. Attractive and eminently quaffable.

84 • Tyrrell's (Australia) 1996 Old Winery, Shiraz,

South Eastern Australia. $9.99.
Dark ruby with a slight garnet fade. Moderately full-bodied. Full acidity. Moderately extracted. Moderately oaked. Mildly tannic. Dried herbs, minerals, earth. Distinctive aromatics lead a rich mouthfeel offset by zesty acidity. Finishes on a lingering herb-tinged note.

84 • McGuigan (Australia) 1998 Bin 2000, Shiraz,
South Eastern Australia. $12.
Bright purple. Medium-bodied. Full acidity. Subtly extracted. Mildly tannic. Black fruits, violets. Primary grapey aromas lead a fresh and lively palate feel. Straightforward, fruity, and deeply flavored, with very slight tannins on the finish.

84 • Marienberg (Australia) 1995 Reserve, Shiraz, South Australia. $12.
Bright ruby-garnet cast. Moderately full-bodied. Low acidity. Moderately extracted. Moderately oaked. Moderately tannic. Brown spices, chocolate, sandalwood. Forward aromas carry a prominent spicy accent. Generous, lush, and velvety, with a sense of richness. Chewy tannins rear up on the finish.

84 • Lindemans (Australia) 1997 Bin 50, Shiraz, South Australia. $9.
Bright ruby purple. Medium-bodied. Balanced acidity. Moderately extracted. Mildly tannic. Red fruits, minerals. Pleasant fruit-centered aromatics carry a slightly earthy note. Light in the mouth with bright brambly flavors and a straightforward herb-tinged finish.

83 • Hermitage Road (Australia) 1997 Shiraz, South Eastern Australia. $10.
Deep ruby cast. Medium-bodied. Balanced acidity. Moderately extracted. Mildly tannic. Minerals, black fruits, tar. Fairly reserved in aromatics, with a lighter styled, lean palate feel. Angular, minerally finish.

81 • Hardys (Australia) 1997 Nottage Hill, Shiraz,
South Eastern Australia. $7.99.
Bright ruby purple. Medium-bodied. Balanced acidity. Moderately extracted. Mildly tannic. Red fruits, minerals, dried herbs. Lean aromas carry an herbal edge. Light in the mouth, with a crisp quality through the berry-flavored finish.

81 • Fergusson (Australia) 1997 Shiraz, South Eastern Australia. $12.99.
Bright ruby-garnet cast. Medium-bodied. Full acidity. Moderately extracted. Mildly tannic. Sweet herbs, overripe red fruits. Forward herbal aromatics lead a lighter-styled palate hinting at overripeness. Falls a bit flat toward the finish.

81 • Bulletin Place (Australia) 1997 Shiraz, South Eastern Australia. $9.99.
Bright ruby cast. Medium-bodied. Balanced acidity. Moderately extracted. Quite tannic. Dried herbs, red fruits, spice. Aromatically reserved, with a lean mouthfeel and compact flavors backed by aggressive tannins that are rather dry through the finish.

Other Aussie "Rhônes"

89 • Yalumba (Australia) 1996 Bush Vine, Grenache, Barossa. $14.
Bright ruby cast. Moderately full-bodied. Balanced acidity. Highly extracted. Mildly tannic. Briar fruits, minerals. Ripe, jammy aromas lead a full, rich palate feel. Lush and generous through the flavorful finish.

86 • Penfolds (Australia) 1996 Bin 2, Shiraz-Mourvèdre,
South Eastern Australia. $10.
Dark ruby cast. Medium-bodied. Balanced acidity. Moderately extracted. Mildly tannic. Earth, dried herbs, minerals. Features a Rhonelike roasted, earthy edge to the flavors. Light in the mouth, but flavorful and concentrated. Lengthy finish.

84 • Tatachilla (Australia) 1997 Grenache-Shiraz, McLaren Vale. $13.99.
Bright ruby cast. Medium-bodied. Balanced acidity. Moderately extracted. Mildly tannic. Black pepper, raspberries, minerals. Quite aromatic, with a convincing array of complex Rhonelike flavors. Light in structure but concentrated in flavor. Interesting.

84 • Rosemount (Australia) 1997 Grenache-Shiraz, Australia. $7.99.

Bright ruby-garnet cast. Medium-bodied. Balanced acidity. Subtly extracted. Mildly tannic. Black pepper, minerals, red fruits. Bright peppery aromas lead a lush but light palate feel. Generous and flavorful through the finish.

84 • Cockatoo Ridge (Australia) 1997 Grenache-Shiraz, Australia. $10.

Pale ruby purple. Moderately light-bodied. Balanced acidity. Subtly extracted. Mildly tannic. Black pepper, minerals, green herbs. Forward peppery aromas carry a green edge. Light and lively in the mouth with a crisp finish. A light, undemanding style.

83 • Marienberg (Australia) 1995 Cottage Classic Red, 65% Cabernet Sauvignon-25% Mourvèdre-10% Grenache, South Australia. $10.

Bright ruby red with a slight fade. Medium-bodied. Full acidity. Subtly extracted. Mildly oaked. Mildly tannic. Cedar, dried herbs, minerals. Shows a mature edge to the flavors. Light in the mouth with firm tannins and an angular finish.

81 • Tim Adams (Australia) 1997 The Fergus, Grenache, Clare Valley. $11.

Bright ruby red with a fade to the rim. Moderately full-bodied. Balanced acidity. Moderately extracted. Mildly tannic. Menthol, sweet herbs, earth. Very unusual high-toned aromas lead a surprisingly lush, almost fat, palate. Supple through the finish it lacks grip.

81 • Goundrey (Australia) 1997 Shiraz-Grenache, South East Australia. $14.

Pale ruby cast. Moderately light-bodied. Balanced acidity. Subtly extracted. Mildly tannic. Black pepper, spice. Crisp spicy aromas lead a light palate with a vibrant peppery array of lean fruity flavors that linger on the finish. Quaffable.

U.S. Syrah

90 • LinCourt (CA) 1996 Syrah, Santa Barbara County. $14.

Opaque, brilliant dark crimson hue to the rim. Intense black fruit cordial, briar, oak spice, pickle flavor elements. Hefty wood tones. Supple entry. Full-bodied with plentiful, velvety tannins. Lingering, rich finish. Lots of everything here in a supple, well-extracted style that is intense, concentrated, and stuffed. Drinkable now, but can improve with age.

88 • Meridian (CA) 1996 Syrah, Paso Robles. $14.

Deep purple-red, limpid, and brilliant to the rim. Generous, fantastic cedar and red currant flavors. A firm entry leads a medium-bodied palate that shows crisp acidity. Moderate, grainy tannins. Well gripped through the lingering finish, with fine structuring acids. Bright and lively, with a nice oak overlay. Drink now.

88 • J. Lohr (CA) 1996 South Ridge, Syrah, Paso Robles. $14.

Dark black cherry color, limpid and brilliant. Generous, sound bramble fruit and vanilla flavors. Subtle wood tones. A smooth entry leads a moderately full-bodied palate with crisp acidity. Moderate, drying tannins. Chunky, rich, and fruity, with a lengthy finish. Drinkable now, but can improve with age.

86 • R.H. Phillips (CA) 1996 EXP, Syrah, Dunnigan Hills. $12.

Dark ruby color, limpid with a slight fade. Medium-bodied. Cooked fruit flavors. Crisp, fruity, and well supported by grainy tannins and bright acids. Fruit-centered, relatively firmly structured. Drink now.

86 • Monterra (CA) 1996 Syrah, Monterey County. $9.99.

Rich purple, limpid, and brilliant with a slight fade. Medium-bodied. Blueberry and vanilla flavors. A softer, rounder, fruit-forward style with fine persistence of fruit flavors. Supple and easy drinking. Drink now.

86 • Hogue (WA) 1996 Genesis, Syrah, Columbia Valley. $15.

Bright, saturated ruby red to the rim. Generous red fruit and spice aromas belie a prominent oak accent. A firm attack leads a medium-bodied palate with astringent tannins. Intense, flavorful finish. A firm, lean, compact style. Drink now or later. Can improve with more age.

86 • *Fox Hollow (CA) 1996 Shiraz, California. $8.99.*

Pale purple, limpid, and brilliant with a slight fade. Subtle, pleasant cherry and vanilla flavors. Hint of wood tones. A smooth entry leads a moderately light-bodied palate showing very mild, silky tannins. Structurally light, with bright fruit flavors up front carried by fruit acidity. Subtle, short finish. Straightforward and quaffable. Drink now.

85 • *McDowell (CA) 1997 Syrah, Mendocino. $12.*

Bright purple-red to the rim. Subdued earth, herb, and red fruit aromas. A firm attack leads a moderately full-bodied palate with aggressive astringent tannins. Lacks somewhat for acidic grip. Tannic, earthy finish. Rather tough at present, with a funky edge that should blow off. Drink within five years.

84 • *Sobon (CA) 1996 Syrah, Shenandoah Valley, California. $15.*

Medium ruby color, limpid with a slight fade. Medium-bodied. Light, bright herb and berry flavors with mild, drying tannins. A touch herbal, but juicy and balanced. Drink now.

84 • *Sea Ridge Coastal (CA) 1996 Shiraz, California. $10.*

Pale red, transparent with a fading rim. Mild, sound baked red fruit, vanilla, cherry flavors. Hint of wood tones. A soft entry leads a moderately light-bodied palate. A lighter style, very quaffable. Drink now.

84 • *Qupé (CA) 1997 Syrah, Central Coast. $13.50.*

Pale purple, limpid with a fading rim. Subtle, clean flower and crisp berry flavors. Firm entry. Moderately light-bodied palate with crisp acidity. Clipped, short finish. Drink now.

84 • *Montpellier (CA) 1997 Syrah, California. $6.99.*

Medium purple, limpid, and brilliant with a slight fade. Mild, pleasant black cherry and vanilla flavors. Mild wood tones. A smooth entry, and moderately light-bodied palate with balanced acidity and bright fruity accents throughout. Mild, silky tannins and a subtle, short finish. Structurally light. Appealingly straightforward with a soft, fruity character. Drink now.

84 • *Hacienda (CA) 1996 Clair de Lune, Shiraz, California. $6.99.*

Medium cherry red, limpid, and brilliant to the rim. Generous, sound cedar and cherry flavors. Generous wood tones. Smooth entry, medium-bodied palate, and moderate, velvety tannins. Oak dominated, with brown spice notes. Subtle finish. Drink now.

84 • *Forest Ville (CA) 1997 Shiraz, California. $5.99.*

Pale cherry purple, limpid, and brilliant with a slight fade. Subtle, pleasant herb, black fruit, vanilla flavors. Hint of wood tones. Soft entry, medium-bodied palate, and light, drying tannins. Subtle short finish. A jammy though light style. Drink now.

84 • *Forest Glen (CA) 1996 Shiraz, California. $9.99.*

Medium reddish purple. Red currant, vanilla, mineral flavors. Hint of wood tones. Firm entry, medium-bodied palate, and a subtle, short finish with moderate, drying tannins. Fruit flavors are rather muted. Dry and lean, this will work best with food. Drink now.

83 • *Rutherford Vintners (CA) 1997 Shiraz, Stanislaus County. $8.99.*

Dark ruby color, limpid with a fading rim. Medium-bodied. Cherry and vanilla flavors. Tart aromas lead crisp fruit flavors through a drying finish. Drink now.

83 • *Parducci (CA) 1997 Syrah, Mendocino. $10.*

Bright ruby red to the rim. Generous herb, red fruit, and vanilla aromas show a subtle wood accent. A soft attack leads a medium-bodied palate showing supple tannins. The finish is angular, with some grip. A lighter-styled quaffer. Drink now.

83 • *Grand Cru (CA) 1997 Syrah, California. $7.99.*

Medium crimson purple, limpid, and brilliant with a slight fade. Subtle, sound cherry and berry fruit and vanilla flavors. Subtle wood tones. Smooth entry to a medium-bodied palate. Moderate, velvety tannins. Lingering rich finish. Peppery, jammy, youthful, and supple. Drink now.

83 • *Charles Shaw (CA) 1996 Shiraz, California. $8.99.*

Medium crimson red, limpid with a slight fade. Subtle, pleasant cherry, vanilla, mineral flavors. Hint of wood tones. Soft entry, moderately light-bodied palate. Mild, drying tannins. Subtle short finish. Jammy and mildly oak spiced—a lighter style. Drink now.

82 • *Silver Ridge (CA) 1996 Syrah, California. $9.99.*

Light purple, limpid with a fading rim. Muted, sound, crisp black fruit flavors. Soft entry, light-bodied. Fruit is a tad muted, with oak dominating. Subtle, abrupt finish. Simple and one dimensional. Drink now.

81 • *Windsor (CA) 1997 Private Reserve, Syrah, Sonoma County. $15.*

Light cherry red with a slight fade. Subtle, sound herb and berry fruit flavors. Generous wood tones with crisp acidity. Mild, drying tannins. Oak dominates the medium-bodied palate. Clipped, short finish. A light herb-accented quaffing style. Drink now.

81 • *Monthaven (CA) 1996 Syrah, California. $9.99.*

Deep garnet hue, opaque and luminous to the rim. Generous blueberry, raisin, vanilla flavors. Hint of wood tones. A smooth entry leads a moderately full-bodied palate, with crisp acidity. Moderate, drying tannins. Lingering finish. Overripe aromas, yet lean on the palate, making it seem bizarre and unbalanced. Drink now.

81 • *Delicato (CA) 1997 Syrah, California. $5.99.*

Deep purple, limpid, and brilliant to the rim. Generous, pleasant herbs, black fruits, mineral flavors. Subtle wood tones. A firm entry leads a medium-bodied palate with a nice mouthfeel. Supple tannins linger on the rich finish. This is a richer style with some commendable complexity. Drink now.

U.S. Petite Sirah

92 • *Bogle (CA) 1997 Petite Sirah, California. $10.*

Dark ruby purple. Moderately full-bodied. Highly extracted. Quite tannic. Plums, chocolate. Floral, bright fruity aromas follow through on the palate with substantial tannins that are not too dry on the finish. This could use a few years, although is approachable now.

87 • *Dos Cabezas (AZ) 1997 Petite Sirah, Cochise County. $15.*

Saturated dark purple. Moderately full-bodied. Highly extracted. Moderately tannic. Prunes, herbs. Complex savory herb and fleshy fruit aromas. A silky mouthfeel has inky, rich black fruit that stands up to the tannic structure. A touch overripe. This is drinking well now.

86 • *Windsor (CA) 1996 Petite Sirah, North Coast. $12.*

Bright red-purple. Moderately full-bodied. Highly extracted. Moderately tannic. Oak spice, red fruits. Heavily oak-accented aromas have a bright fruit underlay that follows through on the palate. Nicely balanced, drinking well now.

83 • *Mirassou (CA) 1996 Petite Sirah, Monterey County. $11.95.*

Opaque purple. Moderately full-bodied. Highly extracted. Quite tannic. Herbal and blueberry aromas follow through on the palate with a thick, textured mouthfeel. Impressive grainy tannins rise on the finish.

83 • *Concannon (CA) 1996 Selected Vineyard, Petite Sirah, California. $11.45.*

Opaque purple-blue. Full-bodied. Highly extracted. Quite tannic. Well-extracted flavors with dark, fleshy fruit character following though on the finish. Dry, thick tannins linger. Monolithic and intense.

81 • *Edgewood (CA) 1995 Petite Sirah, Napa Valley. $14.*

Opaque blackish-ruby hue. Full-bodied. Highly extracted. Quite tannic. Anise, earth, black fruits. Heavyweight extraction delivers substantial mouth-drying tannins that make this tough at present. Needs years of patient cellaring.

Scale: Superlative (96-100), Exceptional (90-95), Highly Recommended (85-89), Recommended (80-84), Not Recommended (Under 80)

80 • *Cilurzo (CA) 1996 Proprietor's Reserve, Petite Sirah, Temecula. $14.95.*
Saturated opaque dark purple. Moderately full-bodied. Moderately extracted. Quite tannic. Dark chocolate, black fruits. Dark fruit aromas have an astringent note that is confirmed by the extremely dry, powdery tannins that rasp the palate. Low acids make this rather tough to drink.

Other U.S. "Rhônes"

89 • *Windsor (CA) 1996 Carignane, Mendocino County. $10.*
Dark crimson with a purple tinge. Moderately full-bodied. Highly extracted. Mildly tannic. Raspberries, cherries. Smooth and fleshy with a fruit-centered character. Supple tannins on the finish. Very approachable, though chewy tannins come through on the finish.

87 • *Trentadue (CA) 1995 Carignane, Sonoma County. $12.*
Dark crimson. Moderately full-bodied. Moderately extracted. Mildly tannic. Plummy, black cherry aromas and flavors. Generous mouthfeel and mouthcoating tannins. Very modern and well extracted, it is drinking nicely now but will develop in the future.

86 • *Rosenblum (CA) 1997 Chateau La Paws, Côte du Bone, Mourvèdre, Contra Costa County. $9.50.*
Pale ruby red with a slight fade. Medium-bodied. Moderately extracted. Mildly tannic. Raspberry, cola, vanilla. Soft, berryish, and fruit centered, with a supple lingering finish. Very high drinkability factor.

86 • *River Run (CA) 1996 Wirz Vineyard, Carignane, Cienega Valley. $15.*
Crimson hue with a pale, fading rim. Medium-bodied. Moderately extracted. Mildly tannic. Raspberry notes. Generous berry fruit aromas show a ripe jammy character. The palate is lively, with good grip and a fruit center, and supple tannins on the finish.

85 • *Mount Palomar (CA) 1996 Rey Sol Le Mediterrane Old Vines Selection Red, South Coast. $10.*
Bright garnet red with a slight fade. Forward earth and leather aromas. A soft attack leads a medium-bodied palate that is somewhat lacking in tannic grip. Flat, earthy finish. This is a wine in search of a bit more structure. Drink now.

85 • *Curtis (CA) 1997 Heritage, Old Vines Red, California. $10.*
Bright purple-red to the rim. Generous red fruit, sweet herb, and mineral aromas. A crisp attack leads a medium-bodied palate with drying, astringent tannins. Clipped, snappy finish. Youthful and compact. Drink now or later. Can improve with more age.

84 • *Wild Horse (CA) 1995 Grenache, Cienega Valley. $13.*
Pale garnet red with a slight fade. Generous overripe red fruit and mineral aromas. A firm attack leads a moderately light-bodied palate with mildly astringent tannins. Lean, angular finish. Solid grip but lacks generosity. Drink now.

84 • *Santino (CA) 1996 Satyricon, California. $11.95.*
Bright garnet red with a slight fade. Attractive, generous leather, herb and mineral aromas. A supple attack leads a medium-bodied palate with drying, mildly astringent tannins. Lean, angular finish. Rather edgy. Drink now.

84 • *Horton (VA) 1994 Stonecastle Red, Orange County. $11.50.*
Bright garnet red. Generous herb, red fruit, and cedar aromas show a hefty oak accent. A soft attack leads a medium-bodied palate with gripping tannins and bright acidity. Fine structure and balance. Lengthy, spicy finish. Drink now.

83 • *Monthaven (CA) 1995 Carignane, California. $14.*
Brick red with a slight fade. Medium-bodied. Moderately extracted. Mildly tannic. Anise, black fruits. Lean and firmly structured with dusty tannins and black fruit flavors lingering through the finish. A flavorful, rustic style.

83 • *Eberle (CA) 1996 Côtes-du-Rôbles, Paso Robles. $13.*
Pale orange-red. Subdued herb and mineral aromas. Moderately light-bodied. A crisp attack leads a light-bodied palate with drying tannins. Clipped, clean finish. A lightweight with grip. Drink now.

82 • *Joseph Swan (CA) 1996 Mourvèdre, Russian River Valley. $15.*
Crimson red. Medium-bodied. Moderately extracted. Moderately tannic. Earth, minerals. Marked herbal, minty aromas follow through on the palate. Well gripped and lean, angular through the finish. Shows a distinctive oak accent throughout.

81 • *Horton (VA) 1995 Mourvèdre, Orange County. $12.50.*
Pale brown-red. Moderately light-bodied. Subtly extracted. Mildly tannic. Cedar, leather. Very aromatic, with a cedar note. Somewhat light and fading, though it shows a lovely supple mouthfeel and a delicate finish. Quite distinctive.

81 • *Horton (VA) 1995 Cotes d'Orange, Orange County. $14.75.*
Pale orange-red. Pungent cedar and spice aromas show a dominant wood accent. A crisp attack leads a light-bodied palate with zesty acidity and gripping tannins. Snappy, vibrant finish. A light and racy quaffer. Drink now.

81 • *Domaine de la Terre Rouge (CA) 1997 Tête-à-Tête, Sierra Foothills. $12.*
Pale garnet red. Forward herb and sweet red fruit aromas. A soft attack leads a medium-bodied palate with surprisingly astringent, drying tannins. Clipped, glycerous finish. Could use a bit more acidic grip. Drink now.

81 • *Beaulieu (CA) 1995 Signet Collection, Grenache, San Benito. $8.*
Brick red with a slight fade. Unusual herb and mineral aromas. A soft attack leads a moderately light-bodied palate somewhat lacking in tannic grip. Soft, flat finish. Drink now.

Other Great Value "Rhônes"

89 • *Delheim (South Africa) 1996 Shiraz, Stellenbosch. $13.*
Deep, saturated ruby hue. Pungent, exotic game and olive aromas. A brisk entry leads a full-bodied palate with sharp acidity and firm tannins. Shows great intensity of flavor. A smoky and wild style, it is not everyone's cup of tea, but is extremely interesting. Drink now or later.

82 • *Carmel (Israel) 1997 Petite Sirah, Shomron. $5.99.*
Bright saturated ruby color with a purple cast. Moderately light-bodied. Balanced acidity. Subtly extracted. Mildly tannic. Briar fruits, black pepper, dried herbs. Pleasantly aromatic. A light-styled, flavorful palate that has a green edge. Crisp and angular finish.

82 • *Bodegas Nekeas (Spain) 1997 "El Chaparral," Vega Sindoa, Old Vines Grenache, Navarra. $8.*
Pale purple. Moderately light-bodied. Balanced acidity. Subtly extracted. Mildly tannic. Pepper, black fruits, olives. Bright grapey aromas lead a straightforward mouthfeel. A stylish quaffer with complex flavors.

seventeen

Stylish Italian Reds

Introduction   198
Reviews   201
   Chianti   201
   Other Tuscan Reds   203
   Piemontese Barbera   204
   Piemontese Dolcetto   205
   Montepulciano d'Abruzzo   205
   Salice Salentino   206
   Rosso Conero   206
   Amarone   206
   Valpolicella   207
   Other Great Value
   Italian Reds   207
   U.S. Sangiovese   209
   Other U.S. Italianates   210

Introduction: Stylish Italian Reds

When a red wine is required, do you find yourself reaching for a coin, tossing it in the air, and calling, "Heads for Cabernet and tails for Merlot"? If so, you're in a rut and in desperate need of the stylish and flavorful red wines of Italy.

Italy is wine. The flavors and textures of Italian reds vary widely—everything from precocious and impossibly purple fruit-oriented styles to dense, stalwart wines that are as much of a chew as they are a drink. No other country offers the sheer volume (roughly 20% of the world's output) or variety of wines that Italy does. The nation is covered with vines, from its cool Alpine districts in the north, to the near desert-like conditions of Sicily. Every one of Italy's 20 provinces has vineyards. If you have been reluctant to try Italian wines, feeling overwhelmed by the staggering number of varieties and confusing labels, don't worry about it. The experts get confused as well; and frankly, so do the Italians.

The Best Values

Value seekers should concern themselves primarily with a handful of Italy's red wines—several reds from Tuscany and Chianti in particular, as well as Barbera, Dolcetto, Valpolicella, and Montepulciano d'Abruzzo. Most of these wines come from Italy's two most important red wine regions—Tuscany and Piedmont. Chianti is best known, and during the 1990s its popularity grew steadily, driving prices upward, especially for the top producers. However, many bargains remain. Although some top wines are priced above the $15 plateau, they still represent a fantastic value when compared dollar for dollar with the first-rank wines of other famed regions. Barbera, Dolcetto, Valpolicella, and Montepulciano d'Abruzzo are generally $15 or less, which consistently makes them some of the world's best wine bargains.

Piedmont

The Piedmont region lies in Italy's northwestern corner at the foot of the Alpine chain bordering France; hence the name Piedmont, meaning "foot of the mountains." This is one of the most important red wine districts in the world. Three red grapes dominate the region—Nebbiolo, Barbera, and Dolcetto. Nebbiolo is responsible for the world-class wine of Barolo and Barbaresco. Unfortunately, examples under $15 are a thing of the past.

Barbera, however, is another matter entirely when it comes to bang for the buck. Barbera is Piedmont's most widely planted variety. It is typically medium bodied and dry with a healthy dose of acidity. Flavors of black cherry and plum framed by earth and the occasional oak barrel are prevalent. The most famous Barberas come from vineyards in and around the towns of Alba and Asti. (Yes, this is the same Asti made famous by Asti Spumante.) Barberas from Alba tend to be biggest of all, showing great power and concentration while maintaining balance and finesse. Barbera d'Alba is capable of aging 10 years and beyond in favorable vintages. Asti, on the other hand, produces a fruity, less tannic Barbera than Alba, and is best consumed within two to six years of the vintage. Barbera, like most Italian reds, is excellent at the table with a variety of foods. It is marvelous with the Piemontese favorite, *bagna cauda*, a dip of olive oil, anchovies, and garlic. Barbera is also a natural with tomatoes. A simple marinara with a young

Barbera is a match made in heaven. The 1995 vintage was very good, while 1996 and 1997 were absolutely outstanding.

Dolcetto, a variety also from Piedmont, is intensely fruity, with less tannin and acid than Barbera. Dolcetto often draws comparison to France's Beaujolais. It varies from village to village but can generally be classified in two basic styles—extraordinarily soft, velvety, and fruity with little tannin; or slightly rugged, with spicy flavors and a nose of toasted almonds. Dolcetto complements slow-cooked stews and roasts, offering fresh and fruity flavors that enliven the dish, but can be equally good as a picnic wine with a light chill. Vintage patterns are quite similar to those of Piemontese Barbera.

Tuscany

Tuscany lies in north-central Italy and is home to the nation's most famous wine, Chianti. In Tuscany, Sangiovese and its close relatives are the primary red varieties of the region, responsible for the wines of Chianti, Brunello di Montalcino, Rosso di Montalcino, Vino Nobile di Montepulciano, and Rosso di Montepulciano.

If you think of Chianti as a cheap and thin wine poured from wicker-covered bottles, think again. Chianti has undergone a tremendous renaissance in the past two decades, and has returned to its rightful place among the world's greatest red wines. Today's Chianti is medium-bodied, crisp, and flavorful. The nose is filled with aromas of dusty cherries, spice, and cedar. The Riservas are more complex, showing less fruit and more spice. Chianti finds a mate with most any game, and like Barbera, it is exemplary with tomato sauces. The 1995 and 1997 vintages were both excellent, as well as 1990, if you should happen to find any older wines lurking in a shop with decent storage conditions. Basic Chianti, however, does not have wild vintage swings and tends to be at least reliable year in and year out.

Unfortunately, the great wines of Brunello di Montalcino are priced from near $20 a bottle to much more, but it is possible to find

Great Value Red Italian Varietals at a Glance

Number of Wines Reviewed:

106

Countries Represented:

2

bargains from southern Tuscany, where these wines originate. Brunello di Montalcino is one of Italy's finest red wines, made around the town of Montalcino from a Sangiovese variant known locally as Brunello. The flavors are similar to that of Chianti, albeit much richer and more tannic, with a ripe fruit sweetness. While Brunello can be great, the real values are in Brunello di Montalcino's younger brother, Rosso di Montalcino. Rosso di Montalcino is most often made from the young vines and/or wines of Brunello di Montalcino that may not fare well when subjected to the lengthy wood aging required by Brunello. The wines are medium bodied and pleasantly fruity, sharing much in common with a high-quality Chianti.

Vino Nobile di Montepulciano—from the hilltop village of Montepulciano, just around the corner from Montalcino but not as famous—can occasionally be found in the value price zone. The wines are also made from a Sangiovese variant and exhibit ripe, concentrated fruit with hints of leather and smoke. Like Brunello, Vino Nobile also has an "everyday" version, Rosso di Montepulciano. These wines usually offer great value for the money, and are made in a somewhat softer, more accessible style than Vino Nobile. Vintage considerations are the same as those for Brunello—1993, 1995, and 1997 are tops, but the vintages in between are quite good in their own right. Vino Nobile or Rosso di Montepulciano marry strikingly well with grilled vegetables and meats.

Other Regions

Outside of Piedmont and Tuscany, value seekers may want to familiarize themselves with the wines of Montepulciano d'Abruzzo. Abruzzo, which is the province to the northeast of Tuscany on the Adriatic Sea, is famous for its wines from the Montepulciano grape. The wines are light- to medium-bodied with tremendous fruit character and crisp acidity. These well-made, cheerful wines can be fantastic bargains, as they are almost always under $10 and can even be found around $5 a bottle.

Finally, northern Italy's Veneto region is home to a number of famous red wines, but perhaps the most popular is the light and refreshing red from Valpolicella. Fragrant and fruit-forward Valpolicella is a light red that can stand a bit of a chill. It is a pleasant quaffer by itself but often has enough character to stand up to strongly flavored foods. It is not a wine to be talked about and pontificated on, but it is one to be enjoyed. As a result, good examples are almost always a good value.

But What to Eat?

All Italian wine varieties are ideal food companions, so while there may be "ideal" combinations, don't sweat the details. This is because they are very rarely overly alcoholic and they tend to have zesty levels of acidity. Both factors are essential if a wine is to complement food as opposed to competing with it or even overshadowing it. These factors also make Italian varieties easy to drink. They are not tiring in the way that a high-alcohol, rich Cabernet or Chardonnay can be. In short, drink what you like with what you want to eat. If you absolutely have to do a little matching, in Italy as in much of Europe, the wines of the region are usually seen as the perfect accompaniment to the food of the region. This adage is perhaps more true of Italy than any other nation. With one of the many fantastic regional Italian cookbooks that are available in hand, it will be almost impossible to go wrong, and practicing will be half the fun.

Italian Varieties in California

Italians, as well as Italian varieties, have been a part of the California wine industry from its earliest stages. Barbera, which was first bottled in California as a distinct variety in 1884, was the first variety to make an impact, although Sangiovese and Dolcetto predate Barbera plantings by 22 years. Italian immigrants played a major role in California's growth, and where they went, the vine was often sure to follow. In California, however, transplanted Italians usually found themselves working with local varieties such as Zinfandel, Carignane, and Petite Sirah as opposed to varieties from their homeland. At the repeal of Prohibition, Italian families owned the majority of bonded wineries in Santa Clara, Sonoma, and Napa counties.

Today the popularity of Barbera has waned, as the variety saw its peak acreage year in 1978, but Sangiovese is currently in fashion as vineyards in Napa, Sonoma, and Mendocino counties are on the rise. It is too early to define what U.S. Sangiovese is all about, though most examples are rich and fruit oriented with a flashy wood accent—more of a nod to Brunello or the "super-Tuscans" than Chianti—with a price tag to match. As for Nebbiolo and Dolcetto, these varieties have proven far trickier to work with, though occasionally a convincing example will pop up.

Reviews

Chianti

89 • San Vincenti (Italy) 1995 Chianti Classico. $14.99.
Garnet red. Medium-bodied. Balanced acidity. Moderately extracted. Moderately tannic. Cherries, pits, minerals. Austere aromas. Quite structured, with solid tannins through the finish. Not a fruit-forward style, but it shows intensity of earthy flavors with fine length. Nice now, though this should age well for a few years.

89 • Dievole (Italy) 1996 Chianti Classico. $13.50.
Bright reddish purple. Medium-bodied. Moderately extracted. Cherries, vanilla, lead pencil. Ripe, fleshy aromas. Generous, juicy red fruit flavors hint at some Cabernet Sauvignon. Well structured; a little reserved right now.

88 • Vagnoni (Italy) 1996 Chianti Colli Senesi. $12.
Bright ruby purple. Medium-bodied. Full acidity. Moderately extracted. Mildly oaked. Mildly tannic. Plums, red fruits, minerals. Reserved aromatically but quite flavorful on the palate, with a burst of ripe red fruit flavors. Well structured and austere, with a focused, lean finish. Excellent grip and intensity.

88 • San Fabiano Calcinaia (Italy) 1996 Chianti Classico. $12.99.
Bright ruby red. Medium-bodied. Full acidity. Moderately extracted. Mildly tannic. Lead pencil, cherries, herbs. High-toned, faintly herbal aromas follow through on the palate. Juicy red fruit flavors have an herbal edge, with bright acids rearing up on the finish. Very characterful.

88 • Castello di Querceto (Italy) 1995 Chianti Classico. $9.99.
Vanilla red. Medium-bodied. Full acidity. Moderately extracted. Mildly oaked. Cherries, vanilla. Bright, gamey, berry-scented aromas follow through on the lively palate. Bursting with character and Sangiovese expression.

88 • Castello di Farnetella (Italy) 1995 Chianti Colli Senesi. $12.
Bright ruby red. Medium-bodied. Balanced acidity. Moderately extracted. Mildly tannic. Red berries. Generous fruity aromas follow through well on the palate, with a gamey hint. Soft tannins provide some grip on the finish. Well balanced.

87 • *Castello di Querceto (Italy) 1996 Chianti. $7.99.*
Bright ruby hue. Medium-bodied. Full acidity. Moderately extracted. Mildly oaked. Mildly tannic. Red fruits, brown spices, dried herbs. Quite aromatic, with a complex array of flavors on the palate. Lean and taut in structure, with excellent balancing acidity and solid grip.

86 • *Castello di Gabbiano (Italy) 1995 Titolato Gabbiano, Chianti Classico. $11.*
Garnet red. Medium-bodied. Balanced acidity. Moderately extracted. Mildly tannic. Leather, earth, red fruits. Mature, spicy, earthy aromas. Flavorful, soft palate has clean acids and a fine layer of dusty tannins on the finish. Rustic but tasty.

86 • *Barone Ricasoli (Italy) 1995 Brolio, Chianti Classico. $11.99.*
Blood red. Medium-bodied. Balanced acidity. Moderately extracted. Moderately tannic. Leather, earth, black fruits. Solid, chewy mouthful of dark fruit flavors, with some chunky dry tannins on the finish. Flavorsome and richly textured.

86 • *Antinori (Italy) 1995 Badia a Passignano, Chianti Classico. $12.50.*
Ruby red. Moderately light-bodied. Full acidity. Moderately extracted. Mildly tannic. Herbs, tart cherries, minerals. Rounded mouthfeel, showing bright, tart fruit flavors. Mild, tart red fruit notes throughout, with a solid, minerally finish.

84 • *Rocca delle Macie (Italy) 1996 Chianti Classico. $11.*
Blood red. Moderately light-bodied. Balanced acidity. Moderately extracted. Mildly oaked. Mildly tannic. Earth, red fruits. Mildly stewed nose. Light, minerally style with an austere character through the finish. Fine finish has some grip.

84 • *Piccini (Italy) 1996 Chianti Classico. $10.99.*
Full cherry red. Medium-bodied. Balanced acidity. Moderately extracted. Mildly tannic. Ripe red berries. Fleshy, berry-scented aromas. Rounded palate showing some glycerous mouthfeel and ripe flavors. Fruit-centered style. A dusting of dry tannin gives this some grip on the finish.

84 • *Luiano (Italy) 1996 Chianti Classico. $11.99.*
Medium ruby hue. Moderately light-bodied. Balanced acidity. Moderately extracted. Mildly tannic. Violets, red fruits. Quite aromatic, with a lively, juicy palate showing bright sour cherry flavors and a lingering minerally finish that belies its lighter style.

84 • *Cecchi (Italy) 1996 Chianti Classico. $12.*
Pale ruby red. Moderately light-bodied. Balanced acidity. Subtly extracted. Juicy red fruit flavors follow through a crisp, clean finish with a mineral accent.

84 • *Castello di Valiano (Italy) 1996 Chianti Classico. $11.99.*
Bright ruby red. Moderately light-bodied. Balanced acidity. Moderately extracted. Dried herbs, red berries, vanilla. Focused, high-toned red fruit aromas lead a bright, nervous palate that concludes with good minerally grip on the finish.

84 • *Castello di Gabbiano (Italy) 1994 Riserva, Chianti Classico. $15.*
Deep garnet cast. Medium-bodied. Full acidity. Moderately extracted. Mildly oaked. Mildly tannic. Spice, minerals, dried herbs. Reserved aromatically, but shows an earthy core of flavors on the lean and focused palate. Austere through the finish. A solid table wine.

83 • *Riccardo Falchini (Italy) 1997 Colombaia, Chianti Colli Senesi. $8.99.*
Bright red-purple. Moderately light-bodied. Balanced acidity. Moderately extracted. Mildly tannic. Candied fruits. Grapey vin nouveau aromas. Soft and supple, with plenty of quick fruity flavors.

83 • *Piccini (Italy) 1997 Chianti. $6.49.*
Bright ruby hue to the rim. Medium-bodied. Full acidity. Moderately extracted. Mildly tannic. Bitter cherries, spice. Somewhat reserved aromatically, with subtle red fruit overtones. Lean and well structured on the palate, with mild astringency through the finish.

82 • *Del Falegname (Italy) 1996 Chianti Colli Senesi. $9.99.*
Bright ruby red to the rim. Moderately light-bodied. Full acidity. Moderately extracted. Mildly tannic. Minerals. Aromatically reserved, with a lean palate feel. Somewhat dilute, with a certain lack of flavor intensity.

81 • *Piccini (Italy) 1994 Riserva, Chianti Classico. $14.99.*
Bright ruby cast. Moderately light-bodied. Full acidity. Subtly extracted. Mildly tannic. Minerals, dried herbs. Reserved aromatically, with a lighter-styled, austere palate feel. Lacks flavor.

81 • *Fattoria Carpineta Fontalpino (Italy) 1995 Gioia,*
Chianti Colli Senesi. $14.
Ruby red with a slight fade. Moderately light-bodied. Balanced acidity. Subtly extracted. Minerals, faint cherry fruits. Weak aromas reveal a tired palate with faint fruit flavors. Poor finish. Charmless. Overcropped.

81 • *Castello di Gabbiano (Italy) 1996 Chianti. $9.*
Pale garnet hue. Moderately light-bodied. Balanced acidity. Moderately extracted. Mildly tannic. Earth, red cherry fruits. Somewhat earthy nose. Crisp, juicy berry fruit flavors have a hint of tannin to support them.

Other Tuscan Reds

87 • *La Palazzetta di Flavio Fante (Italy) 1995 Rosso di Montalcino. $14.*
Saturated red-purple. Medium-bodied. Moderately extracted. Mildly tannic. Red berries, vanilla, mushrooms. Succulent aromatics. Bright, juicy palate with an open-knit structure and easy fruity flavors. A very textured, modern style.

87 • *Fattoria di S. Angelo (Italy) 1996 Lisini, Rosso di Montalcino. $12.*
Bright ruby purple. Medium-bodied. Moderately extracted. Mildly oaked. Mildly tannic. Black berry fruits. Generous, fleshy, fruity aromas follow through well on the palate, with very elegant, finely wrought flavors. Sound, juicy, and drinking nicely now.

85 • *Terrabianca (Italy) 1995 Scassino, Toscana. $15.*
Bright ruby cast. Medium-bodied. Full acidity. Moderately extracted. Mildly tannic. Red fruits, dried herbs. Reserved aromatically, with a lighter-styled, lean palate feel. Finishes with some mildly astringent tannins. Unyielding.

83 • *Fazi Battaglia (Italy) 1993 Fassati, Vino Nobile di Montepulciano. $15.*
Garnet red. Medium-bodied. Balanced acidity. Moderately extracted. Moderately tannic. Earth, minerals, tomatoes. Mature tertiary aromas. Dry and minerally, with full grip on the finish. Fading somewhat.

83 • *Ecco Domani (Italy) 1997 Sangiovese, Toscana. $10.*
Deep red-purple. Medium-bodied. Balanced acidity. Moderately extracted. Violets, black cherries. Fruit-centered aromas reveal an open-knit, modern wine with easy drinking appeal.

83 • *Cecchi (Italy) 1995 Vino Nobile di Montepulciano. $15.*
Ruby red. Moderately light-bodied. Balanced acidity. Moderately extracted. Mildly tannic. Red fruits, minerals. Crisp, angular flavors with a dusting of dry tannins on the finish. Straightforward.

83 • *Barone Ricasoli (Italy) 1996 Formulae, Sangiovese, Toscana. $14.*
Bright cherry red. Medium-bodied. Balanced acidity. Moderately extracted. Red fruits, minerals, dried herbs. Lean, crisp style with brash red fruit flavors up front, and a dry, minerally finish.

82 • *Rigoli Carmignano (Italy) 1995 Ambra, Vigna di Santa Cristina,*
Carmignano. $15.
Dark blackish ruby hue. Moderately full-bodied. Balanced acidity. Highly extracted. Moderately tannic. Dried herbs, minerals, red fruits. Quite aromatic, with a distinct herbal edge. Firm and compact, with unyielding tannins on the finish. More than a bit tough.

82 • *Fatoria dei Barbi (Italy) 1996 Brusco dei Barbi, Toscana. $13.99.*
Deep blackish purple. Medium-bodied. Balanced acidity. Moderately extracted. Mildly tannic. Overripe red fruits, minerals. Shows a distinct portlike note on the nose, with a firm, well-structured palate feel. Turns rather austere through the finish.

82 • *Capezzana (Italy) 1994 Conti Contini, Sangiovese, Toscana. $9.*
Blood red with a garnet rim. Medium-bodied. Balanced acidity. Moderately extracted. Leather, brown spice, black fruits. Quite aromatic, with a mature character showing tertiary aromas. Earthy, dry flavors make for a solid, somewhat rustic wine.

81 • *Ruffino (Italy) 1996 Fonte Al Sole, Sangiovese, Toscana. $14.*
Medium ruby red. Moderately light-bodied. Balanced acidity. Moderately extracted. Mildly oaked. Cherries, vanilla. Sweet oaky accents with a fruity center. Shows good grip and a firm, minerally backbone.

**81 • *Fazi Battaglia (Italy) 1996 Fassati Selcaia,
Rosso di Montepulciano. $9.50.***
Deep ruby hue. Medium-bodied. Balanced acidity. Moderately extracted. Leather, cherries, herbs. Woody aromas lead high-toned red fruit flavors with a minerally finish.

81 • *Cecchi (Italy) 1996 Sangiovese, Toscana. $9.*
Medium ruby hue. Medium-bodied. Balanced acidity. Moderately extracted. Tart cherries, minerals. Crisp, fruity aromatics lead a simple palate. Good grip on the finish.

Piemontese Barbera

90 • *Coppo (Italy) 1996 Avvocata, Barbera D'Asti. $11.*
Bright ruby hue. Moderately light-bodied. Full acidity. Moderately extracted. Mildly tannic. Red fruits, minerals. Aromatic and light in style though quite well balanced. Mineral-tinged fruit flavors are pure and expressive. Sharp acidity lends brightness throughout. Fine length on the clean finish.

87 • *Gianni Gagliardo (Italy) 1995 La Matta, Barbera d'Alba. $15.*
Bright purple-ruby to the rim. Medium-bodied. Full acidity. Moderately extracted. Mildly tannic. Black fruits, minerals. A little subdued aromatically, but opens up on the palate with a wave of flavor. Firmly structured acidity lends vibrancy to the clean, precise finish. Fine length.

87 • *Castelvero (Italy) 1996 Barbera d'Asti. $11.*
Bright ruby red to the rim. Medium-bodied. Full acidity. Moderately extracted. Mildly tannic. Red fruits, minerals. Pure and expressive, with razor-sharp red fruit flavors brought into focus by an edge of acidity. Well balanced, and quite modern.

85 • *Prunotto (Italy) 1996 Fiulot, Barbera D'Asti. $11.*
Bright blackish ruby to the rim. Medium-bodied. Full acidity. Moderately extracted. Mildly oaked. Mildly tannic. Black fruits, minerals. Quite austere and tightly wound with a compact minerally character. Sharp and angular acidity makes for a very precise finish. Fruit and oak nuances linger. Well balanced and focused.

84 • *Castelvero (Italy) 1995 Barbera d'Asti. $13.*
Bright blackish ruby with a slight fade to the rim. Medium-bodied. Full acidity. Moderately extracted. Mildly oaked. Mildly tannic. Vanilla, red fruits. Oak influence on the nose. Straightforward and focused on the palate though a trifle dilute. Well-structured acidity with dusty tannins and a mildly astringent note to the finish.

81 • *Castelvero (Italy) 1996 Barbera, Piemonte. $9.*
Bright ruby red to the rim. Moderately light-bodied. Full acidity. Moderately extracted. Mildly tannic. Black cherries, earth, mulberry. The aromatics are slightly funky. Clean, focused palate feel. Comes across a tad neutral in flavor. Well structured, however, with zesty acidity.

80 • *Carlo Giacosa (Italy) 1996 Vigna Mucin, Barbera d'Alba. $14.*
Bright blackish ruby to rim. Medium-bodied. Full acidity. Moderately extracted. Mildly tannic. Earth, minerals. A tad funky in the nose with an austere and sharp palate feel. A bit unyielding, but pleasant enough with food.

Scale: Superlative (96-100), Exceptional (90-95), Highly Recommended (85-89), Recommended (80-84), Not Recommended (Under 80)

Piemontese Dolcetto

88 • *Punset (Italy) 1996 Dolcetto d'Alba. $12.99.*
Bright purple. Medium-bodied. Full acidity. Moderately extracted. Mildly tannic. Black fruits, black pepper. Quite aromatic and flavorful with a rounded and lush palate feel. Structural acidity buoys a crisp, clean finish.

88 • *Banfi (Italy) 1995 Argusto, Dolcetto d'Acqui. $14.*
Bright ruby hue. Moderately light-bodied. Full acidity. Subtly extracted. Heavily oaked. Mildly tannic. Vanilla, red fruits, brown spices. Quite redolent of oak and very nontraditional, with some signs of barrel maturity. Almost Rioja-like, with a very aromatic quality and a juicy sense of lightness. Quite tasty, with fine length.

87 • *Azienda Agricola Cantine Del Castello Neive (Italy) 1996 Basarin, Dolcetto, Piemonte. $12.*
Bright purple. Moderately light-bodied. Full acidity. Moderately extracted. Mildly tannic. Black fruits, minerals. Pleasantly aromatic with a very clean and precise palate feel. Finishes with a slightly dusty note to the tannins.

84 • *Prunotto (Italy) 1996 Dolcetto d'Alba. $14.50.*
Bright purple. Moderately light-bodied. Full acidity. Moderately extracted. Mildly tannic. Minerals, anise, black fruits. Crisp, clean, and direct, with a focused quality on the palate. Angular through the mildly tart finish.

84 • *Carlo Giacosa (Italy) 1996 Vigna Cuchet, Dolcetto d'Alba. $14.*
Very deeply saturated purple. Moderately full-bodied. Full acidity. Highly extracted. Moderately tannic. Minerals, black fruits. Full and almost muscular for a Dolcetto, with a sense of richness and good extraction. Quite firmly structured and a little closed in at present.

83 • *Giuseppe Cortese (Italy) 1996 Trifolera, Dolcetto. $12.*
Very deeply saturated purple. Moderately light-bodied. Full acidity. Moderately extracted. Mildly tannic. Minerals, black fruits. Not overly flavorful, but extremely clean and focused with a nervy edge of acidity and a tart angular finish.

83 • *Casetta (Italy) 1996 Magallo Vigna in Treiso, Dolcetto d'Alba. $14.*
Bright saturated purple. Moderately light-bodied. Balanced acidity. Moderately extracted. Mildly tannic. Black fruits, minerals. Somewhat reined in aromatically, with a rounded impression and a very minerally character. Finishes on an angular note.

80 • *Massolino (Italy) 1996 Barilot, Dolcetto. $14.50.*
Very deeply saturated purple. Moderately light-bodied. Full acidity. Subtly extracted. Mildly tannic. Dried herbs, minerals, earth. Crisp, clean, and focused, with a slightly earthy note throughout. The finish is tart and angular.

Montepulciano d'Abruzzo

85 • *Umani Ronchi (Italy) 1995 Jorio, Montepulciano d'Abruzzo. $11.99.*
Deep blackish ruby hue. Moderately full-bodied. Balanced acidity. Moderately extracted. Mildly oaked. Mildly tannic. Black fruits, brown spices, minerals. Very aromatic, with a rich, lush, mouthfilling character. Full and chunky through the finish with good grip and some tannic bite.

84 • *Fattoria la Valentina (Italy) 1994 Montepulciano d'Abruzzo. $7.99.*
Deep blackish ruby hue. Moderately full-bodied. Balanced acidity. Moderately extracted. Mildly oaked. Cinnamon, chocolate, black fruits. Very aromatic, with a pleasant wood accent to the core of ripe fruit flavors. Soft and lush palate with a solid dose of acidity at the finish.

83 • *Scarlatta (Italy) 1996 Montepulciano d'Abruzzo. $4.25.*
Bright purplish ruby cast. Moderately light-bodied. Balanced acidity. Moderately extracted. Red fruits, minerals. Features forward, primary, grapey aromas. Soft and supple on the fruit-centered palate, with low acidity that turns linear toward the finish.

82 • Illuminati (Italy) 1997 Riparosso, Montepulciano d'Abruzzo. $9.
Bright purple. Medium-bodied. Balanced acidity. Moderately extracted. Mildly tannic. Black fruits. Forward, grapey aromas hint at a Beaujolais-like style. Quite full and rich on the palate with great grip and real depth of flavor.

82 • Casal Bordino (Italy) 1994 Colimoro, Montepulciano d'Abruzzo. $9.99.
Bright blackish ruby cast. Moderately light-bodied. Low acidity. Moderately extracted. Earth, minerals. Muted aromas, with a soft entry and distinctive earthy flavors. Easy-drinking style, though not very fruity.

81 • Zonin (Italy) 1996 Montepulciano d'Abruzzo. $7.99.
Bright ruby-garnet cast. Moderately light-bodied. Low acidity. Subtly extracted. Dried herbs, minerals. Aromatically reserved with a simple supple palate feel. Highly quaffable, straightforward style.

81 • Casal Bordino (Italy) 1996 Collegiata, Montepulciano d'Abruzzo. $8.99.
Bright blackish ruby hue with a garnet cast. Moderately light-bodied. Balanced acidity. Moderately extracted. Spice, red fruits. Pleasantly aromatic with a lush, low-acid entry. Picks up a bit of grip through the linear finish.

Salice Salentino

84 • Vallone (Italy) 1994 Riserva, Salice Salentino. $8.99.
Deep blackish garnet hue. Moderately full-bodied. Balanced acidity. Moderately extracted. Stewed fruits, earth, spices. Quite aromatic and extremely flavorful with a complex melange of flavors. Full and quite ripe, yet very well balanced, with a solid structure and good acidity through the finish.

84 • Leone de Castris (Italy) 1995 Riserva, Salice Salentino. $8.99.
Deep blackish ruby hue with a slight fade. Medium-bodied. Balanced acidity. Moderately extracted. Earth, chocolate, black fruits. Very aromatic, with a complex array of flavors. Quite rich and ripe, but carries a sense of lightness on the palate. Linear acidity makes for a clean finish. Well balanced.

83 • Conti Zecca (Italy) 1992 Cantalupi, Salice Salentino. $10.
Bright ruby garnet hue with a fade to the rim. Medium-bodied. Full acidity. Moderately extracted. Stewed fruits, spice, minerals. Very fragrant, with a well-balanced, light, though flavorful palate feel. Bright acidity provides a lively, clean finish.

Rosso Conero

86 • Umani Ronchi (Italy) 1996 Rosso Conero. $6.99.
Bright blackish ruby hue. Medium-bodied. Moderately extracted. Mildly oaked. Mildly tannic. Minerals, red fruits, vanilla. Engagingly aromatic in a modern fashion, with well-integrated fruit and wood flavors. Lean and crisp in the mouth, with a sturdy, angular finish.

84 • Umani Ronchi (Italy) 1995 San Lorenzo, Rosso Conero. $8.99.
Bright, saturated blackish ruby hue. Moderately full-bodied. Balanced acidity. Moderately extracted. Mildly oaked. Mildly tannic. Black fruits, minerals, vanilla. Pleasantly aromatic, with a well-structured, flavorful mouthfeel. Lean and firm through the finish, showing solid grip and intensity.

Amarone

85 • Zonin (Italy) 1994 Amarone della Valpolicella. $10.99.
Bright ruby-garnet hue. Moderately full-bodied. Low acidity. Subtly extracted. Mildly tannic. Black fruits, tar, dried herbs. Aromatically reserved, with a fat and ripe mouthfeel. Turns rather linear toward the finish, showing solid grip.

Valpolicella

83 • _Corte Sant'Alda (Italy) 1994 Superiore, Valpolicella. $14.99._
Pale ruby with a slight garnet cast. Medium-bodied. Balanced acidity. Moderately
extracted. Mildly tannic. Dried herbs, red fruits. Aromatic, with a lean and flavorful
palate feel. Soft on the entry but shows good grip through the finish.

81 • _Remo Farina (Italy) 1996 Valpolicella Classico Superiore. $7.99._
Bright ruby-garnet hue. Medium-bodied. Full acidity. Moderately extracted. Mildly tannic.
Red fruits, minerals. Reserved aromatically, with a soft and lush mouthfeel buoyed by
vibrant acidity. Straightforward but nicely structured.

81 • _Masi (Italy) 1996 Superiore, Valpolicella Classico. $7.99._
Pale ruby cast. Moderately light-bodied. Full acidity. Moderately extracted. Mildly tannic.
Red fruits, dried herbs. Fairly aromatic, with a distinctive herbal overtone. Light and crisp
through the finish.

81 • _Corte Sant'Alda (Italy) 1996 Valpolicella. $11.99._
Bright blackish ruby hue. Moderately light-bodied. Full acidity. Moderately extracted.
Mildly tannic. Black pepper, dried herbs, minerals. A forceful peppery nose leads a
bright, zesty palate. A light, lean, tart style.

81 • _Bolla (Italy) 1994 Le Poiane Jago, Valpolicella Classico. $14._
Bright ruby-garnet cast. Medium-bodied. Low acidity. Moderately extracted. Mildly
tannic. Stewed fruits, dried herbs, minerals. Aromatic, with a soft, slightly dilute entry.
Shows nice grip with solid acidity perking up through the finish.

Other Great Value Italian Reds

**89 • _Umberto Cesari (Italy) 1995 Liano, Sangiovese-Cabernet Sauvignon,
Emilia. $14.99._**
Bright blackish ruby cast. Medium-bodied. Full acidity. Moderately extracted. Moderately
oaked. Mildly tannic. Red fruits, minerals, vanilla. Aromatic, with a modern-styled, flavorful palate feel. Light in the mouth and well balanced, with a clean, angular finish.

89 • _Umberto Cesari (Italy) 1994 Riserva, Sangiovese di Romagna. $9.99._
Deep blackish ruby cast. Moderately full-bodied. Balanced acidity. Moderately extracted.
Mildly oaked. Cinnamon, red fruits. Spicy oak nuances are readily apparent on the nose
and buttressed by a solid core of fruit flavors. Rich and flavorful with low acidity on the
entry that picks up on the linear finish. Quite tasty for near-term to mid-term drinking.

**86 • _Tenuta Cocci Grifoni (Italy) 1995 Vigna Messieri,
Rosso Piceno Superiore. $12.99._**
Deep blackish ruby cast. Moderately full-bodied. Full acidity. Highly extracted.
Moderately oaked. Mildly tannic. Minerals, brown spices, earth. Aromatically reserved,
with a taut, minerally palate feel. Lean, focused, and austere through the angular finish.

86 • _Riunite (Italy) NV Lancellota, Emilia. $5._
Deep blackish purple. Moderately light-bodied. Full acidity. Moderately extracted.
Raspberries, minerals. Aromatic and deeply flavored with a cordial-like intensity to
the flavors. Light and racy with a hint of sweetness to the semi-sparkling finish.

86 • _Lizzano (Italy) 1995 Primitivo, Tarantino. $9._
Bright blackish ruby cast. Moderately full-bodied. Full acidity. Moderately extracted.
Mildly tannic. Briar fruits, minerals. Aromatic, with a deeply flavored, fruit-centered
palate. Lush and rich in the mouth, with vibrant acidity through the finish.

86 • _Caravaglio (Italy) NV Salina Rosso. $14._
Bright blackish purple. Moderately light-bodied. Full acidity. Subtly extracted. Mildly
tannic. Red fruits, minerals. Pleasantly aromatic with a light-styled, fruit-forward
personality. Crisp and delicate in the mouth with a racy finish.

85 • *Moletto (Italy) 1995 Cabernet Franc, Lison Pramaggiore. $11.99.*
Bright blackish ruby cast. Medium-bodied. Full acidity. Highly extracted. Mildly tannic. Mint, dried herbs, minerals. Pungent, with an array of herbal, almost medicinal aromas. Light in style though well structured on the palate, with a firm, extremely flavorful finish. An attention-grabbing style that may not appeal to all.

85 • *Fazi-Battaglia (Italy) 1995 Vino de Tavola, Sangiovese delle Marche. $8.99.*
Bright ruby cast with a slight fade. Moderately light-bodied. Balanced acidity. Moderately extracted. Bitter cherries, minerals. Bright fruity aromas lead a lush, ripe mouthfeel. Finishes with a zesty note of acidity.

84 • *Tenuta Cocci Grifoni (Italy) 1995 Rosso Piceno Superiore. $8.99.*
Bright blackish ruby cast with a garnet edge. Medium-bodied. Full acidity. Moderately extracted. Mildly oaked. Mildly tannic. Minerals, black fruits. Aromatically reserved, with a lean and focused palate feel. Tightly wound flavors emerge on a lengthy, angular finish.

84 • *Sella e Mosca (Italy) 1993 Riserva, Cannonau di Sardegna. $11.99.*
Bright ruby-garnet cast. Medium-bodied. Full acidity. Highly extracted. Moderately oaked. Moderately tannic. Minerals, brown spices, dried herbs. Pleasantly aromatic with an intense and flavorful entry. Lean, well structured, and quite focused through the finish.

84 • *Lizzano (Italy) 1993 Il Taurus, Tarantino. $11.*
Deep garnet cast. Medium-bodied. Full acidity. Moderately extracted. Mildly oaked. Mildly tannic. Leather, prunes. Extremely aromatic in a very Old World, rustic manner. Light on the palate with vibrant acidity and a lean, flavorful finish.

84 • *Antonelli (Italy) 1995 Montefalco Rosso. $11.99.*
Bright garnet cast. Medium-bodied. Full acidity. Moderately extracted. Mildly oaked. Mildly tannic. Overripe red fruits, minerals. Quite aromatic with a subtle portlike overtone. Light on the palate and quite lean, with a clean and vibrant finish.

83 • *Umberto Cesari (Italy) 1997 Il Poggio, Superiore, Sangiovese di Romagna. $6.99.*
Bright, pale ruby with a purplish cast. Medium-bodied. Balanced acidity. Moderately extracted. Dried herbs, bitter cherries. Forward and attractive, with a straightforward low-acid, fruit-centered palate feel. Turns a little lean on the finish. A quaffer.

83 • *Umberto Cesari (Italy) 1995 Riserva, Sangiovese di Romagna. $9.99.*
Bright ruby red with a slight fade to the rim. Moderately full-bodied. Balanced acidity. Moderately extracted. Dried herbs, bitter cherries, green tomatoes. Very aromatic with decisive herbal overtones. Shows soft acids on the entry, but turns more angular toward the finish. Flavorful and interesting.

82 • *Riunite (Italy) NV Lambrusco, Emilia. $5.*
Bright blackish ruby cast. Medium-bodied. Full acidity. Moderately extracted. Briar fruits, minerals. Quite aromatic, in a jammy, fruit-centered way. Light and zesty on the palate with a vibrant, semi-sparkling mouthfeel. A solid quaffer.

81 • *Savese (Italy) 1996 Terrarossa, Primitivo di Manduria. $15.*
Bright blackish ruby cast. Moderately full-bodied. Full acidity. Moderately extracted. Mildly tannic. Earth, briar fruits. Rather unusual aromatics have a distinctive earthy edge and lead a bright, fruit-centered palate. Rich but lively, with elevated acidity through the finish.

81 • *Pino (Italy) 1996 Rosso, Salento. $8.99.*
Bright garnet cast. Moderately light-bodied. Full acidity. Moderately extracted. Mildly tannic. Minerals, black pepper. Reserved aromatically, with a firm and austere palate feel. Somewhat ungenerous but well structured.

Scale: Superlative (96-100), Exceptional (90-95), Highly Recommended (85-89), Recommended (80-84), Not Recommended (Under 80)

81 • Mastroberardino (Italy) 1996 Lacryma Christi del Vesuvio. $15.
Bright blackish purple. Medium-bodied. Full acidity. Moderately extracted. Mildly tannic. Dried herbs, minerals. Forward and aromatic with an herbal edge throughout. Well structured, lean, and angular through the finish.

U.S. Sangiovese

88 • Pugliese (NY) 1997 Sangiovese, North Fork of Long Island. $13.99.
Bright raspberry pink. Intense, striking berry fruit and spice aromas. A supple entry leads a medium-bodied palate with silky tannins. Generous, lush, and stylish. Lighter in style, but quite interesting. Drink now.

87 • Obester (CA) 1995 20th Anniversary, Sangiovese, Mendocino County. $13.95.
Bright ruby with a pink rim. Medium-bodied. Full acidity. Moderately extracted. Moderately oaked. Mildly tannic. Red fruits, bitter cherries, vanilla. High-toned fruity aromas lead a brisk, minerally palate with dry oak notes on the finish. Lively style.

87 • Forest Glen (CA) 1996 Sangiovese, California. $9.99.
Bright cherry red. Moderately light-bodied. Balanced acidity. Moderately extracted. Moderately oaked. Mildly tannic. Red berries, vanilla. Soft, rounded, and supple. Finishes with velvety tannins and vanilla flavors.

87 • Amador Foothill Winery (CA) 1995 Sangiovese, Shenandoah Valley. $12.
Deep ruby cast. Moderately full-bodied. Balanced acidity. Highly extracted. Mildly oaked. Moderately tannic. Overripe red fruits, herbs, wood. Shows a slight portlike quality and a touch of heat throughout. Rustic and full framed, with tannins that bite down on the finish.

86 • Albertoni (CA) 1996 Sangiovese, California. $13.99.
Bright cherry red. Medium-bodied. Balanced acidity. Moderately extracted. Mildly tannic. Cherries, minerals, vanilla. Sweet berry aromas. Engaging and straightforward, with a soft, lingering finish.

83 • Beaulieu (CA) 1995 Signet Collection, Sangiovese, Napa Valley. $9.99.
Dark ruby red with a lightening rim. Medium-bodied. Balanced acidity. Moderately extracted. Moderately oaked. Moderately tannic. Earth, minerals. Austere aromas show some maturity. Uncompromisingly dry, assertive palate shows fine-grained tannins through the finish.

83 • Arciero (CA) 1995 Sangiovese, Paso Robles. $14.99.
Bright ruby-garnet cast. Medium-bodied. Balanced acidity. Moderately extracted. Mildly oaked. Mildly tannic. Overripe red fruits, sweet herbs. Quite aromatic, with a slight portlike note. Light and soft in the mouth, with some edgy acidity that props up the finish. Interesting.

81 • Shenandoah Vineyards (CA) 1996 Sangiovese, Amador County. $12.
Bright cherry red. Medium-bodied. Balanced acidity. Moderately extracted. Mildly oaked. Moderately tannic. Cooked red fruits. Lush berry flavors lack supporting acidity. Flavors are a tad jammy. Finishes with some powdery tannins.

81 • Perry Creek (CA) 1996 Sangiovese, El Dorado. $15.
Ruby red with a garnet rim. Medium-bodied. Balanced acidity. Moderately extracted. Mildly tannic. Brown spice, earth, red fruits. Mature aromas. Solid, earthy flavors are to the fore, with gentle, fast-fading fruity flavors in the background. Drink soon.

80 • Martin Brothers (Renamed Martin & Weyrich, Spring 1999) (CA) 1996 Il Palio, Sangiovese, Central Coast. $12.
Bright blackish ruby cast. Moderately full-bodied. Full acidity. Highly extracted. Mildly tannic. Red fruits, sweet herbs. Features a slightly overripe note to the thick, jammy, fruit-centered palate feel. Finishes with an overlay of spritzy acidity.

Other U.S. Italianates

89 • *Chameleon (CA) 1996 Barbera, Amador County. $14.*

Bright pale ruby cast with a purple edge. Moderately light-bodied. Full acidity. Moderately extracted. Mildly oaked. Mildly tannic. Red fruits, minerals. Pleasantly aromatic and lighter in style, with a super-concentrated wave of briar fruit flavors. Vibrant acidity lends brightness throughout, and provides a clean, angular finish.

87 • *Louis Martini (CA) 1994 Heritage Collection, Barbera, Lake County. $12.*

Bright blackish ruby cast. Medium-bodied. Full acidity. Moderately extracted. Mildly tannic. Red fruits, minerals. Rather reserved aromatically, but flavorful and very well structured on the palate. Finishes on an austere, minerally note, and shows admirable restraint. Will be excellent at the table.

84 • *Windwalker (CA) 1996 Cooper Vineyard, Barbera, Amador County. $12.50.*

Bright ruby cast. Medium-bodied. Balanced acidity. Moderately extracted. Mildly oaked. Mildly tannic. Vanilla, red fruits. Rather reserved aromatically, with a flavorful, rounded palate feel. Finishes on a lean note.

84 • *Via Firenze (CA) 1995 Dolcetto, Napa Valley. $14.99.*

Bright ruby cast. Medium-bodied. Full acidity. Moderately extracted. Mildly tannic. Red fruits, minerals. Somewhat reserved aromatically, but turns quite flavorful on the palate. Lean, concentrated, and focused, with a firm, angular finish. Intense and well balanced.

81 • *Martin Brothers (Renamed Martin & Weyrich, Spring 1999) (CA) NV Insieme Red, Central Coast. $10.*

Bright blackish garnet cast. Moderately full-bodied. Full acidity. Moderately extracted. Mildly tannic. Red fruits, dried herbs. Pleasantly aromatic, with a lean, high-acid palate feel. Crisp and vibrant.

81 • *Callaway (CA) 1996 Dolcetto, Temecula. $15.*

Pale ruby-garnet cast. Medium-bodied. Low acidity. Subtly extracted. Mildly tannic. Overripe red fruits, green herbs. Shows a portlike note with strangely green accents. Thin and dilute on the palate.

81 • *Callaway (CA) 1994 Nebbiolo, California. $15.*

Deep blackish ruby cast. Moderately full-bodied. Low acidity. Moderately extracted. Mildly tannic. Black fruits, earth. Shows an earthy, vegetal quality with a lush mouthfeel. Low levels of acidity make for a fat impression.

81 • *Albertoni (CA) 1996 Barbera, California. $13.99.*

Bright ruby with a purple cast. Moderately light-bodied. Balanced acidity. Subtly extracted. Mildly oaked. Mildly tannic. Red fruits, sandalwood. Quite aromatic, with a pleasant spicy touch. Light and clean on the palate, with a lean, angular finish.

80 • *Arciero (CA) 1994 Nebbiolo, Paso Robles. $9.95.*

Bright reddish garnet cast. Medium-bodied. Full acidity. Moderately extracted. Mildly tannic. Flowers, red fruits, spice. Exotically aromatic, with a very light palate feel. Lean and angular in the mouth, with a clean finish. Interesting.

eighteen

Red Spanish Varietals

Introduction   212
Reviews   214
   Rioja   214
   Ribera del Duero   216
   Navarra   217
   Penedés   217
   Other Great Spanish Values   218

Introduction: Red Spanish Varietals

Spain has played an important role in the development of the New World, but when the New World looks back to Europe, Spain is all too often neglected. It is unfortunate that we have been so remiss in unearthing Spain's bountiful culture, cuisine, and wines. For the value seeker, Spain is a must. Spain gives us Sherry, the world's number one fortified wine bargain; Cava, the world's greatest sparkling wine value; and a staggering number of flavorful, easy-drinking reds. Perhaps the mellow and subtle flavors of Spanish reds seem odd when compared to the assertive characteristics of New World wines. U.S. wine drinkers may feel at a loss without homegrown equivalents to use as references to Spanish red varieties. Flavors range from playful wines, filled with flavors of blackberry and blueberry, to wines exhibiting subtle fruit married with cedar, vanilla, smoke, and earth. In Spain, maturity and a mellow, spicy character are often sought in a quality red wine.

For wine lovers, Spain offers an incredible range of styles and prices. Bargains can be found in virtually every wine region. Pinpointing those bargains is not, however, as easy or logical as it is with many wine-producing nations and regions. Moderately priced producers can neighbor the most expensive. Shoppers must get acquainted with producers that fit both budget and style concerns. You will find the tasting notes a valuable tool when hunting a desired style.

Spain as a whole is a moving target, developing swiftly as we head into the next millennium. Equipment upgrades and new techniques are enabling winemakers to produce wines with broader appeal and greater consistency. The future seems very bright indeed.

Rioja

Rioja, Spain's most prestigious red wine region, demonstrates this bright future better than any other Spanish region. Rioja is located in north-central Spain, a four-hour drive north from Madrid. The main grapes used for these reds are Tempranillo, Garnacha (the Grenache of France's Rhône Valley), Mazuelo, and Graciano. Rioja reds are a blend of these varieties, with Tempranillo accounting for at least 75% of the blend. As is the case with most Spanish reds, Rioja reds are categorized by their length of aging. A *Crianza* is a red wine aged at least 12 months in oak barrels. A *Reserva* is a red wine aged at least 36 months, of which a minimum of 12 months must occur in oak barrels. *Gran Reservas* are aged at least 24 months in the barrel and an additional 36 months in the bottle before release. The oak of choice in Spain is American oak, which imparts signature smoky, sweet, vanilla flavors.

Ribera del Duero

The appellation of Ribera del Duero in northwestern Spain is perhaps the nation's most promising wine region. Like much of Spain, Ribera del Duero is masterfully combining progressive equipment and techniques with time-honored traditions and grape varieties. The vineyards are planted at a high altitude, over 800 meters, which provides a short growing season with warm days and cool nights. The primary local variety, Tinto Fino, a variant of Tempranillo, matures perfectly here, maintaining a healthy dose of natural acidity even when fully ripe. The wines are fuller bodied than those of Rioja. Flavors of blackberry, cedar, roasted nuts, and chocolate are prevalent. Government regulations demand a minimum of 75% Tinto Fino along with Cabernet Sauvignon, Garnacha Tinta, Malbec, Merlot, and Albillo. Wines labeled as "Joven" see little if any wood and are released the year following the vintage. These wines are wonderfully fresh and fruity with a remarkable raspberry character. Crianza is aged a minimum of two years, of which one year must be spent in oak. Reserva and Gran Reserva wines share the same aging requirements as Rioja. Although not a value wine, one of Spain and Europe's most renowned reds, Vega Sicilia, is from Ribera del Duero.

Navarra

The region of Navarra adjoins Rioja to the east. It is best known both for its reds and rosés. Garnacha is the principal variety, with Tempranillo, Cabernet Sauvignon, and Merlot used to a lesser degree. Tempranillo is becoming more widely planted recently, being bottled both as a single variety and in blends with Cabernet Sauvignon. These wines can be quite lovely, showing good fruit concentration with the classic Spanish flavors of earth, tobacco, and cedar.

Penedés

The region of Penedés, near Barcelona, is best known for Cava—sparkling wines made according to the Champagne method. Until recently, the red wines of this region warranted little attention. Today they are among the very best in Spain. The Torres firm must be credited for much of Penedés's quality transformation. They introduced modern techniques such as temperature-controlled fermentation and careful varietal and clonal selection in the vineyards. The region's principal red varieties are Garnacha, Cariñena, Tempranillo, and Monastrell, with a relatively small but growing presence of Cabernet Sauvignon and other international varieties. The wines range in style from light and fruity—reminiscent of Beaujolais—to rich and full-bodied with complex flavors of cedar, leather, and brown spices.

Great Value
Red Spanish
Varietals
at a Glance

Number of Wines
Reviewed:
68

Countries
Represented:
1

Buying and Drinking

When buying the red wines of Spain, you are initially likely to be struck by the wide range of vintages available. Producers often surpass legal aging requirements for Crianzas and Reservas. Vintages can be a significant concern. In recent vintages, since 1994, the wines have been uniformly very good to exceptional. The 1994 and 1995 reds of Rioja and the 1995 and 1996 reds of Ribera del Duero are classic vintages of unsurpassed quality.

Spanish reds have many uses, as they marry well with a variety of foods. They show an affinity for a variety of cured meats and spicy sausages that are an important staple of the Spanish diet. Hearty casseroles and stews, as well as grilled meats and vegetables, are also at home with Spanish reds. These are excellent food wines; however, they are typically soft and approachable and can be quite enjoyable with nothing more than good crusty bread and a little olive oil.

Reviews

Rioja

89 • Bodegas Franco-Españolas (Spain) 1991 Bordon Reserva, Rioja. $12.99.
Pale orange-brick cast. Medium-bodied. Full acidity. Moderately extracted. Heavily oaked. Mildly tannic. Brown spices, tea, leather. Very traditional Rioja with light color and body that belies a mellow, oak-dominated character. Spicy, gamey flavors linger through the finish.

89 • Baron de Ley (Spain) 1994 Reserva, Rioja. $13.99.
Brickish ruby hue with a gentle fade. Medium-bodied. Full acidity. Moderately extracted. Moderately oaked. Mildly tannic. Leather, spice, earth. Traditional in style, with a fragrant, woody character and a light, lean palate feel. Angular and flavorful through the finish.

89 • Abel Mendoza (Spain) 1995 Jarrarte, Rioja. $15.
Deep ruby cast. Moderately full-bodied. Full acidity. Moderately extracted. Moderately oaked. Mildly tannic. Red fruits, vanilla, sweet herbs. Forward aromas carry an attractive oak accent. Rich and intense in the mouth with a powerful core of fruit flavors. Unusually full, though admirably balanced by bright acidity through the finish.

88 • Finca Allende (Spain) 1995 Rioja. $15.
Deep blackish ruby cast with purple highlights. Full-bodied. Full acidity. Highly extracted. Moderately oaked. Moderately tannic. Vanilla, minerals, black fruits. Brooding aromas portend a ripe and extracted palate feel. Dark, rich flavors emerge from a shroud of firm tannins through the finish. Structured for a lengthy stay in the cellar.

88 • Bodegas Martinez Bujanda (Spain) 1995 Conde de Valdemar, Crianza, Rioja. $8.50.
Bright ruby cast. Moderately light-bodied. Full acidity. Moderately extracted. Moderately oaked. Mildly tannic. Sweet oak, minerals, red fruits. Generous woody aromas lead a lean and angular palate feel. Flavorful and zesty through the wood-accented finish.

86 • Marques de Riscal (Spain) 1994 Reserva, Rioja. $10.99.
Bright ruby with a fade to the rim. Medium-bodied. Balanced acidity. Moderately extracted. Mildly oaked. Mildly tannic. Spice, minerals. A subtle woody fragrance leads a lean palate with plenty of grip. Angular and firm with a drying finish.

86 • Marques de Griñon (Spain) 1997 Rioja. $10.
Pale ruby cast. Medium-bodied. Full acidity. Moderately extracted. Moderately oaked. Mildly tannic. Brown spices, toasted oak, red fruits. Forward aromas are attractive and spicy. Crisp and stylish in the mouth with a zesty quality through the flavorful finish.

Scale: Superlative (96-100), Exceptional (90-95), Highly Recommended (85-89), Recommended (80-84), Not Recommended (Under 80)

86 • Bodegas Martinez Bujanda (Spain) 1993 Conde de Valdemar, Reserva, Rioja. $12.
Bright ruby cast. Medium-bodied. Full acidity. Moderately extracted. Moderately oaked. Mildly tannic. Vanilla, red fruits. Quite modern in style, with a fragrant, fruit-centered personality and toasty oak accents. Lean and zesty through the finish.

86 • Bodegas Faustino Martinez (Spain) 1993 Faustino V, Reserva, Rioja. $13.99.
Deep ruby cast. Medium-bodied. Full acidity. Moderately extracted. Mildly oaked. Mildly tannic. Red fruits, spices, minerals. Aromatically reserved, with a bright and youthful quality on the palate. Lean and crisp through the finish. Straightforward and clean.

85 • Marques de Caceres (Spain) 1995 Vendimia Seleccionada, Rioja. $7.99.
Bright ruby cast. Medium-bodied. Balanced acidity. Moderately extracted. Mildly tannic. Minerals, red fruits. Bright aromas carry a dusty fruity quality. Lean in the mouth with an angular finish.

85 • Bodegas Solabal (Spain) 1995 Crianza, Rioja. $10.
Deep ruby cast. Moderately full-bodied. Low acidity. Highly extracted. Moderately oaked. Mildly tannic. Earth, pickle barrel, black fruits. Quite aromatic, with earthy accents and a core of oak-derived flavors. Rich in the mouth, with low acidity levels giving a thick impression through the finish.

84 • Marques de Arienzo (Spain) 1992 Reserva, Rioja. $14.99.
Bright ruby with an orange hue. Medium-bodied. Full acidity. Moderately extracted. Moderately oaked. Mildly tannic. Brown spices, minerals, sweet herbs. Traditional in style, with a lean, lighter-styled palate and wood-driven flavors. Spicy and intense through the lengthy finish.

84 • CVNE (Spain) 1995 Viña Real, Rioja. $12.99.
Bright ruby with a slight fade. Medium-bodied. Full acidity. Subtly extracted. Mildly oaked. Mildly tannic. Minerals, red fruits, wood. Forward aromas carry a spicy accent. Lean and lively in the mouth with a zesty, angular finish.

84 • Cosme Palacio y Hermanos (Spain) 1996 Rioja. $11.
Deep ruby cast. Medium-bodied. Balanced acidity. Moderately extracted. Mildly oaked. Mildly tannic. Minerals, red fruits. Aromatically reserved, with a full yet lean palate feel. Zesty through the finish. A clean and modern style.

84 • Bodegas Palacio (Spain) 1995 Glorioso, Rioja. $14.
Bright ruby cast. Medium-bodied. Balanced acidity. Moderately extracted. Mildly tannic. Dried herbs, minerals, red fruits. Quite lean in style with a minerally backbone of flavors. Crisp and zesty through the finish.

84 • Bodegas Palacio (Spain) 1994 Glorioso, Reserva, Rioja. $10.
Deep ruby cast. Moderately full-bodied. Balanced acidity. Moderately extracted. Moderately oaked. Mildly tannic. Cherry cordial, chocolate, dried herbs. Ripe and lush in flavor with a full and structured palate feel. Lean through the flavorful finish.

84 • Bodegas Martinez Bujanda (Spain) 1997 Valdemar, Vino Tinto, Rioja. $6.
Bright ruby purple. Moderately light-bodied. Full acidity. Subtly extracted. Mildly tannic. Briar fruits, sweet herbs. High-toned aromas feature an attractive fruit accent. Light and lively in the mouth. A snappy, fruity quaffer.

84 • Bodegas Bilbainas (Spain) 1993 Viña Pomal, Rioja. $11.
Pale garnet cast. Moderately light-bodied. Full acidity. Subtly extracted. Moderately oaked. Mildly tannic. Brown sugar, brown spices, minerals. Forward aromas carry a big sweet oak accent. Light in the mouth with a snappy zesty quality. Old-fashioned and flavorful Rioja.

83 • Puelles (Spain) 1995 Crianza, Rioja. $14.
Dark ruby cast. Moderately light-bodied. Balanced acidity. Moderately extracted. Mildly tannic. Briar fruits, minerals. Ripe and fruity aromas lead a lighter-styled mouthfeel. Crisp and zesty through the finish. A modern interpretation.

83 • *Marques de Arienzo (Spain) 1994 Crianza, Rioja. $12.*
Pale ruby cast. Moderately light-bodied. Balanced acidity. Moderately extracted. Mildly oaked. Mildly tannic. Minerals, red fruits. Lean and reserved in style with a minerally backbone and a touch of oak. Crisp and zesty through the finish.

83 • *CVNE (Spain) 1995 Clarete, Rioja. $10.99.*
Deep ruby cast. Moderately full-bodied. Full acidity. Moderately extracted. Mildly oaked. Mildly tannic. Dried herbs, wood, minerals. Rather reserved, with a slight herbal edge. Lean and crisp in the mouth with a vibrant finish.

83 • *Campo Viejo (Spain) 1990 Reserva, Rioja. $11.*
Bright ruby with a brick-red rim. Medium-bodied. Full acidity. Moderately extracted. Moderately oaked. Mildly tannic. Brown spices, minerals. Forward woody aromas lead a lighter-styled palate. Marked acidity makes for an angular, juicy finish.

83 • *Bodegas Montecillo (Spain) 1995 Viña Cumbrero Crianza, Rioja. $8.99.*
Pale ruby cast. Moderately light-bodied. Full acidity. Moderately extracted. Mildly oaked. Mildly tannic. Minerals, brown spices. High-toned aromas carry a sweet wood influence. Light in the mouth, with a lean and angular finish.

83 • *Bodegas Franco-Españolas (Spain) 1995 Bordon Crianza, Rioja. $7.99.*
Pale ruby-garnet cast. Moderately light-bodied. Full acidity. Moderately extracted. Moderately oaked. Mildly tannic. Brown spices, minerals. Forward oaky aromas lead a lean and zesty palate feel. Clean and crisp through the finish.

83 • *Bodegas Consejo de la Alta (Spain) 1995 Alta Rio, Crianza, Rioja. $12.*
Ruby with a fading rim. Medium-bodied. Moderately extracted. Mildly tannic. Raspberry aromas follow through on the palate with a lighter structure and gentle dry tannins that invite early drinking.

82 • *Baron de Ley (Spain) NV El Meson, Seleccion Especial, Rioja. $8.99.*
Deep ruby cast. Medium-bodied. Full acidity. Moderately extracted. Mildly tannic. Earth, minerals. Distinctive earthy aromas lead a lean palate feel. The finish is quick and angular.

81 • *Siglo (Spain) 1994 Crianza, Rioja. $9.99.*
Pale brickish garnet cast. Light-bodied. Balanced acidity. Subtly extracted. Mildly oaked. Mildly tannic. Earth, brown spices. Lean and zesty with an earthy accent. The lighter-styled finish shows good grip.

81 • *Bodegas Consejo de la Alta (Spain) 1997 Alta Rio, Cosecha, Rioja. $9.*
Bright cherry red. Medium-bodied. Moderately extracted. Mildly tannic. Cherry, vanilla. Bright fruity aromas lead a juicy, attractive palate with an accessible structure and firm finish.

Ribera del Duero

90 • *Hijos de Antonio Barcelo (Spain) 1995 Viña Mayor Crianza, Ribera del Duero. $11.*
Ruby red with a fading rim. Medium-bodied. Moderately extracted. Moderately tannic. Blackberries. Chunky black fruit flavors are generous and juicy, with modestly dry tannins lingering on the finish. Has a firm edge, though it is supple enough for current drinking.

88 • *Bodegas Peñalba López (Spain) 1995 Torremilanos Crianza, Ribera del Duero. $13.99.*
Saturated dark ruby with a brickish hue. Medium-bodied. Moderately extracted. Moderately tannic. Black fruits, earth, anise. Dusty, attractive aromas. Earthy, fleshy flavors, solidly structured. The finish is well gripped by dry, grainy tannins.

88 • *Bodegas Gormaz (Spain) 1995 Doce Linajes Crianza, Ribera del Duero. $11.99.*
Ruby hue with brightening rim. Medium-bodied. Moderately extracted. Moderately tannic. Attractively aromatic with cedary, minerally complexity. Well-developed, juicy, generously fruity flavors with leathery tannins through the finish make this very approachable.

85 • Ibernoble (Spain) 1997 Ribera del Duero. $13.99.
Bright ruby purple. Medium-bodied. Moderately extracted. Mildly tannic. Herbs, red berries. Soft, ripe, fleshy aromas. Rounded and supple with ripe flavors and velvety tannins making for an attractive, forward, lighter style that is drinking well now.

84 • J. Garcia Carrion (Spain) 1997 Mayor de Castilla, Ribera del Duero. $9.
Ruby red with a fading rim. Medium-bodied. Moderately extracted. Mildly tannic. Pepper, red fruits. Moderately aromatic. Light on the palate with lean, crisp flavors that have subtle fruit character.

84 • J. Garcia Carrion (Spain) 1994 Mayor de Castilla Crianza, Ribera del Duero. $12.
Dark ruby red with a subtle fading rim. Medium-bodied. Moderately extracted. Moderately tannic. Herbal, olive-tinged, dark fruit aromas are quite complex. Juicy fruit and mouthwatering acids carry the flavors through a slightly short finish.

83 • Bodegas Gormaz (Spain) 1997 Doce Linajes Tinto, Ribera del Duero. $7.99.
Bright purple. Medium-bodied. Highly extracted. Moderately tannic. Youthful, floral, berry fruit aromas. Cordial-like flavors with an herbal edge and gripping tannins on the finish.

Navarra

83 • Bodegas Ochoa (Spain) 1995 Tempranillo, Navarra. $11.99.
Pale ruby-garnet cast. Moderately light-bodied. Full acidity. Subtly extracted. Moderately oaked. Mildly tannic. Wood spice, minerals. Aromatically subdued with a spicy woody quality throughout. A light style with a lean finish.

83 • Bodegas Nekeas (Spain) 1996 Vega Sindoa, Cabernet-Tempranillo, Navarra. $7.
Deep ruby cast. Medium-bodied. Balanced acidity. Moderately extracted. Mildly oaked. Mildly tannic. Red fruits, minerals, wood. Modern in style with deep color, a core of red fruit flavors, and a judicious oak overlay. Tannins have grip through the finish.

83 • Bodegas Marco Real (Spain) 1994 Homenaje Reserva, Navarra. $12.
Pale ruby cast. Moderately light-bodied. Balanced acidity. Moderately extracted. Mildly tannic. Red fruits, minerals, dried herbs. Unusual aromas lead a crisp and zesty mouthfeel. Lean and angular through the finish.

82 • Bodegas Marco Real (Spain) 1995 Homenaje Crianza, Navarra. $7.99.
Deep ruby cast. Medium-bodied. Low acidity. Subtly extracted. Mildly tannic. Anise, minerals. High-toned aromas lead a rather lean palate feel. Angular through the finish.

81 • Bodegas Marco Real (Spain) 1996 Homenaje, Navarra. $6.99.
Pale ruby cast. Moderately light-bodied. Full acidity. Moderately extracted. Mildly tannic. Red fruits, minerals. Forward fruity aromas lead a crisp and stylish palate feel. Flavorful and zesty through the finish.

80 • Bodegas Ochoa (Spain) 1992 Reserva, Navarra. $13.99.
Deep ruby cast. Medium-bodied. Balanced acidity. Moderately extracted. Moderately oaked. Mildly tannic. Vanilla, red fruits. Generous aromas show a sweet oak accent and a core of red fruit flavors. A modern style that is ripe and flavorful with a clean and zesty finish.

Penedés

86 • Torres (Spain) 1996 Coronas, Tempranillo, Penedés. $7.99.
Pale cherry red with a fading rim. Medium-bodied. Moderately extracted. Moderately oaked. Mildly tannic. Pleasing oaky aromas follow through on the palate with juicy fruit flavors up-front, and lingering fruit acids. Drinking well now, showing some bottle development.

86 • Jaume Serra (Spain) 1995 Tempranillo, Penedés. $5.
Pale cherry red. Medium-bodied. Balanced acidity. Subtly extracted. Mildly tannic.
Cherries, spice. Berry fruit aromas follow through with crisp cherry flavors. Well
balanced and highly drinkable, with bright acids lingering through the finish.

84 • Torres (Spain) 1995 Gran Sangre de Toro, Reserva,
Garnacha-Cariñena, Penedés. $10.99.
Bright cherry red. Medium-bodied. Moderately extracted. Mildly oaked. Vanilla,
red berries. Subtle oaky aromas reveal a supple, generously fruity mouthful of
lingering flavors.

Other Great Spanish Values

87 • Corte Real (Spain) 1992 Cabernet Sauvignon-Tempranillo,
Vino de Extremadura. $12.99.
Pale cherry red. Medium-bodied. Moderately extracted. Mildly tannic. Spice, minerals,
cherries. Scented spice box and cherry aromas follow through on an elegant, subtle
palate with a lingering finish. Very harmonious, drinking well now.

86 • Castillo de Valdestrada (Spain) 1991 Vino de la Tierra de Barros. $9.99.
Pale cherry red. Medium-bodied. Moderately extracted. Mildly tannic. Vanilla, red fruits.
Mellow oak-accented aromas lead a supple, brightly acidic palate with precise fruit acids
persisting through a vanilla-scented finish. Harmonious.

85 • Vinicola del Priorat (Spain) 1997 Onix, Priorat. $9.
Bright opaque purple. Medium-bodied. Highly extracted. Mildly tannic. Cherries, red
fruits. Ripe, almost overripe aromas lead a richly extracted and well-gripped palate,
with generous alcohol and supple tannins suggesting early drinking. Quaffable.

84 • Monasterio de Tentudia (Spain) 1989 Tradicion,
Vino de Extremadura. $13.95.
Pale ruby cast. Medium-bodied. Full acidity. Subtly extracted. Heavily oaked. Mildly
tannic. Vanilla, brown spices, red fruits. An extraordinarily fragrant nose features an array
of spicy wood flavors. Lean and crisp in the mouth with a lengthy flavorful finish.

84 • Hijos de Antonio Barcelo (Spain) 1995 Peñascal, Castilla Leon. $6.
Bright pink-crimson. Medium-bodied. Moderately extracted. Mildly tannic. Raspberries,
minerals. Juicy, forward fruity flavors conclude with light tannins and clean fruit acids.
Best suited to early drinking.

84 • Casa Castillo (Spain) 1997 Monastrell, Jumilla. $8.50.
Saturated purple. Medium-bodied. Highly extracted. Quite tannic. Black fruits. Inky,
floral-scented nose leads a tightly wound core of black fruit flavors with powdery, dry
tannins clamping down on the finish.

84 • Bodegas Ayuso (Spain) 1993 Estola Reserva, La Mancha. $6.75.
Pale cherry red. Medium-bodied. Moderately extracted. Mildly tannic. Leather, soft
red fruits. Elegant spice, faint leather aromas. Mature and elegant, with muted tannins
lingering on the finish.

84 • Bodegas Aragonesas (Spain) 1994 Coto de Hayas Crianza,
Campo de Borja. $7.
Bright crimson with a pinkish hue. Medium-bodied. Moderately extracted. Moderately
tannic. Mildly portlike aromas. Firm, well-extracted, subtle black fruit flavors have a dry
character, restrained by dry tannins. Robust style that needs food.

83 • Casa de la Viña (Spain) 1996 Cencibel, Valdepeñas. $5.99.
Bright crimson hue. Medium-bodied. Moderately extracted. Mildly tannic. Flowers, red
fruits. Youthful, high-toned, thin aromas follow through on a crisp but light palate. The
vibrant floral personality is best suited to early drinking.

83 • *Bodegas Farina (Spain) 1996 Colegiata Tinto, Toro. $7.99.*
Bright ruby purple. Medium-bodied. Balanced acidity. Subtly extracted. Mildly tannic. Black fruits, minerals. Forward, primary, grapey aromas lead a lush, open-knit mouthfeel. Features just enough acidity for balance. A quaffer.

83 • *Bodegas 1890 (Spain) 1997 Mayoral, Jumilla. $5.*
Saturated purple-red. Medium-bodied. Moderately extracted. Moderately tannic. Black cherries, bramble fruits. Crisp fruity aromas lead a light-styled palate with vibrant acids, berry fruit flavors, and mild, dry tannins on the finish.

82 • *Vega Adriana (Spain) 1991 Vino de La Tierra de Barros. $9.99.*
Pale cherry red. Medium-bodied. Moderately extracted. Mildly tannic. Herbs, red fruits. Tart, herbal-accented aromas lead a crisp mouthful of red fruit flavors with mild but tough green-edged tannins lingering.

82 • *J. Garcia Carrion (Spain) 1992 Castillo San Simon Reserva, Jumilla. $8.*
Bright ruby purple. Medium-bodied. Full acidity. Moderately extracted. Mildly tannic. Anise, red fruits, minerals. Forward aromas carry a bright, high-toned quality. Lean and flavorful in the mouth with an angular finish.

82 • *Hijos de Antonio Barcelo (Spain) 1997 Realeza, Tempranillo, Castilla Leon. $6.*
Bright red-purple. Medium-bodied. Moderately extracted. Moderately tannic. Bramble fruits, herbs. Fleshy, brambly aromas follow through on the palate with minimal dry tannins and bright acidity. A youthful, appealing style.

82 • *Bodegas Farina (Spain) 1991 Gran Colegiata Reserva, Toro. $14.99.*
Pale garnet cast. Moderately light-bodied. Balanced acidity. Subtly extracted. Mildly tannic. Licorice. Mature aromas lead a lean, drying palate. Rather ungenerous through the finish.

82 • *Bodegas Farina (Spain) 1991 Fin del Rio Reserva, Toro. $12.99.*
Bright ruby-garnet cast. Medium-bodied. Low acidity. Moderately extracted. Mildly oaked. Earth, wood, minerals. Aromatically subdued with an earthy quality throughout. Lean through the finish with brief tannins.

82 • *Bodegas Farina (Spain) 1991 Dama de Toro Reserva, Toro. $11.99.*
Pale garnet cast. Moderately light-bodied. Low acidity. Moderately extracted. Mildly tannic. Minerals, dried herbs. A muted nose leads a lean palate. Light in style with some spicy flavors in the finish.

81 • *Palacio de Valdeinfante (Spain) 1992 Private Collection, Spain. $11.99.*
Bright ruby-garnet cast. Moderately light-bodied. Full acidity. Subtly extracted. Mildly oaked. Anise, minerals, brown spices. Subdued but fragrant, with an unusually high-toned quality and a spicy accent. Lean and crisp with a zesty finish. Very light in style.

81 • *Monasterio de Tentudia (Spain) 1989 Vino de Extremadura. $11.*
Pale ruby-garnet cast. Moderately light-bodied. Balanced acidity. Subtly extracted. Moderately oaked. Mildly tannic. Brown spices. Fragrant sweet wood flavors lead a very light palate. Tasty but rather dilute through the finish.

81 • *J. Garcia Carrion (Spain) 1989 Castillo San Sinon Gran Reserva, Junilla. $10.*
Pale ruby cast. Medium-bodied. Full acidity. Subtly extracted. Moderately oaked. Mildly tannic. Brown sugar, minerals. Sweet wood notes dominate the flavor profile. Light in the mouth with a crisp and zesty finish.

81 • *Casa Solar (Spain) 1995 Tempranillo, Sacedon-Mondejar. $4.*
Translucent pinkish red. Moderately light-bodied. Subtly extracted. Vanilla, red fruits. Mildly oaky, fruity aromas lead a light, precise, and vibrant mouthful. Very straightforward and direct.

81 • Bodegas Farina (Spain) 1997 Toro. $6.99.
Bright ruby purple. Light-bodied. Low acidity. Moderately extracted. Pepper, black fruits. Unusual aromas feature a slightly funky quality. Light in the mouth and lacks grip on the finish.

81 • Bodegas Farina (Spain) 1996 Tinto Zamora, Vino de la Tierra de Zamora. $5.99/L.
Bright ruby red with a slight fade. Medium-bodied. Balanced acidity. Moderately extracted. Mildly tannic. Dried herbs, earth, minerals. Earthy aromas lead an angular and flavorful mouthfeel. Lean through the finish.

80 • Casa Solar (Spain) 1994 Red Wine, Sacedon-Mondejar. $5.
Pale cherry red, with a fading rim. Moderately light-bodied. Subtly extracted. Vanilla, faint red fruits. Oak-scented aromas lead a minerally, somewhat austere mouthful of flavors that finish rather quickly.

nineteen

Sherry: The World's Best Wine Value

Introduction	222
Reviews	226
Manzanilla	226
Fino	226
Amontillado	227
Palo Cortado	229
Oloroso	229
Cream Sherry	230
Moscatel	231
Pedro Ximénez	232
U.S. "Cream Sherry" Style Wines	232

Introduction: Sherry

Produced only in a tiny and strictly defined area in the southwestern corner of Spain, Sherry is one of the world's greatest yet least understood wines. Its zone of production is known as the Sherry Triangle. This triangle has its vertices at three towns, in which stocks for the entire world are vinified and aged. The most important of these centers is the hot and dusty city of Jerez de la Frontera, which lies some 15 miles inland from the Atlantic Ocean. Indeed, the term Sherry is the 18th-century anglicization of this city's name. It is here that the majority of wineries, or bodegas, have their cellars.

The other two towns, Puerto de Santa María and Sanlúcar de Barrameda, are situated on the coast. While Jerez swelters through the long Andalucian summer, the moderating influence of the ocean's breezes offers welcome relief for the coastal towns that lie just down the road. These climatic differences are responsible for the conditions that create the not-so-subtle differences between wines produced in towns only miles apart from each other.

With its hot climate, Jerez has long been known for producing rich and heavily roasted "brown Sherries," which have been favored for so long by people in colder climates. At the opposite end of the scale is Sanlúcar, whose Sherries are matured only steps from the open ocean. It is here that one of the preferred drinks of the Andalucians themselves is produced, Manzanilla. Distinctly light and fresh, with a characteristic tang, this delicious wine is only recently being discovered outside the region. As for the third town, unlike Sanlúcar, Puerto de Santa María's view of the sea is slightly more sheltered, looking across a bay to a peninsula on which lies the ancient city of Cádiz. Thus the sea's influence is somewhat tempered, and the resulting wines lie somewhere in style between Jerez and Sanlúcar. Puerto Fino is its best-known product, a lighter style of Sherry that makes an excellent aperitif in addition to pairing well with the region's abundant supply of fresh seafood.

A Wealth of Styles

Sherry is a fortified wine that is produced almost exclusively from the Palomino Fino grape. There are two basic types of Sherry: Fino and Oloroso, with all styles being variations thereof. The dividing line between the two can be attributed largely to one unique indigenous type of yeast known as *flor*. Flor grows spontaneously on the surface of wines in the Fino family while they are in barrel, and forms a layer that provides a barrier to oxidation. The resultant wines retain a sense of freshness, and the flor imparts a distinctive set of aromas and flavors. It grows more evenly throughout the year in the cooler coastal towns and has a particular affinity for Sanlúcar.

Those wines that do not develop flor belong to the Oloroso family and are matured in contact with outside air. This controlled method of oxidation results in darker, richer, mellower wines. After the vintage, experienced tasters evaluate the newly made white wines and classify them according to their expected development. This is the first step a young Sherry takes on its way to being bottled in one of a range of styles derived from the two basic types. These include:

Manzanilla

Manzanilla is a variation of Fino that is made only in Sanlúcar. It is the lightest, palest, and most delicate of all Sherries. Cellared next to the sea, it is often characterized by a distinctive salty tang and vibrant acidity. Manzanillas are fabulous aperitifs and pair brilliantly with shellfish in particular. These wines should be served chilled.

Manzanillas should be consumed as soon as possible after bottling, as they degrade rather quickly in the bottle. Bottles that have been languishing on shelves for over a year will bear little resemblance to the original, and should be avoided. This may be tricky, however, as bottling dates are not on the labels. This is where a conscientious retailer with a high-volume turnover becomes invaluable. Do not be afraid to ask how long your prospective bottle has been in stock. If your Manzanilla or Fino tastes overly maderized or is dark in color, it should be returned.

Fino

Finos are the flor-affected wines produced in Puerto and to a lesser degree in Jerez. They are a shade fuller than Manzanillas and have a characteristic bitter almond note. Jerez Finos tend to be the fullest of these lighter-styled Sherries. Like Manzanillas, they make excellent aperitifs, but are versatile companions to the table as well.

Tio Pepe and La Ina are two famous brand names of Fino Sherry. The freshness caveat about Manzanillas applies equally to Finos, and it is imperative to purchase Fino in the freshest state possible and serve it chilled.

Amontillado

If a Fino Sherry is left to age, the flor will gradually consume nutrients in the wine until it can no longer replenish itself. This can take six to eight years and sometimes longer under optimum conditions. Once the flor dies, the old Fino will begin to oxidize, and evaporation will gradually raise the alcohol content. Depending upon the length of this second phase of aging, the wine will attain a natural level of alcohol between 16% and 23%. The resultant Sherry will gradually darken in color and take on a perfumed nutty character.

Great Value Sherry at a Glance

Number of Wines Reviewed:

60

Countries Represented:

2

At this point it is an Amontillado, the result of many years of labor-intensive aging. Totally dry in its natural state, some Amontillados are sweetened with Pedro Ximénez or Moscatel (see section further on) to one degree or another, while others are bottled dry. The drier and moderately sweet Amontillados can be revelations at the table and pair well with a range of foods. Sweeter versions are a delight taken after a meal as a digestif. Both should be served at room temperature in order to maximize the bouquet.

Palo Cortado

Palo Cortado is a very rare Sherry that is a style of Oloroso, in that it breeds little or no flor. In other ways, however, it is a bit of a hybrid. Its bouquet is deep and complex, yet the wine retains a sense of clarity and crispness on the palate, showing great similarity to a fine Amontillado.

In order to avoid confusion, it must be noted that a Palo Cortado produced in Sanlúcar will be labeled Jerez Cortado, and some houses choose to classify their Palo Cortados by age using the designations Dos, Tres, or Cuatro Cortado and so on. This designation varies from house to house, however, and is not an accurate guide to various producers' wines. Most Palo Cortados are bottled dry although a few are lightly sweetened. All match beautifully with a wide range of foods, whereas richer versions make ideal sipping wines. They are best enjoyed at room temperature.

Oloroso

Oloroso, in Spanish, means fragrant, and a good Oloroso will be intensely aromatic in a way that is similar to an Amontillado yet more rounded. Unlike an Amontillado, however, which had a sense of lightness imparted by its development as a Fino, an Oloroso is richer and develops further viscosity with age. Some are bottled dry, and these make particularly fine matches for richly flavored foods, though most exports are destined to be sweetened, and these make appealing after-dinner drinks as well. Those that have been lightly sweetened are known to the Spanish as *Amorosos*, but are not often labeled as such. These are ideal as winter warmers and have long been favored by the British to ward off their chilly climate. Like Amontillados, Olorosos show best at room temperature.

Cream

A Cream Sherry is generally an Oloroso that has been heavily sweetened. It was originally developed in Bristol, England, and made famous as Harvey's Bristol Cream. These are truly dessert Sherries in that, unlike an Amoroso, the initial complexity of the Oloroso is largely masked by the Pedro Ximénez or Moscatel usually used to sweeten it. Developed for export, this style is most often consumed much as a Port would be after a meal.

A relatively recent phenomenon, Pale Cream Sherry, was pioneered only in the 1970s by the then newly established firm of Croft's. In order to make a light-colored blend with a sweetness level akin to traditional Cream Sherries, Fino replaces Oloroso as the base wine. This lightens up the style overall, and adds the interesting nuances that are generated by a flor-accented wine. For those who are very familiar with dry Finos, the taste can be quite disarming and a trifle odd.

Pedro Ximénez and Moscatel

Pedro Ximénez and Moscatel are the minor grape varieties grown in the Sherry Triangle and more prominently in provinces to the east. They are extremely rich sweet wines that form the preferred base for sweetening dry Sherries. Much more rarely they are bottled on their own, and Pedro Ximénez in particular is one of the world's best hedonic dessert wines.

Once picked, the grapes are generally left to shrivel in the hot sun for a period of time, thus concentrating their intense sugars. Pedro Ximénezes of great age, such as those from the rare soleras of Osborne and Gonzalez Byass, reach an unbelievable level of viscosity that can be compared to motor oil, and the straightforward raisined character turns deeper, becoming quite complex and brooding. These wines can best be described as desserts in their own right.

The Solera

Once a Sherry's general style has been established, the wine needs to be aged. In the Sherry towns, this is accomplished in a unique and ingenious way known as the *solera* system. Developed as a method of fractional blending, it assures a consistent house style from year to year and avoids the vagaries of vintage. Thus the solera system is the reason Sherries are virtually never vintage dated.

A solera consists of a series of 500-liter oak casks, called butts, arranged in rows on several levels. The row closest to the floor is referred to, somewhat confusingly, as the solera level, while the rows on top of the solera level are referred to as criaderas. The first row above the solera level, or second above the ground, is the first criadera, while the second is the second criadera, and so on. The solera as a whole will contain wines only of a certain type, such as Fino, Amontillado, Oloroso, and so on. Depending upon the type of Sherry being produced, a solera will have a variable amount of criaderas. Manzanillas, for instance, will often have 10 or 11 levels in the solera.

Several times a year, a small amount of wine is drawn from the barrels in the solera level for bottling. These are replenished with an equal amount of Sherry from the first criadera, which in turn is replenished by the next level up. The last criadera will be replenished by younger wines that have been chosen for their likeness to the wines in this particular solera. In the case of Fino and Manzanilla, this may be wine from the new vintage, while an Amontillado solera may be refreshed by a suitable wine that has made its way through the scales of an entire Fino solera.

This fractional blending of younger wines into older wines is what produces uniformity and consistency. The wine that is ultimately bottled from the solera will thus have an average age that varies from one solera to the next. Where freshness and lightness is a key, as in the case of Finos and Manzanillas, the Sherries are moved through the criaderas at a rapid pace, and the resultant wine is still relatively young, though imparted with great complexity derived from contact with the flor. Where oxidation is the key to aging, the pace is more relaxed, and some soleras will have average ages upwards of 50 years or more.

Many of these great soleras were founded in the 1700s and 1800s, and as such would take generations to replace. Understandably, a shipper's old soleras are his most prized and valuable possessions. Many of these wines used to be reserved for family and friends, but some are now bottled in minute quantities and offered for sale as single solera wines. Lustau's Almacenistas, Osborne and Gonzalez Byass's Rare Soleras, and certain Valdespinos are examples; they offer some of the greatest values in the world. Wines of similar ages from Bordeaux or Oporto would fetch hundreds of dollars per bottle, yet these Sherries are often sold between $20 and $40 per bottle—at the moment.

Glassware: A Final Note

Just as consumers as a whole are recognizing that table wines show best when served in proper glassware, the same needs to be said for Sherry. Like Port, it should never be relegated to tiny liqueur or cordial glasses. The secret of Sherry lies in its inimitable and complex bouquet, and in order to experience it, one must use the proper glass. The best glass is similar to one that has been designed for Port, having a tulip shape that narrows slightly at the top. This type of glass is known to the Jerezanos as a copita. A white wine glass works nearly as well, but the glass should not be filled beyond one-half to one-third full.

Reviews

Manzanilla

95 • Hidalgo (Spain) La Gitana Manzanilla, Sanlúcar de Barrameda. $9.99.
Very pale straw appearance. Medium-bodied. Dry. Reminiscent of citrus zest, petrol, brine. Crisp, fragrant rancio aromas with petrol hints lead a crisp palate as clean as a whistle, with a hint of mild astringency and a subtle salty note through the finish.

92 • Sanchez Romate (Spain) Manzanilla, Sanlúcar de Barrameda. $8.99.
Pale gold. Medium-bodied. Moderate acidity. Dry. Reminiscent of roasted nuts, toast, sweet herbs. Fuller in body and a touch darker than a standard manzanilla, this wine exhibits slightly oxidative characteristics, perhaps a function of the age of the samples. Nonetheless, the flavors are fully developed and quite attractive, with a thoroughly cleansing brisk finish.

85 • Gonzalez Byass (Spain) Elegante Manzanilla Sherry, Jerez de la Frontera. $5.99.
Straw colored. Moderately light-bodied. Full acidity. Dry. Reminiscent of lacquer, citrus zest, wheat toast. Fresh and lively, with cleansing acidity and an attractive array of flavors. Features a lovely green note throughout.

84 • Antonio Barbadillo (Spain) Very Dry Manzanilla Sherry, Sanlúcar de Barrameda. $7.99.
Very pale straw appearance. Moderately light-bodied. Dry. Reminiscent of salted almonds, brine. Smooth and rounded mouthfeel with a briny note through the finish. Flavors overall are quite austere but clean in character.

Fino

93 • Sandeman (Spain) Don Fino, Superior Dry Fino, Jerez de la Frontera. $11.99.
Very pale clear straw hue. Moderately light-bodied. Full acidity. Dry. Reminiscent of citrus, flowers, savory herbs. Should it be possible to describe color with aroma, this wine would serve as green in the aromatic dictionary. Bright, fresh, lively, and crisp, this is a sherry of superlatives. Exquisite snap with an attractive astringency to the finish. Just the thing to tame the oppressive heat of an Andalucian summer's afternoon.

91 • *Emilio Lustau (Spain) Puerto Fino, Puerto de Santa Maria. $10.95.*
Pale gold with green highlights. Moderately light-bodied. Moderate acidity. Dry.
Reminiscent of petrol, earth, blanched almonds. Extremely complex and flavorful,
with a fresh and lively palate feel. Has a particularly fine finish with a lingering faintly
roasted note. An ideal table companion.

**90 • *Emilio Lustau (Spain) Jarana, Light Fino Sherry,
Jerez de la Frontera. $9.95.***
Very pale straw cast. Moderately light-bodied. Moderate acidity. Dry. Reminiscent of
flowers, citrus zest, green olives. Extremely fresh and lively, with a delectable perfumed
character. Finishes crisply to round out the package.

**89 • *Gonzalez Byass (Spain) Tío Pepe Fino Sherry,
Jerez de la Frontera. $12.99.***
Pale straw hue with traces of green. Medium-bodied. Moderate acidity. Dry. Reminiscent
of blanched almonds, petrol, beechwood. Attractive aromatics lead a broad range of flavors on the mildly weighty palate. Well-balanced acidity. This sherry would be better
described as complex rather than light and delicate.

87 • *Valdespino (Spain) Inocente Fino Sherry, Jerez de la Frontera. $14.*
Light straw. Medium-bodied. Moderate acidity. Dry. Reminiscent of citrus, green apple,
smoke. Quite pungent on the attack, with well-balanced acidity and a tangy finish.
Forceful in style.

86 • *Sanchez Romate (Spain) Fino Sherry, Jerez de la Frontera. $6.99.*
Pale straw appearance. Medium-bodied. Balanced acidity. Dry. Reminiscent of flowers, citrus, blanched almonds. Light floral aromas. Crisp, greenish entrance with a clean
character and delicate flavors through a simple finish. Best served well chilled; makes
a fine aperitif.

**86 • *Emilio Lustau Almacenista (Spain) Jose Luis Gonzalez Obregon,
Fino del Puerto 1/143, Puerto de Santa Maria. $13.95.***
Deep straw color. Moderately light-bodied. Mild acidity. Dry. Reminiscent of dried herbs,
toast, sake. Distinctively pungent in aromatics with a soft palate feel. Quite a bit richer
than most finos.

84 • *Antonio Barbadillo (Spain) Fino Dry Sherry, Jerez de la Frontera. $8.99.*
Deep straw cast. Moderately light-bodied. Balanced acidity. Yeast, bread, minerals.
Fragrant, but rather light in style, with a sense of softness to the palate. Tasty but lacking
somewhat for grip.

84 • *Alvear (Spain) Fino, Montilla-Moriles. $8.*
Bright yellow-straw cast. Medium-bodied. Full acidity. Blanched almonds, acetone.
Intensely fragrant with a clean and edgy palate feel. Rather unusual in flavor, but crisp
and linear through the finish.

83 • *Harveys (Spain) Dune, Pale Dry Fino Sherry, Jerez de la Frontera. $12.99.*
Pale gold with a greenish cast and brilliant clarity. Moderately light-bodied. Full acidity.
Moderately extracted. Forcefully aromatic, showing a hint of acetone character, with a
vibrant attack on the palate. Snappy, pleasantly bitter almond finish with good grip.

80 • *Jose de Soto (Spain) Tío Soto Fino Sherry, Jerez de la Frontera. $7.99.*
Medium straw appearance. Medium-bodied. Dry. Reminiscent of brown spice, nuts.
Heavy, rather dull aromas. Quite crisp and flavorsome with some nutty qualities and
a little heat on the finish.

Amontillado

90 • *Valdespino (Spain) Amontillado, Jerez de la Frontera. $13.99.*
Deep, rich tawny amber hue. Moderately full-bodied. Moderate acidity. Mild sweetness.
Reminiscent of sweet malt, caramel, roasted nuts. Attractively perfumed, with a viscous
and slightly sweet presence on the palate. It is warm and quite complex, with a compari-
tively dry finish due to its sprightly acidity. Classic roasted character.

90 • Hidalgo (Spain) Napoleon Amontillado, Sanlúcar de Barrameda. $11.99.
Bright amber with a greenish copper tinge. Moderately light-bodied. Moderate acidity.
Dry. Reminiscent of sea salt, dried herbs, smoked peat. The maritime influence in the
nose of this sherry suggests its years of cellaring in Sanlúcar on the bay of Cádiz as
opposed to inland Jerez. It has definite similarities in its crispness and austerity to the
Manzanillas of Sanlúcar. A product of further aging, it has subtle peaty notes that are
not unlike an Islay whisky, yet nonetheless is very light and fresh. Not for everyone, but it
would make an excellent full-flavored aperitif.

*90 • Emilio Lustau (Spain) Rare Amontillado Solera Reserva Escuadrilla,
Jerez de la Frontera. $15.*
Pale amber with a copper-green cast. Medium-bodied. Moderate acidity. Dry.
Reminiscent of brown spices, toasted nuts, flowers. Very enticing overall, with a
well-integrated character. Fully flavored yet quite crisp in the mouth, with snappy
acidity that lends an extremely fresh green note. Fine lengthy finish. A definite
match for rich seafoods and smoked meats.

*89 • Valdespino (Spain) Hartley & Gibson's Amontillado, Jerez de la
Frontera. $7.99.*
Rich and inviting mahogany hue. Moderately full-bodied. Moderate acidity. Mild
sweetness. Reminiscent of salted pecans, molasses, smoke. Classic roasted Amontillado
character is displayed on a moderately viscous and warm palate. Fully flavored, this
sherry has a hint of sweetness that is admirably offset by fresh acidity, and is very lengthy
and elegant through the finish. Could go with food, but may be best as a more delicate
alternative to Oloroso while relaxing in front of the fireplace.

*89 • Sandeman (Spain) Character, Medium Dry Amontillado,
Jerez de la Frontera. $13.99.*
Brilliant pale amber with a subtle bronze cast. Medium-bodied. Mild acidity. Mild
sweetness. Reminiscent of citrus peel, vanilla, dried herbs. Quite fresh and lively with a
crisp green note to the nose. Refreshing and elegantly wrought, with a touch of sweetness
that is met with a dash of acidity in the finish, where it picks up a warming roasted note.
Clean, crisp and complex.

*87 • Emilio Lustau (Spain) Dry Amontillado Solera Reserva Los Arcos,
Jerez de la Frontera. $9.95.*
Tawny amber with bronze highlights. Medium-bodied. Moderate acidity. Dry.
Reminiscent of toasted pecans, honey, minerals. A pleasantly perfumed nose leads
a full, warming mouthfeel, with an attractive roasted character. Crisp acidity makes
for a clean, drying finish. This would make an excellent companion to the table.

*87 • Alvear (Spain) Solera Abuelo Diego, Amontillado,
Montilla-Moriles. $14.*
Full gold-straw color. Medium-bodied. Dry. Reminiscent of brown spice, roasted almonds,
smoke. Spicy, subtly oxidized nose leads a long, dry palate. Delicate roasted flavors linger
through a teasingly long finish that does not become too dry.

*86 • Williams & Humbert (Spain) Dry Sack Superior Medium Dry Sherry,
Jerez de la Frontera. $13.99.*
Brilliant amber with copper highlights. Moderately full-bodied. Moderate acidity. Mild
sweetness. Reminiscent of wild mushrooms, toast, honey. Straightforward and well made
with an unusual but enticing nose. The mild sweetness is balanced nicely by a touch of
acidity, which keeps the finish fresh.

*84 • Antonio Barbadillo (Spain) Medium Dry Amontillado Sherry,
Jerez de la Frontera. $7.99.*
Brilliant amber cast. Medium-bodied. Full acidity. Moderately extracted. Roasted nuts,
brown spices. Pleasantly fragrant, with a lighter-styled, zesty palate feel. Shows just a hint
of sweetness that serves to round off the clean finish.

Scale: Superlative (96-100), Exceptional (90-95), Highly Recommended (85-89),
Recommended (80-84), Not Recommended (Under 80)

83 • Gonzalez Byass (Spain) Elegante Medium Dry Amontillado Sherry, Jerez de la Frontera. $5.99.
Deep amber with a subtle green cast. Medium-bodied. Mild acidity. Mild sweetness. Reminiscent of pumpkin, raisins, earth. Relatively unusual but nonetheless attractive flavors. Clean and straightforward mouthfeel. The mild sweetness gets the best of the very subtle acidity, lending a lingering sweetness to the finish.

83 • Alvear (Spain) Amontillado, Montilla-Moriles. $7.50.
Amber with light copper-red highlights. Medium-bodied. Mild sweetness. Reminiscent of toffee, brown spice, almonds. The sweetness stays in the background. A subtle oxidized character is perceptible on the nose and lingers through the finish. Straightforward and well balanced.

80 • Sanchez Romate (Spain) Amontillado Sherry, Jerez de la Frontera. $6.99.
Deep amber color. Medium-bodied. Mild sweetness. Reminiscent of vanilla, dates, walnuts. Clean and well made, with a touch of viscosity and a mild impression of sweetness. Crisp, lingering finish.

80 • Harveys (Spain) Harveys Club Classic Medium Dry Sherry, Jerez de la Frontera. $12.99.
Deep amber cast. Medium-bodied. Balanced acidity. Subtly extracted. Caramel, brown spices. Aromatically reserved, with straightforward caramel flavors in the mouth. Supple and round, with a hint of sweetness.

Palo Cortado

85 • Emilio Lustau (Spain) Palo Cortado Peninsula, Jerez de la Frontera. $14.95.
Clear, brilliant amber hue. Moderately light-bodied. Mild acidity. Dry. Reminiscent of dried fruits, green tea, old leather. Perfumed, with a soft and seamless mouthfeel. This is a very well-integrated sherry, with exotic flavors offered on an undemanding framework.

Oloroso

88 • Antonio Barbadillo (Spain) Very Old Oloroso Sherry, Jerez de la Frontera. $11.99.
Dark amber with reddish highlights. Moderately full-bodied. Medium sweetness. Reminiscent of dates, brown spice, raisins. Rich caramelized aromas lead an unctuous, relatively viscous palate. The sweetness of the palate is balanced by a touch of acidity. Subtle burnt herbal overtones add complexity to this straightforward wine.

86 • Alvear (Spain) Solera Abuelo Diego Oloroso, Montilla-Moriles. $14.
Bright amber cast. Medium-bodied. Balanced acidity. Moderately extracted. Roasted nuts, brown spices, orange peel. Subtle aromatics have pleasant fruitcake-type overtones. Light in the mouth, with good grip and intensity. Drying through the finish.

85 • Antonio Barbadillo (Spain) Dry Oloroso Sherry, Jerez de la Frontera. $7.99.
Deep amber with a subtle copper cast. Moderately full-bodied. Mild sweetness. Reminiscent of marzipan, toffee, walnuts. Attractively flavored and relatively full in the mouth, with well-balanced acidity. Maintains an enticingly roasted character throughout, with the faintest suggestion of sweetness in the finish.

83 • Emilio Lustau (Spain) Solera Reserva, Don Nuño Dry Oloroso, Jerez de la Frontera. $14.95.
Brilliant amber with greenish copper highlights. Moderately light-bodied. Moderate acidity. Dry. Reminiscent of leather, brown spices, citrus peel. Pleasantly aromatic, with a tinge of greenness on the palate. Sprightly acidity has a focusing impact on the clean, snappy finish.

Cream Sherry

92 • Sandeman (Spain) Armada, Rich Cream Oloroso, Jerez de la Frontera. $11.99.
Tawny amber with a greenish cast. Medium-bodied. Moderate acidity. Mild sweetness. Reminiscent of leather, salted pecans, dried herbs. Full and complex in the nose with a pungent note; nonetheless, the palate is fairly delicate. Moderate sweetness is well accented by pleasant acidity. Lengthy through the clean finish. Enjoy after a meal with cheeses and nuts.

91 • Emilio Lustau (Spain) Deluxe Cream Solera Reserva Capataz Andres, Jerez de la Frontera. $10.95.
Deep mahogany with a tawny rim. Moderately full-bodied. Moderate acidity. Medium sweetness. Reminiscent of salted pecans, brown spices, chocolate. Quite aromatic and flavorful, with a lovely roasted character. Zesty acidity balances the sweetness and maintains a sense of freshness. Rich in the mouth, with a delicate, warming finish. Pair with cheeses to enjoy after a meal.

90 • Valdespino (Spain) Hartley & Gibson's Cream Sherry, Jerez de la Frontera. $7.99.
Chestnut color with a greenish hue. Medium full-bodied. Moderate acidity. Medium sweetness. Reminiscent of oriental spices, dried fruits, redwood. Exotically perfumed, the nose is quite enticing. In the mouth, this sherry is moderately sweet and very flavorful. Lengthy and lingering finish.

89 • Gonzalez Byass (Spain) San Domingo, Pale Cream Sherry, Jerez de la Frontera. $12.99.
Light gold with a subtle green hue. Moderately full-bodied. Mild acidity. Mild sweetness. Reminiscent of minerals, blanched almonds, stone fruits, savory spices. Distinctively aromatic, this sherry surprises with a range of classic fino flavors. Mouthfilling, with just a hint of sweetness, and a very attractive nutty complexity that rides out a lingering finish. Striking a pleasant balance between richness and lightness, this is an impressive all-purpose sipping sherry.

89 • Emilio Lustau (Spain) Rare Cream Solera Reserva Superior, Jerez de la Frontera. $14.95.
Deep mahogany with ruby highlights and a greenish rim. Moderately full-bodied. Moderate acidity. Sweet. Reminiscent of dried fruits, leather, salted nuts. Aromatic and flavorful,with a well-balanced marriage of sweetness and acidity. Pleasant and lingering through the finish.

88 • Alvear (Spain) Cream, Montilla-Moriles. $7.50.
Light chestnut-amber color. Moderately full-bodied. Dry. Reminiscent of raisins, caramel, toasted nuts. Full, rich, sweet, smoky nose leads a rounded, lush palate with a sweet entry. Tapers to a surprisingly dry finish, with plenty of rich flavors on the midpalate. Not the least bit cloying.

87 • Gonzalez Byass (Spain) Elegante Cream Sherry, Jerez de la Frontera. $5.99.
Glossy deep brown with ruby highlights. Medium-bodied. Moderate acidity. Medium sweetness. Reminiscent of ginger, molasses, toasted grains. Moderately complex aromatics play out on a balanced palate. Crisp acidity reigns in the sweetness for an uplifting finish.

87 • Bodegas Robles (Spain) Robles Extra Cream, DO Montilla-Moriles. $7.
Deep tawny hue with a bronze cast. Medium-bodied. Balanced acidity. Moderately extracted. Extremely complex and interesting aromatics lead a well-balanced and vibrant palate. A hint of sweetness is offset by acidity, for a refreshing and flavorful finish.

86 • Croft (Spain) Original Rare Pale Cream Sherry, Jerez de la Frontera. $10.
Gold with a bright yellow hue. Medium-bodied. Moderate acidity. Mild sweetness.
Reminiscent of blanched almonds, dried herbs, petrol, lacquer. A classic petrol note
often associated with Fino sherries from Puerto de Santa Maria is distinctly evident in
the nose. The palate has a well-balanced marriage of sweetness and acidity that results
in a refreshing sense of crispness.

84 • Sanchez Romate (Spain) Cream Sherry, Jerez de la Frontera. $5.99.
Bright copper cast with a greenish tinge. Medium-bodied. Full acidity. Subtly extracted.
Roasted nuts, citrus, toffee. Forward aromas show a candied nutty quality and a touch
of heat. Light in the mouth, with sweetness offset by vibrant acidity. Flavorful and
straightforward.

**84 • Harveys (Spain) Harveys Isis Pale Cream Sherry,
Jerez de la Frontera. $12.99.**
Pale straw cast. Medium-bodied. Moderately extracted. Blanched almonds, lacquer.
Forward aromas carry a fino-like quality throughout. Shows a touch of viscosity in the
mouth, with a hint of sweetness through the finish.

84 • Antonio Barbadillo (Spain) Cream Sherry, Jerez de la Frontera. $7.99.
Bright amber cast. Moderately light-bodied. Balanced acidity. Subtly extracted. Roasted
nuts, caramel. A rather light style with sweet caramel flavors. Clean and straightforward
with lingering nutty flavors.

83 • Osborne (Spain) Cream Sherry. $7.99.
Brilliant deep amber with a greenish cast. Moderately full-bodied. Moderate acidity.
Medium sweetness. Reminiscent of brown spices, charred wood, roasted nuts. This wine
is forceful in aromatics, with a distinctive burnt character that winds its way to the finish.
Moderately viscous, it is balanced by crisp acidity.

**82 • Antonio Barbadillo (Spain) Pale Cream Sherry,
Jerez de la Frontera. $7.99.**
Bright pale straw color. Moderately light-bodied. Medium sweetness. Reminiscent of
dried herbs, green grapes, citrus. Crisply defined aromatics play out on an angular and
snappy palate. Lingering sweetness is moderated by a hint of acidity.

82 • Alvear (Spain) Festival Pale Cream, Montilla-Moriles. $7.
Very pale appearance with a green tint. Medium-bodied. Balanced acidity. Medium
sweetness. Reminiscent of lavender, sweet citrus, toasted nuts. Floral rancio aromas lead
juicy sweet flavors on the palate with a touch of nutty character through the finish.

**81 • Harveys (Spain) Harveys Bristol Cream Sherry,
Jerez de la Frontera. $12.99.**
Pale amber cast. Moderately light-bodied. Balanced acidity. Moderately extracted.
Roasted nuts, caramel. Shows a touch of heat to the nose. Straightforward and flavorful,
with a lighter-styled mouthfeel. Sweet caramel flavors through the finish.

80 • Jose de Soto (Spain) Cream Sherry, Jerez de la Frontera. $7.99.
Brown with reddish highlights. Medium-bodied. Mild sweetness. Reminiscent of apricot,
raisin. Unusual aromas for a cream sherry. The tart/sweet balance of flavors that lingers
through the mildly burnt finish gives this a simple character.

Moscatel

**89 • Antonio Barbadillo (Spain) Pale Sweet Moscatel Sherry,
Jerez de la Frontera. $7.99.**
Bright yellow-gold. Medium-bodied. Balanced acidity. Dry. This curious sherry delivers
the orange-blossom and ginger aromas of a good Muscat, and the sweetness of a cream
sherry. A little low in acidity to be quaffable, it is more of a contemplative sipper.

**88 • Emilio Lustau (Spain) Moscatel Superior Emilin,
Jerez de la Frontera. $14.95.**
Deep, dark mahogany with ruby overtones. Moderately full-bodied. Moderate acidity.
Sweet. Reminiscent of raisins, molasses, flowers. Very aromatic with a full, viscous palate
feel. A touch of acidity lightens up the lengthy finish.

87 • *Alvear (Spain) Moscatel, Montilla-Moriles. $7.50.*
Dark chestnut-brown appearance. Medium-bodied. Dry. Reminiscent of caramelized brown sugar, sweet peach, brown spice. Big caramel aromas with floral nuances that are well expressed on the surprisingly fresh and balanced palate, with a certain lightness to the mouthfeel. Not at all cloying. Probably best with a slight chill.

Pedro Ximénez

92 • *Alvear (Spain) Solera Abuelo Diego, Pedro Ximénez, Montilla-Moriles. $14.*
Deep chestnut-amber color. Full-bodied. Dry. Reminiscent of brown sugar, golden raisins, caramel. Sweet, heavy caramel aromas lead a thick mouthful of intensely rich flavors with a sweetness that will find any lurking cavities. Long sweet finish. All the cloying character one expects from a Pedro Ximénez, with a very pure expression of flavors.

90 • *Emilio Lustau (Spain) Pedro Ximénez, Solera Reserva San Emilio, Jerez de la Frontera. $14.95.*
Deep mahogany with a tawny rim. Moderately full-bodied. Moderate acidity. Sweet. Reminiscent of golden raisins, dates, exotic spices, blackened nuts. Intriguing and quite complex, with a highly roasted character. This sherry is extremely viscous, with a zesty note throughout that keeps it from becoming overwhelming. A brilliant after-dinner drink.

89 • *Osborne (Spain) Pedro Ximénez, Jerez de la Frontera. $10.99.*
Dark opaque brown with a tawny rim and subtle greenish highlights. Full-bodied. Mild acidity. Sweet. Reminiscent of golden raisins, mocha, dates. Broadly aromatic, with deep and attractive flavors. Large scaled but not cloying. Lovely and quite lengthy through the finish.

88 • *Bodegas Robles (Spain) Robles Seleccion Pedro Ximénez, DO Montilla-Moriles. $12.*
Very deep mahogany color. Full-bodied. Low acidity. Highly extracted. Quite rich and viscous. Features straightforward golden raisin, molasses, and date flavors with an interesting vinous quality. A solid Pedro Ximénez of mid-term age.

80 • *Antonio Barbadillo (Spain) Rich Sweet Pedro Ximénez Sherry, Jerez de la Frontera. $10.99.*
Rich, opaque mahogany cast. medium-bodied. Dry. Reminiscent of treacle, raisins, dried flowers. Quite viscous though not cloying, with light fruit-oriented flavors. The acidity helps maintain a sense of balance through the lingering finish.

U.S. "Cream Sherry" Style Wines

88 • *St. Julian (MI) Solera Cream Sherry, Michigan. $12.*
Deep mahogany color with a slight greenish cast. Moderately full-bodied. Balanced acidity. Salted nuts, caramel, toffee. Shows attractive and authentic rancio-accented aromatics, with genuine complexity. Lush and sweet in the mouth, with a lengthy finish. Impressive.

80 • *Meier's (OH) No. 44 Cream Sherry. $7.49.*
Bright amber cast. Moderately light-bodied. Full acidity. Moderately extracted. Salted nuts, caramel. Pleasantly aromatic, with a straightforward, lighter-styled palate feel. Clean and refreshing, with zesty acidity through the finish.

twenty

Port

Introduction   234

Reviews   236

  Portuguese Originals:
    Ruby and Vintage
    Character Port   236

  Portuguese Originals:
    Tawny Port   237

  Portuguese Originals:
    White Port   238

  Aussie "Port"   238

  U.S. "Port"   239

Introduction: Port

Port is the best known of the triumvirate of famed fortified wines (the other two being Sherry and Madeira). Port is sweet, almost always red, and usually enjoyed after dinner. The name is derived from the city of Oporto, Portugal's second largest, from which the wine has historically been shipped. Port has suffered the same plight of name larceny that has befallen the great wine regions of Champagne, Burgundy, and Chablis, to name but a few. Fortunately, New World wine producers have for the most part stopped pirating the use of famous wine region names, with the glaring exception of fortified wines. This fact so troubled the original Portuguese shippers that in 1968 they began to specially label their wines destined for the United States with the name "Porto." This was to no avail, as the name Porto has never caught on, and wine producers in the New World continue to label their sweet red fortified wines as Port.

There are several different styles of Port, many of which are beyond value considerations. New World examples vary greatly in style and price; however, the United States and Australia still offer the best values, as highly rated wines from both nations are often in the $10 range. Portuguese values can generally be found in Vintage Character or Ruby Ports.

Port is made by crushing red grapes and beginning fermentation in the usual way. In three to four days the fermenting grapes have reached an alcohol content of about 6%, with 10% residual sugar remaining. At this point the juice is drained to vats containing a very strong (77% alcohol by volume, according to law) neutral grape spirit. The ratio of wine to spirit is typically 4 to 1. The high-alcohol environment is very inhospitable to yeast, thus stopping fermentation. The resulting Port contains 19% to 21% alcohol and 9% to 10% residual sugar.

Portuguese Styles

There are two basic types of Port, Vintage Port and wood-aged Port.Vintage Port is the rarest, being made from selected lots of wine in only the best years. A vintage year is declared approximately three to four times a decade and is usually done in agreement by the major houses, though not always. The wine spends only two years in neutral casks before it is bottled. It retains its fresh grapey character, having been affected minimally by wood. Vintage Ports are to be aged in the bottle, and it is customary to enjoy them when they have matured for a decade or more. Fine examples can improve over a span of five decades and beyond. True Portuguese Vintage Port is expensive, starting at roughly $25 and rising sharply from there.

Wood-aged Ports are influenced by extended periods of cask aging, resulting in a wine that is ready to drink upon release. They are most often a blend from several Port vineyards and vintages, with the exception of Late-Bottled Vintage Port (LBV). Late-Bottled Vintage Port is a blend from various vineyards in the same vintage. These wines are handled much like Vintage Port but are typically aged for five to six years in cask before being bottled. Sadly, most LBV Ports have exceeded $15. Serve these Ports at room temperature and don't be alarmed by a little sediment, it is perfectly natural. You can minimize sediment in the glass by standing the bottle upright for several hours before serving, and then pouring very slowly.

Scale: Superlative (96-100), Exceptional (90-95), Highly Recommended (85-89),
Recommended (80-84), Not Recommended (Under 80)

Ruby Port, and its finer incarnation of Vintage Character Port, is a house-styled blend. These wines are deeply colored, fruity, and sweet. Ruby Port typically sees three years of cask aging, whereas Vintage Character Port is aged as long as an LBV. Vintage Character Ports are the best of the Ruby Ports, coming just shy of standards necessary for Vintage Port. These wines are often great bargains.

Tawny Port is an extreme departure in style from the others, as extended wood aging alters both appearance and flavor. These wines are a blend of several vintages. The color ranges from ruby to soft amber or "tawny" for which the style is named. Tawny Port varies greatly in price, escalating with age. The best examples give an indication of age, typically in increments of decades from 10 to 40 years, which gives the average age of the wines in the blend. Value-priced Tawny Port rarely gives an indication of age and may be "made" by blending red and white Ports. Tawny is lighter and drier than other Port styles, exhibiting a wonderful nutty flavor. A Tawny may be ideal for those who generally find Port to be too grapey and cloying.

Australian Ports

In Australia, Port is an important style with a long-standing tradition. In the earliest days of the industry, Port-style fortified wine was produced by virtually every vintner because large quantities were exported to England. Until the 1960s, fortified wines made up roughly 75% of domestic wine sales. Today, as in the past, Aussie Port is typically made with the nation's top red grape variety, Shiraz. This grape is well suited to the task of fortified wine because its rustic brambly flavors are accentuated by the elevated sugar and alcohol of Port. Be careful when pairing these wines with desserts or cheeses, as many examples are twice as sweet as their Portuguese counterparts.

U.S. Ports

U.S. Port can be a great value, largely due to the fact that it is under-appreciated. Ports from U.S. producers can be surprisingly good. In California, the style accounts for about

Great Value Port at a Glance

Number of Wines Reviewed:

45

Countries Represented:

3

3% of total wine production. Many varieties have been used by winemakers, including a few stalwarts who persist with traditional Portuguese grapes. More often, however, Zinfandel, Cabernet Sauvignon, and even Merlot find their way into the Port vat. In eastern states, Port varieties and subsequent styles vary greatly. Consult the accompanying tasting notes for flavor, sweetness, and stylistic information.

It is likely that we will always have value Port, as the major Portuguese houses seem committed to offering an "everyday" Port. Port in the value price range will not improve in the bottle and is therefore ready to drink the moment it is purchased. Typically, these wines will not vary from year to year. Port is most often enjoyed after a meal, either with or as dessert. Serve at a cool room temperature. Be sure to try the classic after-dinner repast of Stilton, an English blue cheese, with some walnuts and a glass of Port.

Reviews

Portuguese Originals: Ruby and Vintage Character Port

85 • Cockburn's (Portugal) Special Reserve, Oporto. $9.99.
Medium body. Mild acid. Lots of fruit. Mild tannins. Sweet. Reminiscent of tobacco, prunes, dates, brown spices. Soft and lush on the palate with a sweet finish.

85 • Churchill's (Portugal) VC Reserve Porto, Oporto. $11.99.
Ruby color. Medium-bodied. Balanced acidity. Medium sweetness. Reminiscent of black cherries, herbs, rubber. Distinctive aromatics lead a palate with some depth and richness, and a few edges.

84 • Warre's (Portugal) Warrior Porto, Oporto. $14.99.
Deep blackish ruby hue. Moderately full-bodied. Moderately extracted. Black fruits, minerals. Fairly aromatic, with a rich and ripe palate feel. Quite deeply flavored and well balanced, with a supple finish.

84 • Smith Woodhouse (Portugal) Lodge Reserve Vintage Character Porto, Oporto. $13.99.
Deep ruby hue. Lean mineral, red fruit, and flower aromas. A lush entry leads a medium-bodied palate with mild acidity and lean tannins, and a firm, angular finish. Rather fiery, but well flavored. Drink now.

84 • Quinta do Noval (Portugal) Porto L.B. House Reserve, Oporto. $14.99.
Deep tawny hue with garnet highlights. Medium-bodied. Balanced acidity. Medium sweetness. Reminiscent of candied cherries, tobacco, cedar. Restrained and straightforward fruit with a nice spicy component through the finish.

84 • Feist (Portugal) Baronial, Oporto. $12.
Medium crimson appearance. Medium-bodied. Moderately extracted. Reminiscent of sweet baked fruits, flowers. Generous floral and black fruit aromas lead a rounded palate with bright fruity flavors that conclude softly. Versatile style.

84 • Barros (Portugal) Ruby Porto, Oporto. $8.99.
Brownish garnet appearance. Moderately light-bodied. Balanced acidity. Medium sweetness. Reminiscent of dark chocolate, cherries. A ripe fruity character on the palate with mild drying components give this a lean touch.

82 • Warre's (Portugal) Fine Selected Ruby Porto, Oporto. $10.99.
Deep blackish ruby hue with a slight fade to the rim. Moderately full-bodied. Moderately extracted. Black fruits, lacquer. Sweet, straightforward, and richly fruity, with good intensity and length. A trifle hot on the finish.

82 • Quinta do Noval (Portugal) Old Coronation Ruby Porto, Oporto. $10.99.
Very deep ruby appearance. Moderately full-bodied. Balanced acidity. Moderately extracted. Medium sweetness. Reminiscent of chocolate, cherries, herbs. Sweet fruit character on the palate stands in contrast to a solid spicy frame and a reasonably lean, dry finish.

82 • Osborne (Portugal) Ruby Porto, Oporto. $10.99.
Moderately full body. Medium acid. Lots of fruit. Mild tannin. Sweet. Reminiscent of black cherry, pipe tobacco, brown spice. Vibrant on the palate with a refreshing touch of acidity.

80 • Sandeman (Portugal) Founders Reserve Porto, Oporto. $15.
Deep blackish ruby hue. Moderately full-bodied. Low acidity. Moderately extracted. Black fruits, minerals. Rather reserved aromatically, with a pronounced minerally palate feel. Lean and straightforward with a drying, mildly hot finish.

80 • Rozes (Portugal) Special Reserve, Oporto. $14.99.
Sweet roasted qualities with chocolate and toffee. A medium body with a silky mouthfeel.

80 • Ramos Pinto (Portugal) Fine Ruby, Oporto. $13.75.
Blackish ruby hue with a garnet rim. Moderately light-bodied. Subtly extracted. Dried herbs, raisins. Shows some subtle oxidation in the nose. Light in the mouth, with a straightforward herb-accented finish.

80 • Martinez (Portugal) Fine Ruby Porto, Oporto. $11.
Pale cherry red with a slight fade. Lean red fruit and mineral aromas. A lush entry leads a moderately light-bodied palate with moderate sweetness and a touch of heat. The finish is straightforward. A lighter style, but competent. Drink now.

80 • Feist (Portugal) Vintage Character, Oporto. $14.
Deep ruby appearance. Medium-bodied. Moderately extracted. Reminiscent of ripe baked fruits, brown spice. Rounded, sweet, fruity, portlike aromas. Easy and accessible with some spirity feel. A letdown on the finish.

80 • Dow's (Portugal) Christmas Porto, Oporto. $13.99.
Deep ruby hue with a slight fade to the rim. Moderately light-bodied. Balanced acidity. Subtly extracted. Black fruits. Straightforward and light in style with a supple, fruit-accented palate feel. Tapers off on the sweet finish.

Portuguese Originals: Tawny Port

88 • Harveys (Portugal) Fine Tawny, Oporto. $14.99.
Medium body. Mild fruit. Medium oak. Medium sweetness. Reminiscent of walnuts, raisins, baked cherries. Well balanced, with focused, pretty flavors.

86 • Barros (Portugal) Quinta D. Matilde Tawny Porto, Oporto. $13.99.
Pale amber color. Moderately light-bodied. Balanced acidity. Dry. Reminiscent of dried strawberries, vanilla. Fragrant aromatics. A light and delicate style with subtle nuances.

82 • Barros (Portugal) Tawny Porto, Oporto. $8.99.
Deep red-amber hue. Medium-bodied. Balanced acidity. Medium sweetness. Reminiscent of cherries, brown spice, nuts, raisins. Fruity aromas translate well onto a warm and supple palate. Fruit-driven style.

81 • Martinez (Portugal) Fine Tawny Porto, Oporto. $11.
Pale cherry-garnet hue. Spirity red fruit and chocolate aromas. A lush entry leads a medium-bodied palate with straightforward wood-accented flavors that retain a fruity overtone. Clean, mildly sweet finish. Drink now.

80 • Ramos Pinto (Portugal) Superior Tawny, Oporto. $13.75.
Mahogany with a ruby cast. Moderately light-bodied. Moderately extracted. Toasted wood, brown spices. Pleasantly aromatic, with a lighter-styled palate feel. Features well-integrated wood-accented flavors, but could use more grip.

80 • *Quinta do Noval (Portugal) Tawny, Oporto. $10.*
Medium body. Medium acid. Mild fruit. Medium oak. Sweet. Reminiscent of figs, brown sugar. Straightforward and flavorful with a warming finish.

80 • *Feist (Portugal) Fine Baronial Tawny Porto, Oporto. $12.*
Very pale cherry red. Medium-bodied. Reminiscent of sweet red berries, brown spice. Rounded fruity aromas are well expressed on the palate with subtle spicy hints on the finish. More vinous fruit flavors than one would expect from a tawny style.

Portuguese Originals: White Port

83 • *Feist (Portugal) Baronial Fine White Port, Oporto. $12.*
Full orange luster. Moderately full-bodied. Reminiscent of pepper, sweet citrus fruits, glycerine. Mildly spicy sweet aromas lead a sweet, silky mouthfeel showing viscosity and richness, with a lingering medicinal, peppery note.

Aussie "Port"

91 • *Seppelt (Australia) Trafford Tawny Port, Barossa Valley. $11.*
Rusty amber color. Medium-bodied. Reminiscent of brown spice, dates, amontillado sherry. A subtle, mature spicy nose hints at the elegance of age. Sweet and spicy flavors are refined and finish like a dry amontillado sherry.

89 • *Queen Adelaide (Australia) Woodley Tawny Port, South Australia. $8.*
Red-amber color. Medium-bodied. Balanced acidity. Moderately extracted. Medium sweetness. Reminiscent of earth, nuts, caramel apples. A balanced, remarkably easy-sipping style with attractive caramel undertones. Sweet notes play in the finish, as alcohol provides pleasing warmth.

88 • *Hardys (Australia) Whiskers Blake Tawny Port, Australia. $14.*
Pale red-amber color. Medium-bodied. Reminiscent of caramel, brown spice, baked apple. Baked, caramelized aromas. Sweet, juicy rich flavors expand on the palate with delicate spice on the finish. Well balanced.

86 • *Yalumba (Australia) Clocktower Tawny Port, Australia. $9.99.*
Tawny amber color. Medium-bodied. Moderately extracted. Reminiscent of caramel, baked fruits, mild brown spice. Mildly vinous quality on the nose reveals flavors of sweet caramelized fruits that expand on the palate and linger through the finish. Vinous fruit flavors are more apparent than spicy wood.

86 • *Penfolds (Australia) Club Port, Reserve, South Australia. $11.*
Chestnut appearance. Moderately full-bodied. Fig, toffee. Heavily spiced aromas lead a toffee- and caramel-like entry, with sweetness lingering through the finish. Rancio qualities are quite subtle.

86 • *Chateau Reynella (Australia) 1992 Vintage Port, McLaren Vale. $12.*
Moderately full body. Medium acid. Medium fruit. Medium oak. Medium tannin. Medium sweetness. Reminiscent of cherries, blueberries, pepper. Nice length, a viscous mouthfeel, and an impression of high alcohol make this a powerful after-dinner drink.

85 • *Marienberg (Australia) 12 Year Old Tawny Port, Australia. $13.*
Bright chestnut hue. Medium-bodied. Moderately extracted. Apricot, nuts. Sweet, spicy, fruity aromas lead a caramel and raisin palate with sweetness remaining on the right side of cloying. Very attractive.

85 • *Benjamin (Australia) Tawny Port, Australia. $12.99.*
Light amber color. Moderately full body. Medium acid. Medium fruit. Medium oak. Mild tannin. Sweet. Reminiscent of caramel, brown sugar, dried fruits, nuts. Has very good balance, an impression of high alcohol, and moderate length. A blend of Cabernet Sauvignon, Shiraz, and Merlot.

84 • *Penfolds (Australia) Club Tawny Port, South Autralia. $9.*
Amber-brown hue. Moderately full-bodied. Caramel, toffee, raisins. Sweet and nectarlike, with raisiny flavors that join sweet toffee notes lingering on the finish. Very generous.

82 • Hardys (Australia) Tall Ships Tawny Port, South Australia. $12.99.
Light amber hue. Moderately full body. Medium acid. Lots of fruit. Medium oak. Mild tannin. Medium sweetness. Reminiscent of baked apples, prunes, cinnamon, flowers. Subtle and attractive, with a nice balance of fruit and oak.

U.S. "Port"

91 • Quady (CA) 1993 LBV Port, Amador County 8.18% rs. $12.
Deep blackish garnet cast. Moderately full-bodied. Balanced acidity. Highly extracted. Chocolate, brown spices, black fruits. Carries a generous wood accent throughout, with deeply flavored, supple palate feel. Shows fine grip and intensity, with excellent length.

90 • Whidbey (WA) 1990 Port, Washington 9.8% rs. $12.99.
Blackish ruby hue with brick rim. Moderately full-bodied. Balanced acidity. Highly extracted. Moderately tannic. Medium sweetness. Reminiscent of mocha, dried plums, grenadine. Intensely concentrated and still quite youthful, with a lengthy palate of sweet-tasting fruit enlivened by tangy spice notes. Shows nice grip in the finish.

89 • Quady (CA) Batch 88 Starboard, California 11.1% rs. $11.50.
Deep ruby-garnet cast. Full-bodied. Balanced acidity. Highly extracted. Chocolate, tea, black fruits. Aromatic and quite complex, with a wide range of flavors throughout. Lush, rounded, and well balanced on the palate, with a lengthy finish.

86 • Meier's (OH) No. 44 American Ruby Port 8.3% rs. $6.95.
Deep brickish garnet hue. Medium-bodied. Balanced acidity. Moderately extracted. Medium sweetness. Reminiscent of nuts, earth, coffee, cherries. Well focused and firmly textured, with sweet fruit nuances that play into the finish. Surprisingly well integrated for a "port" of this price.

86 • Lonz (OH) 3 Islands American Ruby Port 9.9% rs. $6.50.
Deep ruby red with brick rim. Moderately full-bodied. Balanced acidity. Moderately extracted. Heavily oaked. Medium sweetness. Reminiscent of dried orange peel, vanilla, raisins. Richly textured and firmly structured on the palate, and layered with distinctive sweet, woody nuances.

86 • Ficklin (CA) Tinta Port, California 8.5% rs. $12.
Deep ruby-garnet cast. Medium-bodied. Balanced acidity. Moderately extracted. Brown spices, toast. Pleasantly aromatic, with a gentle woody note and a touch of heat. Ripe and full in the mouth, with a lingering, flavorful finish.

85 • Windsor (CA) Rare Port, California 11.9% rs. $13.
Deep blackish garnet cast. Moderately full-bodied. Balanced acidity. Moderately extracted. Brown spices, raisins. Made in more of a tawny style, with an obvious wood accent to the flavors. Ripe, thick, and lush. Well-balanced finish with a touch of heat.

85 • Mount Pleasant (MO) JRL's Barrel Select Port,
Augusta 6.75% rs. $11.95.
Reddish brick color with a distinctly browning rim. Medium-bodied. Highly extracted. Mildly tannic. Reminiscent of earth, dates, coffee. A caramelized coffeelike note runs through this. Somewhat tawny in style, it still has plenty of stuffing.

82 • Paul Masson (CA) Rich Ruby Port, California 10.2% rs. $5.99.
Black ruby hue. Moderately full-bodied. Balanced acidity. Highly extracted. Medium sweetness. Reminiscent of black fruits, tar, cherry, tobacco. Sturdy and straightforward, with well-concentrated flavors and fairly weighty texture.

81 • St. Julian (MI) Catherman's Port, Michigan 16% rs. $12.
Opaque blackish purple cast. Medium-bodied. Full acidity. Highly extracted. Cassis, flowers. Pleasantly aromatic, with brooding dark fruit flavors. Surprisingly bright on the palate, with tangy acidity and balanced sweetness. Intense, berryish, and flavorful.

twenty-one

Sweet
Table Wines

Introduction   242

Reviews   243

    Great Value Sweet Wines   243

Introduction: Sweet Table Wines

Sweet wines come in many different styles and flavors. Some are not even made from grapes, but rather from fruits, such as apricots, peaches, and blackberries. With the exception of sweet Sherry and selected styles of Port, there are no general categories of sweet wines that offer good value. In fact, many of the renowned sweet wine categories from around the world can be quite expensive.

What makes a sweet wine sweet? The obvious answer is residual sugar. How this is achieved is often as great a determination of flavor as the grape variety used. Some methods are entirely orchestrated by man while others involve the cooperation of Mother Nature. Relying upon aid from nature is uncertain. In the wine industry, as in life, risk demands reward, and reward comes in the form of higher prices. However, when one considers the incredible risk and effort expended to produce these wines, it is a marvel that many are not even more costly.

Several of the world's most celebrated sweet wines clamor for the assistance of nature. A naturally occurring mold, *Botrytis Cinerea* (often shortened to just *Botrytis*), affects vineyards around the world. Depending on the mold's timing, and the producer's intentions, it can be either the winemaker's greatest ally or worst enemy. In most instances its presence is devastating, particularly when it attacks unripe grapes, rendering them useless. In this circumstance *Botrytis* is the goat; winemakers refer to this occurrence as "gray rot" due to the mold's color. In the fall when the grapes have ripened, a select group of winemakers pray for the mold to descend upon their vineyards. When the mold obliges, it forms on the grapes, perforating the skin and causing rapid evaporation of the fruit's water. This results in a shriveled grape that is super concentrated, sweet, and delightfully accented with the flavor of the mold itself. In this instance *Botrytis* is the hero, as winemakers in France refer to it as *pourriture noble*. In Germany it is called *Eddelfäule*, and Americans concur as the fore mentioned moniker translates to "noble rot." Noble rot does not occur in every vintage. Wines made with this technique include French Sauternes, German Beeranauslese and Trockenbeeranauslese, Hungarian Tokay, and many others, including select wines from North America (both the United States and Canada).

Another popular method of creating sweet wine involves the risky practice of leaving grapes on the vine until well after the normal harvest. No mold is needed, only plummeting temperatures, as the winemaker waits for his grapes to freeze. These wines are aptly named Ice Wine or *Eiswein* as they say in Germany. The grapes must be crushed while frozen, at 20° F or less, to extract only concentrated grape sugars, flavor extracts, and acid, leaving the frozen water behind. This method is extremely popular in Germany, Austria, and Canada where wines of this style can rank among the very best in the world.

Many sweet wines in the New World are simply labeled as "Late Harvest," denoting grapes with unusually high natural sugar levels picked well after the normal harvest. These may, or may not, be made from grapes affected with noble rot. Popular varieties for Late Harvest wines include Gewürztraminer, Riesling, Sauvignon Blanc, and Semillon.

Scale: Superlative (96-100), Exceptional (90-95), Highly Recommended (85-89), Recommended (80-84), Not Recommended (Under 80)

242

Sweet wines are best served cool, as this helps the wine's acid keep it from becoming cloying and flat on the palate. Always serve sweet wines after dry wines, as the elevated sugars tend to exhaust the palate and mask the more subtle flavors of dry wines while leaving an impression of bitterness.

Reviews

Great Value Sweet Wines

(Note: "rs" indicates residual sweetness)

93 • Ackerman (IA)
Apricot Wine 9% rs. $6.50.
Very deep yellow-gold. Full-bodied. Full acidity. Highly extracted. Apricots, spice, mint. Complex and pungent aromatics have a botrytis-like edge. Full and viscous in the mouth, with marked sweetness balanced by razor-sharp acidity. Structured almost like an ice wine.

89 • Osprey's Dominion (NY) NV Spice Wine, North Fork of Long Island. $8.99.
Light garnet hue with a slight fade. Powerful cinnamon, spice, and berry aromas. A smooth entry leads a full-bodied palate with a hint of sweetness and drying tannins. Rich, supple, extremely flavorful and very tasty. Drink now.

88 • St. Julian (MI) Raspberry Champagne, Michigan 6% rs. $8.50.
Bright ruby-garnet cast with a slight fade. Medium-bodied. Full acidity. Highly extracted. Red fruits, minerals. Pleasantly aromatic, with gentle fruit overtones. Fully sparkling on the palate, with spritzy acidity balanced by a hint of sweetness. Flavorful and intense.

86 • Quady (CA) 1997 Essensia, Orange Muscat, California 13.9% rs. $12.
Deep copper hue. Exotic, spirity orange peel and mineral aromas. A lush entry leads a moderately full-bodied, sweet palate with a pithy finish. This vintage of Essensia is moving toward the rustic side, with an herbal overtone. Drink now.

86 • Quady (CA) 1997 Elysium, Black Muscat, California 14% rs. $12.
Saturated pale cherry-garnet hue. Generous herb and red fruit aromas carry a spirity accent. A lush entry leads a full-bodied palate with lots of sweetness and lean acidity. Perfumed through the finish. A full-throttle style ready to drink now.

❧

Great Value Sweet Wines at a Glance

Number of Wines Reviewed:

22

Countries Represented:

2

❧

86 • Perrin (France) 1996 Muscat de Beaumes de Venise. $14.
Bright straw cast. Medium-bodied. Balanced acidity. Moderately extracted. Minerals, citrus, tropical fruits. Pleasantly aromatic, with a decided fruit accent. Crisp and lively on a lighter-styled palate, with a clean, flavorful finish.

86 • Martin Brothers (Renamed Martin & Weyrich, Spring 1999) (CA) 1998 Moscato Allegro, California 10% rs. $10.
Bright gold with a slight spritz. Forward melon and pear aromas. A vibrant entry leads a flavorful palate with juicy acidity and mild sweetness. Lively and refreshing. Drink now.

86 • Bargetto (CA) Chaucers Mead 10% rs. $9.
Deep yellow-straw cast. Moderately full-bodied. Low acidity. Moderately extracted. Honey, cream, vanilla. Fragrant and extremely pure in flavor, with a well-balanced, rounded mouthfeel. Finishes with fine length and mild sweetness.

85 • V. Sattui (CA) 1997 Muscat, California 8% rs. $12.
Brilliant yellow-straw hue. Reserved orange blossom and lacquer aromas. A vibrant entry leads a medium-bodied palate with crisp acids and moderate sweetness. Clean, flavorful, refreshing finish. Drink now.

85 • Gan Eden (CA) 1997 Black Muscat, San Joaquin County 8% rs. $14.
Pale cherry red. Exotic rose and black cherry aromas jump from the glass. A crisp entry leads a moderately light-bodied palate with mild sweetness. Snappy and flavorful. Drink now.

85 • Eola Hills (OR) NV Vin D'Or, Late Harvest Sauvignon Blanc, Willamette Valley 19% rs. $15.
Bronzed gold. Full-bodied. Full acidity. Highly extracted. Dried herbs, citrus. Sweet citrus aromas, with an amazingly sweet, viscous, acidic palate. Impressive, but perhaps a bit much; only for the true sugar junkie.

85 • Ackerman (IA) Blackberry Wine 8% rs. $6.50.
Bright garnet cast. Full-bodied. Balanced acidity. Highly extracted. Red fruits, minerals. Forward and unusual aromatics lead a ripe and viscous mouthfeel. Quite sweet, though an edge of acidity lends a sense of balance to the finish. Fine length.

84 • Columbia Winery (WA) 1998 Cellarmaster's Reserve, Riesling, Columbia Valley 6% rs. $7.
Pale straw hue. Moderate applelike aromas. A sweet, juicy entry leads a medium-bodied palate with ripe, tangy flavors through the finish. Drink now.

83 • Husch (CA) 1998 Muscat Canelli, Mendocino 5.5% rs. $14.
Bright straw hue with a slight spritz. Subdued mineral and talc aromas. A zesty entry leads a moderately light-bodied palate with mild sweetness offset by racy acidity. Lighter in style, but clean and refreshing. Drink now.

83 • Erath (OR) 1997 Late Harvest White Riesling, Willamette Valley 5.1% rs. $9.
Pale gold. Bright apple and mineral aromas. An off-dry attack leads a medium-bodied palate with smooth, pure, fruity flavors. Acids are quite soft through the finish. Drink now.

83 • Eberle (CA) 1998 Muscat Canelli, Paso Robles 5.2% rs. $11.
Bright yellow-straw hue. Attractive orange blossom and honeyed citrus aromas. A rich entry leads a medium-bodied palate with mild sweetness. Soft and lush. Drink now.

82 • Silvan Ridge (OR) 1998 Semi-Sparkling, Early Muscat, Oregon 11% rs. $13.
Bright platinum hue with a slight spritz. Lean, steely, minerally aromas. A zesty entry leads a medium-bodied palate with lots of sweetness. Tasty, but on the simple side. Drink now.

82 • Joseph Zakon (CA) 1998 Muscatini, Sweet White Muscat,
California 13.9% rs. $8.50.
Brilliant straw hue. Subdued mineral and honey aromas. A lean entry leads a sweet, medium-bodied palate with soft acidity. Clean, rounded finish. Straightforward and glycerous. Drink now.

81 • Paul Thomas (WA) 1997 Reserve, Riesling, Columbia Valley 5.5% rs. $7.
Pale straw hue. Tart citrus-zest aromas. A bright, vibrant entry leads a medium-bodied palate with tangy, pure stone-fruit flavors. Subtle herbal overtones emerge on the finish. Drink now.

80 • Tualatin Estate (OR) 1997 Semi-Sparkling Muscat,
Willamette Valley 11.3% rs. $14.
Bright green-straw hue with a slight spritz. Unusual grapey, lemon grass aromas. A vibrant entry leads a flavorful, medium-bodied palate with marked sweetness. A bit off-center, with a foxy edge. Drink now.

80 • Joseph Zakon (CA) 1998 Muscatini, Sweet Red Muscat,
California 11.8% rs. $8.50.
Deep cherry red. Candied chocolate and flower aromas. A lush entry leads a crisp, medium-bodied palate with Tootsie Roll flavors. A tad artificial, with a moderately sweet finish. Drink now.

80 • Gan Eden (CA) 1997 Late Harvest, Gewürztraminer,
Monterey County 8% rs. $14.
Pale straw hue. Forward, earthy, funky aromas. A lean entry leads a medium-bodied palate with sharp acidity and moderate sweetness. Clean, straightforward finish. Drink now.

Index and Bibliography

Brand Index

A

Abarbanel, 34, 86, 110, 133, 189
Abbey Vale, 37, 55, 149
Abel Mendoza, 214
Ackerman, 243-244
Adler Fels, 86
Alain Cailbourdin, 53
Alain Geoffroy, 33
Alain Graillot, 187
Alamos Ridge, 152
Albertoni, 209-210
Albola, 94
Alice White, 36
Alvear, 227-232
Amador Foothill Winery, 209
Anapamu, 41, 159
Angeline, 180
Antinori, 38, 103, 105, 202
Antonelli, 208
Antonio Barbadillo, 226-229, 231-232
Apex, 88
Arbor Crest, 123
Arciero, 150, 209-210
Autumn Hill, 150

B

Backsberg, 39
Bagnoli, 134
Balbi, 152
Bandiera, 140
Banfi, 93, 103, 205
Baobab, 39, 141
Barboursville, 97, 126
Barefoot, 113
Bargetto, 96, 244
Barnard Griffin, 43
Baron de Bellac, 26
Baron de Ley, 214, 216
Baron zu Knyphausen, 72, 74
Barone Fini, 133
Barone Ricasoli, 202-203
Barros, 218-219, 236-237
Batasiolo, 103
Beaucanon, 42, 126, 139
Beaulieu, 59, 112, 179, 196, 209
Bedell, 46-47
Bel Arbor, 111, 140
Bella Vigna, 137
Belvedere, 157, 179
Benjamin, 238
Benziger, 46
Bera, 28
Bergstrasser Winzer, 89
Beringer, 46, 57, 59, 112, 157, 169, 179

Bernard Defaix, 33
Bestheim, 76, 86
Bidwell, 81
Bigi, 103-104
Biltmore, 46, 126, 140
Black Opal, 149
Blackstone, 138
Bodega Norton, 152
Bodegas 1890, 219
Bodegas Aragonesas, 218
Bodegas Ayuso, 218
Bodegas Bilbainas, 215
Bodegas Consejo de la Alta, 216
Bodegas Escorihuela, 66, 151
Bodegas Farina, 219-220
Bodegas Faustino Martinez, 215
Bodegas Franco-Españolas, 214, 216
Bodegas Gormaz, 216-217
Bodegas Marco Real, 136, 217
Bodegas Martinez Bujanda, 214-215
Bodegas Montecillo, 216
Bodegas Nekeas, 136, 196, 217
Bodegas Ochoa, 217
Bodegas Palacio, 215
Bodegas Peñalba López, 216
Bodegas Piedemonte, 127, 136
Bodegas Robles, 230, 232
Bodegas Solabal, 215
Boeckel, 75
Bogle, 123, 139, 175, 194
Bolla, 103, 133, 207
Bollini, 38, 94, 133
Bommarito, 139
Bonterra, 125
Bonverre, 132
Bookwalter, 46, 81, 148
Borie-Manoux, 133
Boschendal, 39, 60
Bott Frères, 75, 95
Bouvet, 25
Bouwland, 152
Bridgeview, 96, 160
Brophy Clark, 58
Brutocao, 179
Buena Vista, 160
Bulgari, 48, 141
Bulletin Place, 36, 191

C

Ca' Montini, 105
Ca'Rugate, 103
Cairel, 102
Calina, 39-40, 121
Caliterra, 40, 56, 121, 134
Callahan Ridge, 111
Callara, 36, 119
Callaway, 58, 96, 210
Calona, 37, 60, 97
Campanile, 94

Campo Viejo, 216
Canoe Ridge Vineyard, 43
Cantine Mezzacorona, 94, 134
Cap Rock, 26
Capezzana, 204
Caravaglio, 207
Carl Graff, 73-74
Carlo Giacosa, 204-205
Carmel, 48, 59, 114, 122, 196
Carmenet, 88
Carneros Creek, 159
Carriage House, 37
Casa Castillo, 218
Casa de la Viña, 218
Casa di Pescatori, 104
Casa Lapostolle, 40, 55, 120, 135
Casa Larga, 122
Casa Solar, 219-220
Casal Bordino, 206
Casetta, 205
Cassegrain, 149, 190
Castello Banfi, 93
Castello di Farnetella, 201
Castello di Gabbiano, 202-203
Castello di Querceto, 201-202
Castello di Valiano, 202
Castello Neive, 102, 205
Castelvero, 204
Castillo de Valdestrada, 218
Castoro, 125, 177, 181
Caterina, 46
Cave de Tain l'Hermitage, 188
Cave Spring, 38, 82, 168
Caves des Papes, 34, 120, 133, 187
Cayuga Ridge, 80
Cecchi, 202-204
Cedar Brook, 179
Cedar Creek, 80, 111
Ceretto, 28
Chalet Debonné, 80-81
Chameleon, 187, 210
Chamonix, 39, 61, 127
Charles Baur, 68, 75-76, 85-86
Charles de Valliere, 161
Charles Krug, 181
Charles Melton, 113
Charles Shaw, 47, 125, 136, 158, 194
Chateau Biltmore, 46
Chateau Dalina, 127, 142
Chateau Frank, 26-27
Chateau Grand Traverse, 79-81
Chateau Julien, 137
Chateau Lafayette Reneau, 79, 81, 111
Chateau Morrisette, 46
Chateau Reynella, 36, 149, 238
Chateau St. Jean, 56-57
Chateau Ste. Michelle, 46, 57
Chimére, 68
Churchill's, 236

Cielo, 94
Cilurzo, 195
CK Mondavi, 181
Claar, 44, 80-81
Cloninger, 122
Clos du Bois, 179
Clos du Lac, 150
Clos du Letzenberg, 86, 96
Clos du Val, 177
Clos Paradis, 53
Cocci Grifoni, 105, 207-208
Cockatoo Ridge, 35, 149, 192
Cockburn's, 236
Colour Volant, 54, 132
Columbia Crest, 43, 46, 57, 59
Columbia Winery, 87, 96, 123, 160, 244
Concannon, 46, 58, 60, 66, 78, 87, 194
Concha y Toro, 40, 120, 134-135
Contadi Castaldi, 105
Conti Zecca, 206
Cook's, 27
Cooper Mountain, 47, 96
Coppo, 204
Corbett Canyon, 126
Corte Real, 218
Corte Sant'Alda, 207
Cosme Palacio y Hermanos, 215
Cote Montpezat, 147
Cousiño Macul, 120
Covey Run, 57, 87, 125, 148
Creston, 179
Croft, 224, 231
Curtis, 111, 195
CVNE, 215-216

D
d'Arenberg, 190
Daniel Lawrence, 42, 138
David Bruce, 175
David Wynn, 35, 118
Davis Bynum, 57
de La Tour, 146, 166
de Lorimier, 60
De Wetshof, 39
Deakin Estate, 35
Deaver, 46, 175, 177
Deer Valley, 140
Del Falegname, 203
Delas, 133, 188
Delheim, 39, 126, 196
Delicato, 60, 138, 194
Deltetto, 102
Diamond Ridge, 37, 132
Dievole, 201
Divinaude, 25
Domaine Borie de Maurel, 189
Domaine Capion, 110
Domaine Constantin Lazaridi, 61
Domaine de la Rossignole, 53

Domaine de la Terre Rouge, 196
Domaine de Montesquieu, 52-53
Domaine de Triennes, 34, 65, 110, 119, 189
Domaine des Beates, 110
Domaine La Chevalière, 66
Domaine Laurier, 45
Domaine Saint Benoit, 188
Domaine Tempier, 110
Doña Consuelo, 121, 134
Dopff & Irion, 68, 76, 95
Dos Cabezas, 96, 194
Dow's, 237
Dr. Konstantin Frank, 78-79, 81, 88, 148
Dr. Loosen, 72
Dry Creek Vineyard, 58
Duckhorn, 148
Dunnewood, 59, 113, 123, 140, 158

E

E.B. Foote, 123, 148
Eberle, 111, 195, 244
Ecco Domani, 203
Edgewood, 177, 194
Elk Run, 81, 88, 125, 151
Emilio Lustau, 227-232
Emilio Lustau Almacenista, 227
Eola Hills, 43, 244
Erath, 97, 244
Erzherzog Johann Weine, 97
Estancia, 58, 136, 158
Estrella, 113, 159, 180
Evans Wine Co., 36
Eyrie, 159

F

Fall Creek, 59
Fatoria dei Barbi, 204
Fattoria Carpineta Fontalpino, 203
Fattoria di S. Angelo, 203
Fattoria la Valentina, 205
Fazi Battaglia, 203-204
Fazi-Battaglia, 208
Feist, 236-238
Fenestra, 151
Fergusson, 191
Fetzer, 58, 77, 87, 113, 123, 137-138, 158
Ficklin, 239
Finca Allende, 214
Firelands, 27, 87
Firestone, 60, 77, 87
Fleith, 76, 95
Foley, 56
Fontana Candida, 105
Fontanafredda, 38
Forest Glen, 41, 138, 193, 209
Forest Ville, 81, 87, 112, 137, 193
Fox Hollow, 125, 137, 158, 193
Foxridge, 45
Framingham, 54

Franciscan, 45
Francois Schwach & Fils, 75-76
Fredericksburg Winery, 125
Freixenet, 25
Frey, 122
Frick, 179
Friedrich Wilhelm Gymnasium, 73
Furlan, 104, 134

G

Gabriel Liogier, 188
Gainey, 80
Gallerie, 33, 119, 133
Gallo Sonoma,
    43, 123, 136, 158, 168, 175, 179
Gamla, 61, 127
Gan Eden, 244-245
Georges Duboeuf, 33-34, 53, 66, 132, 164,
    166-168, 189
Geyser Peak, 179
Gianni Gagliardo, 204
Giesen, 54
Ginestet, 146-147
Giuseppe Cortese, 205
Gleeson's Ridge, 76
Glen Ellen, 169
Glenora, 26, 44, 68, 79-80
Gloria Ferrer, 26-27
Golan, 48, 127
Gonzalez Byass, 225-227, 229-230
Good Harbor, 77
Goundrey, 36, 192
Grand Cru, 67, 71, 75, 80, 85-86, 88, 92, 137,
    160, 179, 193
Grande River, 136, 148
Grandin, 25
Granite Springs, 177
Gristina, 43, 111, 137
Gruet, 26-27
Guenoc, 177
Guglielmo, 45
Guigal, 65, 109, 188
Gundlach Bundschu, 88

H

Hacienda, 125, 138, 157, 193
Hagafen, 78
Hahn Estates, 147, 150
Hardys, 36, 191, 238-239
Hargrave, 47, 68, 150
Harmony, 47, 79
Hartweg, 76
Harveys, 227, 229, 231, 237
Haskovo Winery, 141-142
Haywood, 137
Heartswood, 45
Hedges, 148
Henke, 78
Henri Miquel, 65

Henry Estate, 42, 79, 87, 139, 159
Hermitage Road, 36, 191
Heron Hill, 80
Herzog, 43, 60, 113, 125, 169, 176
Hess Collection, 42
Hester Creek, 142, 153
Hidalgo, 226, 228
Hijos de Antonio Barcelo, 216, 218-219
Hill of Content, 118
Hinman, 81
Hogue, 45, 138, 149-150, 192
Hoodsport, 140
Hopler, 67, 88
Horton, 150, 152, 195-196
Hostens-Picant, 53, 146
House of Nobilo, 48, 55
Huntington, 59, 138
Husch, 59, 87, 244

I

Ibernoble, 217
Icardi, 28
Illuminati, 104, 206
Indian Creek, 45, 79
Indigo Hills, 43, 158
Ingleside Plantation, 137, 150

J

J.C. Chassagne, 188
J. Garcia Carrion, 217, 219
J. Lohr, 41, 192
J.L. Wolf, 74
Jackson-Triggs, 82, 89, 113, 141
Jacob's Creek, 35, 77, 118, 132
Jaja de Jau, 153, 189
Jamesport, 56
Jaume Serra, 218
Jean Baptiste Thibault, 53
Jean Michel Arcaute, 53
Jean-Marc Bernhard, 25, 68, 76
Jean-Pierre Bechtold, 25, 86, 95-96
Jefferson, 151
Jekel, 79, 138, 158
Jenard, 34, 53, 120, 133
Jepson, 42, 66
Jerome Geschickt & Fils, 86
Joan Raventos Rosell, 127, 136
Jose de Soto, 227, 231
Josef Brigl, 94, 134
Joseph Swan, 160, 196
Joseph Zakon, 245
Joullian, 59
Justin, 57

K

Katnook Estate, 55
Kendall-Jackson, 59, 78
Kenwood, 176
Kestrel, 42

Kientzheim-Kayersberg, 75, 95
Kim Crawford, 54
King Estate, 96
Kiona, 148
Korbel, 26-27
KWV, 39, 61, 127, 141

L

L. Mawby, 27
l'Eglise Vieille, 147
L'Ormarins, 39
l'Orval, 34, 133
La Baume, 34, 120, 132, 189
La Colombaia, 94, 133
La Grande Clotte, 147
La Palazzetta di Flavio Fante, 203
La Palma, 40, 120, 134-135
La Playa, 40-41, 120-121, 135
La Vieille Ferme, 65, 188
Labegorce Zede, 146-147
Lagrange les Tours, 146-147
Lamoreaux Landing, 80, 151
Lang, 181
Latcham Vineyards, 178-179
Laurel Lake, 45, 47, 110, 137
Laurier, 43, 45
LaVelle, 78, 96
Lawson's, 54
Leasingham, 77, 190
Lenz, 47, 86, 113, 158
Leon Beyer, 76, 86, 95
Leone de Castris, 206
Les Graves de Viaud, 146
LinCourt, 42, 192
Lindemans, 34, 118, 131, 149, 191
Livio Felluga, 94
Lizzano, 207-208
Lockwood, 45
Lolonis, 56
Lonz, 239
Lorane Valley, 159
Los Vascos, 120
Louis Jadot, 166-168
Louis Latour, 33, 167-168
Louis Martini, 176, 210
Lucien Albrecht, 95
Lucien Deschaux, 34, 188-189
Luiano, 202

M

M.G. Vallejo, 112, 159
Macari, 43, 58-59, 111
Maddalena, 139
Madroña, 147
Magnotta,
    28, 37-38, 61, 89, 127, 141, 153, 161
Maison Blanche, 146
Marcel Deiss, 95
Marcus James, 113

Marega, 38, 94, 104
Marienberg, 36, 119, 191-192, 238
Mariposa, 135, 151-152
Mark West, 42
Marques de Arienzo, 215-216
Marques de Caceres, 114, 215
Marques de Gelida, 25
Marques de Griñon, 214
Marques de Riscal, 214
Marquise de Lassime, 34
Martin Brothers, 209-210, 244
Martinelli, 86
Martinez, 214-215, 237
Martini & Prati, 68, 96, 180
Martini & Rossi, 28
Mas de Gourgonnier, 109
Masi, 207
Massolino, 205
Mastroberardino, 104, 113, 209
Matthias Altenburger, 47
Matua, 55
Maurice Carrie, 59, 80
McDowell, 66, 112, 193
McGuigan, 37, 55, 118, 132, 191
Meier's, 232, 239
Meridian, 42, 125, 157, 176, 192
Michel Barat, 32-33
Michel Lynch, 53, 119, 132
Michel Picard, 33, 119, 132, 189
Michele Satta, 104
Midnight Cellars, 149
Milano, 180
Mirassou, 79, 113, 158, 194
Mission Hill, 37-38, 160-161
Mission View, 140, 150, 176
Moletto, 94, 208
Mommessin, 189
Monasterio de Tentudia, 218-219
Mondoro, 28
Monterey Peninsula Winery, 177
Monterra, 45, 123, 138, 192
Montes, 135
Montevina, 111
Monthaven,
    44, 125, 151-152, 175, 181, 194-195
Montinore, 96
Montpellier, 112, 137, 181, 193
Montsarra, 24
Moulin des Sablons, 153
Mount Palomar, 195
Mount Pleasant, 239
Murfatlar, 97
Murphy-Goode, 59, 68
Mystic Cliffs, 123

N
Naked Mountain, 81, 125, 151
Napa Creek, 140
Napa Ridge, 122

Napa Wine Co., 59
Naturnaher Weinbau Alfred Deim, 77
Nautilus, 54
Neil Ellis, 60
Norman, 148
Nozzole, 38

O
Oak Knoll, 45, 97
Oakencroft, 124
Obester, 209
Opici, 28
Orlando, 28, 76
Osborne, 225-226, 231-232, 237
Osprey's Dominion, 81, 122, 136, 243
Ostertag, 68
Oxford Landing, 36, 55

P
Palacio de Valdeinfante, 219
Palmer, 68, 151
Paradise Ridge, 56, 58
Paraiso Springs, 77, 87
Parducci, 124, 140, 193
Paul Masson, 239
Paul Thomas, 124, 245
Pedroncelli, 43, 110, 123-124, 158, 175-176
Peirano, 140
Pellegrini, 45
Peller Estates, 37
Penfolds, 35, 37, 191, 238
Pepperwood Grove, 139, 158, 181
Perrin, 65, 188, 244
Perry Creek, 139, 181, 209
Pesenti, 124
Peter Dolle, 77
Peter Lehmann, 189
Peters' Hill, 48
Peterson, 178
Pfaffenheim, 67, 75, 85, 95, 160
Piccini, 202-203
Pierre Sparr, 68, 75-76, 85, 95
Pighin, 94
Pillitteri, 37, 141
Pindar, 149, 168
Pino, 208
Pionero, 55, 121, 135
Piper Sonoma, 26-27
Pitray, 147
Powers, 124, 147
Pra'di Pradis, 103
Prejean, 88
Premiat, 141, 160
Preston Premium, 112
Prinz zu Salm-Dalberg'sches Weingut, 73
Prunotto, 204-205
Puelles, 215
Pugliese, 140, 150, 209
Punset, 205

Q

Quady, 239, 243
Quatro, 136
Queen Adelaide, 238
Quinta do Noval, 236-238
Qupé, 193

R

R.H. Phillips, 192
R. Zimmermann, 47
Ramos Pinto, 237
Raymond, 44, 57
Redbank, 34, 190
Reine Pedauque, 33, 65, 187
Reliz Canyon, 136
Remo Farina, 207
Renaissance, 81, 199
Riccardo Falchini, 104, 202
Richemont, 132, 189
Riddoch, 190
Riefle, 75
Rigoli Carmignano, 203
Riunite, 207-208
River Run, 195
Robert Mondavi, 51, 58, 60, 137, 157, 180
Rocca delle Macie, 202
Roccadoro, 103
Rockbridge, 44, 148
Rodney Strong, 58
Rosemount, 161, 192
Rosenblum, 66, 177, 180, 195
Rothrock, 74
Round Hill, 139
Rozes, 237
Rudolf Muller, 73
Ruffino, 105, 204
Rutherford Vintners, 46, 111, 137, 178, 193

S

Saddleback, 68
Saint Clair, 47, 54
Saint Sulpice, 147
Sakonnet, 87, 159
San Fabiano Calcinaia, 201
San Vincenti, 201
Sanchez Romate, 226-227, 229, 231
Sandeman, 226, 228, 230, 237
Santa Alicia, 41, 135
Santa Amelia, 40-41, 56, 121, 135
Santa Carolina, 41, 121, 134
Santa Ema, 41, 121, 153
Santa Julia, 41, 55, 121, 135, 152
Santa Marvista, 134
Santa Monica, 122, 135
Santino, 112, 178, 195
Savese, 208
Scarlatta, 94, 105, 126, 134, 205
Schlegel Boeglin, 75, 85

Schloss Saarstein, 72
Schlumberger, 153
Schuetz Oles, 178
Sea Ridge Coastal, 124, 159, 180, 193
Seaview, 28, 35, 119
Seghesio, 178
Segura Viudas, 25
Sella e Mosca, 208
Seppelt, 34-35, 119, 238
Seth Ryan, 151
Seven Peaks, 123
Shale Ridge, 44, 138
Sheldrake, 35, 132, 190
Shenandoah Vineyards, 124, 176, 178, 209
Shingle Peak, 47, 54, 97, 161
Sichel, 52, 146
Siduri, 159
Sierra Vista, 56, 175-176
Siglo, 216
Silvan Ridge, 97, 244
Silver Lake, 139
Silver Ridge, 43, 139, 157, 194
Simonnet-Febvre, 32
Skouras, 48
Smith Woodhouse, 236
Sobon, 66, 110, 178, 181, 193
Spalletti, 104
Spencer Hill, 54
St. Clement, 56
St. Julian, 79, 232, 239, 243
St. Supéry, 44
St. Ursula, 73
Staton Hills, 56
Ste. Chapelle, 26-27, 44, 78-79, 122, 124
Ste. Genevieve, 60, 112, 158
Stellenryck, 39
Sterling, 42
Stevenot, 180
Stival, 38
Stone Creek, 122
Stonehedge, 126, 152, 175
Sumarroca, 24-25
Swanson, 111
Swedish Hill, 78
Sybille Kuntz, 72

T

Taft Street, 59
Taltarni, 55, 190
Tarara, 151
Tatachilla, 37, 190-191
Tenuta Carretta, 102
Tenuta Cocci Grifoni, 207-208
Tenuta di Caparzo, 105
Terlano, 93
Terrabianca, 203
Thomas Fogarty, 86
Thomas Moillard, 187-188

Thornton, 110
Tim Adams, 192
Topolos, 58
Torre Rosazza, 126
Torres, 136, 213, 217-218
Torresella, 38
Tosti, 28
Tour du Pas St. Georges, 146
Tour Grand Colombier, 146
Trapiche, 40, 121-122, 151
Treleaven, 41
Trentadue, 195
Tri Vento, 152
Tribaut, 26-27
Trimbach, 95
Trumpeter, 120
Tualatin Estate, 80, 245
Turning Leaf, 139, 159
Twin Hills, 181
Tyrrell's, 35, 149, 160, 191

U

Umani Ronchi, 104, 205-206
Umberto Cesari, 207-208
Undurraga, 41, 56, 120, 122, 161

V

V. Sattui, 78-79, 87, 112, 244
Vagnoni, 201
Valdemar, 113, 214-215
Valdespino, 227-228, 230
Valley of the Monks, 141
Vallone, 206
Van Asperen, 138, 180
Van Roekel, 57, 66, 112, 181
Vavasour, 54
Vega Adriana, 219
Veramonte, 40, 120, 134
Via Firenze, 210
Vichon, 34, 66, 119
Vigil, 178
Villa Bel-Air, 53, 146
Villa Frattina, 93, 133
Villa Mt. Eden, 42, 178
Villa Rosa, 103
Villa Sparina, 103
Villanova, 93
Villiera, 28, 39
Viña Santa Carolina, 121, 134
Viña Tarapaca, 40, 55, 121
Viña Undurraga, 56
Vini Winery, 127
Vinicola del Priorat, 218
Vinterra, 40, 152
Viu Manent, 39, 153
Von Lade, 72

W

W.B. Bridgman, 44, 124, 150
Walnut Crest, 40, 135
Warre's, 236
Washington Hills, 88, 124, 139, 148
Waterbrook, 58
Weingut Dr. Bürklin-Wolf, 73
Weingut Dr. H. Thanisch, 72
Weingut Familie Markowitsch, 61
Weingut Heinrich Schmitges, 72-73
Weingut Hermann Huber, 47, 61
Weingut Heyl zu Herrnshelm, 73
Weingut Johannishof, 73
Weingut Paul Braunstein, 89
Weingut R & A Pfaffl, 77
Weingut Schildhof, 77
Weingut Schreiber Zink, 88
Weingut Studert-Prum, 73
Weingut Umathum, 161
Weingut Zull, 77
Weinkellerei P.J. Valckenberg, 88, 97
Weinstock, 57, 111, 168
Wente, 26
Whidbey, 239
White Hall Vineyards, 138
Wild Horse, 169, 195
Wildhurst, 176
Willamette Valley Vineyards, 42, 44, 80, 159
William Hill, 44
Williams & Humbert, 228
Windsor,
    27, 44, 57, 112, 176-177, 180, 194-195, 239
Windwalker, 210
Wolf Blass, 35, 118
Wollersheim, 78, 110, 157
Woodbridge, 133, 139
Woodward Canyon, 78
Wyndham, 36, 119, 161, 190
Wynns, 35, 118, 190
Yakima River, 111, 148
Yalumba, 66, 118, 190-191, 238
Yarden, 61, 82
Yarra Ridge, 160
York Mountain Winery, 180
Yorkville, 150
Yvon Mau, 52
Zabaco, 41, 177
Zayante, 175
Zonin, 206

Bibliography

Baldy, Marian W. 1997. *The University Wine Course*. San Francisco, Calif.: The Wine Appreciation Guild.

Boulton, Roger B., Vernon L. Singleton, Linda F. Bisson, Ralph E. Kunkee. 1996. *Principles and Practices of Winemaking*. New York: Chapman and Hall.

Clarke, Oz. 1991. *Oz Clarke's New Classic Wines*. New York: Simon and Schuster.

———. 1995. *Oz Clarke's Wine Atlas*. London: Little, Brown and Company.

Gladstones, John. 1997. *Viticulture and Environment*. Adelaide, South Australia: Winetitles.

Halliday, James. 1991. *Wine Atlas of Australia and New Zealand*. North Ryde, New South Wales: Angus and Robertson.

———. 1993. *Wine Atlas of California*. New York: Viking.

Hanson, Anthony. 1995. *Burgundy*. London: Faber and Faber.

Johnson, Hugh, and James Halliday. 1992. *The Vintner's Art*. New York: Simon and Schuster.

Macaluso, Roberto. 1994. *La vita ed il vino nella provincia Granda*. Brescia: Edizione Internazionale.

Meredith, Ted Jordan. 1990. *Northwest Wine*. Kirkland, Wash.: Nexus Press.

Morton, Lucie T. 1985. *Winegrowing in Eastern America*. Ithaca, N.Y.: Cornell University Press.

Robinson, Jancis. 1994. *The Oxford Companion to Wine*. Oxford: Oxford University Press.

Vine, Richard P., Ellen M. Harkness, Theresa Browning, and Cheri Wagner.1997. *Winemaking*. New York: Chapman and Hall.

Winkler, A.J., James A. Cook, W.M. Kliewer, and Lloyd A. Lider. 1974. *General Viticulture*. Los Angeles: University of California Press.

The authoritative
buying guide
to wine, beer,
and spirits.

Tastings ▮ Before You Buy

⇌ The Journal of The Beverage Testing Institute ⇌

*If you enjoyed this book, you'll love "Tastings." This bimonthly journal
includes the same comprehensive, professional panel reviews of wine, beer,
and spirits that BTI has been known for since 1981. Features:*

- More than 1,000 reviews per issue
- Guaranteed to help you find better products for less
- Insider's Club – advance news of top-scoring products on the web
- Meet "Scout," our exclusive beverage locator
- User-friendly and entertaining

Tastings provides both the beverage industry and consumer with timely
information on new and existing brands, where to find them, and how to buy them.

For More Information:

*Visit our web-site at: www.tastings.com
Email: journal@tastings.com*

Beverage Testing Institute,
310 South Peoria Street
Suite 504
Chicago, IL 60607 USA

More than 7,000 wines, beers, and spirits rated annually!